Global Perspectives on Anti-Feminism

Global Perspectives on Anti-Feminism

Far-Right and Religious Attacks on Equality and Diversity

Edited by
JUDITH GOETZ AND
STEFANIE MAYER

EDINBURGH
University Press

Edinburgh University Press is one of the leading university presses in the UK. We publish academic books and journals in our selected subject areas across the humanities and social sciences, combining cutting-edge scholarship with high editorial and production values to produce academic works of lasting importance. For more information visit our website: edinburghuniversitypress.com

Edinburgh University Press Ltd
13 Infirmary Street
Edinburgh EH1 1LT

First published in hardback by Edinburgh University Press 2023

Typeset in 10/13 Giovanni by
IDSUK (DataConnection) Ltd

A CIP record for this book is available from the British Library

ISBN 978-1-3995-0539-0 (hardback)
ISBN 978-1-3995-0540-6 (paperback)
ISBN 978-1-3995-0541-3 (webready PDF)
ISBN 978-1-3995-0542-0 (epub)

CONTENTS

ACKNOWLEDGEMENTS

This anthology would not have been possible without the important work and analyses of colleagues who study anti-feminism, the invisible support of numerous people as well as the diverse struggles that feminist activists worldwide wage against anti-feminism. We would therefore like to take this opportunity to thank all those who have accompanied the process of editing this book, be it through support in the search for authors, through feedback, the possibility to discuss individual contributions in advance, e.g. at conferences, but also through moral support from our friends and colleagues. Of course, we would also like to thank the authors of the chapters for their valuable contributions and their patience. At this point we cannot mention all the relevant people by name and therefore we only want to highlight the often forgotten, invisible work, such as that of the two interns at the Institute for Research on Male Supremacism, Vanessa Berthold and Duncan Coltharp, who helped with the proofreading. Last but not least, we would like to thank the publishers, especially Ersev Ersoy, Sarah Foyle and Joannah Duncan, for their excellent cooperation and for making this book possible.

Global Perspectives on Anti-Feminism

Stefanie Mayer and Judith Goetz

A spectre is haunting Europe [. . .]. All the powers of old Europe have entered into a holy alliance to exorcise this spectre: Pope and Tsar, Metternich and Guizot . . . . (Marx and Engels, 1848, *Manifesto of the Communist Party*)

Today not just Europe but most of the world seems to be haunted by a spectre that's even less clearly defined and less tangible than the 'spectre of communism' Marx famously conjured. Feminism, 'genderism', the 'homo-lobby' or leftist and liberal elites are today's bogeymen that unite the Vatican, right-wing conservatives, Christian fundamentalists, authoritarian leaders and the far-right. Anti-feminist, anti-queer and anti-LGBTIQ+ positions have become ubiquitous in right-wing campaigns, spanning different religious and secular backgrounds and ideologies. 'Gender' – or rather: a specific distorted reading of the term – became a major issue in a variety of seemingly unrelated policy fields including, inter alia, US domestic politics, the Columbian peace process or the Russian invasion of Ukraine.

The apparent success of these anti-feminist campaigns – including huge civil society mobilisations in the form of demonstrations and petitions as well as successes at the polls and in referenda – makes them a disquieting topic for gender and sexuality researchers as well as feminist researchers in other disciplines, including political science, the editors' home discipline. So, in recent years, anti-feminism and far-right gender politics have become important topics at international conferences,[1] a number of leading journals published special issues[2] and a growing number of edited volumes debate different perspectives on the issue.[3] Apart from these broader publications that mostly focus on comparing case studies from different European countries, an immense number of smaller-scale publications are available to readers of different languages. Some authors have focused on the transnational dimension of anti-feminist organising (for example

Kuhar and Paternotte, 2017; Korolczuk, 2014), thereby preparing the ground for the more global outlook this publication sets out to provide.

Global Discourses and Local Articulations

Contemporary anti-feminist and anti-LGBTIQ+ rhetoric and strategies seem to transcend different national, religious and political contexts. For example Jair Bolsonaro's rhetoric during the Brazilian presidential election campaign (see Arguedas-Ramírez in this volume) seems to mirror the Polish PiS party's stance on homosexuality as well as the German AfD's fear of 'gender', while right-wing actors in Japan stoke fears of the impeding 'abolishment' of the sexes (see Kawasaka in this volume), which are also catered to in German anti-feminist books and speeches, for example by Birgit Kelle and Gabriele Kuby. Given these similarities it is striking that a global perspective on these developments is still largely absent from the literature.[4] Most of the scholarly work on contemporary anti-feminism focuses on Europe, sometimes including ties to Russia and/or the United States with regards to specific groups of actors like the World Congress of Families or the US alt-right (Blee, 2017; Moss, 2017; Stern, 2019). Other than that, there has been little attention in English-language literature on the transnational ties of anti-feminist actors beyond Europe. In order to foster a more comprehensive debate this volume brings together perspectives from five continents that show how anti-feminism as a transnational ideology and movement is articulated in local contexts, thereby rendering anti-feminism a global phenomenon.

Like any other global (political) phenomenon and discourse anti-feminism is not simply one singular, homogeneous entity that exists independently of time and space, but needs to be realised – to be 'made real' – in specific local contexts. As the chapters in this volume show, the local and the global dimensions of anti-feminism are neither opposites, nor is one simply a part or an example of the other. In order to become relevant, global discourses need to be articulated in concrete local practices, policies and movements, with these local articulations in turn shaping and recreating the global phenomenon (Laclau and Mouffe, 2014). Therefore any analysis of the global or transnational dimension of anti-feminism needs to situate its object in local or national political contexts in order to grasp the significance transnational discourses gain when they are brought to life in specific situations.

The set-up of the book reflects this intricate relationship by approaching the phenomenon from two angles. In the first part transnational discourses – the concept of 'gender ideology', fights about sex education, the backlash against feminist activism, transnational strategising of anti-feminist actors and masculinist discourses – are analysed as they gain meaning in concrete embodiments, practices and politics (for more information see the introduction to Part One of the book). In the second part of the book national contexts take centre stage as the authors explore anti-feminism in the respective countries under study. While the anthology can in no way claim to provide a comprehensive view, our selection of cases was designed to offer insights into divergent cases thereby offering possibilities for comparison beyond the existing English-language literature (for more information see the introduction to Part Two of the book). As editors we also selected different analytical perspectives in order to capture the variety of anti-feminism's diverse articulations. We try to provide some preliminary conclusions and avenues for further investigation in the conclusions to this volume.

Before readers dive into the different studies presented in this volume, we want to use the rest of this introduction to descriptively outline some of the key features of anti-feminism in our current moment, take a look at some of the explanations and analytical concepts presented in the literature so far, and define a number of common starting points for the following analyses.

Anti-gender Mobilisations – Anti-feminism's New Clothes

Emancipatory movements tackling gender relations and sexuality regimes have always been met by reactionary counter-movements, aiming to safeguard the status quo or to restore a mythical 'natural' or 'God-given' order from an imagined past. In this sense there is nothing new about anti-feminism. Similarities and continuities seem especially pronounced with regard to the turn of the nineteenth to the twentieth century, which – just like the present moment – was marked by profound social and political changes. For right-wing political formations at that time, anti-feminist thought was an integral part of a broader anti-modern ideology, deeply intertwined with antisemitism, anti-urbanism, and the rejection of egalitarianism (Baumeister et al., 2020; Klammer and Bechter, 2019; Planert, 1998; Schenk, 1992; Stögner, 2014; Volkov, 2000).

Just like their predecessors, women's and LGBTIQ+ movements during the second half of the twentieth century met fierce opposition from religious as well as secular political actors, some of whom are still at the forefront of today's anti-feminist mobilisations. But even though continuities abound, there have also been important developments in anti-feminist thought and practice that need to be taken into account in order to understand our current political moment. One of the most important innovations was the invention of the concept of 'gender ideology' that provides the blueprint for today's anti-feminist discourses.

Inventing 'gender ideology'

The invention and development of 'gender ideology' is a typical example of how continuities and modernisation intersect in contemporary anti-feminism. In the mid-1990s declarations from UN-conferences (Cairo 1994 and Beijing 1995) used the term 'gender' instead of 'sex' with regard to equality initiatives and referred to the concept of 'gender mainstreaming'. The Vatican and Catholic intellectuals took this opportunity to reframe their long-standing opposition to sexual and reproductive rights – most notably abortion and homosexuality (Heß, 2017; Kuhar and Paternotte, 2017; Paternotte, 2015). Rather than taking a defensive position against the liberalisation of gender and sexuality regimes as well as family planning the Vatican now took an offensive stance and positioned itself as the true representative of women, especially poor women from the global South, whose well-being was allegedly threatened by a powerful alliance of feminist elites, Western governments and the UN bureaucracy. The term 'gender' was supposed to signify this alleged neo-colonial feminist attack on the poor (Paternotte, 2015).

During the 1990s this re-invention of religious anti-feminism, which included alliances with a number of conservative and Islamist governments, could not influence the outcome of the UN conferences, but publications like *The Gender Agenda: Redefining Equality* (1997) by US-American Catholic Dale O'Leary started the global distribution of anti-feminism disguised as a criticism of 'gender ideology'. From today's point of view, it is astonishing how many of the cornerstones of anti-feminist discourses, which are used by the far-right or nationalist groups in a secularised manner, were already present in O'Leary's work. Most importantly she provided a definition of 'gender' as an attack on human nature as well as God's creation and helped create the self-perception of anti-feminists as an embattled minority fighting an overwhelming conspiracy of powerful elites in the name of 'real' women and men. In the following years especially conservative Catholic as well as evangelical groups read, translated and spread O'Leary's work (Heß, 2017, pp. 9–11). Even though it has now been more than twenty-five years since these initial debates on 'gender', they still resonate not only in terms of the content of anti-feminist discourses but also in terms of the self-definition of anti-feminists as defenders of 'real women' (as opposed to feminists), of 'families' (as opposed to LGBTIQ+) and of 'normal, simple people' (as opposed to elites). The same holds true for the picture of an elitist conspiracy promoting 'gender ideology' for its own benefit.

In the early 2000s the Vatican's position on 'gender' as an 'ideology' threatening traditional families, heterosexuality and the religious understanding of the essence of human beings as men and women was consolidated through several publications that were translated in different languages (for the German editions see Päpstlicher Rat für die Familie, 2000; Reis and Päpstlicher Rat für die Familie, 2007). In 2004 the *Letter to the Bishops of the Catholic Church on the Collaboration of Men and Women in the Church and in the World* (Congregation for the Doctrine of the Faith, 2004) authored by Cardinal Ratzinger (who later became Pope Benedict XVI) gave it global outreach and in many cases introduced this (mis-)understanding of the term 'gender' to public debates for the first time, while also bringing divergent positions within the Catholic Church to the fore. Feminist, liberal and socially progressive theological interpretations have been challenging this reactionary stance ever since. Certain tensions within Catholic discourse on issues of gender and sexuality are also visible in the position taken by Pope Francis. On the one hand he argues for a slow liberalisation of a number of tenets of Catholic doctrine, for example with regards to homosexuality, and partly changed the Vatican's rhetoric on issues of gender equality, while on the other hand he calls gender a 'daemonic ideology' (Lauer, 2016) and a threat to the God-given complementarity of men and women (Congregation for Catholic Education, 2019).

Secularisation and right-wing politics

While Catholic actors started the discourse on 'gender ideology' in the 1990s and religious groups in many cases remain its most outspoken representatives (Kuhar, 2015), the range of actors relying on this notion broadened significantly since the mid-2000s, when anti-feminist men's rights activists as well as right-wing (populist) groups and politicians adopted it for their own ends (Mayer and Sauer, 2017). In the beginning most of the energy of political right-wing actors was focused on the term 'gender' itself, on gender mainstreaming (which was mistakenly associated with a deconstructivist approach to gender) and on gender studies. Since then topics connected to anti-gender discourses as well as alliances of different actors (from religiously grounded conservativism to right-wing extremism) have proliferated on a global scale, reaching a first peak with the 'Manif pour tous' against same-sex marriage in France in 2012–13 (Stambolis-Ruhstorfer and Tricou, 2017).

Since then we have witnessed right-wing (populist) and nationalist attacks on 'gender', that is on queer and feminist achievements, which have often but not necessarily used religious symbols and/or the support of organised religion. While some of the most outspoken anti-feminist actors cannot hide their deep investment in religious thinking (see Vega and Mayer and Goetz in this volume), there is also a clear trend of secular actors using this originally religious discourse for secular political ends. Anti-feminism has therefore been instrumental in the renewed importance of religion for the type of politics that have been deemed 'right-wing populist' (Graff and Korolczuk, 2021) or 'illiberal' (Hennig and Weiberg-Salzmann, 2021). Of course, as we have stated above, these campaigns are always attuned to regional, national and local circumstances, rely on different religious convictions and focus on different topics, and therefore they need to be analysed with regard to their respective contexts, that is as local articulations of the transnational trends they articulate. Still, there seem to be three interconnected features that render anti-feminist, anti-gender discourses especially attractive for contemporary right-wing politics. First, the intersectionality of anti-feminism, which makes it easy to link it to racist and nationalist biopolitics, that is to the core of right-wing (extremist) ideologies. In this respect today's anti-gender discourse strongly mirrors the 'old' anti-feminism of the beginning of the twentieth century – we will discuss this in a bit more detail below. Second, anti-feminism fits perfectly the turn to populist strategies within right-wing politics. A number of structural characteristics of contemporary anti-feminist discourses make them a prime example of populist discursive strategies employing 'gender' as an 'empty signifier' (Mayer and Sauer, 2017) in a discourse that is not only open to political alliances but also to 'common sense', that is to a specific political construction of everyday experiences. The alleged 'naturalness' of sex translates to the 'nature' and 'normality' of gender, sexuality and patriarchal family relations, which in turn provide the common basic rationale for different anti-feminist actors. According to anti-feminist discourse God, nature and biological science as well as common sense coalesce in a shared understanding of 'normal' ways of being a man or woman and in the definition of 'normal' families. Third, anti-feminist discourses offer right-wing actors the possibility to stylise their own position in terms of a defender of ordinary people from a malevolent and uncaring elite, rather than as aggressors targeting women and/or sexual minorities.

Academic Perspectives on Anti-feminism

While there seems to be broad consensus as far as the empirical description of recent developments in anti-feminist discourse – as presented above in an extremely condensed and necessarily inadequate fashion – is concerned, academic literature differs widely when it comes to the analysis of contemporary anti-feminism, especially current anti-gender mobilisations. Even though this short introduction will not be able to do justice to the multitude of approaches and concepts in the rapidly expanding literature, we want to revisit a few of the main arguments in order to delineate our own approach.

Continuities

As stated above, feminist thought and women's activism as well as movements for sexual rights and equality have always been confronted with resistance. At times these counter-movements have explicitly called themselves anti-feminist and openly opposed women's emancipation (Planert, 1998), more regularly they have shifted the discourse to issues of sexual morals, the family and child well-being. As Herrad Schenk (1992) and Ute Planert (1998) already stated in their analyses, anti-feminism in this sense can be understood as conscious opposition against women's emancipation, against women's and feminist movements and their political struggles, and as the rejection of improvements to the social status of women. Today opposition against queer politics and the liberalisation of sexuality regimes and gender identities need to be added. Anti-feminism therefore needs to be distinguished from misogyny, the idea of the inferiority of women, as well as from sexism, which signifies the structural discrimination of women and non-heteronormative genders as well as social and political practices that serve to safeguard traditional gender relations and enforce men's privileged role (Kreisky, 2004). While misogyny is located on the level of individual attitudes and sexism at the level of societal structures and corresponding practices, anti-feminism is a political position and a discourse that is consciously developed by specific actors. Of course, these phenomena are mutually dependent and do not usually occur in isolation from each other, but still this delineation offers a first important insight into the political nature of anti-feminism. Contrary to what many anti-feminists argue, anti-feminism is therefore not a question of individual convictions or lifestyle-choices, but a political ideology and its corresponding movements. From today's point of view the early scholarly works on the anti-feminist movements of the late nineteenth and early twentieth century referred to above are especially interesting for the parallels they show to the current situation. The fights of sexual minorities, which historically have not been visible, take centre stage in anti-gender mobilisations around the globe today, but the 'moral panic' (Hall, 1978) created around historic women's movements seems to mirror many of today's discourses around same-sex parenting, sex education and gender transitions.

Taking what we might call the continuity perspective, anti-feminism can be understood as a political phenomenon with a history lasting for more than a century. Until today, anti-feminist movements aim to perpetuate gender-based discrimination and oppression by reinstating traditional gender norms. Therefore, their main goal remains to defend male privileges by maintaining a patriarchal gender differentiation that legitimates male supremacy. Contemporary examples of masculinist groups such as incels[5] or Pickup Artists show that the idea of women's subordination and of a male entitlement to women's bodies and sexuality is still salient (Armengol and Kimmel, 2009; Kaiser, 2020; Kimmel and Aronson, 2003; O'Neill, 2018; Stoltenberg, 2005). Similar patriarchal ideas can be found among some activists, especially in men's and father's rights groups. They denounce the alleged preferential treatment of women in family courts and through quota and anti-discrimination programmes, thereby defending male privileges and positions of paternal power (Bates, 2020; Dietze, 2019; Manne, 2018; Stern, 2019). Katharina Wiedlack and Iain Zabolotny in their contribution in this volume explore oppressive and violent reactions to feminist activism that clearly show that the idea to 'put women in their place' is not a thing of the past.

Despite these striking continuities there are very important discursive and strategic shifts that mark contemporary anti-feminist debates. One of those is the change of objects of attack as today's anti-feminist campaigns focus on 'gender' rather than 'women', which more often than not translates into a focus on the liberalisation of sexuality regimes and the demands of LGBTIQ+ movements rather than gender equality per se. Accordingly, gender discrimination is often externalised or historicised, that is located in 'other' societies or in a distant past, rather than outright denied. Imke Schmincke coined the term 'neosexism' for this discursive strategy, which serves anti-feminists to deny ongoing discrimination based on gender and/ or sexuality (Schmincke, 2018, p. 30). Neosexism turns into anti-feminism as it delegitimises current feminist and queer demands. As allegedly equal rights have long been achieved, today's demands are framed as excessive and as instances of 'gender ideology', which follows a hidden agenda of creating 'sexless' human beings and destroying 'the family' along the way.

Shifting strategies

Strategic shifts of discourse have long been part of anti-feminist activism. One case in point are so called 'pro-life' mobilisations, which for the most part do not openly negate women's sexual and reproductive rights, but rather reframe the foetus' right to life as being more important than the mother's right to self-determination (Achtelik, 2015). Today we see similar strategies that allow for positive (for example 'family-friendly', 'child-friendly') self-depictions rather than negative (for example 'anti-women', 'anti-gay') ones. One sign of this trend is current discourses which oppose feminism not because of its alleged detrimental effects on men and (heterosexual, patriarchal) gender relations, but because of its alleged abolishment of (biological) sex as such, the ensuing destruction of 'the family' and the threat this poses to children. This strategic de-centring of gender relations in anti-feminist discourse serves to enhance moral legitimacy as it seemingly puts children first, who are regarded as the most vulnerable members of society, rather than powerful (hetero-/cis-)men. Some researchers have analysed this as a shift from a 'men-centred' to a 'family-centred anti-feminism' (Scheele, 2016), but the label might be problematic as it risks taking anti-feminist strategies at face value and downplaying the role the defence of male supremacy still plays for parts of anti-feminist movements. Upon closer inspection the concern about families and children often proves to be a thinly veiled concern for male privileges and a patriarchal gender order (Mayer and Goetz, 2019; Notz, 2015).

Other researchers have named the phenomenon 'anti-genderism' because of anti-feminists' preoccupation with the notion of 'gender' (Hark and Villa, 2015; Strube et al., 2021) in the wake of the Catholic invention of 'gender ideology' depicted above. While this terminology aptly captures a very important discursive modernisation that occurred within anti-feminist movements since the 1990s, it also reproduces anti-feminist claims that today's feminism is spreading 'genderism' or 'gender ideology' rather than advancing women's rights and gender equality. As mentioned above, there is sometimes even a rhetorical distancing from 'old' anti-feminism, while its concerns are confirmed and further dis-seminated at the same time (Mayer and Sauer, 2017). This apparent dis-tancing enables anti-feminists to portray themselves in a more positive light and fosters acceptability in broad parts of the political spectrums that share a diffuse discomfort with 'gender' and the alleged 'excesses' of equality policies. Research using the term 'genderism' – even in a criti-cal sense – therefore runs the risk of strengthening anti-feminists' claims to modernisation and the historicisation of anti-feminism as something Western societies overcame in the distant past. It thereby makes it more difficult to analyse continuities of anti-feminism as an ideology that has always been intersectional (Stögner, 2017).

Anti-feminism as a reactive ideology

Anti-feminism can be understood as a reactionary ideology in the truest sense of the term, i.e. as a reaction to societal changes. In its simplest form this explanation points to recent successes of feminist and LGBTIQ+ mobilisations, to feminist achievements and (legal) improvements, as well as the liberalisation of sexuality regimes that enabled comprehensive sexual education and allowed for critical gender pedagogy. In sum, these efforts shake dichotomous gender concepts in favour of more diverse lifestyles and question the traditional heteronormative nuclear family as the only viable option. Anti-feminists react to these developments by (re-)constructing gender as a natural given, which in turn stabilises social relations in an 'attempt to restore security that has become precarious' (Hark and Villa, 2015, p. 10).[6]

Although anti-feminism without doubt reacts to feminist and queer successes, research has convincingly shown that this explanation would be too simple. Just like its historic predecessor, current anti-gender mobilisations can rather be understood as reactions to broad social changes, which do not necessarily originate in the realm of gender and sexuality.[7] Economic and social deprivation (Wimbauer et al., 2015), the crisis of care (Fraser, 2017) and a specific form of subjectivation that enforces self-reliance and competition and hinders solidarity (Fassin, 2020) are among the most important factors in many explanations of the success of contemporary anti-feminism.

Schmincke speaks of 'anti-feminism as a modern crisis symptom' (Schmincke, 2018, p. 33), in which gender and sexual diversity are used as stand-ins for fundamental fears and insecurities linked to social change, globalisation and neoliberalism. Importantly, these fears are not an automatic reaction to problematic social conditions, but are stoked by conservative and right-wing actors, who shift the conversation from the economic and social consequences of neoliberal policies and austerity measures to the liberalisation of gender and sexuality regimes that liberal policies often entail. Esther Kováts and Maari Põim in turn define 'gender' as 'symbolic glue' (Kováts et al., 2015) that is used by right-wing groups and parties to address the discomfort of many people with the neoliberal restructuring of their societies in the wake of the transformation of Central and Eastern Europe following the model of Western, liberal democracies. They stress the fact that anti-feminism addresses real grievances, especially of poor and rural women, who were largely overlooked by liberal gender equality policies and to whom the pro-family stance of contemporary anti-feminism is appealing. Focusing on the German context and on men rather than women Christine Wimbauer, Mona Motakef and Julia Teschlade analyse the success of anti-gender campaigns as a 'reaction to [the] precarisation of male privileges' (Wimbauer et al., 2015, p. 44), that is the end of family wages that supported a male breadwinner-model and the growing precarisation of labour in general. In these analyses, gender is constructed as a symbol of this crisis of social reproduction on an individual as well as a collective level. Especially in right-wing (extremist) interpretations it also functions 'as a code for a misguided development that is detrimental to the "nation's body" (*Volkskörper*) and a program imposed from above' (Ganz and Meßmer, 2015, p. 73).

According to these analyses, anti-feminism's success follows from the function it fulfils for its addressees. Contemporary anti-feminism contains a longing for an imagined past security and stability that is turned into a political weapon. Anti-feminism implies a prefabricated, rigid concept of heteronormative gender dualism as a 'natural' alternative to the complexities of diversity and thereby seems to offer an alternative to neoliberal self-optimisation and to a meritocratic measurement of success that is always rigged against the common people. By calling on its addressees as 'natural' men and women, it seemingly provides relief from the stream of demands to continuously re-imagine oneself and rationalise one's life.

Anti-feminism in the culture wars

Taking the argument of anti-gender mobilisations as a reaction to neoliberalism one important step further, some authors have strongly argued against the continuity view depicted above. In a nutshell: in this view anti-gender mobilisations are a consequence of and a reaction to the devastations of neoliberalism, rather than to feminism and the emancipation of women and LGBTIQ+ (Graff and Korolczuk, 2021). In line with the approaches discussed before, they argue that 'gender' became the privileged signifier to symbolise resistance to neoliberal ideas and policies, with liberal equality policies and especially the liberalisation of sexuality regimes serving as central foci. However, rather than focusing on their reactive side, these analyses put forward a view of anti-gender mobilisations as strategies in the 'culture wars' (Korolczuk, 2014). These are fought between a vaguely defined liberal hegemony on the one hand, which has associated itself with specific feminist and queer demands (e.g. equality policies, anti-discrimination, diversity), while firmly rejecting more radical claims for social justice and redistribution of wealth and power. And, on the other hand, an equally ill-defined coalition of right-wing forces that spans ideological differences and includes the religious and conservative right as well as right-wing extremists. Therefore 'anti-genderism' became central to right-wing populist attacks on a real or perceived (neo-)liberal hegemony – not in the sense of a mere tool, but as the unifying lens that provides common ground as well as a common language to different actors. In this view, although the term 'gender' is referred to constantly, anti-gender discourses are not so much about gender relations, but rather about social relations in general, about societal power and political hegemony in a broad sense. Anti-feminism in this perspective forms one specific part of anti-gender mobilisations, where they directly challenge women's rights (Graff and Korolczuk, 2021), while 'gender' functions as an 'empty signifier' (Laclau, 2013; Laclau and Mouffe, 2014; Mayer and Sauer, 2017) that allows to link different grievances.

While we agree with many parts of this conceptual outlook, we see two important risks with this focus on anti-gender mobilisations as a front for right-wing attacks on (neo-)liberal hegemony: first, the risk of following anti-feminists in their conflation of feminist and LGBTIQ+ movements with neoliberal equality policies, thereby devaluing the feminist critique of and opposition to neoliberalism (Fraser, 2013). Second, the risk of promoting an ahistorical view that underestimates the role anti-feminism played in anti-modern ideologies throughout the twentieth century and especially during its tumultuous beginning. Volkov's (2000) reflections on anti-feminism in the Weimar Republic as a 'cultural code' that implies an ideological position rather than an opinion on specific policies (Klammer and Bechter, 2019; Volkov, 2000) are a strong argument to understand even this feature of anti-feminism in its continuity rather than as a distinct feature of current anti-gender mobilisations. Last, there is a risk of defining anti-feminism too narrowly in terms of geographic and political contexts. Anti-feminism shows a degree of consistency and continuity across times, places and actors that cannot be explained when analyses are focused solely on the current neoliberal conjuncture.

In this volume we therefore put forward a slightly different approach that takes anti-feminism rather than 'anti-genderism' to be one of the central ideological tenets of current anti-democratic and anti-liberal attacks. In our view anti-feminism has proven to be changeable and capable of modernisation and adaptation. Its current form therefore can be understood as a 'modern variety' (Lang and Peters, 2018, p. 18), a 'variant' (Schmincke, 2018, p. 29) or a 're-articulation' (Mayer and Sauer, 2017, p. 36) of anti-feminism, rather than its replacement.

Anti-feminism as Discourse and Ideology

Having established 'anti-feminism' as our central object of enquiry and located our research within ongoing academic debates, we now want to conclude this introduction by highlighting two features of current anti-feminism that are of special importance to most of the following studies as they provide the basic rationale for anti-feminism as an ideology and help to explain its salience in different contexts. First, we discuss the relationship of current anti-feminist discourses to feminist and more specifically queer-feminist theory (and the ensuing feminist controversies). Second, we delineate our understanding of the intersectionality of anti-feminism, which enables it to function in different political contexts and for actors with different ideologies, thereby rendering it such an important weapon in the 'culture wars' depicted above.

Queer theory in reverse

Leo Löwenthal famously defined the work of manipulative political agitation as 'psychoanalysis in reverse' (Löwenthal and Guterman, 1949, p. 18). He showed how agitators mobilised their audiences' (latent) antisemitic attitudes by whipping up emotions and aggression and through that very process blocking the way to any meaningful insight into the true causes of these emotions. Even though anti-feminist resentments are of course very different from antisemitism, there are certain similarities regarding the processes in which antifeminists' objects of hate are constructed and emotions of pain, fear and anger are drawn up and directed to political ends.

As stated above, current anti-gender mobilisations use the term 'gender' as a 'negative foil for interpretation' (Bartz and Schulz, 2017, p. 8) and build on a specific (mis-)reading of queer-feminist theory to construct threat scenarios for the nation, society or the family. While their objects of attack may vary greatly and might include equality and anti-discrimination policies that do not question the gender binary at all, the refuting of deconstructivist feminist and queer theories forms the argumentative basis of these mobilisations.

Summarising very roughly, deconstructivist feminist stances disrupt the seemingly self-evident connection of sex, gender and desire (Butler, 1990) and analyse the (everyday) violence that is embodied in becoming 'real' men and women (Debus, 2017; Hechler and Stuve, 2015). This revolution within feminist philosophy and theory that went global in the early 1990s entailed politically salient consequences for feminist movements. It put sexuality/desire centre stage regarding the social construction of gender (Butler, 1990). Queer-feminist theory revolves around the question of how (biological) sex, (social) gender and (sexual) desire are forcefully constructed as one seemingly 'natural' entity that defines a person's identity. It therefore entails an understanding of the violent character of the gendering of human beings as 'real' (that is heterosexual, gender-compliant) men and women and a deconstruction of that seemingly natural entanglement of sex, gender and desire. This is where the second, presumably even more important effect comes to play. From a queer-feminist point of view, becoming and being a woman (de Beauvoir, 2011) means to performatively re-enact one of the cornerstones of hetero-patriarchal relations over and over again. Queer theory therefore separated feminism from 'women' in the sense of a political identity in which feminist politics could be grounded.

Within the (still ongoing) feminist debate this shift remains the main point of contention. Feminist politics can no longer be based on a specific gender identity but rather on shared experiences with the violence embedded in the 'heterosexual matrix' (Butler, 1990) and a shared conviction that stable gender identities that presuppose a 'fitting' sex are themselves part of the problem. Fears that were voiced in this context early on included the 'disembodiment' of women (Duden, 1993), the impossibility to voice political demands once the feminist 'we, women' became problematic (Niekant, 1999) and a more general fear of losing sight of ordinary women's problems in favour of a rather abstract theory (Jeffreys, 1993). In activist practice theoretical debates turned to fights over issues of inclusion or exclusion of trans people, with essentialist feminists constructing a link between sex (as ascribed at birth), gender and political position. Named 'TERFs' (trans-exclusionary radical feminists)[8] by their opponents, these activists call themselves 'gender-critical feminists'.While we do not want to equate essentialist feminism with right-wing or conservative anti-feminism, similarities can be seen between both approaches in terms of content as well as effects. Both favour the term 'sex', which centres the biology of human beings, both result in transphobia as people defying the 'natural' relationship between sex and gender become prone to pathologisation. There are even similarities in the form of discourse as gender-critical feminists just like anti-feminists argue for the protection for children – in this case mostly 'saving' girls from medical treatment for gender dysphoria. In some cases these similarities in content have even translated to unlikely alliances between trans-exclusionary feminists and right-wing anti-feminist actors (see Kawasaka in this volume).

Even though anti-feminists will exploit debates within feminism whenever possible, for anti-feminist actors a different consequence of the queer-feminist upheaval appears much more frightening: from a queer-feminist point of view 'gender' is no longer just the socio-cultural side of 'sex', but an arbitrary norm that is violently enforced on bodies, which only through this gendering come to embody a specific sex. Queer-feminism therefore entails a radical de-naturalisation of the sex-gender nexus as well as of sexuality. 'Nature' (which in right-wing thinking is understood as a timeless and unchanging entity which draws its normative power from exactly this ascribed eternal state) ceases to be a legitimate reason for unequal gender relations or the unequal treatment of sexualities and is instead analysed as a powerful social construction. Without the seemingly apolitical and pre-social status of 'nature', social inequalities regarding gender or sexuality can only be legitimised on ethical grounds in their own right, which is a politically difficult endeavour in modern societies that are based on the idea of political equality among citizens. Anti-feminists therefore cling to the 'naturalness' of gender and sexual differences as well as heterosexuality in order to legitimise a hierarchically structured, unequal society.

This discursive strategy gains credibility by capitalising on the highly uneven transfer of feminist theory into feminist practices and equality policies. The radical deconstruction of gender and sex envisioned by queer theory offered relatively few blueprints for feminist practices and equality policies, but it strengthened a move to replace 'sex' with the socially oriented, more flexible concept of 'gender' that had already been underway. In many cases – including policy papers and declarations – 'gender' displaced the notion of 'sex' in order to stress the focus on lived experience rather than anatomy. One case in point is 'gender mainstreaming', which as a management tool in policymaking works mainly with a male/female dichotomy and has little connection to the radical theoretical ideas of queer-feminism (Schmidt, 2005, p. 68). Nevertheless, its use of the term 'gender' is enough to put the concept into the anti-feminists' spotlight as they frame the use of the term 'gender' itself as a deconstruction of sex.[9]

In a similar manner queer-feminism's de-construction of the 'natural' link between sex/gender and sexuality is turned around in anti-feminist agitation and framed as an attack on heterosexuality per se. While in queer-feminist analysis the entanglement of gender, sex and desire is addressed in a critical fashion, anti-feminism reverses this critical move in order to re-enforce the alleged natural fit of body, identity and sexuality within 'real' (heterosexual, gender-compliant) men and women. Within these discourses 'gender' does not only signify an attack on patriarchal gender relations, but also on heterosexuality as the only 'natural' – therefore the only 'normal', that is normatively acceptable – form of sexual desire (Davis and Greenstein, 2009; Mayer and Goetz, 2019; Mayer and Sauer, 2017). 'Gender ideology' is therefore not only used to attack women's emancipation and women's rights, but equally entails attacks on LGBTIQ+ people and movements.

This is also the reason, why we decided to use anti-feminism as an umbrella term for attacks against women's rights, reproductive and sexual rights, the rights of sexual minorities, transgender and intersex people. Concerns about gender identity in anti-feminist discourse cannot be separated from concerns about sexuality as it is exactly the re-naturalisation of the relation between sex/gender and sexuality that drives current anti-feminist mobilisations. This usage in no way diminishes the specific experiences and specific vulnerabilities of straight women and queer people (inter alia trans and non-binary people, gay men, lesbian women) but rather points to the commonalities in anti-feminist reasoning that need to be analysed.

Anti-feminism as an intersectional ideology

In order to clarify what we mean by an 'intersectional ideology' we first need to acknowledge that of course anti-feminism is intersectional in the sense that – like any oppressive ideology – it affects people differently depending on their situatedness in society (see Beeson in this volume on the especially instructive case of South Africa). Anti-feminism is never independent of racism, nationalism or classism (to name just the 'big three' of the multitude of unequal power relations that shape our world), because as Audre Lorde (2007) famously put it 'we don't live single issue lives'. For feminist researchers and activists this is tremendously important as an understanding of these intersectional effects must shape our policies and strategies. But when we talk about anti-feminism as an intersectional ideology, we propose to slightly shift our focus to the articulations of anti-feminism and how different ideologies come to shape what anti-feminism actually means. This issue is taken up with different foci in all the articles in this volume, but is most pronounced in Mareike Fenja Bauer's work on the interdependence of corona conspiracy myths and anti-feminism in Germany.

The anti-feminist preoccupation with the 'natural fit' between sex, gender and desire explains why the (heterosexual, patriarchal) family is so central in this agitation as it forms the privileged point of convergence of gender and sexual relations. It is also one of the fields in which the intersectionality of anti-feminism as an ideology plays out. What Karin Stögner (2017) suggests with regard to antisemitism, namely to understand it as an intersectional ideology, 'which is permeated by sexist, racist and nationalist elements and which derives its lasting social and individual effectiveness from this entanglement' (Stögner, 2017, p. 26), also applies to anti-feminism. Based on Stögner's considerations, anti-feminism can be described as an intersectional ideology pervaded by other ideologies of inequality, which are often specific to certain actors. One example is the link that right-wing extremists draw between nativist and nationalist (*völkisch*) population policies and anti-feminist family-oriented policies.

Many of their conservative and Christian allies would probably not stand for the former but are more than happy to support the latter.

Talking about 'intersectionality' as an analytical term means to embrace complexity, as the interweaving of ideologies of inequality might take different forms (Kerner, 2009). Anti-feminism often appears as racialised or ethnicised – directly for example when sexual and reproductive rights are labelled a 'Western' and/or 'colonial' import (see Fuller in this volume; Korolczuk and Graff, 2018), but also indirectly, when sexism and sexual violence are projected onto 'others' in order to foster racism and refute feminist claims (Dietze, 2016). Interestingly this 'ethnicisation of sexism' (Jäger, 2004) is a second issue on which anti-feminists unite with some essentialist feminists that follow the same us-vs.-them understanding of social relations. Like 'gender-critical' feminism that excludes trans and intersex people this racist feminism excludes racialised 'others', including racialised women and LGBTIQ+ people, and plays into modernised anti-feminist discourse with its historisation and projection of anti-feminism into a distant past and/or onto geographically or culturally removed 'others'.

While racism leads some feminists to embrace this externalisation of gendered hierarchies, anti-feminist activists on the right of the political spectrum take this argument several steps further: if 'other' men threaten 'our' women, the deeper problem is supposed to be migration as such, which is redefined in terms of invasion, siege and war. There are a number of culprits – effeminate 'weak' men, assertive women, failing families – for which an alleged 'feminisation' of society is to blame that has been brought upon us by feminism. And there is one remedy: manly men, who are ready to fight for what is theirs, including 'their' women and their nation (see Simon Copland in this volume). This discursive chain – that started with issues of (sexualised) male violence against women – firmly links anti-feminism to racism and nationalism, blames feminism for immigration and thereby for violence against women, and promotes patriarchal gender relations as the way to safety. For feminist researchers and activists it is of high importance to understand how this interlinking of different discourses renders anti-feminism a highly effective intersectional ideology. While concrete links and examples will of course vary greatly in different contexts and between different actors the overall logic seems to apply in many cases.

As we have hinted above in relation to the fostering of alliances, the intersectional quality is also one of the reasons why anti-feminism is such a successful tool in struggles for hegemony. Debates about 'gender ideology' allow actors to gain 'cultural power by creating an anti-hegemonic approach against the equality and emancipation of women and LGBTIQ+ people as well as against the liberalization and pluralization' of societies

(Mayer and Sauer, 2017, pp. 36–7). We therefore start this book from an analytical working definition of anti-feminism as a distinctive, albeit not completely coherent, ideology which is always already intersectional. As an ideology that aims to naturalise social inequality (in this respect similar to racism, nationalism or antisemitism) it is articulated differently in accordance with the broader framing it is given by different political actors.

Notes

1. E.g. ECPR – European Consortium for Political Research and ECPG – European Conference on Politics and Gender in 2019 and 2022.
2. E.g. *NORMA: International Journal for Masculinity Studies, 15*(1), 2020: Political Masculinities and Populism; *Signs, 44*(3), 2019: Gender and the Rise of the Global Right; *European Journal on Politics and Gender, 1*(3), 2018: Contemporary Crises in European Politics: Gender Equality+ Under Threat; *Politics and Governance, 6*(3), 2018: The Feminist Project under Threat in Europe; *Feminist Media Studies, 18*(4), 2018: Online Misogyny; *Patterns of Prejudice, 49*(1–2), 2015: Gender and Populist Radical-right Politics.
3. Inter alia Dietze and Roth (2020); Henninger (2020); Köttig et al. (2017); Kováts et al. (2015); Kuhar and Paternotte (2017); Näser-Lather et al. (2019); Strube et al. (2021).
4. Since the finalisation of the manuscript an anthology with a global approach has been published (Scheele et al., 2022).
5. So called incels – involuntary celibates – are mostly young men who turn their involuntary celibacy into a misogynist ideology. Individuals affiliated with incel communities have been responsible for terrorist attacks in the past.
6. All quotes originally in German have been translated by the authors.
7. Some authors have convincingly argued that anti-feminist mobilisations are in no way limited to contexts that have previously seen legal and political gains for women and/or sexual minorities (Graff and Korolczuk, 2017).
8. Although widespread, the notion seems a bit off as many of these feminists are without doubt transphobes, but can hardly be deemed 'radical'. This points to one of the problems of queer-feminist critique, which often paints a one-dimensional picture of 'essentialist feminism' without bothering with the different conceptions of 'woman' salient within different strands of second-wave-feminism.
9. This is helped by the fact that many languages – including the editors' native German – do not offer separate terms for 'sex' and 'gender'. Referring to the academic term 'gender' plays well into the idea of an elitist conspiracy.

References

Achtelik, K. (2015). *Selbstbestimmte Norm: Feminismus, Pränataldiagnostik, Abtreibung.* Verbrecher Verlag.
Armengol, J. M. and Kimmel, M. (2009). *Debating Masculinity.* Men's Studies Press.

Bartz, A. and Schulz, C. (2017). Genderfragen und ihre Verunglimpfung: Kirchliche Positionierungen und Handlungen als Gegenstand von Hate Speech. *Ariadne. Forum für Frauen- und Geschlechtergeschichte, 33*(71), 46–53.

Bates, L. (2020). *Men who Hate Women: From Incels to Pickup Artists, the Truth about Extreme Misogyny and How it Affects Us All.* Simon & Schuster.

Baumeister, M., Lenhard, P. and Nattermann, R. (2020). *Rethinking the Age of Emancipation: Comparative and Transnational Perspectives on Gender, Family, and Religion in Italy and Germany, 1800–1918.* Berghahn Books.

Beauvoir, S. de (2011). *The Second Sex.* Vintage Books.

Blee, K. (2017). Similarities/Differences in Gender and Far-Right Politics in Europe and the USA. In M. Köttig, R. Bitzan and A. Petö (eds), *Gender and Far Right Politics in Europe* (pp. 191–204). Springer International Publishing.

Butler, J. (1990). *Gender trouble: Feminism and the Subversion of Identity.* Routledge.

Congregation for Catholic Education. (2019). *'Male and Female He Created Them'. Towards a Path of Dialogue on the Question of Gender Theory in Education.* https://www.vatican.va/roman_curia/congregations/ccatheduc/documents/rc_con_ccatheduc_doc_20190202_maschio-e-femmina_en.pdf

Congregation for the Doctrine of the Faith. (2004). *Letter to the Bishops of the Catholic Church on the Collaboration of Men and Women in the Church and in the World.* https://www.vatican.va/roman_curia/congregations/cfaith/documents/rc_con_cfaith_doc_20040731_collaboration_en.html

Davis, S. N. and Greenstein, T. N. (2009). Gender Ideology: Components, Predictors, and Consequences. *Annual Review of Sociology, 35*(1), 87–105. https://doi.org/10.1146/annurev-soc-070308-115920

Debus, K. (2017). Dramatisierung, Entdramatisierung und Nicht-Dramatisierung von Geschlecht und sexueller Orientierung in der geschlechterreflektierten Bildung. Oder: (Wie) Kann ich geschlechterreflektiert arbeiten, ohne Stereotype zu verstärken? In U. Glockentöger and E. Adelt (eds), *Gendersensible Bildung und Erziehung in der Schule* (pp. 25–42). Waxmann.

Dietze, G. (2016). Ethnosexismus. Sex-Mob-Narrative um die Kölner Sylvesternacht. *movements. Journal for Critical Migration and Border Regime Studies, 2*(1). http://movements-journal.org/issues/03.rassismus/10.dietze--ethnosexismus.html

Dietze, G. (2019). *Sexueller Exzeptionalismus: Überlegenheitsnarrative in Migrationsabwehr und Rechtspopulismus.* Transcript.

Dietze, G. and Roth, J. (eds). (2020). *Right-wing Populism and Gender: European Perspectives and Beyond.* Transcript.

Duden, B. (1993). Die Frau ohne Unterleib. Zu Judith Butlers Entkörperung. *Feministische Studien, 11*(1993)2, 24–33. https://doi.org/10.1515/fs-1993-0204

Fassin, É. (2020). Anti-gender Campaigns, Populism, and Neoliberalism in Europe and Latin America. *LASA Forum, 51*(2). https://forum.lasaweb.org/files/vol51-issue2/Dossier1-12.pdf

Fraser, N. (2013). *Fortunes of Feminism: From State-Managed Capitalism to Neoliberal Crisis.* Verso Books.

Fraser, N. (2017). Crisis of Care? On the Social-Reproductive Contradictions of Contemporary Capitalism. In T. Bhattacharya (ed.), *Social Reproduction Theory* (pp. 21–36). Pluto Press.

Ganz, K. and Meßmer, A.-K. (2015). Anti-Genderismus im Internet. Digitale Öffentlichkeiten als Labor eines neuen Kulturkampfes. In S. Hark and P.-I. Villa (eds), *Anti-Genderismus* (pp. 59–78). Transcript.

Graff, A. and Korolczuk, E. (2017). 'Worse than communism and nazism put together': War on Gender in Poland. In R. Kuhar and D. Paternotte (eds), *Anti-Gender Campaigns in Europe* (pp. 175–94). Rowman & Littlefield.

Graff, A. and Korolczuk, E. (2021). *Anti-Gender Politics in the Populist Moment.* Routledge.

Hall, S. (1978). *Policing the Crisis: Mugging, the State, and Law and Order.* Macmillan.

Hark, S. and Villa, P.-I. (eds). (2015). *Anti-Genderismus: Sexualität und Geschlecht als Schauplätze aktueller politischer Auseinandersetzungen.* Transcript.

Hechler, A. and Stuve, O. (2015). *Geschlechterreflektierte Pädagogik gegen Rechts.* Verlag Barbara Budrich.

Hennig, A. and Weiberg-Salzmann, M. (eds). (2021). *Illiberal Politics and Religion in Europe and Beyond: Concepts, Actors, and Identity Narratives.* Campus Verlag.

Henninger, A. and Birsl U. (eds). (2020). Antifeminismen. 'Krisen'-Diskurse mit gesellschaftsspaltendem Potential. In *Antifeminismen. 'Krisen'-Diskurse mit gesellschaftsspaltendem Potential* (pp. 9–41). Transcript.

Heß, R. (2017). Anti_Gender_ismus? Hintergründe und Konturen der aktuellen Front gegen 'Gender' – Erkundungen in einer (kirchen-)politischen Kampfzone. *Epd-Dokumentation, 42(2017),* 4–24.

Jäger, M. (2004). Die Kritik am Patriarchat im Einwanderungsdiskurs. Analyse einer Diskursverschränkung. In R. Keller, A. Hierseland, W. Schneider and W. Viehöver (eds), *Handbuch Sozialwissenschaftliche Diskursanalyse.* VS Verlag für Sozialwissenschaften. https://doi.org/10.1007/978-3-322-99764-7_15

Jeffreys, S. (1993). *The Lesbian Heresy: A Feminist Perspective on the Lesbian Sexual Revolution.* Spinifex.

Kaiser, S. (2020). *Politische Männlichkeit: Wie Incels, Fundamentalisten und Autoritäre für das Patriarchat mobilmachen.* Suhrkamp.

Kerner, I. (2009). Alles intersektional? Zum Verhältnis von Rassismus und Sexismus. *Feministische Studien, 27*(1), 36–50. https://doi.org/10.1515/fs-2009-0105

Kimmel, M. and Aronson, A. (2003). *Men and Masculinities: A Social, Cultural and Historical Encyclopedia.* ABC Clio.

Klammer, C. and Bechter, N. (2019). 'Anti-Gender' als kultureller Code? Theoretische Überlegungen zum gegenwärtigen Antifeminismus. In Forschungsgruppe Ideologien und Politiken der Ungleichheit (eds), *Rechtsextremismus. Band 3: Geschlechterreflektierte Perspektiven* (pp. 248–78). Mandelbaum.

Korolczuk, E. (2014). *'The War on Gender' from a Transnational Perspective – Lessons for Feminist Strategising.* Proceedings of III International Gender Workshop 'Are We Moving Forward or Backwards? Strategizing to Overcome Gender Backlash in Central and Eastern Europe'. https://pl.boell.org/sites/default/files/uploads/2014/10/war_on_gender_korolczuk.pdf

Korolczuk, E. and Graff, A. (2018). Gender as 'Ebola from Brussels': The Anticolonial Frame and the Rise of Illiberal Populism. *Signs: Journal of Women in Culture and Society*, *43*(4), 797–821. https://doi.org/10.1086/696691

Köttig, M., Bitzan, R. and Pető, A. (eds). (2017). *Gender and Far Right Politics in Europe*. Palgrave Macmillan.

Kováts, E., Põim, M. (eds). (2015). *Gender as Symbolic Glue: The Position and Role of Conservative and Far Right Parties in the Anti-gender Mobilization in Europe*. Friedrich-Ebert-Stiftung. http://library.fes.de/pdf-files/bueros/budapest/11382.pdf

Kreisky, E. (2004). Geschlecht als politische und politikwissenschaftliche Kategorie. In S. Rosenberger and B. Sauer (eds), *Politikwissenschaft und Geschlecht: Konzepte, Verknüpfungen, Perspektiven* (pp. 23–43). WUV.

Kuhar, R. (2015). Playing with Science: Sexual Citizenship and the Roman Catholic Church Counter-narratives in Slovenia and Croatia. *Women's Studies International Forum, 49*, 84–92.

Kuhar, R. and Paternotte, D. (eds). (2017). *Anti-gender Campaigns in Europe: Mobilizing Against Equality*. Rowman & Littlefield.

Laclau, E. (2013). *Emanzipation und Differenz*. Turia + Kant.

Laclau, E. and Mouffe, C. (2014). *Hegemony and Socialist Strategy: Towards a Radical Democratic Politics*. Verso.

Lang, J. and Peters, U. (eds). (2018). *Antifeminismus in Bewegung: Aktuelle Debatten um Geschlecht und sexuelle Vielfalt*. MARTA PRESS.

Lauer, J.-M. (2016). *Gleichstellungsgarantie oder Ideologie?* katholisch.de. https://www.katholisch.de/artikel/8235-gleichstellungsgarantie-oder-ideologie

Lorde, A. (2007). *Sister Outsider: Essays and Speeches* (revised edition). Crossing Press.

Löwenthal, L. and Guterman, N. (1949). *Prophets of Deceit: A Study of the Techniques of the American Agitator*. Harper.

Manne, K. (2018). *Down Girl: The Logic of Misogyny*. Oxford University Press.

Mayer, S. and Goetz, J. (2019). Mit Gott und Natur gegen geschlechterpolitischen Wandel. Ideologie und Rhetoriken des rechten Antifeminismus. In FIPU (eds), *Rechtsextremismus Band 3: Geschlechterreflektierte Perspektiven* (pp. 205–47). Mandelbaum.

Mayer, S. and Sauer, B. (2017). 'Gender ideology' in Austria: Coalitions around an Empty Signifier. In R. Kuhar and D. Paternotte (eds), *Anti-Gender Campaigns in Europe. Mobilizing against Equality* (pp. 23–40). Rowman & Littlefield International.

Moss, K. (2017). Russia as the Saviour of European Civilization: Gender and the Geopolitics of Traditional Values. In R. Kuhar and D. Paternotte (eds), *Anti-gender Campaigns in Europe* (pp. 195–214). Rowman & Littlefield International.

Näser-Lather, M., Oldemeier, A. L. and Beck, D. (eds). (2019). *Backlash?!: Antifeminismus in Wissenschaft, Politik und Gesellschaft*. Ulrike Helmer Verlag.

Niekant, R. (1999). Zur Krise der Kategorien 'Frauen' und 'Geschlecht': Judith Butler und der Abschied von feministischer Identitätspolitik. In C. Bauhardt and A. von Wahl (eds), *Gender and Politics: 'Geschlecht' in der feministischen Politikwissenschaft* (pp. 29–45). VS Verlag für Sozialwissenschaften

Notz, G. (2015). *Kritik des Familismus: Theorie und soziale Realität eines ideologischen Gemäldes*. Schmetterling Verlag.

O'Leary, D. (1997). *The Gender Agenda: Redefining Equality.* Huntington House Publishers.

O'Neill, R. (2018). *Seduction: Men, Masculinity and Mediated Intimacy.* Polity.

Päpstlicher Rat für die Familie. (2000). *Family, Marriage and 'de facto' Unions.* Libreria Editrice Vaticana.

Paternotte, D. (2015). Blessing the Crowds: Catholic Mobilisations against Gender in Europe. In S. Hark and P.-I. Villa (eds), *Anti-Genderismus: Sexualität und Geschlecht als Schauplätze aktueller politischer Auseinandersetzungen* (pp. 143–7). Transcript.

Planert, U. (1998). *Antifeminismus im Kaiserreich: Diskurs, soziale Formation und politische Mentalität.* Vandenhoeck & Ruprecht.

Reis, H. and Päpstlicher Rat für die Familie. (2007). *Lexikon Familie: Mehrdeutige und umstrittene Begriffe zu Familie, Leben und ethischen Fragen.* Ferdinand Schöningh Verlag.

Scheele, S. (2016). Von Antifeminismus zu 'Anti-Genderismus'? Eine diskursive Verschiebung und ihre Hintergründe. *Tagung 'Gegner*innenaufklärung – Informationen und Analysen zu Anti-Feminismus'.* Gunda-Werner-Institut in der Heinrich-Böll-Stiftung. https://www.gwiboell.de/sites/default/files/uploads/2016/08/scheele_diskursive_verschiebung_antifeminismus.pdf

Scheele, A., Roth J. and Winkel H. (eds). (2022). *Global Contestations of Gender Rights.* Bielefeld University Press.

Schenk, H. (1992). *Die feministische Herausforderung: 150 Jahre Frauenbewegung in Deutschland* (2nd, revised edition; first published 1981). Beck.

Schmidt, V. (2005). *Gender Mainstreaming – An Innovation in Europe?: The Institutionalisation of Gender Mainstreaming in the European Commission.* Verlag Barbara Budrich.

Schmincke, I. (2018). Frauenfeindlich, sexistisch, antifeministisch? Begriffe und Phänomene bis zum aktuellen Antigenderismus. *APuZ, 17(2018),* 28–33.

Stambolis-Ruhstorfer, M. and Tricou, J. (2017). Resisting 'Gender Theory' in France: A Fulcrum for Religious Action in a Secular Society. In R. Kuhar and D. Paternotte (eds), *Anti-Gender Campaigns in Europe* (pp. 79–98). Rowman & Littlefield.

Stern, A. M. (2019). *Proud Boys and the White Ethnostate: How the Alt-right is Warping the American Imagination.* Beacon Press.

Stögner, K. (2014). *Antisemitismus und Sexismus: Historisch-gesellschaftliche Konstellationen.* Nomos.

Stögner, K. (2017). 'Intersektionalität von Ideologien' – Antisemitismus, Sexismus und das Verhältnis von Gesellschaft und Natur. *Psychologie & Gesellschaftskritik, 41(2),* 25–45.

Stoltenberg, J. (2005). Sexual Objectification and Male Supremacy. In J. Stoltenberg (ed.), *Refusing to be a Man: Essays on Social Justice* (2nd edition). Routledge. https://doi.org/10.4324/9780203980828

Strube, S. A., Perintfalvi, R., Hemet, R., Metze, M. and Sahbaz, C. (eds). (2021). *Anti-Genderismus in Europa: Allianzen von Rechtspopulismus und religiösem Fundamentalismus: Mobilisierung – Vernetzung – Transformation.* Transcript.

Ṿolḳov, S. (2000). *Antisemitismus als kultureller Code: Zehn Essays*. Beck.

Wimbauer, C., Motakef, M. and Teschlade, J. (2015). Prekäre Selbstverständlichkeiten. Neun prekarisierungstheoretische Thesen zu Diskursen gegen Gleichstellungspolitik und Geschlechterforschung. In S. Hark and P.-I. Villa (eds), *Anti-Genderismus*. (pp. 41–58). Transcript.

Part One

Global Patterns of Contemporary Anti-Feminism

As stated in the general introduction to this volume our main goal is to provide insights into transnational patterns of contemporary anti-feminist discourse and movement strategies, which lead to striking similarities across very different national, local, religious and political contexts. However, these similarities cannot be grasped in the abstract, but need to be analysed as specific, localised articulations of a transnational and even global discourse, which is in turn shaped, reiterated and changed by these local practices and embodiments. We therefore do not conceptualise the global and the local in opposition to each other, but rather need to understand these dimensions as intertwined. The first part of the book therefore provides analyses of dominant discourses and prevalent strategies, which are used by different anti-feminist actors globally. Still, all chapters are situated in geographically, politically and historically specific contexts, thereby allowing the authors to analyse these transnational strategies with a view to their effects in these specific contexts. With this collection of different research perspectives and foci we try to show the multidimensionality of anti-feminism.

Gabriela Arguedas-Ramírez' analysis of the role the invention of 'gender ideology' plays in the crusade against democracy in Latin America provides the starting point for this endeavour. In line with our understanding of the entanglement of the transnational and the local this chapter does not just provide insights into contemporary political developments in this region, but can (and in our view, should) be read as an analysis of local/regional articulations of a global discourse, which in turn takes on new meaning in these situated struggles. Even though the origins of this discourse can be pinned down to the position of the Holy See vis-à-vis

'gender' it has been profoundly changed through its transnational dif-
fusion, thereby coming to signify a much broader attack on secularism
and democracy that fosters tangible (and worrying) political changes. In
a somewhat similar vein, Regina Fuller's chapter on discourses on CSE in
Ghana as compared to Uganda, South Africa and Senegal explores one of
anti-feminism's global issues of contestation. There is no doubt that the
struggles Fuller analyses are shaped by the specific circumstances of Ghanaian political, educational and religious systems, but it is exactly through
this situated analysis that the author can show how CSE becomes a means
to situate the nation in religious terms rather than being 'just about the
children'. Katharina Wiedlack and Iain Zabolotny turn to the post-Soviet
sphere comparing attacks on feminist activists in Russia, Kyrgyzstan and
Kazakhstan and the role patriarchal norms about female bodies and their
behaviour played in each of these, while refuting simplified accounts of
Russian dominance in the region. This chapter most clearly emphasises
the importance of the local in the transnational, i.e. it underlines that
an analysis of transnational ties needs to be supplemented by an equally
thorough understanding of local contexts and their situated logics. This
chapter highlights the adaptability of anti-feminist discourse and movements to different contexts and different issues, which is one of the conditions for its transnational success.

The first part of the book concludes with two chapters detailing research
on two very different spectre of anti-feminist actors, who both organise
transnationally. The editors analyse the European Christian-conservative
network Agenda Europe and its manifesto on a 'natural' social order,
which provides a consistent blueprint for a Christian conservative utopia.
This transnationally organised network is not only working on a common
platform in terms of content, but also in terms of strategies that are either
applicable transnationally or are directly targeting international politics
and international law. Different anti-feminist communities take centre
stage in Simon Copland's analysis of the manosphere and their influence
on far-right discourse. In this case actors are transnationally connected
online, sharing ambivalent constructions of masculinity that fuel fear and
rage about an alleged 'feminisation of society'. Yet again, it is through an
in-depth analysis of two Australian cases that the meaning and relevance
of this discourse as well as its possibly devastating effects in the offline
world come into focus. There can be no doubt that this selection of foci
is far from all-encompassing, but we hope to provide insights into some
of the most crucial issues and dynamics in contemporary anti-feminist
discourse and movement.

ONE

The Twenty-First-Century Crusade against Democracy in Latin America: 'Gender Ideology' at the Frontline

Gabriela Arguedas-Ramírez

In this chapter, my purpose is to describe and explain how, in Latin America, a neoconservative religious-political alliance has deployed a rhetorical strategy based on what they have labelled 'gender ideology', to gather support for their political purposes in a way that endangers fundamental democratic principles and processes. The notion of 'gender ideology' (which I'll explain in the following sections) is, despite being fallacious, compelling for many people in Latin America. It does this by taking advantage of commonplace prejudices against women and non-heteronormative people as well as of the strong and long-standing political influence of the Catholic Church and, more recently, of neo-Pentecostalism.

I understand neoconservatism, following Kerwick's (2015) analysis, as a political ideology that originated in the US and has influenced political thinking all around the world. Kerwick characterised neoconservatism as 'a militant, imperialistic form of political rationalism'. As Murray Douglas, quoted by Kerwick (2015) describes, neoconservatism is a 'revolutionary conservatism'. Central to this political ideology is the belief in American exceptionalism, which is considered by its followers to be rooted in Judaeo-Christian values. Robbins (2011) highlights that a relevant aspect of neoconservatism is that its political theology overlaps easily with a neo-liberal laissez-faire economic policy. According to Brown (2006, p. 697) 'The open affirmation of moralized state power in the domestic and international sphere is what sets off neoconservatism from an older conservatism, what makes it neo.'

I will argue that the current transnational neoconservative alliance (Haynes, 2020; Archer and Provost, 2020) can be characterised as a twenty-first-century crusade, not just against feminism, women's and LGBTQI people's rights, but against the very idea of democracy. The religiosity in this alliance comes from two very well defined and identifiable socio-religious phenomena: Catholic neo-Integralism and neo-Pentecostal fundamentalism. The term 'crusade' functions not only as a metaphor to convey what this neoconservative alliance looks like, but as a symbolic description of the emotions and longings at play. During their political campaigns, Trump's and Bolsonaro's followers created memes and other sorts of viral visual messages of them in crusaders' regalia, accompanied by the phrase 'Deus Volt!' (God's will) and there were public gatherings where followers displayed a variety of medievalist religious symbols (Gabriele and Perry, 2020; Kanji and Kalmar, 2018).

My central argument is that this neoconservative alliance, these twenty-first-century crusaders, pursue three mains political goals: first, to re-establish – at least some – of the most fundamental political prerogatives religious authorities used to have before the secularisation[1] of the state and the consolidation (at least formally) of liberal democracies. Second, to reform the state, make it coherent with the neoliberal functioning of the economy and public policy, and, third, to further a process of de-secularisation of society at large, that consequently will restore legitimacy to a traditional patriarchal gender hierarchy. Anti-feminism is a crucial tool to accomplish these three aims, given the fact that the neoliberal-religious state they aspire to build requires the 'traditional' family to procure all the care work and assistance the state will no longer provide. All other social services that are needed and cannot be procured by the family might be delivered (with certain limitations and under specific conditions) by religious institutions (Cooper, 2019). In other words, social justice and the welfare state will be substituted by the naturalised reproductive labour of women and by religious institutions. This agenda is not new, but it is entering a new, more religiously authoritarian, phase that I argue appears as a new crusade, a 're-conquest' of a territory (both material and symbolic) that has been under constant dispute for more than four decades.

To understand how this anti-democratic neoconservative alliance has emerged and operates in Latin America, it is indispensable to situate the analysis in a historical perspective. First, it should be considered that despite different national histories all countries in this region have been shaped by complex political, military, economic and cultural confrontations that have evolved over the course of five centuries, after the Conquest and colonisation of these territories under the banner of the Spanish Catholic monarchy. It was not until 200 years ago that the first republics were declared, however many of them became confessional states. Some countries are, up to this day, constitutional confessional states.[2] The political, symbolic and cultural power of the Catholic Church continues to be strong, even though the secularisation process (that began in the second half of the nineteenth century) put limits to some of its political and economic privileges. Nonetheless, the Catholic Church has played a determining role in most important political events and transformations in the region, such as the coups d'état in Chile, Argentina, Honduras and Guatemala.

In order to understand the advance of this new anti-democratic neoconservative alliance in Latin America, it is necessary to see the ongoing historical process. The US neoconservative project encountered a fertile ground in Latin America, where the conservative idea that the state has a moral purpose and that this purpose must be guided by religious institutions still prevails.

Political events in Brazil, Mexico and Colombia illustrate the political confrontations in democratic settings, where the neoconservative alliance has deployed the war on 'gender ideology' – taking advantage of popular anti-feminism and homophobia, to agitate the masses and mobilise them during electoral processes. The selected cases are paradigmatic and illustrative of the political climate in the region. In Brazil, the re-emergence of the extreme right, openly defending the dictatorship and the political power of religion, was a major turn of events; as were the first results of the peace referendum in Colombia, where moral panic was stronger than the collective desire to put an end on the armed conflict. On the other hand, in Mexico, the populist-religious turn of López Obrador, was a significant blow against secularisation, which paradoxically came from a politician who was framed as a leftist.

A Brief Historical Overview of Religion and the State in Latin America

In this section I will briefly provide some historical details on the relation between religion and the state in Brazil, Mexico and Colombia.

Brazil is a vast country with a powerful economy, notwithstanding alarming levels of inequality and exclusion. However, the two left-wing governments, before Bolsonaro came to power in 2018, successfully improved the general quality of life and life expectancy. Nonetheless, during that time, a politically ambitious neo-Pentecostal fundamentalist movement was growing, which burst out during the impeachment of President Dilma Rousseff in 2016. One of the key issues behind Rousseff's impeachment was the political-religious weaponising of homophobic and anti-feminist popular sentiments. This conservative religious-political narrative was also instrumental for Bolsonaro during his political campaign (Løland, 2020).

To grasp the profound effects that religious beliefs, organisations and narratives have in Brazil, it is essential to consider the relationship between church and state. Secularisation has been superficial and incomplete, limited mostly to mere restrictions in the use of religious symbols by state officials in public events or the prohibition to favour a particular religious community over the rest. The current constitution allows the financing of religious organisations, recognises as important the collaboration between the state and religious communities for the convenience and interest of the public, and provides civil effects to religious marriages. By a constitutional provision, religious organisations are not required to pay taxes. Additionally, Brazil has signed three agreements with the Holy See (Gomes, 2014).

Mexico is one of the most interesting cases of a secular state. As Patiño Reyes (2015) compellingly states: 'It is not irrelevant to remember that there were two conquests: the military and the spiritual. The first was achieved by Spanish soldiers, and the second was made by the Franciscans, Dominicans and Jesuits' (p. 507). The secular state in Mexico was fervently championed by liberal intellectuals, who perceived a secularised political order as a necessary step in the process of independence and sovereignty. President Benito Juarez García proclaimed the separation between the state and the Catholic Church in the constitution of 1857, along with the recognition of religious freedom, then understood as religious tolerance. This reform asserted the independence and political sovereignty of the state over the Catholic Church, which had excessive economic power (ibid.).

After the Mexican Revolution, the confrontation with the Catholic Church that still exercised important political power ended with the 1917 constitution that limited religious influence to the private sphere. As explained by Carlos Monsiváis (2008), the constitutional mandate of a secular public education, which promotes science and critical thinking, was an endorsement of the profound importance the secularity of the state had at that moment. Even more, it was an instrument to prevent religious fanaticism and intolerance. But the Catholic Church rejected the secularisation of the constitution, state and education, and this reaction triggered a violent conflict known as the 'Cristero' War (1926–9). The aftershock of this tragic conflict permeated the relations between Church and state for many decades (Amuchástegui et al., 2010).

Colombia has suffered one of the world's longest-running violent internal conflicts, driven by land rights disputes, growing inequality and exclusion, and lack of confidence in government (Vitale and Cohen, 2013). In the last thirty years, besides suffering from this intense armed conflict, and probably in part due to that tragedy, there have also been significant changes in the religious landscape. Still a profoundly Catholic country, in Colombia the religious competition has intensified during the last decades (Prieto, 2020).

As in the case of Brazil, the secular state is understood, essentially, not as a separation between two spheres – the political and the religious – but as an open door for cooperation between the state and the different religious communities under equal conditions. Since the 1991 constitutional reform, the state has extended to all religions the prerogatives that before had been reserved for the Catholic Church. In fact, ending the inequality among religious denominations was the most important demand that drove the push to eliminate the confessionality of the state. That means that the constitutional reform was not motivated by a liberal conviction that politics and religion should be separated, as happened in Mexico (ibid.).

In June 2017, one year before the peace agreement referendum, there was an intense debate concerning the relation between religion and politics. The episode that prompted this discussion was the decision by the mayors of two rural towns to offer those municipalities to Jesus Christ by means of official governmental decrees. These were unconstitutional acts that were received with indignation by part of the public but were also applauded by anti-secular religious communities. Manrique (2019) explains that these were symptomatic expressions of the intensifying militancy of conservative evangelical churches in electoral politics.

Conceptual Apparatus and Historical Context

'Gender ideology': a product of Catholic neo-Integralism

Several authors such as Garbagnoli (2016) and Kuhar and Paternotte (2018) have developed theoretical and conceptual analysis of the term 'gender ideology'. But as I have argued before (Arguedas-Ramírez, 2019) I am interested in exploring the notion of 'gender ideology' as a product of strategic counter-argumentation developed by intellectuals in the Catholic neo-integralist movement, in close communication with the Holy See. The concept of 'gender ideology' has an enormous symbolic power that has helped political-economic interest groups to bring together different social sectors that share three key aspects: (1) social conservatism, (2) a deep distrust of liberal democracy, for several reasons, including opening spaces for feminist and sexual diversity claims and (3) opposition to what they consider to be left-wing policies.

The concept of 'gender ideology' and the movement that it has furthered have been characterised as anti-rights or anti-gender by several activists and authors such as Sonia Côrrea, David Paternotte and Roman Kuhar (2018). Even though this concept was developed to counteract and discredit gender and feminist theories, the social movement that has declared the so called 'war against gender' aspires to control more than the bodies of women and sexually diverse people. And that is why I consider it essential to frame this term as an attack on democracy.

As I have previously discussed (Arguedas-Ramírez, 2020) in 2012 Pope Benedict XVI delivered a Christmas speech in which he critiqued Simone de Beauvoir's philosophy of gender, strategically referring to the interpretation made by a non-Catholic spiritual authority, the Chief Rabbi of France, Gilles Bernheim. This was a clever way to signal that he was not only addressing the Catholic community but delivering the message that gender theory should be considered a threat for all of human society. In his commentary, the former Pope said that,

> according to this philosophy, sex is no longer an original given of nature that man must accept and personally make sense of and fulfil with meaning, but rather a social function that each one can choose autonomously (. . .) The profound falsehood of this theory and of the anthropological revolution it contains is glaring. Man is now contesting the fact of having a nature, constituted by his corporeality, which characterizes the human being. (Benedict XVI, 2012)

Ratzinger is not just performing a metaphysical or spiritual exhortation but a rational counter-argumentation, appealing to a seemingly self-evident biological truth. Even more, he is finding common ground between non-believers and believers. This is a distinctive sign of Catholic neo-Integralism, as I will describe in more detail in the following section. His discursive repertoire is not limited to religious symbolism, because this is not useful in a secularised debate about gender theory. Rather, he is providing a narrative that looks reasonable enough to debate gender and feminist theory and prevents the risk of been discredited a priori for using religious references in a secular public sphere. The notion of 'gender ideology', though fallacious, serves the purpose of defending a moral truth in a way that can be perceived as universal and rational.

At the end of this speech, Ratzinger equates the defence of the traditional family, according to God's will, with the defence of all human beings. Here lies the fundamental opposition between 'good and evil', that is to say, between de Beauvoir's thesis of the social construction of women's subalternity and gender, and the divine creation. The line of thought in Ratzinger discourse is that to deny the unquestionable immutability of gender is to deny nature, and, therefore, gender theory is a fundamentally destructive ideology that must be rejected by all people – believers and non-believers – who defend the very nature and dignity of human beings. In this way, Ratzinger elaborates a rhetorical scheme in which the reasonable, the truth and the moral are one thing and cannot be divided.

This is how the term 'gender ideology' has been circulating in Latin America, the US and some European countries. Neo-integrist scholars have contributed to legitimising this concept and to disguising its implicit religious moral judgement. Since the beginning of the twenty-first century the term 'gender ideology' has been increasing its presence in academic settings, mostly through the work of professors and researchers in Catholic universities.[3]

Jane Adolphe's (2003) article entitled ,The Case Against Same-Sex Marriage in Canada: Law and Policy Considerations', presented at The Future of Marriage and Claims for Same-Sex Unions Symposium can serve as a paradigmatic example. Adolphe, who is employed at the Ave Maria School of Law, cites a speech that Joseph Ratzinger delivered in 1999, denouncing that the status of family and marriage was in danger because the law allegedly was no longer based on stable, immutable and true principles but on what the majority decided to be true or just at any given moment. He was, in a way, denouncing the coming of a post-truth era, using ideas that can be assimilated into academic language. Adolphe takes up his argumentation and transforms it into a conservative – but secular – legal reasoning, in which the notion 'gender ideology' is central:

> In the same-sex marriage debate, a judicial minority has so far largely determined what is to be regarded as just and true. When the Parliament and other legislatures fail to override judicial overreaching, Canadians live under an altered constitutional system based on a new ideology not defined or desired by government but rather developed in an ad hoc manner through case law (. . .) Certainly, in the same-sex debate, gender ideology has been promoted through the courts with the assistance of rights rhetoric. In the case of same-sex marriage, one may argue that the Charter of Rights and Freedoms is 'being used as a tool of cultural genocide' to condemn cultural, religious, and moral beliefs and practices which do not conform. (2003, pp. 515–16)

Catholic neo-Integralism and neo-Pentecostal fundamentalist movements have combined their strengths to make 'gender ideology' the new detonator of moral panic. Their rhetoric strategy is based on deploying this concept in a way that will convince people they must oppose feminist theory, gender theory, and feminist and LGBTQI movements, to protect the common good.

In this way, the call for social mobilisation appears as a sensible position based on reason and not on religious bigotry. This enables these political-religious movements to reach broader audiences, beyond the boundaries of the communities of faith, advancing the re-conquest (like a Reconquista or a crusade to regain control over the Holy Places during the Middle Ages) of the public sphere.

Catholic neo-Integralism and anti-secularism

Catholic neo-Integralism is rooted in the Catholic Integrism of the nineteenth century in Spain. This movement advocated for the centrality of the Catholic tradition both in private life and the public sphere. It was also a significant influence in the Catholic nationalist movement during Franco's dictatorship (Pace and Guolo, 2006).

Its moral and political agenda is based on the idea that moral tradition should govern all individual behaviour, even in democratic republics. Former Pope Benedict XVI supported the view that the Church should still act as society's director of conscience and that this fundamental task was key in the preservation of Europe's historical identity, which has profound Catholic foundations.

At the end of the nineteenth century, Catholic Integrism marked a sharp contrast to the social progressive side of Catholicism that supported Pope Leo XIII and his encyclical Rerum Novarum, issued in 1891 and considered by many conservative Roman Catholics to be extremely liberal. In Spain, Catholics deeply committed to tradition were opposed to what they viewed as the influence of liberal and socialist thought within the Catholic Church and fought those proposals inspired by modern ideals, such as the separation between the political sphere and the religious realm (Van der Krogt, 1992; Poulat, 1985).

Two foundational documents of Catholic neo-Integralism are the encyclical letters Quanta Cura and Syllabus Errorum that were issued by Pope Pius IX in 1864. These documents motivated a conservative reaction against all forms of adaptation of Catholicism to modernity. For instance, the Syllabus Errorum defines beliefs such as naturalism and absolute rationalism, freedom of religion and political doctrines like socialism and communism as errors and distortions of modernity. This encyclical letter affirms that it is a fundamental mistake to admit civil powers to determine the rights of the Church and their limits and rejects the secularisation of education and civil law.

All those ideas, though expressed in a subtler manner, are incorporated in Catholic neo-Integralism and shape today's neoconservative agenda. The transition process from Catholic Integrism towards Catholic neo-Integralism has moved forward through the continuous and systematic work of lay organisations such as Opus Dei, which have consolidated a strategic opposition against the secularisation of the public sphere, while accepting a more flexible position towards capital accumulation than Catholic Integrism did in the nineteenth century. Through the apostolate, which is the call upon Catholics to claim and transform everyday spaces to sites of political faith-based resistance, a common individual is ontologically transformed into an active participant in the divine plan.

According to Escrivá de Balaguer, founder of Opus Dei, a true Catholic must always act in coherence with their faith. Nothing is above the religious mandate, not even the law. Thus, religious mandates not only govern Catholics' private personal choices, but also dictate all other facets, including their professional duties. This moral conviction is incompatible with the separation between personal religious beliefs and civic duties (Escudier, 2013).

Both neo-Pentecostalism and Catholic neo-Integralism share core ideas about how political organisations, including the state, should work. Essentially, these movements envision a state that includes some features of contemporary life (i.e. the dominant economic system) while re-establishing the indivisibility of religious morality and civil law. Hence, the legitimacy of political authority would require a harmonious relation with moral and religious authority. This situation would mean that religious organisations would have privileges like no other civil or political actor.

Neo-Pentecostal fundamentalism and the US Christian Right

Religious fundamentalism is defined as a flexible but coherent arrangement of groups that ground their ideology on the literal word of sacred texts and actively seek to make their world-view and institutions adopted in the public sphere. It is characterised by an inflexible confrontation with modernity (Ozzono, 2007). Neo-Pentecostal fundamentalist organisations react against the political marginalisation of religion with a selective reinterpretation of sacred texts, moral absolutism and messianism (Ozzano, 2009).

Neo-Pentecostalism in Latin America is linked to the evangelical revival in the United States during the post-Second World War period, which became known as the Christian Right. For decades, this political-religious movement has been doing political activism by means of missionary work throughout Latin America (Sotelo and Arocena, 2021). In the US, it has established strong connections with the Republican Party since the 1960s, promoting an agenda against LGBTQI people and women's rights and against the secularisation of education. In the US, during the last five decades, famous preachers have risen from their churches to political-electoral roles, thus creating an even more explicit link between religion and politics (Armstrong, 2001).

This anti-secular strategy applied in several Latin American countries with the support of their US counterparts has also promoted free enterprise and free trade, while strongly opposing social justice policies. By connecting their churches with political parties, they have been successful in translating their religious precepts into policy agendas and expanding complex networks of actors who can influence multiple spheres of public life. Evangelical churches (including but not limited to neo-Pentecostal) have also created a vast international conglomerate of media outlets, including radio stations, television studios and digital media.[4] It could be said that their communication strategy is an expression of the Society of the Spectacle (Debord, 1995). To put on an attractive show is central in neo-Pentecostal religiosity. This savoir-faire is key for the neoconservative alliance in its crusade against 'gender ideology'.

If Catholic neo-Integralism is the intellectual source of the conceptualisation of 'gender ideology' as a tool to oppose gender theory, feminist theory and sexual diversity, neo-Pentecostal fundamentalism is the communication network that has reached even the most rural areas in Latin America.

García-Ruiz and Michel (2010), framing their analysis as a political anthropology of globalisation, describe neo-Pentecostalism in Latin America as an indicator of the social reorganisation propelled by the economic and cultural process of globalisation, as well as a means people use to navigate that reorganisation. For these authors, the individuation process produced in neo-Pentecostal communities is compatible with the demands of neoliberal globalisation. That is to say, the subjectivity of the neo-Pentecostal individual is fully integrated into the market logic. Through religion, they have created new communities and loyalties, linked to opportunities for social mobility and to a sense of political relevance.

The 'trinity': Catholic neo-Integralism, neo-Pentecostal fundamentalism and neoliberalism

In moral terms, Christianism exercises control over the community of believers through the moral superiority of pastors and priests who act as 'shepherds' (conscience directors). With the ethical revolution prompted by the ideas of enlightenment, individuals became aware of their capacity for acting as moral subjects[5] without relinquishing their autonomy to religious or moral authorities.

The emergence of the individual subject as someone that can discern the complexities of moral issues produced a profound cultural transformation. The process of secularisation is one of its most transformative consequences. Democratisation and republicanism both depend on the secularisation of the public sphere and political institutions, as well as on the protection of individual freedom of conscience and belief. The significant difference between a regime where political and religious authority are indistinguishable from each other, and a regime where both are separated and political authority defines the rules of coexistence, resides in the principle of individual moral autonomy. That is the fundamental idea that nineteenth-century Catholic Integrism vehemently opposed. Catholic neo-Integralism maintains at its core that integralist conviction in a moral authority that must guide all citizens (not just believers) to create what they consider a good society (in political-theological terms). Consequently, secularity is still considered an obstacle, and so is a democratic order that embraces the legacy of the enlightenment.

The political objective shared by conservative religious and neoliberal groups that have deployed the concept of 'gender ideology' is to gain control over the state and its institutions by democratic means and then, from within, impose their social and economic vision on societies. As Brown (2006) and Cooper (2019) have extensively analysed, the common ground between economic elites, the neoliberal agenda and the political-religious movements I have described previously lies in the shared conviction that social justice and welfare policies should be substituted by charity and philanthropy. Catholic neo-Integralism's and neo-Pentecostal fundamentalism's response to inequality and poverty is what I call disciplinary charity. The services that religious organisations provide to vulnerable people are not truly free of charge. The price to pay is a disciplinary – in Foucauldian terms – process of moral transformation guided by the religious authority.

Both neoliberals and religious neo-integralist/fundamentalists consider religious organisations to be better at attending to populations in need. In this way, a faith-based clientelism is produced in the form of an instrumental exchange of compassionate actions such as food for poor families for moral conformity. Religious organisations expect moral discipline and gratitude from their beneficiaries. They believe that vulnerability is not caused by structural injustice but by individual lack of moral strength. Clearly, this approach is compatible with the neoliberal demand for a minimal state.

The neoconservative alliance enthusiastically supports the idea that all social problems can be eradicated by supporting and promoting the formation of traditional families and values. For them the ultimate responsibility of caring and protecting vulnerable individuals does not lie with the state but with the family. Therefore, the concept of 'gender ideology' can be constructed as a threat against the traditional family and the natural order that determines the social places that men and women should occupy in a good society. Even more, it has been used to engender fear of an attack on the founding values of the nation, in this way capturing the attention of more potential neoconservative followers and sympathisers, many of whom are traditional men who have not found an outlet for their frustration and anger (Hochschild, 2016).

During the 1960s and 1970s in Europe and the Americas, the process of secularisation, democratisation and inclusion continued to move forward. Civil rights, social justice, and sexual and reproductive rights were part of the political demands that were gaining more support in the West. The legalisation of abortion in the US and in some European countries, such as France, marked a critical moment in the separation of moral dogma and public policy. As a result of these transformative social movements, conservative actors were responding in many ways (Faludi, 1991). A diverse anti-feminist group was created at the UN, uniting Muslim countries, the Vatican, Russia and the United States. This alliance found a way to use the language of human rights, citizen participation, free exchange of ideas and non-discrimination to validate their belligerent opposition to sexual and reproductive rights and to justify the de-secularisation of liberal democracy (Cupać and Ebetürk, 2020).

The War on 'Gender Ideology' in Latin America

For more than twenty years, a political and religious counter-offensive against feminism and LGBTQI social movements has been underway in Latin America, through a well-articulated and financed assemblage of neo-conservative religious actors. They have succeeded in creating considerable obstacles to sexual and reproductive rights (Arguedas-Ramírez and Morgan, 2017). Over the last decade, this offensive has added to its rhetorical arsenal the concept of 'gender ideology'. The strategic weaponising of widespread anti-feminist and homophobic sentiments has had significant political results favourable to the neoconservative agenda.

Here I will present three Latin American examples of how this alliance, using the war against 'gender ideology', has influenced the political landscape in the region doing considerable damage to women and LGBTQI people as well as democratic principles.

Brazil

During the electoral campaign (2017–18) Jair Bolsonaro insisted that God should be given more space in politics because most Brazilian people are Christian, and therefore the faith of the great majority should not be ignored (Zilla, 2020). Almost 70 per cent of the evangelicals and 50 per cent of the Catholics in Brazil voted for Bolsonaro in 2018. But it should be noted that the politicisation of religious discourse for electoral purposes is anything but new. As Zilla (2020) explains,

> since re-democratization, many politicians with presidential ambitions have actively sought the support of spiritual authorities and their communities. Some have even founded 'Evangelical committees' within their campaign machinery to gain the favour of Evangelical voters.

In 2018, the evangelical support was crucial in Bolsonaro electoral success, which brought back the right in Brazilian politics.

According to Løland (2020, p. 63), his success 'can partly be understood as an effect legitimated by this new political alliance of conservative Christian forces and their theologies: traditional Pentecostalism, neo-Pentecostalism and neoconservative Catholicism'. His campaign used cyber-activism to circulate misinformation and animosity towards women and sexually diverse people. As Løland (2020, p. 71) puts it, their fight against 'gender ideology'

> may be said to lead to continuous devaluation of political liberty in the field of reproductive rights. At the very least, the Christian right's valorization of state power for particular moral ends stands in potential tension with the liberal culture of constitutional democracy.

Bolsonaro was also backed by the political right, which found in him the perfect candidate; one that was willing to justify human rights violations during the military regime of 1964–85.

Corrêa and Kalil (2020) demonstrate the effects of the radical politicisation of religious beliefs during the process of re-democratisation and the neoliberal transformation of public policies in Brazil. Aggressive disputes against feminist and LGBTQI demands in the Brazilian Congress exemplify how invested the neoconservative religious forces are in their quest to dismantle women's and LGBTQI rights. The situation has been getting more acrimonious since the beginning of the twenty-first century. Issues such as the decriminalisation of abortion and same-sex unions induced a peak of moral outrage and consequently have been weaponised for political purposes. Strongly opposing these demands and agitating popular sectors using the war against 'gender ideology' in electoral campaigns, the Brazilian Christian Right gained votes and extensive social support.

During the presidential campaign of 2010 in Brazil, when Dilma Roussef was the candidate for the Partido dos Trabajadores (Workers Party), her position in favour of the legalisation of abortion became the main target. Her opponent from Partido da Social Democracia Brasileira (Social Democratic Party) and many conservative organisations raged against her for supporting sexual and reproductive rights. After she won the election, the attacks against her for expressing even the slightest support for feminist and sexual diversity causes became more and more aggressive. A neoconservative alliance was formed to obstruct any legal reform or public policy that was linked to women's rights or sexual diversity issues. For instance, it boycotted the Third National Human Rights Plan, which was a public policy backed by a wide network of progressive civil society organisations. This plan included the decriminalisation of abortion, the secularisation of public space, and the creation of the National Truth Commission to investigate crimes committed by the Brazilian Army during the military regime of 1964–85. In 2011 the issue of LGBTQI rights became the focus of neoconservative attacks as a reaction against the School Without Homophobia campaign. The neo-Pentecostal branch in Congress used the slur 'gay kit' to refer to it. Jair Bolsonaro was then a member of parliament and became a key political actor during the intense conflict between Dilma Rousseff and the parliament that ended in the withdrawal of the campaign (Corrêa and Kalil, 2020).

Neo-Pentecostal fundamentalist organisations were also responsible for the impeachment of Dilma Rousseff. This movement was getting more audacious as its political representatives (who had managed to gather most votes) were gaining more and more disputes at parliament. The LASA report (Chalhoub et al., 2017) on the impeachment of President Rousseff points out:

> In July 2016, senator and evangelical pastor Magno Malta authored a bill titled 'Escola Sem Partido' (School Without Political Parties), which would prohibit teachers from promoting 'party-political' interests or 'inciting' pupils to take part in protests. The project also established that gender ideology and sexuality 'should not be part of the didactic materials'. (p. 51)

This campaign also encouraged parents and the public to take legal action against teachers they thought were indoctrinating children with 'gender ideology' or any other deviant political discourse. The Escola Sem Partido movement was motivated not only by this religious defence of conservative values but also by a neoliberal agenda against the legacy of social justice policies of Lula da Silva.

Mexico

During post-revolutionary governments, traditional protestants supported the principles of secular liberalism. Evangelicals, in general, usually kept aside from electoral activism as they considered these activities to be deviations from their faith. However, as social movements such the feminist and the LGBTQI-movements were gaining more political and social relevance in the late twentieth and early twenty-first centuries, conservative evangelicals' disapproval of that significant social transformation took a political turn. And despite the historic hostilities between the Mexican Catholic Church and evangelical organisations, they found common ground in their shared adversary: feminist and LGBTQI movements. United against what they perceived as moral deviance, Catholics and evangelicals have come together to protest the decriminalisation of abortion, same-sex marriage, sexual education, reclaiming in this way a political voice in the public space (Gómez-Peralta, 2020).

In the context of democratic transition, at the beginning of the twenty-first century, evangelicals moved to the political arena, through most political parties. Moreover, some evangelical leaders created their own political organisations, such as the Social Encounter Party (PES). Even though evangelicals in Mexico account for no more than 10 per cent of believers, their activism (carried out mostly by Pentecostal and neo-Pentecostal churches) is quite conspicuous. They have succeeded in converting to the faith a number of political leaders, and persuading many others to adopt their religious-political agenda, as in the case of President Andrés Manuel López Obrador (known in Mexico as AMLO) (Pérez Guadalupe and Grundberger, 2018).

The PES is the most prominent and openly religious (strongly leaning to neo-Pentecostalism) political party in Mexico. It is characterised by two main features of the neo-integralist/fundamentalist assemblage previously described: a strong defence of traditional moral Christian values regarding sexuality, gender and the family, and an economic agenda based on the neoliberal doctrine (defence of a free market economy, a strong defence of private property and minimal state regulation of business activity). PES benefited as well from the support of wealthy religious organisations that own several media outlets such as radio stations and TV channels (Careaga and Aranda, 2020). However, they claim to be liberals, and even 'juaristas'.[6]

Catholics and neo-Pentecostals (not so traditional Protestants), have been allies since the 1980s, defending a common social conservative agenda. Gómez-Peralta (2012) concludes that 'although they may have had serious differences in the economic field (. . .) this has been the breeding ground for the formation of a new Mexican Christian right-wing, composed of a Catholic and Evangelical side' (p. 10).

In this context of growing religious-political participation based primarily on opposing the advance of sexual and reproductive rights and the defence of the 'natural and traditional family', the coalition of evangelical churches, Confraternidad Nacional de Iglesias Cristianas Evangélicas (CONFRATERNICE), gave its full support to AMLO during the 2018 electoral campaign. AMLO's political party, MORENA, negotiated with PES the creation of an electoral alliance called Juntos Haremos Historia (Together We Will Make History) (Gómez-Peralta, 2020). And they did. AMLO won the presidential election and the electoral coalition MORENA won a parliamentary majority. PES held a strong presence in some key states and won eight senators and fifty-six federal congressmen. During the last four years PES has been an important political player, decisive in approving the constitutional reforms proposed by AMLO (Careaga and Aranda, 2020).

According to Díaz Domínguez (2020) AMLO's electoral strategy consisted in connecting with popular religious sensitivity. His continual appeals to traditional and religious values were an attempt to soften the radical-left image he had from previous electoral campaigns. In his public discourse he often mentions the importance of religious faith and values while insisting that issues such as same-sex marriage and decriminalisation of abortion should be decided via referendum.

One of AMLO's first presidential acts was to officially endorse a conservative pamphlet from the 1940s called Cartilla Moral (Moral Textbook). He publicly said that a good moral education was fundamental to fight the generalised corruption in Mexican society. In contrast, while AMLO has opened up his government to religious organisations, he has closed the door to feminist and LGBTQI organisations. In addition, on many occasions he has used derogatory and offensive terms against women and feminist organisations, in a clear gesture of anti-feminist complicity with the neoconservative alliance (Careaga and Aranda, 2020).

Colombia

Latin-Americanists Beltrán and Creely (2018) explain that

'Gender ideology' came to the forefront of the Colombian public consciousness in a series of mass protests which took place on 10th August 2016 in major Colombian cities. The protests were against the use of a new manual for sex education in primary schools called 'Ambientes escolares libres de discriminación' ('School environments free from discrimination') (Albarracín 2016; Vélez 2016a). The manuals were designed in response to sentence T.478 of 2015 of the Colombian Constitutional Court, in which the Court tried to establish the responsibility of the high school Gimnasio el Castillo for the suicide of homosexual teenager Sergio Urrego. In this sentence, the Constitutional Court acknowledged faults in the Colombian school system which created situations of intolerance and discrimination on the basis of 'sexual orientation' and 'gender identity'. For this reason, the Court required the Colombian Ministry of Education to implement measures that would 'incentivize and strengthen the school community and the exercise of students' human, sexual and reproductive rights'. (p. 7)

The Ministry of Education published the manual two months before the peace referendum of 2016 and the negative reaction was unprecedented. Thousands of people took to the streets to protest what neo-Pentecostal leaders named a manual that incentivised homosexuality. Catholic neo-integralist organisations also joined the protests, accusing the Ministry of Education of indoctrinating children into 'gender ideology', destroying the family and corrupting children.

This account serves as an illustration of the prelude to the peace referendum. Hagen (2016) points out that the Colombian peace process was the first one to include LGBTQI groups alongside with a thorough gender perspective. According to Hagen (2016), only 4 per cent of participants to peace processes are women. Many feminist and women's organisations advocate for the inclusion of a gender perspective into peace negotiations to understand to what extend an armed conflict affects women's lives, in all its dimensions. Moreover, nearly 40 per cent of FARC combat forces were women. For that reason, the Colombian peace negotiating team created a gender subcommission to safeguard the inclusion of a gender perspective in the process.

However, as noted by Mazo (2019) and Beltrán and Creely (2018) among other scholars, religious actors fallaciously and deliberately called the inclusion of a gender perspective 'gender ideology', to create confusion and fear towards the peace negotiations in public. Affirmative action and reparations based on gender or sexual orientation were not welcomed by neoconservative organisations, specifically neo-Pentecostal churches that have a close relationship with right-wing political parties. But it was just after the aforementioned protests against the Ministry of Education that the campaign against the gender perspective in the peace negotiations started. These three scholars agree that the peace referendum opposition movement identified the term 'gender ideology' as an efficient catchphrase in their pursuit for attention and sympathisers. Soon, there were discussions all around the country denouncing how 'foreign' interests were meddling with the peace negotiations, introducing ideas against Colombians' dearest moral values, the 'natural' family, marriage and the innocence of children; and even that Colombia was at risk of sliding towards a communist-atheist dictatorship that would destroy freedom of religion.

Finally, the 'No' against the peace agreement won the referendum. As Hagen (2016) concludes: 'Disagreements over sexual orientation and gender identity ultimately played a key role in the social perception of the peace deal after four years of negotiations between the Colombian government and Revolutionary Armed Forces of Colombia (FARC) rebels.' The role played by the neoconservative alliance against the peace agreement was decisive in the outcome. After so much suffering during more than fifty years of armed conflict, the result of the referendum came as a shock for many in all Latin America. Manrique (2019) explains: 'In the perplexity generated by this shock, exhilarating for the opponents and heart-breaking for the supporters of the peace process, the electoral force of the evangelical churches showed itself as having an unexpected, and yet relentless reach.'

García Molina and Chicaíza (2018) underline the similarities between the triumph of the 'No' against the peace agreement, the election of Donald Trump in the US and the vote in favour of Brexit in the United Kingdom. All those controversial events happened in 2016 and, as I see it, there are important similarities also with the election of Bolsonaro, in Brazil, in 2018, such as the strategic use of social media and references to fictitious enemies such as 'gender ideology'. Once installed, those kind of false but well-designed narratives are almost impossible to counteract.

Conclusion

The twenty-first-century crusade against liberal democracy, LGBTQI and women's human rights and social justice is a very complex problem. In this chapter, I used the example of Latin America to highlight the way in which neoconservative discourses are deployed in different scenarios to further broaden and diversify social alliances against a perceived common adversary. In the case of 'gender ideology', that worldwide common adversary is feminism, gender theory and sexual diversity. Not all of those who are convinced that 'gender ideology' is a real political strategy to overturn the family and destroy moral values are religious. Many are non-believers or non-Christian believers. What believers and non-believers who have joined the movement against 'gender ideology' have in common is that they respond to anti-feminist propaganda. The fact that discourses associated with the anti-feminist enemy image 'gender ideology' are not limited to religious actors, but are integrated into their respective narratives by different anti-feminist spectra in different parts of the world, is also demonstrated by other contributions in this anthology, including Copland for the manosphere and Bauer with regard to opponents of COVID-19 measures in Germany.

Based on how the idea of 'gender ideology' has been used in the three cases I presented (Brazil, Mexico and Colombia), I conclude that anti-feminism is the motor that keeps neoconservative narratives circulating and makes them so easy to adopt as common sense. Catholic and neo-Pentecostal conservativism are particularly fertile grounds for anti-feminist emotions to grow and expand, because those religious traditions still maintain dogmatic sexist views that are incompatible with feminist claims. The cases analysed in this chapter show the three main political goals pursued by this twenty-first-century crusade: to restore the political prerogatives of religious authorities (de-secularise the state and public sphere), to reform the state according to the neoliberal ideology, and to validate the patriarchal gender hierarchy.

However, the findings presented in this chapter are not limited to the Latin American context; similar developments are taking place in many countries around the world, where the process of secularisation has also remained superficial and incomplete, causing massive resistance to the profound cultural and democratic changes that have accompanied it. For example, in France the 'Manif pour tous' marked one of the first major anti-gender mobilisations in Europe, which in turn provided a vehicle to strengthen the political influence of religious (in this case Catholic) actors in the public discourse of a secular society. That is why understanding the process of secularisation in a particular society seems to be relevant not only for the comprehension of how the neoconservative movement emerges and advances in the analysed specific contexts, but can also contribute to a better understanding of this anti-democratic 'crusade' in secularised societies. If in a specific society the process of secularisation has taken place in a way that promotes what Spanish philosopher Adela Cortina (2020) has conceptualised as 'minimal ethics', that is a shared basic set of civic values for coexisting in pluralistic democracies, then that society will be less vulnerable to neoconservative and anti-democratic strategies such as the one described in this chapter. Cortina's idea is based on the recognition of moral difference that, in order to be accepted by all individuals in a democratic society, requires also from all individuals the acceptance of a common set of ethical principles, duties and reciprocity that are the sine qua non requirement for moral diversity to exist. In that sense, a secularised public sphere will be valued by all individuals as the common ground on which pluralism and diversity can thrive.

Notes

1. Here I do not understand secularisation as a mere lack of religious symbols, but as a process that leads to a democratic community based on shared civic

values and respect for diversity, where religious beliefs do not interfere in public or political affairs.
2. Costa Rica, for instance, is a confessional state according to the constitution.
3. The University of Navarra Press, for example, publishes a vast number of documents, books and articles on the so-called 'gender ideology'. It has also supported projects and publications which defined homosexuality as a pathological condition that can be therapeutically treated and cured. Further, it has also published research documents to prove the risks of adoption by homosexual people and a supposedly scientific rational for rejecting in-vitro fertilisation and other assisted reproduction techniques. Also located at the University of Navarra, the Institute of Sciences for the Family was responsible for organising the 1st International Congress on Gender Ideology in 2011.
4. See for instance the news outlet Mundo Cristiano: https://www1.cbn.com/mundocristiano
5. As understood in ethics and moral philosophy.
6. Appealing to former president Benito Juárez (1858–72), considered in Mexico as the most important liberal-progressive historical leader, and defender of the secular state.

References

Adolphe, J. (2003). The Case Against Same-Sex Marriage in Canada: Law and Policy Considerations. *Brigham Young University Journal of Public Law, 18*(2), 479–542. https://digitalcommons.law.byu.edu/jpl/vol18/iss2/7/

Amuchástegui, A., Cruz, G., Aldaz, E., Mejía, M. C. and Equality, G. (2010). The Complexities of the Mexican Secular State and the Rights of Women. Geneva: United Nations Research Institute for Social Development. https://www.unrisd.org/80256B3C005BCCF9/(httpAuxPages)/7E3249044579CB6EC1257769004 45C2F/$file/Mexico19July10.pdf

Archer, N. and Provost, C. (2020, 27 October). *Revealed: $280m 'Dark Money' Spent by US Christian Right Groups Globally.* openDemocracy. https://www.opendemocracy.net/en/5050/trump-us-christian-spending-global-revealed/

Arguedas-Ramírez, G. (2019). ¿Ideología de género?: Alianza entre el neointegrismo católico y fundamentalismo evangélico frente a los feminismos y la diversidad sexual. Un análisis desde América Latina. In Los feminismos latinoamericanos ante los retos del milenio. In M. Castañeda, M. L. González and P. Rodríguez (eds), *Los feminismos latinoamericanos ante los retos del milenio* (pp. 163–204). UNAM.

Arguedas-Ramírez, G. (2020). *Ideología de género, lo 'post-secular', el fundamentalismo neopentecostal y el neointegrismo católico: la vocación anti-democrática.* Observatorio de Sexualidad y Política.

Arguedas-Ramírez, G. and Morgan, L. M. (2017). The Reproductive Rights Counteroffensive in Mexico and Central America. *Feminist Studies: FS, 43*(2), 423–37.

Armstrong, K. (2001).*The Battle for God: A History of Fundamentalism*. Ballantine Books.

Beltrán, W. M. and Creely, S. (2018). Pentecostals, Gender Ideology and the Peace Plebiscite: Colombia 2016. *Religions*, *9*(12), 418.

Benedict XVI (2012). *Address of His Holiness Benedict XVI On the Occasion of Christmas Greetings to The Roman Curia*. Holy See. https://www.vatican.va/content/benedict-xvi/en/speeches/2012/december/documents/hf_ben-xvi_spe_20121221_auguri-curia.html

Brown, W. (2006). American Nightmare: Neoliberalism, Neoconservatism, and De-Democratization. *Political Theory*, *34*(6), 690–714.

Careaga, G. and Aranda, L. (2020). *Políticas antigénero en América Latina: México*. Observatorio de Sexualidad y Política (SPW).

Chalhoub, S., Collins, C., Llanos, M., Pachón, M. and Perry, K. Y. (2017). Report of the LASA Fact-Finding Delegation on the Impeachment of Brazilian President Dilma Rousseff.

Cooper, M. (2019). *Family Values: Between Neoliberalism and the New Social Conservatism*. The MIT Press.

Corrêa, S. and Kalil, I. (2020). *Políticas antigénero en América Latina: Brasil*. Observatorio de Sexualidad y Política (SPW).

Corrêa, S., Paternotte, D. and Kuhar, R. (2018, 31 May). The Globalisation of Antigender Campaigns. *IPS Journal*. https://www.ips-journal.eu/topics/democracy-and-society/the-globalisation-of-anti-gender-campaigns-2761/

Cortina, A. (2020). *Ética Mínima*. Tecnos.

Cupać, J. and Ebetürk, I. (2020). The Personal is Global Political: The Antifeminist Backlash in the United Nations. *British Journal of Politics and International Relations*, *22*(4), 702–14.

Debord, G. (1995). *La Sociedad del Espectaculo*. E. Naufragio (ed.). Ediciones Naufragio Press. http://serbal.pntic.mec.es/~cmunoz11/Societe.pdf

Domínguez, A. D. (2020). ¿Votó la ciudadanía religiosa por AMLO en 2018?. *Política y gobierno*, *27*(2). http://www.politicaygobierno.cide.edu/index.php/pyg/article/view/1336

Escudier, J. J. T. (2013). *Las enseñanzas de San Josemaría Escrivá de Balaguer sobre la libertad política de los católicos*. Doctorate in Sacred Theology, Pontificia Universitas Sanctæ Crucis. https://www.unav.edu/documents/3511980/804ba08e-069d-4566-b197-e1becc556760

Faludi, S. (1991). *Backlash: The Undeclared War against American Women*. Crown.

Gabriele, M. and Perry, D. (2020, 7 January). Donald Trump Jr.'s rifle shows how obsessed the right still is with the Crusades. *The Washington Post*. https://www.washingtonpost.com/outlook/2020/01/07/donald-trump-jrs-rifle-shows-how-obsessed-right-still-is-with-crusades/

Garbagnoli, S. (2016). Against the Heresy of Immanence: Vatican's 'Gender' as a New Rhetorical Device Against the Denaturalization of the Sexual Order. *Religion and Gender*, *6*(2), 187–204.

García Molina, M. and Chicaíza, L. A. (2018). Brexit, paz y Trump: enseñanzas para los economistas. *Revista de Economía Institucional*, *20*(38), 129.

García-Ruiz, J. and Michel, P. (2010). Neopentecostalism in Latin America: Contribution to a Political Anthropology of Globalisation. *International Social Science Journal*, 61(202), 411–24.

Gomes, Evaldo Xavier, O. C. (2014). *Religion and the Secular State in Brazil*. https://classic.iclrs.org/content/blurb/files/Brazil%202014%20FINAL.pdf

Gómez-Peralta, H. (2012). The Role of the Catholic Church in Mexico's Political Development. *Politics and Religion*, 6(1), 17–35.

Gómez-Peralta, H. (2020). The Rise of Evangelical Conservatism in Mexican Politics. *Journal of Religion & Society*, 22.

Hagen, J. J. (2016, 19 December). *Did Sexual Orientation and Gender Identity Play a Role in the Rejection of the Colombian Peace Deal?* LSE Women, Peace and Security Blog. https://blogs.lse.ac.uk/wps/2016/12/19/did-sexual-orientation-and-gender-identity-play-a-role-in-the-rejection-of-the-colombian-peace-deal/

Haynes, S. (2020, 27 October). U.S. Christian Right groups are pouring millions into conservative and anti-LGBTQ causes in Europe, new report says. *Time*. https://time.com/5903931/christian-right-conservative-agenda-europe-report/

Hochschild, A. R. (2016). Strangers in Their Own Land. The New Press. Papal Encyclicals (1864, 9 June). *The Syllabus of Errors*. https://www.papalencyclicals.net/pius09/p9syll.htm

Kanji, A. and Kalmar, I. (2018, 15 November). *Trump the 'White Power Crusader' Defends Christianity Against a Jewish-Muslim Plot*. https://www.haaretz.com/us-news/.premium-trump-feeds-global-conspiracy-theories-of-a-jewish-muslim-plot-against-christianity-1.6654389

Kerwick, J. (2015). Conservatism vs. Neoconservatism: A Philosophical Analysis. *E-LOGOS – Electronic Journal for Philosophy*, 22(1), 15–27.

Kuhar, R. and Paternotte, D. (eds). (2018). *Campagnes anti-genre en Europe*: Des mobilisations contre l'égalité. Presses universitaires de Lyon.

Løland, O. J. (2020). The Political Conditions and Theological Foundations of the New Christian Right in Brazil. *Ibero-Americana (Stockholm, Sweden: 1971)*, 49(1), 63–73.

Manrique, C. A. (2019). Religious Practices, State Techniques and Conflicted Forms of Violence in Colombia's Peacebuilding Scenarios. *Revista de Estudios Sociales*, 67, 56–72.

Mazo, S. (2019). ¿La Religión como Política? *SUR*, 29. https://sur.conectas.org/wp-content/uploads/2019/12/10-sur-29-portugues-sandra-mazo.pdf

Monsiváis, C. (2008). *El estado laico y sus malquerientes: (crónica/antología)* (No. Sirsi) i9789703251339).

Ozzano, L. (2007). Una prospettiva politologica sul fondamentalismo. *Teoria Politica*, 23(2), 103–17. http://www.francoangeli.it/Riviste/SchedaRivista.aspx?IDarticolo=31052&lingua=IT

Ozzano, L. (2009). Religious Fundamentalism and Democracy. ПОЛИТИКОЛОГИЈА РЕЛИГИЈЕ III. *Politics and Religion*, 3(1), 127–53.

Pace, E. and Guolo, R. (2006). *Los fundamentalismos*. Siglo XXI.

Patiño Reyes, A. (2015). Religion and the secular state in Mexico. *Religion and The Secular State: National Reports*, 522–36. https://sistemadeinvestigacion.ibero. mx/es/publications/religion-and-the-secular-state-in-mexico-3

Pérez Guadalupe, J. L. and Grundberger, S. (eds). (2018). *Evangélicos y Poder en América Latina*. Instituto de Estudios Social Cristianos and Konrad Adenauer Stiftung.

Poulat, É. (1985). La querelle de l'intégrisme en France. *Social Compass*, *32*(4), 343–51.

Prieto, V. (2020). Colombia as a Secular State. In R. V. Souza Alves (ed.), *Latin American Perspectives on Law and Religion* (pp. 145–64). Springer International Publishing.

Robbins, J. W. (2011). *Radical Democracy and Political Theology*. Columbia University Press.

Sotelo, M. V. and Arocena, F. (2021). Evangelicals in the Latin American Political Arena: The Cases of Brazil, Argentina and Uruguay. *SN Social Sciences*, *1*(7), 180.

Van der Krogt, C. (1992). Catholic Fundamentalism or Catholic Integralism? In J. Veithc (ed.), *To Strive and not to Yield: Essays in Honour of Colin Brown* (pp. 123–35). The Department of World Religions. Victoria University.

Vitale, R. and Cohen, M. J. (2013). *Colombia Contested Spaces Briefing Paper*. https:// s3.amazonaws.com/oxfam-us/www/static/media/files/contested-spaces-colombia-briefing-paper.pdf

Zilla, C. (2020). *Evangelicals and Politics in Brazil: The Relevance of Religious Change in Latin America*. SWP Research Paper. German Institute for International and Security Affairs.

TWO

'Comprehensive Sexuality Education is Satanic': Homosexuality, Politics and Christian Nationalism in Ghana

Regina Fuller

'The Ghana Pentecostal and Charismatic Council [seeks] to address and state our official position on the raging debate and controversy on the Comprehensive Sexuality Education, which I have termed Comprehensive Satanic Engagement because of the impact it can have on our children', declared Council President Rev. Frimpong-Manso, during a press conference on Comprehensive Sexuality Education (CSE) (Frimpong-Manso, 2019). With their press conference, the Ghana Pentecostal and Charismatic Council joined a host of national Christian religious councils in not only rejecting but also demonising CSE in Ghana's schools. CSE, a hallmark of sexual and reproductive health and rights (SRHR), aims to equip young people with scientifically accurate information on gender, human rights and human reproduction. In the last three decades, contemporary debates on CSE have raged in the US, with Christian Right organisations stoking claims that it undermines the Christian heterosexual family, sexualises children, teaches homosexuality and endorses lesbian, gay, bi and transgender rights (Buss, 2004; Irvine, 2000; Kendall, 2013; Luker, 2006). While debates on sex education are common in the global North, only in the last decade have fierce public battles over sex education proliferated in Africa. For example, public and religious outcry against CSE has erupted in Ghana, Uganda (Moore et al., 2021) and South Africa (Ellerbeck, 2019), forcing leaders and communities to discuss the place of CSE, heterosexuality and faith in their countries. Africanist research demonstrates how these anti-homosexual discourses are ignited by either Pentecostal leaders with support from US Christian Right organisations (Kaoma, 2016a; Muse-Fisher, 2014) or by local Christian leaders seeking to expand their political influence, resulting in transnationally informed, locally instantiated fights over sexuality, power, God and the nation.

The sex education debates in Africa illustrate the continued politicisation of sexuality education and the growing religious opposition to sexual and reproductive health and rights on the African continent. Engaging African feminist theory, this chapter attends to sexuality and gender as a political, national project (Oinas and Arnfred, 2009; Tamale, 2011b). As Oinas and Arnfred (2009) aptly note, 'sexualities and gendered power relations are central in the shaping and making of political power on the level of national politics' (p. 151). My study of sexual politics in Ghana highlights how sexuality and Christianity are mobilised and contested to assert Christian nationalism. I chose to focus exclusively on Christian organisations because of their strong influence over Ghanaian culture and politics and because Christianity is the largest religion in Ghana. In this chapter, drawing on Christian councils' press releases and engaging an African feminist conceptual frame, I argue that Christian faith organisations used the sex education debates as an opportunity to further Christian heterosexual nationalism – the ideal of Ghana as a culturally Christian heterosexual nation incompatible with the tenets of CSE and unaccepting of non-normative sexualities. Next, I illustrate how Christian leaders gained more moral, political influence over the future of sex education policy and sexual politics. My analysis demonstrates that the sex education debates have ushered in a new period in Ghana's sexual politics in which Christian leaders are actively using their political power and religious influence to shape public discourses on sexuality with the goal of policing non-normative sexualities through public policy and legislation.

To set the stage for analysis, I frame the sex education debates in postcolonial Ghana through African feminist scholarship, politicised homophobia and public religions in Africa. Next, I show my methods of content analysis. Then I highlight the movement for sexual and reproductive health and rights and trace how religious, heterosexual family movements have existed alongside SRHR since the 1990s. Next, I illustrate how conservative religious movements have driven public debates on sex education across Africa. The subsequent section provides background on Christianity and the sex education debates in Ghana. Finally, an analysis of Christian rhetoric on CSE illustrates how leaders mobilised Christian nationalism and strengthened Christianity's role in education and sexual policymaking.

Framing the Sex Education Debates in Ghana

Queer African feminist scholarship guides this analysis of religious discourse in Ghana. Gender and sexuality are socially constructed and 'influenced by and implicated within social, cultural, political, and economic forces' (Tamale, 2011a, p. 2). African feminist scholars such as Ekine and Abbas (2013), Spronk and Nyeck (2021), Epprecht (2008) and Tamale (2013) call for a queer lens for the study of gender, sexuality and politics in Africa. Following Ekine and Abbas (2013), I use a queer lens as a political and analytical frame 'to underscore a perspective that embraces gender and sexual plurality and seeks to transform, overhaul and revolutionise African order rather than seek to assimilate into oppressive hetero-patriarchal-capitalist frameworks' (p. 3). Queer African feminist scholarship rejects the notion of a singular, heterosexual Africa and recognises the diverse sexualities, both normative and non-normative, present on the continent and within national borders. I use non-normative sexualities and LGBT interchangeably as an umbrella term to encompass sexualities that sit outside of the heterosexual norm (Nyeck and Epprecht, 2013). Finally, queer African feminism examines how sexual politics and laws reinforce heteronormativity and regulate non-normative sexualities within African countries (Nyanzi, 2014; Nyeck and Epprecht, 2013).

The concepts of politicised homophobia, public religions and Christian nationalism best reflect the relationship between sexuality, politics and Christianity in Africa. Currier (2019) contends that African elites employ 'politicized homophobia' in public discourses to police sexuality, to make claims of an African heterosexual identity and to identify people with non-normative sexualities as 'enemies of the state, culture, and the family' (p. 15). Politicised homophobia is mobilised through anti-homosexual logics such as homosexuality being culturally 'un-African' and an amnesia of the existence of non-normative sexualities in African societies. This amnesia results in an imagined heterosexual Africa. Another common anti-homosexual discourse is the belief in an international gay agenda or a concerted campaign for gay and lesbian rights in international human rights arenas (Buss, 2004). Second, the concept of public religions in Africa (Casanova, 1994; Gifford, 1998) explains how religious organisations exert powerful influence over national politics and policymaking in African countries. According to Gifford, African Christianity, unlike forms of Christianity in the global North, operates in both private and public spheres, with Christian organisations speaking publicly on national issues such as the economy, political elections and development. Third, Christian nationalism as a framework adds how Christian organisations, as public religions, rally around nationalism, heterosexuality and Christianity in their world-view. Scholars Whitehead and Perry (2020) define Christian nationalism in the US as a 'cultural framework . . . that idealizes and advocates for a fusion of Christianity with American civic life . . . it includes assumptions of . . . patriarchy and heteronormativity' (p. 10).

Likewise, van Klinken (2014) finds in Zambia that Pentecostal organisations, as public religions, promoted Pentecostal nationalism in public debates on gay rights by positioning Zambia as a Christian heterosexual nation incompatible with homosexuality. In short, heteronormativity and homophobia are central to Christian nationalist views of the nation state. In essence, some Christian councils, as active public religions in Africa, marshal politicised homophobia and Christian nationalism in national sexual politics in defence of the perceived Christian, heterosexual nation.

Methods of Content Analysis

This chapter is based on content analysis of four press releases and press conferences on CSE in Ghana. The press statements were published by Christian councils and a religious national coalition group between October 2019 and January 2020 when CSE and homosexuality were major issues of public and political debate. In Ghana, there are three religious councils that collectively represent Christian faith traditions: the Christian Council of Ghana (CCG), the Ghana Catholic Bishops Conference (GCBC), and the Ghana Pentecostal and Charismatic Council (GPCC). CCG, the oldest council in the country, is composed of Protestant denominations of Methodist, Presbyterian and Anglican; collectively these churches are known as mission or mainline churches since they were founded by missionaries in the 1800s. GCBC is the second oldest council in the country. CCG and GCBC combined own most of the country's public schools, which were historically mission schools, and frequently collaborate to influence Ghana's political culture (Gifford, 2004). Following Gifford, I refer to Protestant and Catholic churches collectively as mainline churches. Since the 1990s, Pentecostalism has grown exponentially in Ghana, and GPCC represents Charismatic and Pentecostal churches. I analysed press releases and press conference transcripts for major themes on CSE and sexuality. I also include a press conference from the National Coalition for Proper Human Sexual Rights and Family Values (National Coalition), which is an umbrella organisation for Christian, Muslim and traditional religious leaders in Ghana who want to 'ensure the preservation of our indigenous African traditional and cultural sexual rights and family values' (National Coalition for Proper Human Sexual Rights and Family Values, 2019). While the National Coalition is ostensibly a coalition organisation for all religious councils in Ghana, National Coalition leaders are Christian and often invoke Christian principles in their statements. GPCC, CCG and GCBC are all members of the National Coalition. I also conducted eight interviews with Christian and Muslim leaders during 2020 as a part of my larger dissertation study. The interviews are not included in this chapter but they do inform my analysis.

History of Movements For and Against Sexual and Reproductive Health and Rights

The rise of sexual and reproductive health and rights and CSE in Africa has been accompanied by the rise of heterosexual family, conservative religious movements which contest sexuality education, reproductive rights and LGBT sexuality. Sexual and reproductive health and rights (SRHR) and gender equality entered international population policy in the 1990s with the 1994 International Conference on Population and Development (ICPD) in Cairo which heralded a shift from population control to reproductive health and rights, gender equality and the empowerment of women (Buss and Herman, 2003; UNFPA, 1994). The resulting ICPD Programme of Action outlined global goals for population and development for the next twenty years with an emphasis on 'empowering women and . . . a broadened approach to reproductive health and rights' (UNFPA, 1994, p. 4). Key to ICPD's focus on adolescent SRHR is access to comprehensive sexuality education. Since then, United Nations agencies such as the United Nations Population Fund (UNFPA) and the United Nations Educational, Scientific and Cultural Organisation (UNESCO) have furthered the vision of the programme of action by providing guidance, insight and monetary support to bring CSE to countries in the global South.

When the UN institutionalised SRHR through ICPD, religious counter-movements against SRHR formed simultaneously. Conservative religious actors such as the Christian Right and the Vatican oppose reproductive rights, abortion and homosexuality in the US, Europe and Africa (Buss, 2004; Kaoma, 2016b). Mobilised by ICPD, the Vatican and Christian Right actors allied to counter gender and reproductive rights at the United Nations level which they saw as a threat to the 'natural' (heterosexual married) family (Buss and Herman, 2003; Paternotte and Kuhar, 2017). Conservative religious alliances between Christian and Islamic leaders are united in their opposition to contraception, homosexuality and gender equality. These actors see women's rights and efforts to empower women as a UN covert strategy to build support for abortion and homosexuality, which they fear will erode the 'natural family' (Buss, 2004). Consequently, CSE, as an offspring of SRHR, also becomes a dangerous threat to the natural family. Conservative religious actors have raised fierce battles against comprehensive sexuality education in the US (Kendall, 2013) and around the world (di Mauro and Joffe, 2007; Marsden, 2008). In the US for example, conservative Christian leaders have found the battles over CSE to be useful to winning local struggles on how abortion, contraception and abstinence are taught in schools and building broader community support for their 'natural' family movement. Sex education policy is a useful, successful target for conservative religious groups because of the taboo nature of sexuality in many countries, societal norms around children as innocent, asexual beings, and perceived infringement on parents' rights to teach children their own values on sexuality (Irvine, 2009). In short, while the sex education debates may seem to only detail sex education policy in schools, these debates are a door for conservative Christian leaders to advocate for wider sexual policy issues against homosexuality, contraception and abortion. Thus, strong opposition to CSE is an integral movement-building strategy for conservative religious natural family groups.

Battles over Sex Education in Africa

Since the early 2000s, UN agencies such as UNFPA have financially supported African countries to upgrade their existing sex education curricula to CSE (Zimmerman, 2015); however, this transition has been met with conservative religious opposition across African countries. As with the battles over sex education in the US, conservative religious actors in Uganda, South Africa and Senegal oppose CSE to 'save' the 'natural' heterosexual family and criminalise non-normative sexualities. I highlight these countries because they have had contentious national debates on CSE within the last five years. Christian and Muslim religious leaders in these countries employed politicised homophobia and asserted the public role of religious doctrine to make political, normative claims on sex education policy and morality. Additionally, religious leaders extended the anti-homosexuality logic of homosexuality as 'un-African' to CSE; CSE is perceived as culturally un-African and foreign and therefore a threat to the nation and the family. For example, in the last decade in Uganda, American evangelical organisations and Ugandan religious organisations have partnered to initiate fierce battles over sex education. In 2016, public and religious leaders united to oppose CSE based on the belief that it was teaching children homosexuality as an acceptable sexual behaviour (Moore et al., 2021; Ninsiima et al., 2019). The CSE debates in Uganda were similar to those in the US: conservative religious leaders claimed sex education promoted bad sexual behaviour for young people, while CSE advocates that said young people have the right to sex education. Integral to Christian opposition to CSE was the anti-homosexual logic of the foreignness of homosexuality and CSE in Ugandan culture. Framed as foreign, CSE supposedly threatened Ugandan Christian cultural and moral values of heterosexuality (Moore et al., 2021; UNESCO, 2021). Ugandan Christian leaders employed politicised homophobia and Christian nationalism against CSE to achieve a greater political role for Christian organisations in Ugandan politics and nation building.

Debates on comprehensive sexuality education have also erupted in South Africa and Senegal. In 2019, conservative Christian leaders rallied against the implementation of CSE in South African schools through anti-homosexual rhetoric; they claimed to protect the innocence of young children, framed CSE as a foreign import imposed by the UN, and argued that CSE did not reflect South African cultural values (Ubisi, 2020). For example, the conservative religious organisation called the Freedom for Religion South Africa warned parents to 'make their voice heard' in opposing CSE so that 'the rights of parents to raise their children according to their own values and beliefs' would prevail (Ellerbeck, 2019). As in Uganda, South African Christian leaders mobilised politicised homophobia and Christian nationalism to 'save' the heterosexual nation from the enemy of CSE. Similarly, conservative religious leaders in Senegal contested the country's family life education programme, based on CSE's principles, as incompatible with Senegalese social and moral values (Chau et al., 2016). Again, leaders used politicised homophobia to promote a culturally heterosexual nation and to reject 'Western' sex education. Across Africa, conservative religious leaders consistently framed CSE as foreign and incompatible with African cultural and moral values and mobilised religious heterosexual nationalism. Religious leaders' opposition to CSE repudiates LGBT rights, gender equality and global SRHR priorities in Africa; instead of SRHR, faith leaders offer a culturally religious (Christian) world-view on political and social issues.

The examples of Uganda, South Africa and Senegal demonstrate that battles over sex education, promoted by religious conservatives, are becoming more common in Africa, just as these battles are regular occurrences in the global North. I contend that recent CSE debates across Africa signal a shift in sex education policymaking and Africa's sexual politics. First, sex education policymaking in Africa is no longer a neutral arena for UN agencies and country ministries of education to develop; it is now a highly contested arena with local and transnational religious organisations working as public religions to influence and shape policies through a normative, heterosexual lens. Second, African religious organisations, learning from the US Christian Right's role in US sex education battles, are borrowing discursive tools such as the 'natural family' and actively using opposition to CSE to garner more political power in Africa's sexual politics. Finally, African religious organisations use debates around CSE to proclaim Christian/religious heterosexual nationalism in their countries. The CSE battles across Africa illustrate the growing role of faith leaders and politicised homophobia in setting and maintaining normative ideals of the family, sexuality and the nation.

The Ghanaian Context

Christianity plays an influential role in public life, politics and nation building in Ghana. In 2000, a Gallup poll declared Ghana as one of the most religious countries in the world, with over 94 per cent of respondents attesting their belief in God (Takyi et al., 2010). According to the latest census data, most Ghanaians are Christian (71.2 per cent), while a minority are Muslim (17.6 per cent) and an even smaller minority (5.2 per cent) believe in traditional religions (Okyerefo, 2019). While Ghana has been a secular state since its founding in 1957, Christianity has played an outsized influence in the public sphere and public discourse on the nation. Culturally, Ghana is a Christian nation (Gifford, 1998). Traditionally, mission or mainline churches, those which form the Christian Council of Ghana and the Ghana Catholic Bishops Conference have exerted the most political and moral impact on Ghanaian discourses and politics (Okyerefo, 2019). However, with the expansion of the Pentecostal-Charismatic population, Pentecostal-Charismatic churches and leaders have a growing influence on politics and nationhood in Ghana (Gifford, 2004). In essence, the strong religiosity of Ghanaians and the historical relationship between Christian and political leaders explain the power religious leaders have in public battles over sexuality and nationhood.

In 2017, the government of Ghana, through the Ministry of Education and its subsidiary agencies, the Ghana Education Service (GES) and the National Council for Curriculum and Assessment (NaCCA), and the National Population Council, an independent government agency, started developing the guidelines for Comprehensive Sexuality Education and updating its existing reproductive health curriculum to CSE. The move to CSE was driven by three factors: first, persistently high teenage pregnancy rates in the country; second, funding from UNFPA Ghana for the new curriculum; and, third, the ten-year curriculum review process. Public education in Ghana is dictated by a national not federal system run by GES. GES funds all public primary and secondary education in the country while NaCCA establishes curricula standards for all public schools. Every ten years, NaCCA, in consultation with GES, updates the national curriculum for all grade levels. With the upcoming curriculum review set for 2020, high teenage pregnancy rates and UNFPA funding, government agencies led by the National Population Council decided it was time to incorporate CSE into the curriculum. By 2018, after a series of consultations with technical experts and with UNFPA support, the government released the *Guidelines for Comprehensive Sexuality Education* (Government of Ghana, n.d.; UNFPA Ghana, n.d.). Over the next two years, 2018–20, UNFPA Ghana planned to train teachers on the new curriculum with the goal of full implementation by 2020.

The National Coalition for Proper Human Sexual Rights and Family Values (National Coalition) ignited the CSE battles in September 2019. The National Coalition, founded in 2013, aims to protect the 'natural family' and respond to what they call the growing threat of LGBT phenomena. On 25 September 2019, the National Coalition announced that it would be hosting the World Congress of Families (WCF) Africa conference in October 2019 and that the introduction of CSE would 'undermine the cultural and moral values of the country' (Noshie, 2019). As the WCF Africa host, the National Coalition was keen to prove to the WCF, a US Christian natural family organisation, that Ghana championed the 'natural' Christian heterosexual family. Ghanaian media outlets unquestioningly carried this accusation forward, and by the following week CSE was on the cover of most newspapers and was the topic of discussion on English and Twi radio stations. Thanks to the National Coalition's assertation that CSE teaches homosexuality as an acceptable sexual behaviour, all religious councils concluded that the goal of CSE is to teach young children about the existence of nonnormative sexualities. Though there were no explicit references to LGBT sexualities within the CSE guidelines (Government of Ghana, n.d.), religious and public leaders promoted the rumour that CSE equals the acceptance of LGBT sexualities. While a curriculum analysis is beyond the scope of this chapter, it is important to note that debates about CSE were more concerned with the perception of what CSE teaches rather than the reality of the guidelines' contents. Thus began Ghana's sex education debates.

Religious Discourse on CSE in Ghana

In Ghana, Christian councils framed some form of sex education as necessary while vilifying and condemning CSE. Christian organisations advanced a normative sexual identity for the nation while employing politicised homophobia and visions of a singular African culture in the sex education debates. By asserting their opinions on sex education policy, religious leaders reaffirmed faith's public and political role in influencing public policy and national politics. Moreover, Christian leaders advanced Christian nationalism in their rejection of CSE to unite the Ghanaian populace around the enemies of CSE and the 'gay agenda'. Finally, faith organisations positioned battles against CSE as a cosmic battle between God and Satan for the nation's soul.

Christian acceptance of reproductive health education

Christian leaders confirmed the need for reproductive health education while rejecting CSE as a suitable form of sexuality education for young people. As with religious leaders in the US (Kendall, 2013), Ghanaian religious organisations desired some form of school-based instruction on reproductive health. Based on interviews with Christian leaders, leaders saw a distinct difference between the country's existing reproductive health education curriculum and CSE; in their opinions, the existing curriculum only included modules on biology and reproduction while CSE included 'unwanted' topics such as reproductive rights, gender and sexuality. The Ghana Catholic Bishops Conference (GCBC), for example, denounced CSE while affirming the existing sex education curriculum. They announced in their communique, 'We would like to implore the President to take further concrete steps to prevent future reintroduction of CSE in any form or guise into our curriculum ... We already have an acceptable sex education in our educational system' (Ghana Catholic Bishops' Conference, 2019, p. 4). The Christian Council of Ghana reflected this agreement that sex education is necessary, but CSE should not be taught to children. They announced:

> Sex education has always featured in the curricula of Ghanaian education. We the CCG therefore welcome any education that seeks to help our children attain healthy sexual reproductive lives. However, we seek to reiterate our earlier position on the Comprehensive Sexuality Education and reject any attempt to introduce them into the syllabus of our primary schools. (Christian Council of Ghana, 2020, p. 3)

CCG reinforced the idea that sex education and CSE are opposed, and while sex education is acceptable and necessary, CSE is not acceptable and should not replace the existing curriculum. Historically, CCG and GCBC have exercised a united voice in national policy issues, and both own most of the public government-run schools in the country (Gifford, 1998). Consequently, it is not surprising that they have the same stance that sex education is beneficial to children. Second, these Protestant-Catholic leaders tend to speak on political issues through a professional, not moral lens (Gifford, 2004). Thus, they initially rejected CSE not on moral grounds but on technical ones. Christian organisations overwhelmingly supported existing forms of sex education in Ghana but opposed the introduction of CSE.

Christian nationalism

As previously mentioned, Christianity plays an outsized role in Ghanaian culture and politics; many Christian and political leaders already believe that Ghana is a Christian nation. Consequently, Christian organisations used the sex education battles to further Christian heterosexual nationalism or an ideal of a Christian, heterosexual nation state (Whitehead and Perry, 2020). Heteronormativity and homophobia are central to Christian nationalism in Ghana. Politicised homophobia, Currier (2019) notes, enables political and religious elites in Africa to punish non-normative sexualities and 'buttress narratives of national sovereignty' (p. 20). Christian leaders employed politicised homophobia to refute CSE, uphold Christian nationalism and show the supposed incompatibility of homosexuality with Christian-Ghanaian cultural norms. Faith organisations advanced this nationalism in their remarks on CSE through two anti-homosexuality logics: references to the 'gay agenda' (Buss, 2004) and a belief in homosexuality being 'un-African' (Currier, 2019; Kaoma, 2016a).

To illustrate, the Ghana Pentecostal and Charismatic Council (GPCC) asserted:

> We reject absolutely the inclusion of Comprehensive Sexuality Education in any form and in any name in our school curriculum now and in the future, as we see the policy as a long-term subtle agenda to target our young population with a liberal mindset to accepting and tolerating LGBT as a normal societal behaviour in the very near future. (Frimpong-Manso, 2019)

GPCC's statement furthered the normative ideal of a heterosexual Ghana. By labelling LGBT as a part of a 'liberal mindset', the council stigmatised LGBT sexualities as outside of the supposed acceptable cultural norm of heterosexuality. The GPCC also endorsed the anti-homosexuality logic that the covert gay agenda is targeting Ghanaian children to accept non-normative sexualities. In short, Pentecostal and Charismatic leaders insisted that CSE should be rejected because homosexuality is supposedly both un-Ghanaian and morally deviant. Protestant leaders advanced religio-cultural arguments against CSE and homosexuality as both 'un-Ghanaian' and 'un-Christian', thereby reversing their usual stance to comment on political issues in a professional, technical manner (Gifford, 2004). For example, the Christian Council of Ghana (Christian Council of Ghana, 2020) endorsed Christian nationalism through their rejection of CSE. They maintained:

> Ghana is a Christian nation but with many other religious beliefs . . . However, we seek to reiterate our earlier position on the Comprehensive

Sexuality Education and reject any attempt to introduce them into the syllabus of our primary schools as they have underneath them a subtle agenda to introduce gay and lesbian rights into our nation. As we indicated in times past, our cultural norms and religious values as a nation do not support LGBT rights and we reject them in all their subtle forms. (pp. 2–4)

CCG rejected LGBT rights and upheld the ideal of a singular, Christian heterosexual nation. They also invoked the anti-homosexuality logics of homosexuality being un-African and the existence of a 'gay agenda'. Since CCG claimed that Christianity and Ghanaian cultural norms only endorse heterosexuality, homosexuality is a supposed affront to Ghanaian cultural and Christian values of (hetero)sexuality. Moreover, the Ghana Catholic Bishops Conference (GCBC, 2019) echoed that CSE should be rejected because homosexuality is supposedly un-Ghanaian and morally deviant. They insisted:

We are aware of the subtle agenda of lobbyists and some NGOs to promote a lifestyle that is against universal natural values and certainly, against Ghanaian cultural and moral values . . . we oppose very strongly any CSE that teaches the acceptance of LGBT and same-sex marriages as normal. (pp. 4–5)

GCBC defended a normative and cultural sexual identity of heterosexuality in Ghana. GCBC also added credibility to existence of a hidden gay agenda that is targeting Ghanaian sexual norms. Combined, mainline councils furthered Christian nationalism in their rejection of CSE by naming heterosexuality and Christianity as exclusive parts of Ghanaian cultural and moral values.

A common retort of religious leaders against homosexuality in Africa is the myth of a heterosexual African past. To these leaders, Africa has been culturally heterosexual from the precolonial period to the present (Currier, 2019). This anti-homosexual logic of homosexuality being 'un-African' continues to resonate with religious organisations. To illustrate, the National Coalition, a coalition of Christian, Muslim and traditional religious councils, in its press conference on CSE maintained that Africa has a deep cultural past of heterosexuality and religiosity that does not align with the CSE curriculum. Like the mainline and Pentecostal councils, the National Coalition advanced a religious nationalism for Ghana and the African continent; though not ostensibly Christian, this religious nationalism was based on heteronormativity and homophobia. In the words of Dr Samuel Onwona, executive member of the Coalition:

Thank God for this coalition. This Society of Ghana and Africa is based on the God factor . . . They don't know that the Ghana Empire predates Europe and North America . . . And that that has remained a taboo, homosexualism (sic) and lesbianism (sic). We are not saying it doesn't exist, we have them. They are there. But they are afraid to show up because it's a taboo. In America, polygamy is not accepted. In Africa, LGBTQ is a no no . . . That God factor is that fundamental key that holds our society together . . . God said male and female when he created humans. That's the God factor. LGBTQ today in CSE is advocating for 15 different genders. It's not male or female any longer. (Onwona, 2019)

He uses history and religion to highlight how Ghana and Africa have deep historical legacies of heterosexuality and a belief in God that predates Western countries. Their cultural argument for the historical legacy of Africa rejected the cultural infantilisation of Africa while defending the myth of heterosexual Africa – despite scholarship that demonstrates that non-normative sexualities have existed on the continent for centuries (Epprecht, 2008). Not only is Africa culturally heterosexual, they argued, but all of Africa's religious traditions disapproved of non-normative sexualities. In addition, their comparison of taboos against polygamy in the US and homosexuality in Africa broadened their cultural claim that US and African sexual norms are distinct. In their formulation, even if homosexuality is culturally acceptable in the US, it is not culturally African since the countries have divergent cultures. Next, they retorted that Africa's belief in God is what unites all religions on the continent. Therefore, LGBT sexualities are not only 'un-Ghanaian' and 'un-African', but they are also against all African religious beliefs. Using this myth of a culturally religious heterosexual past, Onwona repudiated CSE based on its supposed instruction on non-normative sexualities and fifteen genders. National Coalition leaders erased the history of same-sex sexualities in Ghana by proclaiming an imagined heterosexual, religious past in Africa.

Christian leaders called for a rejection of CSE to preserve Ghana's presumed Christian, heterosexual heritage, thereby furthering Christian heterosexual nationalism. In short, Protestant, Catholic and Pentecostal leaders united their voice in the debates to protect the supposed Christian nation from the 'hidden' gay agenda. I contend that the sex education battles ushered in a new era in Christian organisations' public role in national politics. Protestant and Catholic organisations, reversing their usual stance to evaluate public policies through a technical, professional lens, joined Pentecostal organisations in evaluating public policies through a Christian nationalist framework based on assumptions of heteronormativity and politicised homophobia.

Public religions and education policy

While Protestant and Catholic councils have been directly involved in politics as public religions, they had historically left sex education policy to be developed by education technocrats and development agencies. For example, religious leaders were invited to review the CSE guidelines in 2018 only after a technical working group of education and health experts had developed all the content; at the time of their review there were no objections to CSE. A year later, the CSE debates ushered in a new era in Ghana's sexual politics in which Christian organisations applied their influential public role to sex education policymaking by engaging with the government. The Ghana Pentecostal and Charismatic Council (GPCC) remarked:

> Government should be transparent with the people of Ghana by publicly committing to completely withdrawing this policy instead of a mere assurance of suspension of implementation. This move is what we believe will engender trust between government and the key stakeholders of our education system. (Frimpong-Manso, 2019)

GPCC directly addressed the government to reaffirm their influential public role as a faith organisation in educational policymaking. From their perspective, it is the prerogative of Christian leaders to not only oppose CSE but to demand that the secular government implements policies in line with Christian values. Likewise, the Christian Council of Ghana (CCG) cautioned political leaders to remember the council's continued public advocacy role in politics. They wrote, 'Be assured that the Council shall continue to provide support for the government and people of Ghana through our public education, advocacy, and dialogue' (Christian Council of Ghana, 2020, pp. 3–4). Similar to the GPCC, the CCG maintained that Christian councils continue to have moral and political influence over policymaking and nation building in the country. Next, the Ghana Catholic Bishops Conference (GCBC) appealed to the president to remove CSE. They stated, 'We would like to implore the President to take further concrete steps to prevent future reintroduction of CSE in any form or guise into our curriculum.' Historically, the GCBC and CCG have been the most influential Christian councils in Ghanaian politics. Through their appeal to the country's foremost political leader, the GCBC reminded the government that their Christian views are not only important but must be addressed in present and future sex education policy. Faith organisations, as public religions, illustrated that sex education policy is not just a technical issue for education experts alone but is a deeply moral, religious issue that must involve the opinions of Christian leaders. Faith organisations united to assert the influential political power of Christianity in Ghanaian politics.

Sex education debates as a cosmic battle

Religious leaders positioned contemporary battles over sex education as a cosmic battle between the devil and God, extending a Christian world-view to regulate education policy. Researchers of Christianity in Africa assert the importance of the dualism of God and Satan to Christian believers on the continent. In Southern Ghana for example, Meyer (1996) finds that the image of the devil for Ewe Christians served as mediator between Christian and traditional religions and between Christian and heathen lifestyles. Gifford (2004) notes that Ghanaian Pentecostal leaders typically address political and economic issues through an enchanted lens in which demons are responsible for political wrongs. Similarly, the dualism of God and Satan played a prominent role in public debates on homosexuality in Zambia. Van Klinken (2014) concluded that Pentecostal leaders framed debates on homosexuality as an eschatological battle or a 'cosmic struggle between God and the Devil', with homosexuality perceived as an evil threat to Christianity (pp. 519–20). In the sex education debates in Ghana, Pentecostal and Catholic leaders viewed discursive battles against CSE as spiritual warfare between God and Satan for Ghana's presumed Christian soul. For example, the Ghana Pentecostal and Charismatic Council (GPCC) renamed CSE 'Comprehensive Satanic Engagement' to show its perceived evil spiritual nature (Frimpong-Manso, 2019). Consequently, no longer is CSE only culturally reproachable, it also represents an evil spiritual combatant to both Christians and the supposed Christian nation. The spiritual association of CSE with the devil is not only present in African Christian discourses but also is a common rhetorical strategy in American evangelical battles over sex education. For example, di Mauro and Joffe (2007) show that American conservatives framed battles against comprehensive sexuality education as a battle between good and evil. GPCC leaders continued to employ demon cosmology throughout their press conference. They stated:

> We shall not as Churches, parents and communities shirk our primary moral upbringing and responsibilities to our children by allowing government and other external interest groups to dilute our long tested traditional values on sexuality and allow the introduction of any demonic policies through CSE. (Frimpong-Manso, 2019)

The GPCC reinforced Christian heterosexual nationalism and a belief in the nation of Ghana being under Satanic attack by the government and other actors. By naming CSE as a demonic policy, the organisation moved CSE and education policy from the realm of the secular to the realms of the sacred and secular. To them, Christian values of good and evil should dictate the policies that the government supports. Accordingly in the sacred Pentecostal realm, CSE can be fought against with spiritual tools as well as political ones. Surprisingly, Catholic leaders adopted the Pentecostal rhetorical tool of Satan/God to assess sex education policy. The Ghana Catholic Bishops Conference (2019) vowed to fight against 'those who propagate this evil agenda' (p.4). In public debates on sexuality education, Christian faith leaders united to spiritually defend the nation from the supposed evil of CSE. By applying the dualism of good/evil to sex education policy, faith organisations affirmed that a Christian nationalist worldview could be used to evaluate sexuality policymaking.

Conclusion

This chapter demonstrates the politicisation of sex education policy in Ghana through an analysis of Christian discourse on CSE. I began the chapter by highlighting recent battles over CSE in other African countries such as South Africa, Uganda and Senegal to show how Christian and Muslim leaders across the continent are directly targeting CSE as a strategy to initiate contentious debates on the place of sexuality and religion in the nation. In short, CSE as an UN-supported form of sexuality education is useful fodder for natural family organisations – not only in Africa, but also in other parts of the world (see Vega's contribution in this anthology) – looking to build momentum for their 'natural' family movement and garner greater public support against non-normative sexualities under the banners of culture, religion and national sovereignty. By highlighting the case of the sex education debates in Ghana, I show that fights over CSE are neither solely 'local' nor solely perpetuated by US Christian Right organisations in passive African countries. Battles over CSE are transnationally informed, locally instantiated fights in which Ghanaian Christian leaders employ Christian Nationalism and 'Ghanaian culture' and borrow rhetorical strategies from US evangelical discourses to counter CSE and defend the nation. First, I illustrated how the sex education debates have changed Protestant and Catholic councils' involvement in political and public life. While Gifford (2004) concluded that mainline and Pentecostal organisations had two distinct forms of involvement in politics, I found that Protestant and Catholic councils adopted a Pentecostal nationalistic tone and spiritual view of sex education policy. Consequently, I contended that now mainline and Pentecostal councils share the same spiritual, Pentecostal approach to politics in Ghana. Second, Christian councils promoted Christian heterosexual nationalism through the anti-homosexual logics of the myth of a heterosexual Africa and the belief in a hidden gay agenda, which has resulted in the vilification of non-normative sexualities as 'un-natural', 'un-Ghanaian' and 'un-Christian'. This politicised homophobia built political and religious opposition to CSE and homosexuality and reinforced Christian nationalism in the country. Third, Christian organisations expanded their roles as public religions in Ghanaian politics through their direct appeal to the government to promote sex education policies that align with a Christian nationalist world-view. While Christian organisations were involved superficially in sex education policy before the debate, their united vocal opposition to CSE has compelled the government to give them more power to decide what subjects are taught and not taught, what grades are included, and the new name of the sex education curricula (observation, 31 January 2020). The sex education debates in Ghana illustrate how heterosexuality, power and Christianity are being contested in contemporary Africa. The 1994 ICPD ushered in a new wave of sexual and reproductive health and rights across the globe. At the same time, global and local religious organisations, united against the ICPD programme of action, are initiating fights against CSE in different parts of the world to defend the 'natural' Christian heterosexual family and to gain greater political power as public religions in national sexual politics. These heated battles against CSE are not accidental or sporadic but a proven movement-building strategy of the natural family movement.

While CSE is no longer in the press or radio, the consequences of the sex education debates reverberate in present-day Ghanaian sexual politics. In response to the national uproar against CSE, Ghana's President Akufo Addo met with Protestant and Catholic leaders in October 2019 to assure them that CSE would not be implemented in schools (*Daily Graphic*, 2019). Since then, the government has distanced itself from CSE by banning its implementation in schools, referring to sex education exclusively as reproductive health education and holding a stakeholder's forum on the future of reproductive health education. I contend that the CSE battles have ushered in a new era in Ghana's sexual politics by bringing homosexuality to the forefront of national debates and by positioning (hetero)sexuality as something to be regulated through law and public policies. By naming CSE and LGBT as supposed enemies of the religious nation state, faith leaders, through politicised homophobia, united the Ghanaian nation around these alleged moral threats and demonstrated to the government that Christian organisations exercise a strong political, normative influence over sexual policymaking. The endeavour to use CSE debates to expand political influence can be seen a transnational strategy in which religious and conservative anti-feminist actors use 'moral panic' to challenge the separation of religion and politics, which Arguedas-Ramírez has already addressed in her chapter, beyond the specific issue at hand. Thus, it becomes obvious that it is never 'just about the children'. The reference to the supposedly threatened children through CSE is also accompanied by the construction of a danger to the nation, which – as the example of Ghana shows – ultimately serves, on the one hand, to crack down on non-normative sexualities and, on the other hand, functions as a means to locate the nation in religious terms. Vega's contribution in this anthology in particular, which also focuses on (religious) resistance to CSE using Ecuador as an example, provides insights into how this strategy has effects in the context she has analysed. Both this analysis on Ghana and Vega's contribution on Ecuador can thus be understood as specific examples of a broader trend of desecularisation and the resulting challenges that Arguedas-Ramírez has highlighted in her chapter. Prior to 2019, the National Coalition was unable to build a public consensus against LGBT in Ghana though Christian and political leaders actively vilified homosexuality (Odoi, 2021). With the CSE debates, the National Coalition and its member religious councils mobilised politicised homophobia to raise the supposed threats of CSE and homosexuality to a national public discourse. The government's ban on CSE defeated one of these so-called enemies in 2019, leaving the supposed threat of homosexuality still alive. From the perspective of Christian leaders, the CSE debates demonstrated the need for anti-homosexuality legislation in order to protect the Christian nation from the 'demonic danger' of LGBT. In June 2021, the parliament of Ghana introduced the Promotion of Proper Human Sexual Rights and Ghanaian Family Values Bill 2021 to eliminate the 'enemy' of homosexuality (Reid, 2021). The bill criminalises non-normative sexual acts and advocacy for homosexuality. Since the bill was introduced, there have been further national debates about homosexuality with leaders employing the same anti-homosexual logics and Christian nationalism used in the sex education battles. LGBT+ Rights Ghana reports increased homophobic attacks on queer people since the introduction of the bill. While sex education may seem peripheral to the nation state, the case of Ghana demonstrates how battles over sex education are used to uphold Christian nationalism, give religions more power in policymaking and sexual politics, and build momentum for anti-homosexuality legislation. If the promises of SRHR in Africa are to be realised, we must pay attention to sex education policy, sexual politics and natural family religious advocacy on the continent.

References

Buss, D. E. (2004). Finding the Homosexual in Women's Rights. *International Feminist Journal of Politics, 6*(2), 257–84.

Buss, D. E. and Herman, D. (2003). *Globalizing Family Values: The Christian Right in International Politics.* University of Minnesota.

Casanova, J. (1994). *Public Religions in the Modern World.* University of Chicago Press.

Chau, K., Traoré Seck, A., Chandra-Mouli, V. and Svanemyr, J. (2016). Scaling up Sexuality Education in Senegal: Integrating Family Life Education into the National Curriculum. *Sex Education, 16*(5), 503–19.

Christian Council of Ghana. (2020, 24 January). *Communique* [Press Release]. http://www.christiancouncilofghana.org/NewsPages/Communique-of-CCG-JAN-2020.php

Currier, A. (2019). *Politicizing Sex in Contemporary Africa: Homophobia in Malawi.* Cambridge University Press.

Daily Graphic. (2019, 7 October). It's Final: No CSE in Ghana. *Daily Graphic.* https://www.graphic.com.gh/daily-graphic-editorials/it-s-final-no-cse-in-ghana.html

di Mauro, D. and Joffe, C. (2007). The Religious Right and the Reshaping of Sexual Policy: An Examination of Reproductive Rights and Sexuality Education. *Sexuality Research and Social Policy, 4,* 67–92.

Ekine, S. and Abbas, H. (2013). Introduction. In S. Ekine and H. Abbas (eds), *Queer African Reader* (pp. 1–5). Pambazuka Press.

Ellerbeck, D. (2019). *New CSE Curriculum Mired in Controversy.* Freedom of Religion South Africa. https://forsa.org.za/new-cse-curriculum-mired-in-controversy/

Epprecht, M. (2008). *Heterosexual Africa?: The History of an Idea from the Age of Exploration to the Age of AIDS.* Ohio University Press.

Frimpong-Manso, P. Y. (2019, 3 October). GPCC Press Conference on CSE. https://www.youtube.com/watch?v=n7z7tW87whk

Ghana Catholic Bishops' Conference. (2019, 15 November). *Communique Issued by the Ghana Catholic Bishops' Conference at the End of its Annual Plenary Assembly* [Communique]. https://www.cbcgha.org/index.php/2019/11/16/communique-issued-by-the-catholic-bishops-conference-at-the-end-of-its-plenary-in-elmina-capecoast/

Gifford, P. (1998). *African Christianity: Its Public Role.* Hurst & Company.

Gifford, P. (2004). *Ghana's New Christianity: Pentecostalism in a Globalizing African Economy.* Indiana University Press.

Government of Ghana. (n.d.). *Guidelines for Comprehensive Sexuality Education in Ghana.* Ghana Education Service.

Irvine, J. M. (2000). Doing it with Words: Discourse and the Sex Education Culture Wars. *Critical Inquiry, 27*(1), 58–76.

Irvine, J. M. (2009). Transient Feelings: Sex Panics and the Politics of Emotions. In G. Herdt (ed.), *Moral Panics, Sex Panics: Fear and the Fight over Sexual Rights* (pp. 234–76). New York University Press.

Kaoma, K. (2016a). An African or Un-African sexual identity? Religion, Globalisation and Sexual Politics in sub-Saharan Africa. In A. van Klinken and E. Chitando (eds), *Public Religions and the Politics of Homosexuality in Africa* (pp. 113–29). Routledge.

Kaoma, K. (2016b). The Vatican Anti-Gender Theory and Sexual Politics: An African Response. *Religion and Gender, 6*(2), 282–92.

Kendall, N. (2013). *The Sex Education Debates.* University of Chicago Press.

Luker, K. (2006). *When Sex Goes to School: Warring Views on Sex – and Sex Education – Since the Sixties.* Norton and Company.

Marsden, L. (2008). *For God's Sake: The Christian Right and US Foreign Policy.* Bloomsbury.

Meyer, B. (1996). Modernity and Enchantment: The Image of the Devil in Popular African Christianity. In P. van der Veer (ed.), *Conversion to Modernities: The Globalization of Christianity* (pp. 199–230). Routledge.

Moore, E. V., Hirsch, J. S., Spindler, E., Nalugoda, F. and Santelli, J. S. (2021). Debating Sex and Sovereignty: Uganda's New National Sexuality Education Policy. *Sexuality Research and Social Policy.*

Muse-Fisher, A. (2014, 9 May). The Struggle for Rights within Uganda's LGBT Community: An American Debate Relocated. *Prospect Journal.* https://prospectjournal.org/tag/homosexual/

National Coalition for Proper Human Sexual Rights and Family Values. (2019, October). *National Dialogue Series: Info Brief* [Brochure]. Author.

Ninsiima, A. B., Coene, G., Michielsen, K., Najjuka, S., Kemigisha, E., Ruzaaza, G. N., Nyakato, V. N. and Leye, E. (2019). Institutional and Contextual Obstacles to Sexuality Education Policy Implementation in Uganda. *Sex Education, 20*(1), 17–32.

Noshie, A. (2019, 25 September). Introduction of Comprehensive Sexual Education will undermine cultural, moral values'. *Ghanaian Times.* https://www.ghanaiantimes.com.gh/introduction-of-comprehensive-sexual-education-will-undermine-cultural-moral-values/

Nyanzi, S. (2014). Queering Queer Africa. In Z. Matebeni (ed.), *Reclaiming Afrikan: Queer Perspectives on Sexual and Gender Identities* (pp. 64–9). Modjaji.

Nyeck, S. N. and Epprecht, M. (2013). Introduction. In S. N. Nyeck and M. Epprecht (eds), *Sexual Diversity in Africa: Politics, Theory and Citizenship* (pp. 3–15). McGill-Queens's University Press.

Odoi, A. (2021). Homophobic Violence in Ghana: When and Where It Counts. *Sexuality Research and Social Policy.*

Oinas, E. and Arnfred, S. (2009). Introduction: Sex & Politics – Case Africa. *NORA – Nordic Journal of Feminist and Gender Research, 17*(3), 149–57.

Okyerefo, M. P. K. (2019). Scrambling for the Centre: Ghana's New Churches as an Alternative Ideology and Power. *Religions, 10*(12).

Onwona, S. (2019). *CSE: Coalition Against Proper Human Sexual Right and Family Values Address Press.* https://www.youtube.com/watch?v=aU7PW-oINFQ&list=PL0NMJE9DpZnB1sndzQprPrHCsYx8OZE_V&index=23&t=641s

Paternotte, D. and Kuhar, R. (2017). 'Gender Ideology' in Movement: Introduction. In R. Kuhar and D. Paternotte (eds), *Anti Gender Campaigns in Europe: Mobilizing Against Equality* (pp. 1–21). Rowan and Littlefield.

Reid, G. (2021, 10 August). *Homophobic Ghanaian 'Family Values' Bill is Odious and Beggars Belief.* https://www.hrw.org/news/2021/08/10/homophobic-ghanaian-family-values-bill-odious-and-beggars-belief

Spronk, R. and Nyeck, S. N. (2021). Frontiers and Pioneers in (the Study of) Queer Experiences in Africa: Introduction. *Africa, 91*(3), 388–97.

Takyi, B. K., Opoku-Agyeman, C. and Kutin-Mensah, A. (2010). Religion and the Public Sphere: Religious Involvement and Voting Patterns in Ghana's 2004 Elections. *Africa Today, 56*(4), 62–86.

Tamale, S. (2011a). Introduction. In S. Tamale (ed.), *African Sexualities: A Reader* (pp. 2–36). Pambazuka Press.

Tamale, S. (2011b). Researching and Theorising Sexualities in Africa. In S. Tamale (ed.), *African Sexualities: A Reader* (pp. 11–36). Pambazuka Press.

Tamale, S. (2013). Confronting the Politics of Nonconforming Sexualities in Africa. *African Studies Review, 56*(02), 31–45.

Ubisi, L. (2020). Analysing the Hegemonic Discourses on Comprehensive Sexuality Education in South African Schools. *Journal of Education,* (81), 118–35.

UNESCO. (2021). *The Journey Towards Comprehensive Sexuality Education: Global Status Report.* https://unesdoc.unesco.org/ark:/48223/pf0000377963?1=null&queryId=79b2917d-16dd-4bf0-8ff3-5b0eec4acebc

UNFPA. (1994). *ICPD Programme of Action.* UNFPA. https://www.unfpa.org/events/international-conference-population-and-development-icpd

UNFPA Ghana. (n.d.). *Empowering Adolescent Girls through Comprehensive Sexuality Education.* Retrieved 16 December from https://www.unfpa.org/empowering-adolescent-girls-through-comprehensive-sexuality-education-and-sexual-and-reproductive

van Klinken, A. (2014). Homosexuality, Politics and Pentecostal Nationalism in Zambia. *Studies in World Christianity, 20*(3), 259–81.

Whitehead, A. and Perry, S. (2020). *Taking America Back for God: Christian Nationalism in the United States.* Oxford University Press.

Zimmerman, J. (2015). *Too Hot to Handle.* Princeton University Press.

THREE

The Backlash against Feminist Body Positive Activism in Russia, Kyrgyzstan and Kazakhstan: A Transnational Post-Soviet Trend?[1]

Katharina Wiedlack and Iain Zabolotny

This chapter offers an analysis of three recent, nationally and internationally discussed cases of anti-feminist violence against body positive activism in the post-Soviet regions: the case against Yulia Tsvetkova in Russia; against the exhibition organisers of the Feminnale and the 8th of March demonstration in 2020 in Kyrgyzstan; and the NGO Feminita in Kazakhstan. We reconstruct the individual cases by piecing together information from national and international Russian and English language news and social media, prioritising independent media, and activists' own accounts. We analyse the three cases against their national context, focusing on how public and structural (administrative and state) violence centred on heterosexist ideas of the female body in relation to 'family values'. Moreover, we ask how these examples are rooted in the respective broader and historic anti-feminist discourses. Comparing the three cases to each other, and reading them against academic literature that compares the backlash against liberal and progressive ideas in the region, we ask if the occurrences of anti-feminist violence are a transnational post-Soviet trend or rather local phenomena.

Anti-feminist Discourses in the Selected Regions

Russia

Russia is often seen as a significant influence to other post-Soviet regions and internationally. Academic analysts have been paying attention to Russian anti-feminist discourses (Sauer, 2019) and cases of violence against feminist activists since the beginning of 2012 and the persecution of the feminist activist group Pussy Riot (Mason, 2018; Sharafutdinova, 2014). Most ana-lysts understand the state and public violence against Pussy Riot as part of the broader national discursive trend towards morality and 'traditional val-ues' that explicitly targets feminist and homophile politics and actors. The Kremlin used the Pussy Riot trial to advance its new 'morality politics' in Rus-sia's domestic and foreign policies to restore its legitimacy after the massive street protests against alleged election fraud and Putin's return to the presi-dency in Moscow in winter 2011–12 (Sharafutdinova, 2014, p. 615). This 'conservative turn' in Russian cultural politics (Laruelle, 2020; Østbø, 2017) and its moralising stance aims at marginalising regime-critical stances and re-consolidating the Russian public 'based on traditional, conservative val-ues' (Sharafutdinova, 2014, p. 615). Not coincidentally, the discourses that position morality and 'traditional values' positively against gender equality, reproductive rights, sex education and the acceptance of homosexuality and trans*gender identifications are decidedly anti-Western (Chebankova, 2016; Edenborg, 2018; Stepanova, 2015; Wilkinson, 2014). One part of the strate-gies to unify the Russian nation is the celebration of traditional gender roles. 'The body is the focal point of these controlling mechanisms. It is simulta-neously the nationalized and the gendered body; it also becomes the space where heterosexual norms are imposed and controlled through discourses of "appropriate behaviour" collectively imagined in the name of the nation' (Kudaibergenova, 2019, p. 365). Restricting sexuality and women's repro-ductive rights became signified as 'traditional values' rather than state inter-ference in personal matters, constructed in opposition to Western European 'sexual democracy' (Stella and Nartova, 2016).

While Russian masculinity discourses have been analysed at length (Makarychev and Medvedev, 2015; Riabov and Riabova, 2014a; Sperling, 2014), not much literature has focused on female gender models. How-ever, scholars studying Russian political masculinity agree that notions of heteronormative masculinity, femininity and homophobia are employed as political tools to gain political legitimacy (Sperling, 2014, p. 3; Slept-cov, 2017, p. 144). The femininity employed by feminist and LGBTIQ+ activists such as Pussy Riot or Yulia Tsvetkova violates these politically instrumentalised 'traditional' gender roles. Moreover, a critical feminist reflection of existing gender roles, female body norms and heteronorma-tivity in an activist or academic fashion becomes framed as anti-Russian. Indeed, the analytical concept of 'gender' is understood as Western ideol-ogy and opposed to 'traditional values' (Moss, 2017).

Following the international affairs scholar Marlene Laruelle, anti-feminism is part of an assemblage of different conservative, partly right-wing, anti-Western, homo- and trans*phobic ideas that must not be understood as a coherent ideology or political tactic. Rather, it is a pattern of values and a 'framework for making sense of the world [and] a genuine producer of common sense' (Laruelle, 2020, p. 116). Moreover, it goes back to the late Soviet era, when 'right-wing social conservatism was prevalent' (Laruelle, 2020, p. 117). While the official Marxist-Leninist doctrine continued to propagate women's rights and gender equality, 'prudishness – preaching "high morals", professing chastity, condemning adultery and premarital sex; criminalizing male homosexuality; practising a virtual ban on talking about sex [. . .] and rigorously censoring art and media for moral and political impropriety' (Lipman as cited in Laruelle, 2020, p. 117) were prevalent. Conservative political views gained broader public support during the 1990s and the traumatising experiences of the abrupt discontinuation of everyday life and commonly shared social values. 'Conservative sentiment in this period centred on the perceived need for stability and predictability, a strong leader able to enforce law and order, and a revival of statism and patriotism' (ibid.). During that time the Russian Orthodox Church advanced into a proponent of Russian patriotism and morality, redefining Russian culture as built around orthodoxy (Turoma et al., 2019), and a variety of far-right, conservative, religious patriotic grass-roots movements formed, sharing their opposition to liberal ideas. Gradually, the regime's amorphous endorsement of conservatism and 'traditional values', including homophobia, the celebration of military masculinity, patriotism and world power status manifested in deliberately turning away from the West. Additionally, from 2013 onwards the state started targeting dissidents through laws such as the 'anti-gay propaganda law' or 'the blasphemy law' which enabled authorities to block websites and ban 'obscene language' in films, books and music. Naturally, the state's actions empowered the existing illiberal sector of civil society (Khazov, 2013; Laruelle, 2020, p. 118; Moss, 2017, pp. 197–9).

Although researchers agree that Russia actively participates in global anti-feminism (Sauer, 2019, p. 340) and the transregional and transnational promotion of 'traditional values' (Edenborg, 2018, p. 69; Moss, 2017, pp. 195–7), comparative studies mostly focus on the intersections between Russia, Western Europe and the USA (Mason, 2019; Murdoch et al., 2020). Only a few address Russia's anti-feminist and homophobic influence and alliances within Central Asia, and the only study that analyses the influence of Russia's political discourses within the regions of Kazakhstan and Kyrgyzstan does not consider anti-feminist or homophobic discourses particularly (Laruelle et al., 2019).

A literature review, however, suggests that anti-feminist discourses in Russia, Kyrgyzstan and Kazakhstan show significant similarities.

Kazakhstan

The Kazakh regime of former president Nursultan A. Nazarbayev, similarly to the Putin regime, created an eclectic set of discourses concerning the nation that legitimises the power of the president as keeper of economic prosperity, stability and inter-ethnic and inter-religious peace. These 'traditionalist discourses [aim at] controlling heterosexual norms to keep order enshrined in the discursive understanding of power, nation and gender, [and] the collective targeting and shaming of "deviant" discourses' (Kudaibergenova, 2019, p. 367) and activists. Conservative actors from the Kazakh civil society support the political regime's anti-feminism, homophobia and nationalism. The 'Uyat' (meaning 'Shame', Kudaibergenova, 2019, p. 364) movement agitates against female nudity in public, arguing that it offends national values. 'What is at the heart of these discussions is the body and its socially acceptable or unacceptable behaviour, as well as the visualization and censorship of images depicting naked, sexualized, objectified, national and nationalized, traditional and retraditionalised bodies' (Kudaibergenova, 2019, p. 365). The 'Uyat' actors exercise control over female (and to a lesser extent male) bodies through shaming 'in the name of and for the national cultural values that they continuously redefine' (Kudaibergenova, 2019, p. 366). They feed into discourses around the Kazakh family, based on a shame-and-honour system to regulate non-normative genders and sexualities.

These illiberal (re)traditionalist discourses are not entirely new to Kazakh culture, but draw on the Soviet heritage that silenced, pathologised, medicalised and criminalised non-normative sexual and gender expression. Kazakhstan is generally understood to be one of the 'most Sovietised' (Akiner, 1995, p. 51) Central Asian cultures. Changing women's role in Kazakh society was a Soviet priority and meant drastically altering the existing regional gender and sexual norms. The traditional Central Asian kinship ideology was gradually replaced with the nuclear heterosexual family (Ashwin, 2000; Zdravolmyslova and Temkina, 2007). During the Soviet period, sex and sexuality were viewed as private matters exclusively, 'references to sex and erotica were considered to be dubious and morally reprehensible' (Stella, 2015, p. 35). A negative attitude towards any discussion of the sexual body, non-reproductive sex and sexual pleasure was at the core of the Soviet ideology around gender (Kon, 1995; Stella, 2015). Public conversations around sex focused exclusively on marriage and reproduction (Kon, 1995). Male and female same-sex desires were pathologised as a 'perverted attraction to persons of the same sex' (Stella, 2015, p. 30; see also Clech, 2018).

While Soviet Russia heavily impacted the gender and sexuality discourses of Soviet Kazakhstan, the Russian influence on post-Soviet Kazakhstan is not as clearly identifiable. While some interpret the Kazakh attempt to pass a regional version of the 'anti-gay propaganda law' as evidence of Russia's 'soft power' (Nye, 2004) in the 'near abroad' (Healey, 2017), other academic work on Kazakh gender and sexuality discourses do not necessarily support this claim (Buelow, 2012; Patalakh, 2018). All of the available research, however, indicates a highly negative general public attitude against homosexuality and gender non-normativity that often manifests itself in discrimination and psychological and psychical violence (Latypov et al., 2013; Buelow, 2012; HRW, 2015; Feminita, 2018; Alma-TQ, 2016). Moreover, LGBTIQ+ people experience systemic violence in medical settings and from the police (HRW, 2015). Yet, the Kazakh domestic legislation 'On the Protection of Children from Information Harmful to their Health and Development' from 2 July 2018 does not mention homosexuality. While the law supports conservative ideas of family and 'traditional values', it does not primarily target non-normative sexual expressions. As Patalakh puts it 'while Russia is positioning itself as a strong opponent of LGBT rights domestically and abroad, Kazakhstan behaves far more neutrally' (2018, p. 37).

Kyrgyzstan

Post-Soviet Kyrgyzstan, similar to Kazakhstan, has been shaped by 'nationalizing' (Suyarkulova, 2016, p. 247) state policies and the 're-traditionalisation' (Werner, 2009, p. 321; see also Gal and Kligman, 2000) of society since the 1990s. Through a recent constitutional reform conservative values have been added 'and the legal definition of family has been changed from "a union of two people" to the gender-specific "a union between a man and a woman"' (Beyer and Finke, 2019, p. 319). This gendered re-traditional nationalism is 'enacted, lived, and understood in the realm of everyday practices, representations, and discourses, whereby ethno-national and gender identities and regimes are routinely (re)produced through banal signifiers that make both gender and nationalism appear natural, common sense, and taken for granted' (Suyarkulova, 2016, p. 247). Moreover, both need to be understood against the history of the paternalistic Soviet discourses of women's liberation in Central Asia, 'the so-called hujum ("assault")' (Suyarkulova, 2016, p. 248) campaign against 'purdah (seclusion of women), child marriage, bride price, bride abduction, and veiling' (Suyarkulova, 2016, p. 249). After the dissolution of the Soviet Union and with the new status of independence, the Soviet national symbols and practices became incorporated into the new state's discourses of sovereign statehood. Part of the Soviet legacy was the high valorising of literacy and women's participation in the workforce. The simultaneous prioritising of high fertility rates and the preservation of the existing family structures, which spanned over multiple generations and followed a strictly gendered division of labour, however, significantly hindered women's participation in the labour market (Kandiyoti, 2007, p. 607). Since the Soviet times, and with the dwindling of the welfare state into a neoliberal economy and part of the global market, the historic patriarchal values and nationalist ideas transformed, influenced by a growing class divide and newly gendered divisions of labour and 'bolstered by the ideas of "proper" Kyrgyz masculinity and femininity' (Suyarkulova, 2016, p. 249).

Within nationalist Kyrgyz politics women are frequently addressed as 'valuable possessions of the nation' (Suyarkulova, 2016, p. 250), as 'nationalist wombs' (ibid.), whose function is to reproduce the 'national "gene pool"' (ibid.). Moreover, women are held as 'symbols of national dignity and honor [and] child-like vulnerable creatures susceptible to defilement, exploitation, [and] manipulation' (ibid.). '[W]omen's mobility, their control over their own bodies, and their political participation [is restricted] through various policies and actions (regarding, for example, social provisioning, clothing, marriage, etc.), and [their agency is restricted] to the frame of the household' (Beyer and Finke, 2019, p. 318).

The wide support of conservative gender models is exemplified by the 2013 law draft that would have prohibited unmarried women under the age of twenty-two to leave the country. It was presented in the Kyrgyz parliament by Yrgal Kydyralieva of the Social-Democratic Party. Kydyralieva defended the bill, arguing that women 'give birth to the nation' and are 'bearers of the nation's honor' (Sultanbekova, 2013). 'Kyrdyralieva's proposal was met with a wave of protests by legal and civil rights organizations, which opposed the initiative as anti-constitutional. As a result, it was not passed' (Suyarkulova, 2016, p. 251). Yet, many read it as a definite sign 'of the rise of paternalistic policies and attitudes in the country [aiming] to control female sexuality and protect the "purity" of Kyrgyz women [and exercise] control over women's bodies' (Suyarkulova, 2016, p. 251). As of 2018 'Kyrgyzstan is ranked #122 on the UN Gender Equality index, behind some of [its] Central Asian neighbours – Kazakhstan, Uzbekistan, and even Turkmenistan' (Herrington-Kobekpaeva, 2018). '[B]ride abduction has become more frequent in Kyrgyzstan in the last two decades' (Beyer and Finke, 2019, p. 318), and LGBTIQ+ are highly stigmatised (Hoare, 2019, p. 172; Wilkinson and Kirey, 2010; Omurov, 2017; Boemcken et al., 2018).

This trend empowered actors, referring to themselves as patriots, violently abusing Kyrgyz women for what they understood as shameful behaviour. They defended their actions as 'patriotic, truly masculine and ethnic', as 'fighting for the honor of the nation' (Ibraeva et al., 2015, p. 3), and protecting the women's honour (ibid.).

In parallel with the existence of a lively non-governmental organisation sector that includes multiple feminist, women's equality oriented and LGBTIQ+ groups, feminism and queer activism are met with 'considerable hostility and came under attack for "destroying" the family and threatening traditional Kyrgyz values, and their employees were at risk of physical violence' (Hoare, 2019, p. 172). The 8th of March parade in 2019, organised by LGBTIQ+ activists and feminists, was met with 'anti-LGBT rhetoric in parliament' (HRW, 2020). An active anti-feminist and anti-LGBTIQ+ group is the nationalist group Kyrk Choro ('40 Warriors'), which held a counter-protest on the same day. Kyrk Choro and others 'perceive the LGBT community as a danger to "traditional" family values and moral norms' (Boemcken et al., 2018, p. 69). A publicly discussed example for this trend is the violence against the young feminist musician Zere Asylbek and her music video 'Kyz' ('Girl'), which calls out gender disparity in Kyrgyz society (Herrington-Kobekpaeva, 2018). Conservatives harshly criticised the video, arguing that it insults national values, and the singer received death threats for it (Talant, 2018). The popularity of Asylbek's music and message online shows that there is a significant part of the population that believes in women's equality and self-determination. Yet, her case also shows 'that feminist liberation meets harsh opposition from the discourses of those who strive to control new understandings of "tradition" and "shame" locally' (Kudaibergenova, 2019, p. 364).

Although the Kyrgyz state partially aligns with Russia in forming a counter-pole to Western liberalism, for example in signing the Russian counter-resolution to the '2011 UN Human Rights Council SOGI resolution [that focuses] on traditional values' (Hoare, 2019, p. 175), there is no evidence that the Russian influence goes further than supporting already prevalent national discourses. The proposed 'anti-homosexual propaganda law', which has been under consideration by the Kyrgyz parliament since 2014 (Hoare, 2019, p. 175), can be viewed in this light. However, Kyrgyz, as in Russian and Kazakh discourses, signifies heterosexuality and conservative gender roles as traditional and patriotic (Commercio, 2015, pp. 529–30), and as cornerstones of 'national culture' which need to be protected from dangerous Western discourses that aim at normalising queer sexuality and gender fluidity (Kudaibergenova, 2019; Tiidenberg, 2015; Mamedov, 2016; Rodulgina, 2016; Riabov and Riabova, 2014b; Stella and Nartova, 2016).

Moreover, as in Russia and Kazakhstan, feminism is understood as Western, hence 'incompatible with traditional gender norms' (Beyer and Finke, 2019, p. 318). In all three regions, nationalism instrumentalises traditionalist views on the gendered body to legitimate a patriarchal social order, spearheaded by the national elite; and establishing hegemonic conservative notions of gender and control over bodies aims at unifying the nation (Kudaibergenova, 2019).

Methodology

In the following we reconstruct the different cases of anti-feminist violence within the three regions by piecing together information from various online media, including national news media, international media as well as blogs and social media. Our search on Google News found approximately 6,320 articles in Russian and 1,610 articles in English on Tsvetkova's case (newspaper reports, analytical articles, interviews, etc.). With regard to the case against the Kyrgyz Feminnale, 139 Russian and 108 English language articles were published . Finally, our Google News search found 181 Russian language articles and 1,150 in English about the Kazakh Feminita. We prioritise independent media sources as well as the feminists' own accounts on the events. We analyse the cases, focusing on the anti-feminism(s) behind them, and using an intersectional lens that considers a variety of variables such as age, gender, class and race or ethnicity. We identify the different levels of power that bring forward anti-feminist discourses and actions, distinguishing between agitators on behalf of the state, religious institutions and civil society. Moreover, we consider the historic context of anti-feminist discourses and actions as well as their intersections with other social and political discourses. Analysing the cases within their historic and contemporary, national and transnational context, we want to know what the content of anti-feminism is. What are the arguments and actions that can be classified as anti-feminist? Who are the protagonists or actors of anti-feminism? Are they acting on behalf of institutions such as the state or the church? Finally, we compare the results to find out how the national anti-feminist discourses are related with each other.

Description of the Cases of Anti-feminism

Russia

The prosecution of the feminist, anti-militarist and LGBTIQ+ activist Yulia Tsvetkova is an example for anti-feminism in Komsomolsk-na-Amure,

Khabarovsk Region, Russia. Starting from early 2019 Tsvetkova was trialled in several cases for both criminal and administrative offences: her body positive sketches of naked women with body hair and stretch marks were investigated as 'pornography', and a play challenging gender stereotypes called 'Pink and Blue' that Tsvetkova directed in a children's theatre was labelled 'gay propaganda to minors'[2] (Kommersant, 2019b). During the investigations, Tsvetkova spent months in home detention, not even allowed to seek medical care (Novaya Gazeta, 2020a). Aside from the investigations conducted by the Russian Federal Security Service (since 'gay propaganda' is considered to be a threat to the state, see Novaya Gazeta, 2020b), the activist reported receiving multiple death threats from homophobic activists such as the group 'Saw against LGBT' (Novaya Gazeta, 2020c) or Timur Bulatov (A pogovorit?, 2020, 41.29–42.54), both of these having a long history of outing and bullying LGBTIQ+ in Russia (Sobaka, 2019).

The trials against Tsvetkova and the absurdity of the accusations have gained wide publicity and led to multiple solidarity actions in Russia and beyond (hashtags #МедиаСтрайкЗаЮлю, Novaya Gazeta, 2020d; #WEAREYULIA, Wonderzine, 2020); a large number of artists as well as feminist and LGBTIQ+ activists publicly demanded the prosecutions to stop (Novaya Gazeta, 2020e); and a personal exhibition of Tsvetkova's art works was organised by activists in Moscow in August 2021 (CCI Fabrika, 2021). Feminist activists demonstrating in solidarity with Tsvetkova in Moscow and Saint Petersburg in June 2020 were arrested (OVD-info, 2020). Tsvetkova went on a hunger strike in May 2021 to protest the lack of transparency of the proceedings against her (OVD-info, 2021).

Now Tsvetkova is facing two fines for 'gay propaganda to minors'. Moreover, the European Court of Human Rights has proposed that Tsvetkova and the Russian Federation settle out of court with regard to these 'propaganda of homosexuality' allegations. After more than a year and four rounds of reinvestigations of Tsvetkova's body positive vagina drawings for allegedly containing pornography, the conviction was affirmed, and the first court hearing took place in March 2021. In June 2021 the activist's online community 'Vagina monologues', on the social media platform Vkontakte, was blocked by the Federal Service for Supervision of Communications, Information Technology and Mass Media (Roskomnadzor) following a court order, and the pornography investigations are still ongoing (OVD-info, 2021).

Kyrgyzstan

The cases of state censorship of the first international feminist art exhibition 'Feminnale' in late 2019 and police brutality against the participants of the 8 March 2020 demonstration, supported by right-wing national-ist groups, are two examples of anti-feminism in Bishkek, Kyrgyzstan. The exhibition included a performance about violence against women and sex workers' rights: the artist appeared naked and slowly put on her clothes (Mamedov, 2020). The demonstration of a naked female body in a state museum during this performance was criticised as 'not align-ing with [Kyrgyz] mentality and traditions' by nationalist groups that demonstrated in front of the 'Feminnale' venue (Kaktus, 2019a), and the president of Kyrgyzstan Sooronbay Jeenbekov spoke of it as 'a humilia-tion of women' (Gezitter, 2019). Finally, the Minister of Culture Azamat Zhamankulov personally visited the exhibition and censored the per-formance along with seven other pieces (Kaktus, 2019b). The director of the museum Mira Dzhangaracheva and the curator of the exhibition Altyn Kapalova were subjected to harassment, both on social media and on TV, and the director of the museum had to resign (Voices on Central Asia, 2020).

The curator Kapalova was part of the demonstration on 8 March 2020 too, when a group of masked men (some of them wearing national Kazakh hats) attacked the peaceful gathering against violence towards women (Interfax, 2020). When police arrived, the attackers dispersed, and the police officers brutally arrested and detained seventy participants of the march for hours without providing any reason for their action and without providing access to lawyers (Meduza, 2020b). The authorities claimed that the police 'prevented a conflict during an illegal demonstra-tion' and argued that local citizens were scandalised since the demonstra-tion took place at a square that is a sacred space for the commemoration of the soldiers who fought in 'the great patriotic war' (Vesti, 2020). A year earlier the right-wing organisation 'Kyrgyz Choroloru' called for the resignation of the head of the City of Bishkek Administration after a rainbow flag and pro-LGBTIQ+ posters were noticed during the women's day demonstration on 8 March 2019 (Kaktus, 2019c).

In May 2020 a draft law which would force more government con-trol of NGOs and independent civic activists was discussed in the parlia-ment of Kyrgyzstan. The proponents of the document used the examples of Feminnale and the 8th of March demonstrations to argue that more government control was necessary to ensure that events that do not cor-respond to the values and traditions of the Kyrgyz people are prohib-ited (Imanaliyeva, 2020). Nevertheless, in March 2021 the women's day demonstration went ahead peacefully without any interruptions, bring-ing together 500 participants, which is the all-time highest number for Bishkek (Malaisarova, 2021).

Kazakhstan

In Almaty, Kazakhstan the women's rights group FemPoint organised a photo-shoot against the taboos around menstruation in 2018 (Azattyq, 2018), during which participants carried hand-drawn posters and menstrual pads covered in red paint. A week later one of the participants, Zhanar Sekerbayeva, was arrested, verbally harassed by police officers and charged with petty hooliganism (Amnesty International, 2019). Sekerbayeva reports receiving a large number of inappropriate messages from strangers that addressed her appearance and sexuality in derogatory terms (ibid.). Together with Gulzada Serzhan, Sekerbayeva is co-founder of the NGO Feminita which supports LBQ women in Kazakhstan. One of the cases Feminita works with is a privacy breach, whereby after a video of two women kissing was uploaded onto the Internet, their relationship with their friends, family and colleagues was damaged and they started receiving threats from strangers in the streets and online. After a year of court procedures on different levels, the Supreme Court ruled that the actions of the man who took and uploaded the video were illegal (Azattyq, 2019; Diapazon, 2020). Feminita is also legally defending several participants of the 8th of March 2020 demonstration (Diapazon, 2020). Sixty activists from different feminist organisations marching for women's rights were detained, and two of them were fined for participating in an illegal demonstration, for petty crime and for not being registered at their place of residence (Kloop, 2020). In 2021 the women's demonstration was approved by the Almaty city officials and went smoothly, uniting more than 500 participants from feminist organisations throughout the country (Mamashully, 2021).

In 2021 Feminita organised a seminar series on women's and LBTQI+ rights in a number of cities in Kazakhstan. In the city of Shymkent the activists were denied the seminar space just before the start of the event, they were attacked by a mob of homophobic men, and were brutally detained by the local police 'for their own safety' and sent back to Almaty (Asylbek, 2021). In Qaraghandy the local authorities forced the activists to leave the building, half an hour after the seminar had started and a violent religious crowd of around fifty people attacked them on the streets, while the police did not interfere (Fergana, 2021). More than 100 people protested against the planned seminar by Feminita in Aktobe (Zhursin and Zhankatov, 2021). The protests in all of the above-mentioned cities were fuelled by misinformation that was spread on social media about Feminita organising a 'gay pride' or a 'gay concert'.

Analysis

What are the actions that can be classified as anti-feminist?

In all of the cases described above, male activists reacted violently to feminists' political and public actions that were intended to address gender inequality and create discourses of social change. To understand the actions as anti-feminist, it is important to point out that all the women involved are self-identified feminists. These women's actions were decidedly feminist acts of self-representation, showcasing female agency. The focus of the respective groups differed. In Kazakhstan the women wanted to break the taboo around menstruation, aiming at normalising it in public discourse. The Kyrgyz activists protested against violence against women and the exploitation of sex workers through images of female nudity, which can be interpreted as an attempt to de-sexualise representations of female bodies. Yulia Tsvetkova posted sketches of different naked female bodies to propagate body positivity and fight normative beauty standards. Her images were presented exclusively online, while the activists in Kyrgyzstan and Kazakhstan chose public spaces for their feminist actions, such as a city square or a state museum. In the latter cases, the feminist actions were a decided intervention into public spaces, whereas in Russia the intervention was virtual. Importantly, in all the cases, men took the most offence from showing female bodies that were not sexualised or did not comply with a male gaze during these feminist actions.

The anti-feminist actors can be classified as anti-feminist because they understood that the women were feminists and that their actions aimed at equality and social change. They sprang into action because the women went into the public sphere and attracted attention, taking up space and bringing forward feminist discourses on female bodies that defy conservative and neo-traditional ideas. In all cases the anti-feminist actors came from civil society, but they were backed up by state institutions such as the police or city authorities. Moreover, all of these anti-feminist actors exercised violence against the feminists, although the form and extent of the violence varied. The Kyrgyz feminists were physically attacked while demonstrating on the streets, both by anti-feminist counter-demonstrators and by the police detaining them. In Kazakhstan, the activists were threatened online, and were arrested and harassed by the police, as was Tsvetkova.

What are the arguments which can be classified as anti-feminist?

In Kyrgyzstan the anti-feminist protestors argued that displaying naked female bodies is a disgrace to women and does not comply with the national traditions and values (Gezitter, 2019; Kaktus, 2019a). Moreover, the anti-feminist actors were offended by a rainbow flag that was carried by the feminist demonstrators, because pro-LGBTIQ+ activism is an even bigger offence to national values (Kaktus, 2019c). Importantly, the anti-feminist agitators focused on the locations of the feminist actions as offensive, a state museum and a city square respectively. They feared that the feminist women 'c[a]me to [their] museum and force[d] things upon [them] that are out of line with [their] mentality and traditions' (Kaktus, 2019a). They stated that they 'are against people getting naked and hanging their underwear in our museum', voicing the concern that their relatives might accidentally visit the museum 'without knowing that such things are happening here' (Kaktus, 2019a). In the case of the 8th March demonstration the authorities reproduced the rhetoric of anti-feminist and nationalist groups in their press releases, arguing that the local citizens were scandalised by the unsanctioned demonstrations at the city square that commemorates the soldiers who died during the Second World War while protecting their Fatherland[3] (Vesti, 2020).

Implicitly, the anti-feminist actors reacted to the appearance of women in a public space on their own terms. These men saw the national social (gender) order as being violated by feminist body-related discourses. Firstly, the women appeared as self-determined political agents within the terrain of the political that is usually determined by men. Secondly, the feminists propagated ideas about the female body that violate conservative and neo-traditionalist ideas. The anti-feminists did not only spring into action themselves, they also called upon the state and its institutions to reinforce the patriarchal social order and punish the women for taking action and violating conservative social norms.

In the case of the Kazakh photo shoot against taboos around menstruation the attacks equally came from civil society actors that seemed even more disorganised than in the Kyrgyz case. Yet, seven days afterwards feminists were detained by the police and accused of petty hooliganism. The argument behind the anti-feminist counter-protest was the women's offensive behaviour in displaying inappropriate images of female body parts in public. As in the case of Kyrgyzstan, the men took offence with women taking political public actions that aimed at demystifying the female body and presenting a female gaze. Importantly, the counter-protesters addressed and took offence with the self-presentation of the feminists. They commented on the activists' 'unfeminine' looks, short hair and non-normative gender representations, mockingly asking about their marital status (Amnesty International, 2019). They argued that women were not to talk about menstruation at all, let alone take public action. They also implied that the feminists' bodily representation and style was inappropriate and their lifestyles should be changed according to the national values, meaning their submission under the patriarchal gender order. One man took offence with two women kissing in public, filmed them and approached them with a homophobic comment to remind them of the expected heteronormative behaviour (Azattyq, 2019). After the women did not react the way the man wanted, he uploaded the video to the internet, outing the women and inviting the general public to sanction their non-normative behaviour. The outing damaged the women's relationships with family, friends and colleagues, and they received threats both online and offline. In this instance too, the man took offence with female agency that did not comply with the heteronormative standards of behaviour.

In both the Kyrgyz and the Kazakh cases the state, in the form of the police and the courts, got involved only after public agents had acted violently against feminist activists, while in the Russian case it was the local administration who acted first. They classified Tsvetkova's play 'Pink and Blue' as 'homosexual propaganda', and forbade its performance at the children's theatre 'Merak' where Tsvetkova was the director. They identified the terms 'pink' and 'blue' as code for homosexuals, as they were used before and during the 1990s. In protest, Tsvetkova reached out to local media to cover the case (A pogovorit?, 2020, 25:01–29.57). This publicity triggered the interest of the police and the Russian Federal Security Service (FSB). According to Tsvetkova's mother, who is the owner of the children's theatre, one of the FSB investigators noted that LGBTIQ+ is a threat to the Russian state, which is why they had to get involved (Novaya Gazeta, 2020b). Through their search, the FSB became aware of Tsvetkova's body positive drawings, and her role as organiser of an online community called the Vagina Monologues[4] that posts vagina drawings by different artists. They started an independent case against Tsvetkova, alleging that the content of the Vagina Monologue posts was pornography, the distribution of which is a criminal offence (Consultant.ru, 2020).

While in Kazakhstan and Kyrgyzstan the body positive representations of female bodies triggered anti-feminist public protest and violence that shifted towards homophobic agitation only when queer symbols and people were discovered among the feminist activists, in Russia it was the other way around. The city administration of Komsomolsk-na-Amure as well as the FSB were first alarmed by the possibility of LGBTIQ+-positive content and only later used allegations of inappropriate body representations that they classified as pornographic to start yet another legal case against Tsvetkova. In other words, they reverted to anti-feminist agitation to support their homophobic persecution.

In all three cases there was a selective coalition between right-wing activists or civil society actors and institutions on different levels of administration that exercised anti-feminist violence. Importantly, in Tsvetkova's case and in that of the members of the Kazakh group Feminita, the political opposition – which usually protests against state or state-sanctioned violence against anybody who expresses a liberal point of view – did not support them as much as they would support other political agents (Novaya Gazeta, 2020d; Azattyq, 2019). This allows for the conclusion that homophobia and anti-feminist sentiments are widespread among civil society in general. In fact, according to Serzhan, the co-founder of Feminita, the group was founded because lesbian activists could not find a home within the liberal opposition because of their homophobia: 'some did not like the way we looked. We felt that our orientation was perceived as strange. After this protest action we wanted to join other civil rights movements too but we had a feeling that people were avoiding us' (Azattyq, 2019).

An interesting detail about the Russian context is that the Russian Orthodox Church, which is often seen as strong proponent within anti-feminist agitation, was not involved in the violence against Tsvetkova. Equally, religion does not play any role in the two other cases, where Islam is the most widespread faith. In 2021, however, the protesters against Feminita's seminars on women's rights explicitly connected their Muslim beliefs with the protest (Zhursin and Zhankatov, 2021).

The representation of the targets of the anti-feminist discourses and actions shows similarities and differences between the three cases. The example of Tsvetkova is the most individualised one, since she does not represent any groups and her prosecution is an attack against her personally (Kommersant, 2019b). What makes this context so similar to the Feminita case is the silence of the official institutions that are exercising the political repressions: no comments from the representatives of power on different levels, no media coverage by state or local government-affiliated media (which is a typical communication strategy of Russian authorities while dealing with ambiguous topics). At the same time there are many media outlets that represent Yulia's and her mother's experiences of street harassment and conversations with the investigators and the police. In the comments to these articles, people comment on her non-conforming looks (shaved hair and lack of make-up) (Meduza, 2020b), while the investigators ask about her connections to the West (Tsvetkova studied in London) (A pogovorit?, 2020, 29:58–30:47). Her age and gender do not seem to play an important role in the anti-feminist narratives; however, they are widely used by her supporters, who appeal to the image of an innocent, brave young girl confronting the anonymous inhumane system (Novaya Gazeta, 2020e).

In the case of the Feminnale the activists are collectivised and ano-nymised; in an official message about the 8th of March demonstration they are referred to as 'representatives of civil groups "Feminale" and "8/365"', completely erasing their gender and the cause they address (Vesti, 2020). The discourses about the exhibition censorship, on the other hand, label the artists and the organisers, no matter their citizenship, age or educa-tion, as 'women' (Kaktus, 2019a; Gezitter, 2019), therefore putting them in a position in a society where they (should) depend on their respective men (fathers, husbands, president or minister of culture). The narrative of the scandal and the disciplining of the outrageous women takes over the individual stories and art pieces presented at the exhibition (Mamedov, 2019). According to the curator of the exhibition, she and the director of the museum were harassed personally on TV and social media (Voices on Central Asia, 2020).

As in case of Yulia Tsvetkova, Feminita's cases are very personalised, focusing on Zhanar Sekerbayeva, due to her gender ambiguous appear-ance, which triggered the online harassment after the photo shoot against the menstruation taboo. Moreover, the legal authorities' representatives questioned her about her marital status and her motivation to participate in the photo shoot, appealing to her high level of education (Sekerbayeva, 2018), implying that only people with little education and understanding of the societal norms would want to be publicly associated with such a shameful topic. Sekerbayeva is also visible in the reporting on the violence connected to the seminars of Feminita in 2021, since she was the one physically attacked and detained by the police (Asylbek, 2021). However, in the reporting about the 8th of March demonstration events, the activists are referred to as 'feminists' or 'feminist groups Kazfem, Svet, Feminita, Femagora and Femsreda' (Azattyq, 2020), collectivising them but still making their cause visible.

Preliminary Conclusion

Our analysis strongly suggests that, although anti-feminism is the trans-nationally and discursively shared sentiment and discourse, the specific local conditions that allowed for the erupting of anti-feminism, its rhe-torical foci and its goals are rooted in local contexts and are not imported from elsewhere. Moreover, while the violence and the censoring of body positive initiatives show significant similarities transnationally, media identifies exclusively local profiteers of the actions. Therefore, the exam-ples we have selected above reveal all the importance of 'the local in the transnational', and thus a second, equally relevant, side of transnational movements, namely the significance of local contexts for the unfolding possibilities of anti-feminist strategies and policies. In this respect, this chapter has focused primarily on the reactive side of anti-feminism, as it examined anti-feminist forms of articulation taking into account the respective national circumstances that relate directly to concrete feminist activism. Accordingly, the first results of our analysis not only underline the complexity of transnational anti-feminist discourses, but also illustrate adaptability to different contexts and issues as one of the conditions for the transnational success of the respective actors.

Furthermore, our study does not support widespread theories of direct state-ordered Russian influence in the post-Soviet regions of Kazakhstan and Kyrgyzstan. Rather than a Russian influence, the violence was reported on as individually regionally enacted measures in support of patriarchal authoritarian social structures that are globally connected through anti-feminism.

Although the three cases have much in common, there are significant differences in how anti-feminists approach the messages of the respective activists and in what the media highlight. For example, there is a clear difference between Tsvetkova in Russia and Feminita in Kazakhstan. While the anti-feminist discourses and actions utilise legal means against the body positive and pro-LGBTIQ+ activities in the case of Tsvetkova, trying to set an example to prevent such politics in the future, the Kazakh anti-feminist discourses focus on the bodies of the feminists as much as on their politics, trying to force conservative body norms on these individuals. Moreover, in Russia the focus on body positivity and the pornography claims were only made after the homophobic claims of endangering children, and can be seen as secondary, while in the Kazakh case the focus on the body was primary. The bodies were addressed as a battlefield for gendered norms themselves, open for disciplining practices and traditionalist inscriptions, and framing non-normative sexual behaviour as unacceptable.

In all three examples, however, media discourses strongly indicate that local actors took issues with feminist and pro-LGBTIQ+ visibility in public spaces. Especially in the Kyrgyz case, anti-feminist discourses negotiated what should and should not be presented in a national museum. While in all three cases questions of national representation and national values were brought forward with regards to individual female body representations, the Kyrgyz discourses most directly discussed national identity and representation. In all the regional media discourses, we could clearly see a selective coalition between right-wing activists or civil society actors and institutions on different levels of administration that exercised anti-feminist violence. Interestingly, religion did not play a major role in the local anti-feminist discourses. In fact, only the reports on the protests against

Feminita's seminars on women's rights in 2021 explicitly mentioned Muslim beliefs at all.

Notes

1. The research for this chapter was developed by the authors within the framework of the project 'The Magic Closet and the Dream Machine: Post-Soviet Queerness, Archiving, and the Art of Resistance' (AR 567), conducted by Katharina Wiedlack, Masha Godovannaya, Ruthia Jenrbekova and Iain Zabolotny, funded by the Austrian Science Fund.
2. All translations from Russian were done by the authors of the chapter, unless noted otherwise.
3. In Russian the term is fatherland (Отечество), not motherland, as in English.
4. The name of the community is a clear reference to the famous American feminist play *The Vagina Monologues* by V (formerly Eve Ensler) that premiered in 1996.

References

Akiner, S. (1995). *The Formation of Kazakh Identity: From Tribe to Nation-State*. Royal Institute of International Affairs.

Alma-TQ. (2016). *Violations by Kazakhstan of the Right of Transgender Persons to Legal Recognition of Gender Identity*. https://tbinternet.ohchr.org/Treaties/CCPR/Shared Documents/KAZ/INT_CCPR_CSS_KAZ_24305_E.pdf (accessed 30 June 2018).

Ashwin, S. (2000). *Gender, State and Society in Soviet and Post-Soviet Russia*. Routledge.

Beyer, J. and Finke, P. (2019). Practices of Traditionalization in Central Asia. *Central Asian Survey, 38*(3), 310–28.

Boemcken, von, M., Boboyorov, H. and Bagdasarova, N. (2018). Living Dangerously: Securityscapes of Lyuli and LGBT People in Urban Spaces of Kyrgyzstan. *Central Asian Survey, 37*(1), 68–84.

Buelow, S. (2012). Locating Kazakhstan: The Role of LGBT Voices in the Asia/Europe Debate. *Lambda Nordica, 4*, 99–125.

Buelow, S. (2015). LGBT in Central Asia: 2014's Most Pivotal Moments. *Anthropology News*. http://www.anthropology-news.org/index.php/2015/06/30/lgbt-in-central-asia/

Chebankova, E. (2016). Contemporary Russian Conservatism. *Post-Soviet Affairs, 32*(1), 28–54.

Clech, A. (2018). Between the Labor Camp and the Clinic: Tema or the Shared Forms of Late Soviet Homosexual Subjectivities. *Slavic Review, 77*(1), 6–29.

Commercio, M. (2015). The Politics and Economics of 'Retraditionalization' in Kyrgyzstan and Tajikistan. *Post-Soviet Affairs, 31*(6), 529–56.

Edenborg, E. (2018). Homophobia as Geopolitics: 'Traditional Values' and the Negotiation of Russia's Place in the World. In J. Mulholland, E. Sanders-McDonagh and N. Montagna (eds), *Gendering Nationalism: Intersections of Nation, Gender and Sexuality* (pp. 67–87). Palgrave Macmillan.

Feminita. (2018). Situation of Lesbian, Bisexual and Transgender Women in Kazakhstan: Alternative Report on Implementation of the International Covenant on Economic, social and Cultural Rights. https://tbinternet.ohchr.org/Treaties/CESCR/Shared Documents/KAZ/INT_CESCR_ICO_KAZ_29944_E.pdf

Gal, S. and Kligman, G. (2000). *The Politics of Gender after Socialism*. Princeton University Press.

Healey, D. (2017). *Russian Homophobia from Stalin to Sochi*. Bloomsbury Publishing PLC.

Herrington-Kobekpaeva, K. (2018). Run the World: Zeré Asylbek Called Out Gender Disparity in Kyrgyzstan and She's Only Getting Started. *Calvert Journal*, 2 October 2018. https://www.calvertjournal.com/articles/show/10689/zere-asylbek- feminist-pop-anthem-interview

Hoare, J. P. (2019). Narratives of Exclusion: Observations on a Youth-led LGBT Rights Group in Kyrgyzstan. In R. C. M. Mole (ed.), *Soviet and Post-Soviet Sexualities* (pp. 171–91). Routledge.

HRW. (2015). 'That's when I realized I was nobody': A Climate of Fear for LGBT People in Kazakhstan. *Human Rights Watch*. https://www.hrw.org/report/2015/07/23/thats-when-i-realized-i-was-nobody/climate-fear-lgbt-people-kazakhstan

HRW. (2020). Kyrgyzstan: Events of 2019. *Human Rights Watch*. https://www.hrw.org/world-report/2020/country-chapters/kyrgyzstan#

Ibraeva, G., Moldosheva, A. and Ablezova, M. (2015). 'We will kill you and we will be equitted!' – Critical Discourse Analysis of a Media Case of Violence Against Female Migrants from Kyrgyzstan. In T. Kruessmann (ed.), *Gender in Modern Central Asia* (pp. 3–26). LIT Verlag.

Kandiyoti, D. (2007). The Politics of Gender and the Soviet Paradox: Neither Colonized, Nor Modem? *Central Asian Survey, 26*(4), 601–23.

Khazov, S. (2013). Russia's Anti-gay Own Goal. *Open Democracy*, 27 September 2013. https://www.opendemocracy.net/en/odr/russias-anti-gay-own-goal/

Kon, I. (1995). *The Sexual Revolution in Russia: From the Age of the Czars to Today.* The Free Press.

Kudaibergenova, D. T. (2019). The Body Global and the Body Traditional: A Digital Ethnography of Instagram and Nationalism in Kazakhstan and Russia. *Central Asian Survey, 38*(3), 363–80.

Laruelle, M. (2020). Making Sense of Russia's Illiberalism. *Journal of Democracy, 31*(3), 115–29.

Laruelle, M., Royce, D. and Beyssembayev, S. (2019). Untangling the Puzzle of 'Russia's influence' in Kazakhstan. *Eurasian Geography and Economics, 60*(2), 211–43.

Latypov, A., Rhodes, T. and Reynolds, L. (2013). Prohibition, Stigma and Violence against Men Who Have Sex with Men : Effects on HIV in Central Asia. *Central Asian Survey, 32*(1), 52–65.

Makarychev, A. and Medvedev, S. (2015). Biopolitics and Power in Putin's Russia. *Problems of Post-Communism, 62*(1), 45–54.

Mamedov, G. (2016). The Illusion of the Soviet: Conservative Turn in Kyrgyzstan. The Law on Prohibiting 'Gay Propaganda' and the Soviet Discourse of Homosexuality. In O. Shatalova and G. Mamedov (eds), *Queer-Communism eto etika* [Queer Communism is Ethics] (pp. 63–84). Svobodnoe Marxistskoe Izdatelstvo.

Mason, C. (2019). Opposing Abortion to Protect Women: Transnational Strategy since the 1990s. *Signs*, 44(3), 665–92.

Mason, J. (2018). Pussy Provocations: Feminist Protest and Anti-Feminist Resurgence in Russia. *Feminist Encounters: A Journal of Critical Studies in Culture and Politics*, 2(1), 1–14.

Moss, K. (2017). Russia as the Saviour of European Civilization: Gender and the Geopolitics of Traditional Values. In R. Kuhar and D. Paternotte (eds), *Anti-Gender Campaigns in Europe: Mobilizing Against Equality* (pp. 195–214). Rowman & Littlefield.

Murdoch, S., Mulhall, J., Lawrence, D. and Hermansson, P. (2020). *The International Alt-Right: Fascism for the 21st Century?* Routledge.

Nye, J. S. (2004). *Soft Power: The Means to Success in World Politics*. Public Affairs.

Omurov, N. (2017). Identity Disclosure as a Securityscape for LGBT People. *Psychology in Russia: State of the Art*, 10(2), 63–86.

Østbø, J. (2017). Securitizing 'Spiritual-Moral Values' in Russia. *Post-Soviet Affairs*, 33(3), 200–16.

Patalakh, A. (2018). Economic or Geopolitical? Explaining the Motives and Expectations of the Eurasian Economic Union's Member States. *Fudan Journal of the Humanities and Social Sciences*, 11(1), 31–48.

Riabov, O. and Riabova, T. (2014a). The Remasculinization of Russia? *Problems of Post-Communism*, 61(2), 23–35.

Riabov, O. and Riabova, T. (2014b). The Decline of Gayropa? *Eurozine*, 1–9. https://www.eurozine.com/the-decline-of-gayropa/

Rodulgina, I. (2016). Russian Homophobia: The History of Production. *Colta.ru*. http://www.colta.ru/articles/raznoglasiya/12008

Sauer, B. (2019). Anti-feministische Mobilisierung in Europa. Kampf um eine neue politische Hegemonie? *Zeitschrift Für Vergleichende Politikwissenschaft*, 13(3), 339–52.

Sharafutdinova, G. (2014). The Pussy Riot Affair and Putin's Démarche from Sovereign Democracy to Sovereign Morality. *Nationalities Papers*, 42(4), 615–21.

Sleptcov, N. (2017). Political Homophobia as a State Strategy in Russia. *Journal of Global Initiatives: Policy, Pedagogy, Perspective*, 12(1), 140–61.

Sperling, V. (2014). *Sex, Politics, and Putin: Political Legitimacy in Russia*. Oxford University Press. https://books.google.com/books?id=M2u6BAAAQBAJ&pgis=1

Stella, F. (2015). *Lesbian Lives in Soviet and Post-Soviet Russia: Post/Socialism and Gendered Sexualities*. Palgrave Macmillan.

Stella, F. and Nartova, N. (2016). Sexual Citizenship, Nationalism and Biopolitics in Putin's Russia. In F. Stella, Y. Taylor, T. Reynolds and A. Rogers (eds), *Sexuality, Citizenship and Belonging. Trans-National and Intersectional Perspectives* (pp. 24–42). Routledge.

Stepanova, E. (2015). 'The Spiritual and Moral Foundation of Civilization in Every Nation for Thousands of Years': The Traditional Values Discourse in Russia. *Politics, Religion & Ideology, 16*(2–3), 119–36.

Sultanbekova, Z. (2013). Interviu: pochemu deputat khochet ogranichit' vyiezd molodykh kyr- gyzstanok za granitsu [Interview: Why a Member of Parliament Wants to Restrict Travel for Young Kyrgyzstani Women]. *Kloop.kg,* 4 March. http://kloop.kg/blog/2013/03/04/ interv-yu-pochemu-deputat-hochet-ogranichit-vy-ezd-molody-h-ky-rgy-zstanok-za-granitsu/

Suyarkulova, M. (2016). Fashioning the Nation: Gender and Politics of Dress in Contemporary Kyrgyzstan. *Nationalities Papers, 44*(2), 247–65.

Tiidenberg, K. (2015). Odes to Heteronormativity: Presentations of Femininity in Russian-Speaking Pregnant Women's Instagram Accounts. *International Journal of Communication, 9,* 1746–58.

Turoma, S., Aitamurto, K. and Vladiv-Glover, S. (eds). (2019). *Religion, Expression, and Patriotism in Russia.* Ibidem.

Werner, C. (2009). Bride Abduction in Post-Soviet Central Asia: Marking a Shift towards Patriarchy through Local Discourses of Shame and Tradition. *Journal of the Royal Anthropological Institute, 15,* 314–31.

Wilkinson, C. (2014). Putting 'Traditional Values' Into Practice: The Rise and Contestation of Anti-Homopropaganda Laws in Russia. *Journal of Human Rights, 13*(3), 363–79.

Wilkinson, C. and Kirey, A. (2010). What's in a Name? The Personal and Political Meanings of 'LGBT' for Non-heterosexual and Transgender Youth in Kyrgyzstan. *Central Asian Survey, 29*(4), 485–99.

Zdravolmyslova, E. and Temkina, A. (2007). Sovetskii Etakraticheskii Gendernyi Kontrakt [Soviet Gender Contract]. In E. Zdravomyslova and A. Temkina (eds), *Rossiiskii Gendenyi Poriadok. Sotsiologicheskii Podkhod* [Russian Gender Order. Sociological Perspective] (pp. 96–137). Izdatel'stvo Evropeiskogo Universiteta v Sankt-Peterburge.

Media sources

A pogovorit? (2020). Дело Юлии Цветковой: как в России сесть за рисунок? Author: Shikhman, I. 3 July. In: https://youtu.be/15zeXbTvy7M

Amnesty International. (2019). My Activism isn't Motivated by Kindness. It's Motivated by Anger. Author: Sekerbayeva, Zh. 2 July. In: https://www.amnesty.org/en/latest/campaigns/2019/07/zhanar-sekerbayeva-from-feminita-on-why-anger-motivates-her-activism/

Asylbek, B. (2021). Нетерпимость и агрессия к ЛГБТ+. В чем причины гомофобии в Казахстане? *Radio Azattyq,* 7 June. In: https://rus.azattyq.org/a/kazakhstan-homophobia-causes-of-aggression/31292952.html

Azattyq. (2018). Суд оштрафовал активистку Feminita. Author: Asautai, M. 20 June. In: https://rus.azattyq.org/a/kazakhstan-feminita-zhanar-trial-fining/29443934.html

Azattyq. (2019). Сложности защиты женщин с нетрадиционной сексуальной ориентацией. Author: Asautai, M. 23 September. In: https://rus.azattyq.org/a/kazakhstan-regusal-to-register-a-feminist-initiative/30178615.html

Azattyq. (2020). Участниц марша в Алматы привлекают к административной ответственности. 12 March. In: https://rus.azattyq.org/a/30481112.html

CCI Fabrika. (2021). Завтра в 19:00! #заЮлю'. *CCI Fabrika Instagram Account*. In: https://www.instagram.com/p/CSZYXGbCffr/

Consultant.ru. (2020). УК РФ Статья 242. Незаконные изготовление и оборот порнографических материалов или предметов. 30 December. In: http://www.consultant.ru/document/cons_doc_LAW_10699/ad5d9196ef8584bf342b4c-10c1eb39fed4ae8745/

Diapazon. (2020). Геев и лесбиянок сажают под домашний арест, отмаливают у муллы. 3 December. Author: Alishbaeva, A. In: https://diapazon.kz/news/106476-geev-i-lesbiyanok-sazhayut-pod-domashnii-arest-otmalivayut-u-mulli

Fergana. (2021). 'Аллах Акбар!' против феминизма. 2 August. In: https://fergana.agency/articles/122560/

Gezitter. (2019). Президент охарактеризовал феминале в музее как 'унижение женщин'. 25 December. In: https://www.gezitter.org/society/84862_prezident_oharakterizoval_feminale_v_muzee_kak_unijenie_jenschin/

Imanaliyeva, A. (2020). Kyrgyzstan: Draft Bill Threatens to Drive NGOs Against the Wall. *Eurasianet*, 22 March. In: https://eurasianet.org/kyrgyzstan-draft-bill-threatens-to-drive-ngos-against-the-wall

Interfax. (2020). В Бишкеке начался стихийный митинг в поддержку женщин, задержанных 8 марта. 10 March. In: https://www.interfax.ru/world/698345

Kaktus. (2019a). У музея несколько мужчин попытались спровоцировать арт-куратора феминнале Алтын Капалову. Author: Ulanova, B. 2 December. In: https://kaktus.media/doc/402009_y_myzeia_neskolko_myjchin_popytalis_sprovocirovat_art_kyratora_feminnale_altyn_kapalovy.html

Kaktus. (2019b). 'Можете называть это цензурой'. Министр культуры запретил на феминнале восемь работ. Author: Ulanova, B. 3 December. In: https://kaktus.media/doc/402045_mojete_nazyvat_eto_cenzuroy._ministr_kyltyry_zapretil_na_feminnale_vosem_rabot.html

Kaktus. (2019c). Азиз Суракматов прокомментировал требование 'Кырк Чоро' об отставке за марш 8 марта. Author: Abduvaitova, A. 11 February. In: https://kaktus.media/doc/388024_aziz_syrakmatov_prokommentiroval_trebovanie_kyrk_choro_ob_otstavke_za_marsh_8_marta.html

Kloop. (2020). Казахстан: Организаторок женского марша 8 марта оштрафовали за 'мелкое хулиганство' и участие в митинге. 12 March. Author: Makhmudova, S. In: https://kloop.kg/blog/2020/03/12/kazahstan-organizatorok-zhenskogo-marsha-8-marta-oshtrafovali-za-melkoe-huliganstvo-i-uchastie-v-mitinge/

Kommersant. (2019a). Многие приходят в активизм, когда видят дичайшую несправедливость. Author: Litvinova, M. 12 December. In: https://www.kommersant.ru/doc/4190328

Kommersant. (2019b). В Комсомольске-на-Амуре нашли порнографию. Authors: Litvinova, M. and Ovsyannikiva, V. 10 December. In: https://www.kommersant.ru/doc/4188956

Malaisarova, A. (2021). Frauenmarsch in Almaty: Gleiche Rechte für alle. *Deutsche Allgemeine Zeitung*. 10 March. In: https://daz.asia/blog/frauenmarsch-in-almaty-gleiche-rechte-fuer-alle/

Mamashully, A. (2021). 'Бесовщина', 'права матки', 'разрушение нацкода': реакция на женский марш и ее причины. *Radio Azattyq*. 10 March. In: https://rus.azattyq.org/a/kazakhstan-marche-for-rights-on-womens-day-reaction/31142780.html

Mamedov, G. (2019). Невидимая Феминнале. Скандал, затмивший выставку. 16 January. In: https://kloop.kg/blog/2020/01/16/nevidimaya-feminnale-skandal-zatmivshij-vystavku/

Meduza. (2020b). В комментариях требовали сжечь ведьму' Интервью Анны Ходыревой — матери ЛГБТ-активистки Юлии Цветковой. Ее дочери грозит тюрьма из-за публикации рисунков вульвы. Author: Kravtsova, I. 27 July. In: https://meduza.io/feature/2020/06/27/v-kommentariyah-trebovali-szhech-vedmu

Meduza. (2020a). В Бишкеке феминистки 8 марта вышли на акцию против насилия над женщинами. Сначала на них напали люди в масках, а потом задержала милиция. 8 March. Author: Gorin, V. In: https://meduza.io/feature/2020/03/08/v-bishkeke-feministki-8-marta-vyshli-na-aktsiyu-protiv-nasiliya-nad-zhenschinami-snachala-na-nih-napali-lyudi-v-maskah-a-potom-zaderzhala-militsiya

Novaya Gazeta. (2020a). ЛГБТ-активистка Юлия Цветкова пожаловалась в СК на отказы дознавателя в посещении стоматолога. Author: Mikisha, V. 26 February. In: https://novayagazeta.ru/news/2020/02/26/159354-lgbt-aktivistka-yuliya-tsvetkova-pozhalovalas-v-sk-na-otkazy-doznavatelya-v-poseschenii-stomatologa

Novaya Gazeta. (2020b). В Комсомольске-на-Амуре на художницу Юлию Цветкову составили второй протокол о гей-пропаганде. Author: Mikisha, V. 2 July. In: https://novayagazeta.ru/news/2020/07/02/162733-v-komsomolske-na-amure-na-hudozhnitsu-yuliyu-tsvetkovu-sostavili-vtoroy-protokol-o-gey-propagande

Novaya Gazeta. (2020c). ЛГБТ-активистка из Комсомольска-на-Амуре Юлия Цветкова подала заявление в полицию из-за угроз 'Пилы'. Author: Mikisha, V. 24 February. In: https://novayagazeta.ru/news/2020/02/24/159311-lgbt-aktivistka-iz-komsomolska-na-amure-yuliya-tsvetkova-v-politsiyu-iz-za-ugroz-pily

Novaya Gazeta. (2020d). Медиастрайк в поддержку Юлии Цветковой. 27 June. In: https://novayagazeta.ru/articles/2020/06/27/86034-mediastrayk-v-podderzhku-yulii-tsvetkovoy

Novaya Gazeta. (2020e). Дело Юли Цветковой – политическое. Author: Mikisha, V. 28 June. In: https://novayagazeta.ru/articles/2020/06/28/86050-delo-yuli-tsvetkovoy-politicheskoe

OVD-info. (2020). На пикетах в поддержку ЛГБТ-активистки Юлии Цветковой начались задержания. 27 June. In: https://ovdinfo.org/express-news/2020/06/27/na-piketah-v-podderzhku-lgbt-aktivistki-yulii-cvetkovoy-nachalis (accessed 27 September 2021).

OVD-info. (2021). Дело Юлии Цветковой. In: https://ovdinfo.org/story/delo-yulii-cvetkovoy

Sekerbayeva, Zh. (2018). После суда. 16 August. In: https://www.facebook.com/zhanar.sekerbayeva/posts/1849427845134121

Sobaka. (2019). 'Пила против ЛГБТ': что известно о гомофобном движении, которое считают причастным к смерти активистки Елены Григорьевой. Author: Morozova, K. 24 July. In: https://www.sobaka.ru/city/society/94002

Talant, B. (2018). Feminist Song Draws Supporters and Death Threats in Kyrgyzstan. *Eurasianet*, 18 September. In: https://eurasianet.org/feminist-song-draws-supporters-and-death-threats-in-kyrgyzstan

Vesti. (2020). УВД Свердловского района: Милиция предотвратила конфликт на митинге. 8 March. In: https://vesti.kg/proisshestviya/item/69264-uvd-sverdlovsk-ogo-rajona-militsiya-predotvratila-konflikt-na-mitinge.html

Voices on Central Asia. (2020). Feminism and Central Asia – What Went Wrong? Author: Ulugova, L. 25 June. In: https://voicesoncentralasia.org/feminism-and-central-asia-what-went-wrong/

Wonderzine. (2020). Нидерландские активистки сняли красивый фотопроект в поддержку Юлии Цветковой. 22 December. In: https://www.wonderzine.com/wonderzine/life/life/254237-we-are-yulia

Zhursin, Z. and Zhankatov, A. (2021). Акция противников ЛГБТ в Актобе и доводы группы Feminita. *Azattyq TV*, 10 August. In: https://rus.azattyq.org/a/kazakhstan-aktobe-rally-against-meeting-of-feminita-group/31401318.html

FOUR

A European Agenda? The Supra-National Dimension of Anti-Feminism in Europe

Stefanie Mayer and Judith Goetz

Attacks on feminism, LGBTIQ+ activism, gender research and equality policies by Christian actors have been on the rise globally (Kuhar and Paternotte, 2017; Mos, 2018; Strube et al., 2021). In Europe, Christian groups have started using a twin-track strategy, consisting on the one hand of grass-roots mobilisations like petitions or citizens' initiatives, facilitating a greater involvement of diverse actors outside the institutionalised churches; and on the other hand of a political strategy to expand their influence in the field of policymaking, e.g. by influencing legislation (Datta, 2018, 2021a). This is evidenced not only by legal changes, for example stricter anti-abortion laws in Poland, but also by large scale anti-gay and anti-queer mobilisations in different European countries in the past few years. Additionally, there have been petitions on a European level, initiated for instance by the CitizenGO foundation, established in 2013, for the 'defence of Christian values'. Christian actors have created their own increasingly professional NGOs, (lobbying) groups and networks in order to increase their influence on political developments across regional and national borders on a trans- and supra-national (European) level. International human rights bodies, especially but not limited to the UN level, are one important target, where anti-feminist actors try to halt or even reverse the process of expanding individual rights and protections.

While recent scholarly research has increasingly studied anti-feminism and anti-gender mobilisations, most studies (including our own work) have referred to country-specific contexts and in many cases concentrated mainly on right-wing extremism and populism (see inter alia Graff and Korolczuk, 2021; Hark and Villa, 2015; Kuhar and Paternotte, 2017; Dietze and Roth 2020). Even though some of these publications considered inter- and transnational organisational aspects as well as shared ideologies, the supra-national European dimension has hardly been analysed in detail. Due to the transfer of political power from the national level to the EU, Christian actors are also trying to expand their influence in this context. Subsequently campaigning and lobbying on the supra-national level as well as transnational networking have become more important.

In order to add to the rather scarce research on the European dimension of anti-feminist movements (for an exception see Mos 2018), this chapter will analyse the programmatic and strategies of the pan-European, Christian network Agenda Europe (AE) as detailed in the strategy paper *Restoring the Natural Order* (RTNO). Far from being the only ultra-conservative network, Agenda Europe is especially important because it brings together influential anti-feminist and anti-queer actors, including among others elected parliamentary representatives, former politicians and high-ranking civil servants from the European Commission, who work with campaigners in order to develop political lobbying strategies and professionalise campaigns.

First, we discuss ongoing trends of secularisation and de-secularisation and define the term 'political Christianity' because it provides an insightful perspective on ultra-conservative Christian activism as exemplified by Agenda Europe. Second, we give a short overview of the network and its activities. Third, taking frame analysis as our starting point, we investigate how problems are being constructed and which solutions are being implied in the main part of the RTNO paper as well as which normative claims are used to legitimate these constructions. This perspective allows us to analyse discursive strategies as well as ideological and normative convictions underpinning Christian anti-feminism. Specifically, we hope to add nuance to the observation of a secularisation of these discourses (Kuhar, 2015; Datta, 2018).

Political Christianity

In order to better understand current developments, it is worth looking at the secularisation of European societies and at Christian efforts to reverse or at least mitigate these social changes. Against the background of a long and highly uneven process of loosening the close ties between the state and church across Europe (starting with the Enlightenment and the French Revolution, but being marked by backlashes and its still unfinished character), the churches' gradual acceptance of a democratic and constitutional state always met resistance. In the nineteenth century during 'culture wars' about the reorientation and restructuring of the relationship between church and state, the main goal of Christian actors was to safeguard and maintain the Christian claim to power over public institutions (e.g. schools) (Green, 1996).

Struggles over cultural and political domination have been ongoing until today, as became apparent in recent opposing trends of secularisation on the one hand and the renewed importance of religion and associated de-secularisation on the other hand (Hennig and Weiberg-Salzmann, 2021; Kuhar and Paternotte, 2017; Kuru, 2009; Paternotte, 2015; Stambolis-Ruhstorfer and Tricou, 2017; Strube et al., 2021; Turner, 2020). Secularised philosophy questions religious reasoning (Paternotte, 2015), thereby representing the 'natural' as well as the 'divine order' as means to secure a hierarchical social order. As Stambolis-Ruhstorfer and Tricou (2017, p. 58) show for the French case, in many European countries secularisation has made 'religious discourse politically illegitimate in the public arena', so that religious actors have to change their strategies and justify their positions 'in secular terms'. In this sense, the Argentine sociologist Juan Marco Vaggione shows that current attempts to strengthen Christian influence go hand in hand with a secularisation of Christian discourse on the one hand and an NGO-isation of religious actors on the other hand (Kuhar and Paternotte, 2017, p. 4). However, in spite of this strategic secularisation, the goal of Christian actors remains 'to "clericalize" society' (Kuhar, 2015) in the sense of a re-strengthening of conservative Christian values in all areas of society and especially with regard to family policies and sexual and reproductive rights. Within this struggle against secularism, gender issues and feminism have become a central battlefield (Paternotte, 2015). The concept of 'gender' itself is accused of erasing sex, promoting secularisation, being the 'work of the devil', destroying the supposedly natural (divine) gender order (Kuhar and Paternotte, 2017) and thus of also hollowing out 'the anthropological basis of the family' (Pope Franciscus, 2016; see introduction to this volume; Mayer and Sauer, 2017).

In order to classify the ideology of these anti-feminist groups, networks and platforms, the concept of political Catholicism or political Christianity is useful because it describes their core objective to reorder politics and society according to conservative religious doctrine (Burghardt, 1967; Kaiser, 2003). While other terms such as Christian fundamentalism and the Christian or conservative right refer primarily to the content of this type of political doctrine, political Christianity draws attention to the fact that these actors want more than just to be accepted as political players within the limits of liberal democracy. They strive to restructure the political field according to their interpretation of Christianity. In this world-view political positions and social practices that contradict Christian beliefs are not merely opposed, but ought to be denied the right to exist. We therefore argue that right-wing Christian (grass-roots) politics need to be understood in the context of this ongoing struggle for political power. To be clear, there is neither 'the Catholicism' nor 'the Christianity' following one uniform political goal (Burghardt, 1967).

Left-wing Christians, who play a tremendously important role in struggles for the human rights of asylum seekers or socially engaged liberation theology in Latin America, do not strive for a re-Christianisation of politics and society in the manner described above, nor do they share the right-wing interpretation of Christian faith. We therefore use political Christianity to describe actors who follow a very narrow, fundamentalist conception of Christianity, which they wish to impose as a general order on society.

In contrast to the (scholarly) discussion of the term 'political Islam', parallel debates and theorisations of 'political Catholicism' or 'political Christianity' have been widely neglected. Apart from a few, mainly histori-cal, studies which according to Kaiser 'have contributed a great deal to a much better understanding of political Catholicism and Christian Democ-racy as a European phenomenon' (Kaiser, 2003, p. 275), this analytical perspective has hardly been applied to current political actors and their discourse, which will be the focus of our following analysis.

In order to provide some context to this analysis the next section will describe the Agenda Europe network.

Agenda Europe

The network Agenda Europe was founded in 2013 with the aim of organ-ising pan-European, non-public summit meetings, which were soon attended by 100 to 150 important conservative and Christian anti-abor-tion, anti-gender and anti-LGBTIQ+ actors and organisations from over thirty European countries (Datta, 2019). The first meeting on strategies was initiated by two Catholic political activists: Gudrun Kugler (member of the conservative Austrian People's Party, ÖVP) and Terrence McKeegan (Legal Adviser for the Permanent Observer Mission of the Holy See to the UN). Both have good connections to the Vatican. In addition to organis-ing strategic meetings, the network hosted a blog. The group and their secret meetings were exposed by the Arte TV channel[1] and the European Parliamentary Forum on Sexual and Reproductive Rights (EPF) in 2018. The strategy paper *Restoring the Natural Order*, which surfaced at the same time, was also attributed to the network by the media and Neil Datta (Dakli, 2021; Datta, 2019; Hecht, 2018). Documents leaked in summer 2021 indicate that the paper was debated at an Agenda Europe summit as early as 2014.

The Secretary General of the EFP, Neil Datta, classifies the participants of Agenda Europe into two groups: transnational actors, the so called 'luminar-ies' – who are developing and implementing strategies for example through citizens' initiatives, campaigns or discursive attempts to reinterpret relevant terms in political debates – on the one hand, and the 'Agenda Europe Insiders' on the other. The latter are important decision-makers in the fields of politics, judiciary, parliaments and also at the EU level (Datta, 2019). One of the network's most important actors is Luca Volonté, an Italian politician and former chairman of the parliamentary group of the European People's Party at the Council of Europe until 2013 (whose prison sentence for bribery was on appeal at the time of writing). Like Gudrun Kugler, founder of the Observatory on Intolerance and Discrimination against Christians in Europe and member of the Austrian National Council for the Austrian People's Party, and Jakob Cornides, Austrian legal expert within the European Commission (Datta, 2018), Volonté belongs to the second group. Ignacio Arsuaga, president and founder of the Spanish ultra-Catholic organisations Hazte Oir (Make yourself heard) and CitizenGO, an online platform managing right-wing citizen's initiatives, as well as board member of the World Congress of Families, can be classified in the first group. Another important activist of the network is Sophia Kuby, co-founder of the NGO European Dignity Watch and daughter of Gabriele Kuby, a German Catholic convert and author of several anti-feminist publications. This brief list shows, as is also stressed by Datta (2019), that the network successfully managed to unite 'the most socially conservative, traditionalist and in some cases, marginal and far-right Christian religious movements and actors into a single organizing network'.[2]

Restoring the natural order

The document *Restoring the Natural Order* itself does not contain any indication as to when and by whom it was written. Thus, we can only speculate about its author(s) for the time being. Agenda Europe themselves even deny having been involved: 'The Agenda Europe network has no links to or control over the Agenda Europe blog (and the Twitter Account), despite use of the same name. The document *Restoring the Natural Order* is not an Agenda Europe publication. It is a paper drafted by an individual person without any involvement of Agenda Europe.'[3] This notwithstanding, there are hints in leaked CitizenGO documents which show that a first draft was discussed at AE's 2014 meeting in Castle Fürstenried near Munich, Germany. The paper became public in 2018 via the EPF and was then posted on the AE's blog for free download. While it is not known how the ideas and strategies were discussed and whether there was broad consensus, three important arguments point towards the relevance of the paper: first, RTNO is an attempt to lay down a comprehensive programme for the implementation of Agenda Europe's political stance. Second, it fulfils exactly what the network was founded to do from the beginning, i.e. develop content and strategies for a right-wing Christian political agenda. And, third, it seems to have been a basis for Agenda Europe's discussions for years.

All in all, the manifesto consists of six chapters on 144 pages; it attempts to analyse the judicial and political situation in order to develop new strategies to redefine questions of sexuality and reproduction, medical practices, especially with regard to the beginning and the end of life, and issues of equality and (anti-)discrimination. Interestingly, it does not argue from a religious perspective but from a legal one, referring to so-called natural law. After a short introduction, the central argument is set out in chapter 2, postulating the existence of a 'Natural Law' applicable regardless of time and place, 'which human reason can discern and understand, but which human will cannot alter' (p. 7).[4] As it is 'pre-existent to all written legislation', it has to be 'the task and purpose of all positive legislation to transpose and enforce Natural Law in a way that adapts to the specific needs and circumstances of a given society at a given time. A positive law that stands in contradiction to the precepts of Natural Law has no legitimacy, and nobody is morally bound by it' (p. 7). A 'cultural revolution' is identified as posing the greatest danger to this natural law. Accordingly, the paper states the necessity for a fundamental change in thinking with regard to marriage, family, protection of life, equality and anti-discrimination – topics which are covered in greater detail in the subsequent chapters.

Chapter 3 focuses on 'Marriage and the Family', chapter 4 on 'The Right to Life' and the fifth chapter covers 'Equality and Anti-Discrimination', before the last chapter deals with political strategies. In terms of discursive strategies, the document's author(s) suggest reinterpreting and redefining the terms, in which the aforementioned topics are debated today.

> It therefore seems to be a much better strategy to use all those words [i.e. terms defined by Agenda Europe's opponents], including neologisms such as 'reproductive rights', but at the same time making clear what meaning those words have for us. If that is done consistently, we might even succeed in 'contaminating' (or in, fact, rectifying) the vocabulary that our opponents have crafted, so that they cannot use them any more. If, for example, a sufficient number of governments clearly state that 'reproductive rights' means that anybody has the right to reproduce, but that they do not imply any right to have access to abortion or artificial contraception, then all existing references to this term could be used in our favour. (p. 127)

This choice of strategies clearly shows the author('s) understanding of politics as a fight for hegemony (Laclau and Mouffe, 2014). Another highly important strategy is to 'Bring the Right People into the Right Positions' (p. 122), including into positions of political decision-making, but also into important courts or human rights-related political bodies. The global aspirations of Agenda Europe shape these strategies insofar as international law is at the centre of their analysis of the current situation and international (UN) human rights bodies are defined as central arenas of struggle. It is in these bodies and the lobbying groups influencing their policies that Agenda Europe identifies its main enemies in the guise of the 'abortion and "reproductive services" industry, the lesbian and gay lobby, the radical feminist lobby, and militant atheist and masonic networks' (p. 111).[5]

Apart from some journalistic articles on the topic – which usually found little resonance outside the national circulation area of the respective period-ical – analyses of the group and the manifesto have been scarce. Important exceptions are two studies by the Secretary of the European Parliamentary Forum for Sexual and Reproductive Rights (EPF), Neil Datta. While *Restoring the Natural Order: The Religious Extremists' Vision to Mobilize European Societies Against Human Rights on Sexuality and Reproduction* (2018) mainly deals with the strategy paper *Restoring the Natural Order*, the analysis *Tip of the Iceberg. Religious Extremist Funders against Human Rights for Sexuality and Reproduc-tive. Health in Europe 2009–2018* (2021) concentrates on the financing struc-tures of right-wing and conservative networks. The author emphasises the 'radically reactionary world view' apparent in the manifesto, 'which, if it was implemented successfully, would dismantle the human rights of all Europe-ans with regard to sexuality and reproduction' (Datta, 2019). 'The targeted changes would have consequences for women*, adolescents and LGBTQI persons in particular.'

These examinations of *Restoring the Natural Order* generally agree that the language used amounts to a 'contortion of religiously-inspired positions on sexuality and reproduction to artificially resemble classical human rights language' (p. 16). In his talk at a 2021 conference in Frank-furt am Main, Datta described the actors, who are 'religiously inspired but appear to have a secular facade'. The main vehicle for this, he continued, was a 'secularisation of the language'. The ideological basis, however, had hardly changed or, as Datta put it, using the metaphor of a washing machine: 'old religious ideas' had been put in and taken out again as a 'new human rights language' (Datta, 2021b). In a similar vein Mos (2018) calls the struggle of the religious right in Europe 'old wine in new bottles' and emphasises similar rhetorical strategies.

The EPF (Datta, 2018, p. 16) recognises this as 'a trend already observed in the Holy See's evolving use of SRR language at the United Nations (UN)'. They refer to Coates et al.'s 2014 study *The Holy See on Sexual and Reproductive Health and Rights: Conservative in Position, Dynamic in Response,* which noticed 'a general shift away from doctrinal arguments towards the use of more secular rhetoric, using sophisticated technical evidence and strategic interpretations of international human rights standards in order to communicate its position'. The Vatican's ideological positions, however, had not changed fundamentally; on the contrary, the selective adoption of UN language had to be interpreted as a strategy for strengthening their influence (ibid.).

These findings provide an important point of departure for our analysis. While a certain 'secularisation' is undeniable as far as choice of words in *Restoring the Natural Order* is concerned, we believe it is worth looking more closely at the rationale and the logic underpinning Agenda Europe's argumentation. To put our central thesis upfront: we think that despite the fact that the document discusses laws, international treaties and court decisions, the argumentation relies solely on the author(s)'s claim to a divine truth that forecloses all deliberation and amounts to a totalitarian vision of society.

Methodology

In our analysis of the document described above we use frame analysis, which was invented by Erving Goffman (1975) and further developed as 'critical frame analysis' (van der Haar and Verloo, 2016; Verloo, 2007). Its focus is an analysis of political discourse and policies with a focus on how political problems are constructed and how these constructions mandate specific solutions. We decided to use the frame approach due to the nature of our material, as the RTNO paper explicitly names the reconstruction of discourses and reframings of societal problems as a strategy for pushing through their world-view. Frame analysis can help to understand these strategies, for it centres around so-called 'frames', which act as 'interpretative schemata', as patterns of explanation and interpretation, and consist of views, narrations, ideas, values and fabrications of meaning that are shared by actors. In the realm of political discourse, they serve as interpretative frameworks of political phenomena and help to construct social and political problems in a way that matches actors' ideological viewpoints and preconceived solutions (Sauer and Pingaud, 2016, p. 33).

Critical frame analysis according to Verloo focuses on two aspects. First, the 'diagnosis', the discursive construction of problems – i.e. what certain actors deem to be the specifically problematic aspects of a given situation, which actors they believe to be responsible and who they see as victims; Second, on the 'prognosis', i.e. the implicit or explicit construction of solutions to these problems. Frame analysis then asks what legitimation strategies actors use, for example which norms, values, ideological or moral stand-points they refer to (Sauer and Pingaud, 2016, p. 35). Frames also aim at mobilising people for the respective agenda by identifying solutions for the problems stated, through the mobilisation of affects and through 'calls for action' (Verloo 2016).

A Matter of Morality

A closer look at the content of the strategic paper *Restoring the Natural Order* shows a high degree of consistency throughout the paper, with similar lines of reasoning and argumentation being applied to different issues. Rather than giving a detailed account of Agenda Europe's position on specific policies, we therefore present a summary analysis of the most important elements that form part of their framing. This analysis should lead to the identification of the master frames that structure problem construction as well as the identification of enemies and victims and proposed solutions.

We structure our findings according to the typical elements of frame analyses, starting with the construction of problems before turning to enemies and victims identified within the paper. The third section deals with solutions that are (in this case often explicitly) presented in the text before concluding with a section on the narratives and concepts used to legitimise these specific constructions.

What's the problem?

Restoring the Natural Order addresses problems on different levels from the mundane to the philosophical and in different policy areas. For reasons of space, we cannot go into the long list of things the author(s) deem 'immoral' and would therefore like to render unlawful, but just mention a few examples.

It is no surprise that Christian conservatives would like to ban abortion in all instances (including pregnancies that are a consequence of rape or incest) (pp. 67–8), nor that homosexual practices – which they prefer to label as 'sodomy' – are considered dangerous. Consequently, they make a case 'for the re-introduction of laws that repress homosexual activity' (pp. 49–50). This choice of words is not accidental as the author(s) try to reframe homosexuality as an issue of 'sinful' practices (p. 41), rather than an issue of identity or sexual orientation. They promote an understanding of homosexuality that Foucault would have relegated to the discourse of the seventeenth and eighteenth centuries (Foucault, 1979, p. 47). While 'sentiments' that are beyond a person's control are not deemed problematic, acting on those is fully condemned: 'The immorality lies in the implication that a sexual act can have the sole purpose of procuring physical pleasure, i.e. that it may be dissociated from its procreative potentiality' (p. 43).

This foundational understanding underpins the paper's stance about all issues touching upon sexuality – or as it is framed in the text, issues of 'marriage and the family' (pp. 23–61). One of the questions the paper deals with in this context is contraceptive practices, which in the author(s)'s view 'undermine . . . *the dignity of the sexual act*' (p. 55). At this point the author(s) also clarify which norm people should not deviate from, as any sexual act not signifying an 'expression of an unconditional love that is oriented towards a common life and shared responsibility as parents of a family' (p. 55) would amount to 'mutual masturbation' (p. 56). States should therefore be encouraged to restrict or prohibit contraceptives (p. 59). Marriage is understood as a lifelong commitment which includes procreation as a necessity and should be the only form of family life being encouraged, recognised and supported by the state. This not only precludes equal rights for same-sex and non-married heterosexual couples as well as single parents, it also translates into a harsh stance on divorce: 'Ideally, divorce should not be possible. Where it is possible, it should be available only under very restricted circumstances' (p. 31).

As these brief examples show, the author(s) do not only formulate policies for specific areas, but rather develop an underlying world-view that links all the aforementioned issues: 'In matters related to life, marriage, and the family, all is interconnected with everything . . . . Whoever finds the use of contraceptives "normal" must also accept homosexuality, and whoever has accepted assisted procreation will find it difficult to argue against abortion' (p. 4).

The central narrative underpinning this world-view is provided by an overarching story of decline: 'The Cultural Revolution that has transformed (deformed?) the West in the course of the last decades' (p. 3) was 'more than anything else, a "sexual" revolution', which severed the link between sexuality and procreation, thereby eroding the basic prerequisite for human dignity (p. 4). Allegedly, this revolution already has devastating consequences ranging from low birth rates to 'social welfare systems on the brink of collapse' (p. 5). The danger of 'irreparable damage' arises if young people grow up with an understanding of sexuality that 'makes them unable to become good spouses and parents' (p. 5). The author(s) arrive at a 'narrow time window of ten to twenty years' in order to reverse the 'Cultural Revolution', or else Western civilisation 'will simply not continue at all' (p. 5).

On top of these past developments, the author(s) address a second broad policy field, namely equality and anti-discrimination, which appear to be the biggest challenges of today, as enemies of the 'natural order' use these to safeguard and deepen the cultural-sexual revolution. Even though this part of the document is less voluminous, it is especially interesting in terms of the political problems constructed. The argument hinges on a formal definition of justice, as 'the constant and perpetual will to render to every man his due', which is expressed by practices that 'treat the equal equally, the unequal unequally, and everything according to its merit' (p. 103). It is evident that this stance leads to a strict rejection of affirmative action in all its forms. But the paper goes much further in its legitimation for discrimination. The author(s) identify 'race, religion, descent, gender, disability, or sexual orientation' (pp. 103–4) as criteria that anti-discrimination policies want to outlaw as grounds for unequal treatment and they take issue with that for two reasons. First, this would mean a 'loss of liberty' as citizens in their private lives – for example in their function as hostel owners – should not be bound to equal treatment. Second, and even more importantly, anti-discrimination policies allegedly serve to impose specific moral views, which refers mainly to the ban on discrimination based on sexual orientation. Interestingly, the other explicit example provided refers to the legitimacy of discrimination against Muslims, as allegedly 'there is a wide difference between tolerance and granting an entitlement to equal treatment to all religious communities irrespective of their beliefs' (p. 104). It is telling that the obvious discrepancy between legitimising the discrimination of LGBTIQ+ people on grounds of Christian religious beliefs and legitimising the discrimination of Muslims because of their beliefs seems to have evaded the author(s). This hints at the equation of Christian belief and 'objective moral truth' as a normative frame of reference that we will analyse below.

Who's to blame?

Rather early on in the text, the author(s) list ideologies that form part of the alleged cultural-sexual revolution. Most of them are typical scapegoats of right-wing anti-feminist discourse more broadly (cf. Mayer and Sauer 2017, pp. 30–5), but with a slightly different emphasis than within the secular political right. Among the typical enemies is Marxism (pp. 11–12) and its alleged direct successors, feminism (pp. 13–14) and 'homosexualism', which is defined as 'the novel ideology that exalts homosexuality/sodomy as "equal", and hence morally acceptable, inclination and behaviour' (pp. 14–15).

In terms of their rejection of feminism the author(s) are quite frank about their wish for women's subordination, as they reject 'emancipation' on the grounds that (economic) independence would be detrimental to marriage as an institution and by extension to the state, which has to provide childcare and welfare benefits, as well as to the economy (p. 14). The devaluation of women and femininity also becomes apparent in the way the association of feminism to Marxism is formulated: 'Just as Marxism wanted wealth (rather than poverty) for everyone, Feminism aims at masculinity for everyone' (p. 14). Of course, the statement is false on a purely factual level as feminism has always been first and foremost about the abolishment of patriarchy and male superiority, but, more importantly, the equation of femininity with poverty and the inability to imagine women as anything else than poor and dependent is telling.

'Gender theory' is defined as yet another enemy, with the author(s) echoing the typical anti-feminist claim that gender theory would argue for a free choice of gender identity and sexual orientation, thereby being an example of 'radical liberalism' and 'hopelessly unscientific' (p. 17; for analyses of these claims see inter alia our introduction to this volume; Graff and Korolczuk, 2017; Hark and Villa, 2015; Kuhar, 2017; Kuhar and Paternotte, 2017). In the section on 'gender theory', the author(s) focus exclusively on this alleged exaltation of 'subjective emotions and personal choices', which is deemed to 'supersede every objective reality' (p. 17). There seems to be no need to explain to readers what this 'objective reality' would look like as the heteronormative gender binary, in which a person's gender has to match the sex assigned at birth, is taken as self-evident.

Last but not least, 'Anti-Discrimination Ideology' is flagged as an enemy, as it allegedly 'seek[s] to turn "equality" into a new human right that supplants and supersedes all the others' (p. 18). The perpetrators of this attack are more clearly identified in later parts of the document as a 'long-standing, mutually supportive coalition between the abortion and "reproductive services" industry, the lesbian and gay lobby, the radical feminist lobby, and militant atheist and masonic networks' (p. 111). While the strategy-oriented part at the end of the document credits these groups with 'clever propaganda' and 'intimidation of those who fail to be persuaded' (p. 114), the more content-oriented parts focus on a specific strategy, namely the 'politically motivated manipulation and distortion' (p. 9) of human rights treaties. Allegedly, pressure groups 'pursue a consistent agenda of judicial activism, "discovering" new abortion and LGBT rights in internationally agreed texts that . . . in fact do not contain them' (p. 9). Here we find the rationale for the author(s) use of a judicial, rights-oriented language, as they understand the content and scope of human rights as the current terrain of their fight against the 'Cultural Revolution'. The quote also underscores the importance Agenda Europe ascribes to the global human rights system, which underpins their endeavour to formulate political strategies for transnational activism and the supra- and international arena.

The alleged victims of the 'Cultural Revolution' receive comparably little attention. This is surprising as a whole sub-chapter is devoted to 'intimidation and physical violence' as an alleged part of the enemy pressure groups' strategies, which nevertheless fails to name any victims besides 'human dignity' and 'defenceless and innocent children' (p. 118; for analysis of this rhetoric see Schmincke, 2015), which refers to foetuses. Heterosexual married couples are defined as victims of the broadening of the definition of 'family' (pp. 25–6). Here the goal of defending privileges and the circular logic this defence requires become obvious as the author(s) argue, that 'a clear and correct definition of the concept of a family [i.e. limiting the definition of family to married heterosexual couples raising or at least planning to raise children] is a pre-condition for any targeted policy for families' (p. 25). At this point the anti-individualist stance seems most pronounced, legitimising not only the discrimination of adults, who for whatever reason cannot or do not want to enter a heterosexual marriage, but also of children living within any other type of family.

What should be done?

In line with the way the author(s) construct problems as consequences of laws that are too permissive in the sphere of sexuality (homosexuality, cohabitation) and family life (birth control, divorce, abortion) and too restrictive in the sphere of anti-discrimination (protection of sexual orientation and non-Christian religions, affirmative action), solutions are sought through a reform of the legal framework.

In this regard there seems to be some discrepancy between the author(s)'s affirmation of classical liberal values like personal freedom (p. 106), self-determination (p. 12), freedom of thought and expression (p. 105) and freedom of contract (p. 104) on the one hand and the wish to regulate people's life down to their most intimate moments on the other hand. Readers get the impression that the author(s) recognised this problem and tried to provide a rationale, which would allow them to define all 'immoral' behaviour as outside the protected private sphere. For example, a couple's family planning is turned into a public matter and therefore deemed fit to be regulated by the state through the assertion 'that the use of artificial contraception . . . severely affects societal interests' (p. 59). While from a feminist point of view one could easily argue that quite a number of the alleged detrimental effects are not problematic, but rather signs of women's emancipation, there is a more important analytical point to be made. As we have seen above, the author(s) understand children's education as highly relevant for society, even proposing that a new generation growing up with liberal sexual values will be the end of Western civilisation. Following the argument just outlined in relation to contraception, it would therefore be logical to assign high priority to the re-regulation of education, but surprisingly this is not the case. On the contrary, the author(s) claim that 'education is a right of parents as the primary educators of their children and the state's role must be limited to providing assistance to the parents' (p. 23). Similar anti-state arguments are made for the economic sphere with regards to anti-discrimination legislation and affirmative action (pp. 105–8) as well as with regards to social benefits, which should only be provided 'if and where family networks and local communities are not capable of providing them' (p. 23).

This argumentative strategy amounts to a double standard concerning people's private lives as well as with regard to state functions. Behaviour that is in line with the author(s)'s moral values is to be protected from intervention and regulation because of that moral verdict – not because of a consistent belief in a private sphere that ought to be protected or because of its possible effects on society. On the other hand, any behaviour – including consensual sexual practices – that does not fit the author(s)'s moral stance is to be legally banned or at least discouraged through legislation. A similar arbitrary stance can be found with regard to social welfare. On the one hand, 'hypertrophic social welfare systems' are blamed for the crisis of the family as they allegedly 'encourage irresponsible and anti-social behaviour' (p. 24). On the other hand, privileges for marriage (in the restrictive sense detailed above) are called for in social and tax laws (p. 130). So despite the judicial language used in most parts of the document and the focus on changes of the legal framework, the logic of the argumentation does not follow from a systematic understanding of state functions and/or different spheres of the legal system. Rather, it subordinates all of those to the implementation of a specific political agenda, that is legitimised by a claim to a single 'truth' (p. 3).

Which truth?

The author(s) spell out their exclusive claim to truth at the very beginning of the document, where they try to convince readers to be less tolerant towards different moral convictions: 'Genuine moral precepts are not based on subjective "values" but on objective truth, and this is why it is not only legitimate, but also necessary, to impose them on those who do not accept them' (p. 3). That of course gives rise to questions about how to distinguish between mere 'subjective "values"' and 'genuine moral precepts'. These are answered by a further equation of 'objective truth' with 'Natural Law', which aims to reposition the discourse. Instead of appealing to morality, which is tinged by association with subjective convictions, ethical and/or religious beliefs, natural law offers discursive bridges to the judicial field and to 'nature', i.e. to two strong institutions lending legitimacy in modern societies.

As the term figures prominently throughout the document, the usage of 'nature' merits some reflection. Tellingly, the author(s) use 'nature' in at least two different ways. One is the 'good' nature of natural law and the natural order, which offers the blueprint for a morally sound life. One example is an argument in favour of traditional marriage: 'If by nature each child has one (biological) father and one (biological) mother, it must be assumed that being raised by . . . its biological father and mother is what is naturally best for a child's healthy development' (p. 27). The second meaning is less favourable, denouncing the 'naturalistic fallacy' (p. 43) of those trying to normalise homosexuality by pointing to examples of same-sex behaviour among animals. In this case, the author(s) interpret this appeal to nature as a 'radical contradiction to the very concept of human dignity' (p. 42). It seems that nature itself cannot be trusted with defining 'natural', therefore morally sound and 'normal' realities, so the author(s) impose a functional logic: 'Our concept of normality must be based on an understanding of the function and purpose of certain aspects of the human body or, in a wider sense, of the human nature' (p. 43). Just as an 'eye that cannot see is not "normal" . . . the homosexual proclivity is not "normal"', because it does not fulfil 'the purpose of sexuality[, which] is procreation' (p. 43). Despite the body metaphors used in this argument, the functional logic of sexuality that is superimposed on nature does not take its legitimation from any scientific, biological or psychological arguments – which would offer a much broader view on the 'functions' of sexuality. In spite of the frequency with which the terms 'nature' and 'natural' are used, upon closer inspection neither the natural, biological world nor the corporeality of the human body and its biological needs provide the legitimation for the author(s) truth claim. 'Nature' rather serves as an argumentative tool, which is itself in need of legitimation through the function it fulfils within some greater plot.

Turning to 'Natural Law', the author(s) offer sweeping claims: 'Natural Law remains the same at all times and in all places, and it is pre-existent to all written legislation' (p. 7) – but little information on where and how this natural law comes about. A short paragraph tells readers that it is not

only a Christian heritage, but one of all religions, and that it has been recognised in antiquity as well as the Age of Enlightenment, but refrains from
a more detailed discussion (p. 7). Still, the grandness of the claims themselves hints at the much more limited tradition the paper is based on. It is
true that there have been predecessors of natural law since antiquity, and
that the 'Declaration of the Rights of Man and of the Citizen' from 1789
('Men are born and remain free and equal in rights') as well as the US Declaration of Independence ('We hold these truths to be self-evident, that all
men are created equal') declare self-evident human rights, but these examples actually do not point to the immutable quality of natural law but
rather to the historic changes it has faced. Whereas antique understandings of the 'natural right' to freedom pertained to a small percentage of
the population, enlightenment had (at least in theory) widened this claim
to the entirety of the adult white male population, before women's and
anti-colonial movements in the course of the nineteenth and twentieth
centuries demanded their equality in being recognised as human beings
(cf. Tönnies, 2011). Broadly speaking, it is exactly because modern natural
law puts equality and freedom of individuals front and centre that it is
necessarily dynamic as it develops 'step by step out of concrete experiences
of injustice' (Kriele, 1993, pp. 18, 22). The idea of an immutable natural
law on the other hand is a specific one that echoes medieval Christian
'natural law' in the tradition of Thomas Aquinas. Rather than concerning
itself with the rights of individuals, its goal is the legitimation of the existing social order. Rather than being an agent of social change, it is an agent
of authority, and rather than taking individual human beings as its point
of departure, it is understood as an expression of the divine will (Kriele,
1993, pp. 9–10). Tönnies mentions the 'persistent damage' of this 'confusion' of the 'rational universal natural law' with this religious understanding (Tönnies, 2011, p. 68). She points to Ernst Bloch, who defended the
'natural rights' of individual liberty – prominent among them the right to
a private sphere, which explicitly should not be regulated by law – against
the encroachment of moral judgement. He stated that 'Even the right to
one's own body and the private life that is related, flourishes only in a
judicial understanding that is moral-free, practical-technical, and does not
aspire to morale' (Bloch, 1977, p. 261). A larger contrast to the paper we
analysed here would be hard to imagine.

Conclusions

Looking at the actors involved in Agenda Europe, there can be no doubt
about the ultra-conservative Christian background of the network. With

regards to the different types of political activism and lobbying many of these individuals and groups are engaged in there can also be no doubt that they work with a broad variety of methods and approaches in order to reconfigure politics in line with Christian doctrine. It is therefore noteworthy that some of the most important actors within these movements funded Agenda Europe to counter a perceived lack of strategy and to devise political tools that cannot only be used transnationally, but even more importantly target international politics especially in the domain of human rights. The programmatic paper *Restoring the Natural Order* is one attempt to do this. It has previously been analysed as a strategic secularisation of Christian political discourse – a verdict that we believe merits some differentiation, as we would like to argue in these concluding remarks.

Our frame analysis showed the paper to be largely coherent, both in terms of content in the construction of problems and solutions and in terms of their contextualisation within the judicial domain. Contradictions arise mainly out of the arbitrary demarcation of the private and public sphere. These contradictions pertain to issues of sexuality and family life where e.g. homosexuality, contraceptives and extra-marital sex should be banned on grounds of their alleged detrimental consequences for society at large, while children's education is deemed a private matter, which the state should not get involved in. They are even more pronounced when it comes to questions of (anti-)discrimination where on the one hand the protection against discrimination is deemed an intrusion into the private sphere, while on the other hand Christian belief should be protected and even privileged in comparison to other religions.

These contradictions point to the deeper logic of the paper, which – despite the references to (international) law, court cases and so on – bears little resemblance to modern judicial reasoning. The one master frame that is repeated over and over again throughout the document demands that 'positive laws must comply with Natural Law' (p. 22) in order to provide the framework for a 'natural' social order that reverses the negative impacts of the 'Cultural Revolution'. At first sight, this recourse to natural law seems to fit well with the author(s) preoccupation with human rights and their fear of treaty monitoring bodies acting as agents of the cultural-sexual revolution, as human rights themselves rest on the idea of natural rights pertaining to each individual human qua our shared humanity. But upon closer inspection, the 'Natural Law' that *Restoring the Natural Order* talks about has little resemblance to this idea of an individual claim to rights and freedom. Rather, it harks back to the medieval Christian tradition of legitimising a hierarchical and unequal social order through a divine and therefore 'natural' plan. Even though the author(s) accept that current positive law is the outcome of political processes, i.e. of negotiations between interest groups, and develop strategies to work within that political arena, their long-term goal is to superimpose an absolute truth that renders deliberation impossible. While in the discussion of the relation between human rights and natural law the status of human rights treaties as outcomes of 'a political process' (p. 8) and implicitly even the possibility of different interpretations is acknowledged, the formulation of the author(s)'s goal leaves no room for deliberation, compromise or interpretation:

> Once we have decided that positive laws must comply with Natural Law, we must follow that approach consistently. In the areas discussed in this paper, everything is intertwined with everything: accepting one single law that disrespects Natural Law means accepting a principle that will ultimately undermine the entire legal order. (p. 22)

Fulfilling this vision would be tantamount to the end of politics and the end of societal change as a social order that is based on an absolute, ahistoric and unchangeable truth would be immune to contestation. This dystopian and totalitarian vision is what political Christianity would amount to, if this ideal of complete coherence between Christian moral values and legal order was allowed to become true. The term 'Natural Law' serves a strategic function as it offers the possibility to locate the discourse in judicial terrain, thereby lending legitimacy to demands in the sphere of positive law.

As stated above the term 'nature' might be misleading in the case of *Restoring the Natural Order* as it has nothing to do with biology, natural science or the embodied nature of human beings, but understands 'nature' as a part of a bigger divine plot, in which it has to fulfil a specific function. Nevertheless, on the discursive surface there are resemblances and parallels to secular right-wing extremism, and the naturalisation of social inequalities that is the core of this ideology (Forschungsgruppe Ideologien und Politiken der Ungleichheit, 2014). The very specific definition of equality as treating 'the equal equally, the unequal unequally, and everything according to its merit' (p. 103) also seems to parallel right-wing extremist Social Darwinism. Although our analysis showed that the secularisation of Christian discourse within the paper remains superficial and does not pertain to the argumentative logic, these superficial changes might have consequences both with regards to conservative Christians' ability to form alliances with secular right-wing extremist forces and with regards to their influence on broader public and political discourse especially in the domain of human rights.

When we started analysing *Restoring the Natural Order* we were most interested in the openly anti-feminist and anti-queer positions that the author(s) formulated and in their attack on virtually all progress made in terms of women's as well as sexual and reproductive rights within the last century. Our analysis revealed the much broader scope of the paper; thereby underscoring that anti-feminism is an ideology of societal change rather than being contained within specific policy fields (Graff and Korolczuk, 2021; Mayer and Sauer, 2017). *Restoring the Natural Order* clearly shows the aspiration to reorder society in line with the convictions of political Christianity. Taking gender relations and the sexual order as its starting point, these anti-feminist actors want far more than just to reverse some the gains of feminist and LGBTIQ+ groups in recent years. While the protection of male, heterosexual privileges is undoubtedly on their agenda, their project is the thorough re-sacralisation of politics and society, which would also be the end of any meaningful democracy.

Notes

1. For a description of the 2018 TV feature see https://programmard.de/TV/arte/pro-life---abtreibungsgegner/eid_28724543597474 and http://www.film-documentaire.fr/4DACTION/w_fiche_film/51802_1
2. The ideological closeness of right-wing extremism and political Christianity can be seen in the compatibility of certain arguments detailed in *Restoring the Natural Order*. The image of a 'demographic winter' (p. 71) as an argument against abortions, for example, resembles right-wing conspiracy myths about the autochthonous population's extinction and its replacement by means of immigration ('The Great Replacement').
3. The statement 'Agenda Europe Position regarding EPFPD Book on Agenda Europe' can be found on a website: http://agendaeurope.org/ which has been set up specifically for this purpose and does not contain any further contributions. The blog https://agendaeurope.wordpress.com/ lacks an impressum. It comments on current political events, promotes campaigns and distributes materials including the paper 'Restoring the Natural Order'.
4. If not stated otherwise, all page numbers in the following sections refer to the document *Restoring the Natural Order*.
5. This is the only time that the Freemasons are mentioned. It seems an indicator of the anti-feminist tendency towards broader conspiracy narratives (cf. Bauer in this volume).

References

Bloch, E. (1977). *Naturrecht und menschliche Würde*. Suhrkamp.

Burghardt, A. (1967). Katholizismus und Katholizismen. Anmerkungen zu einem Begriffsnotstand. *Neues Forum, 159*, 233–5.

Dakli, L. B. (2021). Europe Goes Right with One Goal: To Erase Completely Human Rights and 'Restoring the Natural Order'. *DonnexDiritti Network*. https://

donnexdiritti.com/2021/04/16/europe-goes-right-with-one-goal-destroy-human-rights-competently-and-restoring-the-natural-order/

Datta, N. (2018). *Restoring the Natural Order. The Religious Extremists' Vision to Mobilize European Societies against Human Rights on Sexuality and Reproduction.* EPF. https://www.epfweb.org/sites/default/files/2020-05/rtno_epf_book_lores.pdf

Datta, N. (2019). 'Agenda Europe': An Extremist Christian Network in the Heart of Europe. *Heinrich-Böll-Stiftung, Gunda-Werner-Institut.* https://eu.boell.org/en/2019/04/29/agenda-europe-extremist-christian-network-heart-europe

Datta, N. (2021a). *Tip of the Iceberg: Religious Extremist Funders against Human Rights for Sexuality and Reproductive Health in Europe 2009–2018.* EFP. https://www.epfweb.org/sites/default/files/2021-08/Tip%20of%20the%20Iceberg%20August%202021%20Final.pdf

Datta, N. (2021b). Ultra-conservative Strategies to Restore a 'Natural Order': The Agenda Europe Networks. Keynote at the public forum *Your body is a battleground. Ultra-conservative strategies to restore a 'natural order'* at Frankfurter Kunstverein. https://www.youtube.com/watch?v=l8kLo8KJKhk

Dietze, G. and Roth, J. (eds). (2020). *Right-wing Populism and Gender: European Perspectives and Beyond.* Transcript.

Forschungsgruppe Ideologien und Politiken der Ungleichheit. (eds). (2014). *Rechtsextremismus Band 1: Entwicklungen und Analysen.* Mandelbaum.

Foucault, M. (1979). *Sexualität und Wahrheit 1. Der Wille zum Wissen.* Suhrkamp.

Goffman, E. (1975). *Frame Analysis: An Essay on the Organization of Experience.* Penguin Books.

Graff, A. and Korolczuk, E. (2017). 'Worse than communism and Nazism put together': War on Gender in Poland. In R. Kuhar and D. Paternotte (eds), *Anti-Gender Campaigns in Europe*, pp. 175–94. Rowman & Littlefield.

Graff, A. and Korolczuk, E. (2021). *Anti-Gender Politics in the Populist Moment.* Routledge.

Green, J. C. (1996). *Religion and the Culture Wars: Dispatches from the Front.* Rowman & Littlefield.

Hark, S. and Villa, P.-I. (eds). (2015). *Anti-Genderismus: Sexualität und Geschlecht als Schauplätze aktueller politischer Auseinandersetzungen.* Transcript.

Hecht, P. (2018). Europas Antifeministisches Netzwerk: Geheim und radikal. *taz.* https://taz.de/Europas-Antifeministisches-Netzwerk/!5498934/

Hennig, A. and Weiberg-Salzmann, M. (eds). (2021). *Illiberal Politics and Religion in Europe and Beyond: Concepts, Actors, and Identity Narratives.* Campus Verlag.

Kaiser, W. (2003). Politischer Katholizismus und christlich-demokratische Parteien in Europa im 19. und 20. Jahrhundert. *Jahrbuch für europäische Geschichte, 4,* 259–76.

Kriele, M. (1993). Das Naturrecht der Neuzeit. In K. G. Ballestrem (ed.), *Naturrecht und Politik* (pp. 9–23). Duncker & Humblot.

Kuhar, R. (2015). Playing with Science: Sexual Citizenship and the Roman Catholic Church Counter-narratives in Slovenia and Croatia. *Women's Studies International Forum, 49,* 84–92.

Kuhar, R. and Paternotte, D. (eds). (2017). *Anti-gender Campaigns in Europe: Mobilizing against Equality.* Rowman & Littlefield.

Kuru, A. T. (2009). *Secularism and State Policies toward Religion: The United States, France, and Turkey.* Cambridge University Press.

Laclau, E. and Mouffe, C. (2014). *Hegemony and Socialist Strategy: Towards a Radical Democratic Politics.* Verso.

Mayer, S. and Sauer, B. (2017). 'Gender Ideology' in Austria: Coalitions Around an Empty Signifier. In R. Kuhar and D. Paternotte (eds), *Anti-Gender Campaigns in Europe*, pp. 23–40. Rowman & Littlefield.

Mos, M. (2018). The Fight of the Religious Right in Europe: Old Whines in New Bottles. *European Journal of Politics and Gender*, 1(3), 325–43.

Paternotte, D. (2015). Blessing the Crowds: Catholic Mobilisations against Gender in Europe. In S. Hark and P.-I. Villa (eds), *Anti-Genderismus: Sexualität und Geschlecht als Schauplätze aktueller politischer Auseinandersetzungen*, pp. 143–7. Transcript.

Sauer, B. and Pingaud, E. (2016). Framing Differences: Theorising New Populist Communicative Strategies on the Internet. In M. Ranieri (ed.), *Populism, Media and Education*, pp. 26–43. Routledge.

Schmincke, I. (2015). Das Kind als Chiffre politischer Auseinandersetzung am Beispiel neuer konservativer Protestbewegungen in Frankreich und Deutschland. In S. Hark and P.-I. Villa (eds), *Anti-Genderismus: Sexualität und Geschlecht als Schauplätze aktueller politischer Auseinandersetzungen* (pp. 93–108). Transcript.

Stambolis-Ruhstorfer, M. and Tricou, J. (2017). Resisting 'Gender Theory' in France: A Fulcrum for Religious Action in a Secular Society. In R. Kuhar and D. Paternotte (eds), *Anti-Gender Campaigns in Europe*, pp. 79–98. Rowman & Littlefield.

Strube, S. A., Perintfalvi, R., Hemet, R., Metze, M. and Sahbaz, C. (eds). (2021). *Anti-Genderismus in Europa: Allianzen von Rechtspopulismus und religiösem Fundamentalismus. Mobilisierung – Vernetzung – Transformation.* Transcript.

Tönnies, S. (2011). *Die Menschenrechtsidee: Ein abendländisches Exportgut.* VS-Verlag.

Turner, C. (2020). *Secularization.* Routledge.

van der Haar, M. and Verloo, M. (2016). Starting a Conversation about Critical Frame Analysis: Reflections on Dealing with Methodology in Feminist Research. *Politics & Gender*, 12(3), 1–7.

Verloo, M. (2007). *Multiple Meanings of Gender Equality: A Critical Frame Analysis of Gender Policies in Europe.* Central European University Press.

FIVE

Weak Men and the Feminisation of Society: Locating the Ideological Glue between the Manosphere and the Far-Right

Simon Copland

Who is truly to blame?

The people who are to blame most are ourselves, european [sic] men. Strong men do not get ethnically replaced, strong men do not allow their culture to degrade, strong men do not allow their people to die. Weak men have created this situation and strong men are needed to fix it.

These words feature prominently in the manifesto of the Christchurch shooter, who killed fifty-one people in cold blood in early 2019. While he did not speak openly about feminism within his manifesto at any point, focusing primarily on anti-Muslim and anti-immigrant sentiment, these words represent an element of far-right thinking that connects directly to prominent anti-feminist ideas. This chapter examines the linkages between the 'manosphere' and the far-right, and how both groups argue that society has been 'feminised'. This feminisation, caused by the changes brought about by feminism, both argue, has not only weakened men but weakened society overall. It has, according to these men, inflicted a collective injury, one primarily against white, Western men whose contributions to society have become devalued to the point of oppression.

I conduct this analysis by looking at three key texts: posts from the manosphere subreddit r/TheRedPill; the manifesto of the Christchurch shooter; and online articles from the Australian far-right organisation the Lads Society. By reading them against each other I study how men theorise the concept of the 'feminisation of society', how this results in anti-feminist sentiment, and the way that this rhetoric is used by far-right activists to justify violence against immigrant, specifically Muslim, communities. Together, I argue that the notion that society has been feminised is one of the clearest links between manosphere groups and the far-right, an ideological connection that highlights significant similarities between the two.

Rather than being a periphery of concern, anti-feminism is a core ideology underpinning each of these groups, meaning it must become a core unit of analysis of each group. This is particularly relevant in studies of the far-right, in which anti-feminism is often not spoken about at all or is seen as a 'precursor' to more extreme far-right ideologies. Here anti-feminism, and the misogyny that follows, is seen as less serious and less extreme in comparison to other elements of the far-right. I argue this underplays the role of anti-feminist ideas and diminishes the real threats that can follow from the misogyny and sexism that form part of these ideals.

I start this chapter by looking at the notion of the 'feminisation of society' as seen through the lens of manosphere through the subreddit r/TheRedPill. I then examine how these beliefs run through the material of the far-right, even if not specifically targeted at feminism. As will be explored below, while feminism is a common target, it is not the only way that men express these arguments. Instead, anti-feminist ideas are based in an argument against the broader 'overreach' of women, and their inability to know their place. The target is not necessarily feminism therefore, but femininity, and the perceived growing influence femininity is having in society.

I explore these trends through an examination of three case studies – the manosphere r/TheRedPill subreddit, the manifesto of the Christchurch shooter, and the website of the Lads Society. In each case I have conducted a close reading of key texts, primarily popular posts (in terms of votes) on the Reddit subreddit, the manifesto of the shooter itself, and introductory material and blog posts from the Lads Society website. Details of each of these three data sources are available in Table 5.1. Through this reading I have drawn key themes, which I explain below.

Table 5.1 Data sources

Data source	Details
r/TheRedPill subreddit	Selected posts from the r/TheRedPill subreddit. I collected a total of 9,842 posts for my PhD thesis ranging from November 2017–December 2018; as well as conducting my own digital ethnography during and around these periods. For this chapter I have analysed three specific posts, with a total of 1,526 words.
Christchurch shooter manifesto	Manifesto published online (15,978 words).
The Lads Society website	Web pages of Lads Society website, including 'about' page and 12 blog posts (13,864 words).

Throughout the chapter I provide quotes and examples from each of these three sources. I have done so carefully, cognisant of ensuring I do not promote the violent, racist, misogynistic and otherwise hateful ideology of these groups or individuals. I reproduce these texts as part of a thorough analysis, believing this to be essential to understand and in turn counteract these movements. In these instances I will indicate where content comes from, but will not link directly back to original sources, partially as some of these sources are no longer available online (in particular the Christchurch shooter manifesto and the website of the Lads Society), but primarily through a desire not to promote these sources further. I will instead treat this data as I would other data such as interviews, reproducing quotes to be analysed but not promoted or elevated.

I close the chapter by looking at how anti-feminism and in particular the notion of the 'feminisation of society' creates linkages between these groups and ideologies.

Injury and the Feminisation of Society

A fundamental argument of much of modern men's rights movement, the 'manosphere' and the far-right is a belief that feminism has taken over the world, to the detriment both of individual men and society in general. As Mayer and Goetz describe in the introduction to this volume, this aligns strongly with the reaction against the idea of 'gender ideology', which has formed much of the basis of anti-feminist ideas since the early 2000s. Gender ideology, and feminism more broadly, has been framed as threatening traditional families, heterosexuality, and understandings of the essentialist essence of human beings, and in turn is seen as taking over the institutions of modern society. In addition, feminism and gender ideology is seen as attacking the normative notions of the strong and invulnerable men through a philosophy of softening masculinity (Kimmel, 2018). This has been viewed as a key means of attacking the inherent strength of men, with feminism in turn both taking over society and injuring men individually and as a collective.

Kimmel (2017, 2018) argues that these changes have created feelings amongst some men of 'aggrieved entitlement'; a situation in which individuals have not received what they have expected, creating a recipe for humiliation. Through this, men seek to rebuild an image of their masculinity through these spaces. While Kimmel's framework is valuable in understanding these communities, I build on it in two key ways – through using Brown's (1995) analysis of 'injury' as a means to analyse identity formation in these communities, and through positioning them specifically in the post-feminist movement.

These groups engage in a politics and collective subjecthood driven by the notion of being injured subjects at the hands of modern society (Brown, 1995). This turn towards injury is based in a reinscribing and reinforcement of what Nietzsche describes as *ressentiment* – the 'moralising revenge of the powerless' – 'the triumph of the weak as the weak' (Brown, 1995, pp. 66–7). *Ressentiment* in modern liberalism is the result of an ongoing sense of failure, one created by the demands placed upon individuals to be self-reliant and self-made. Through this constant failure, individuals and collectives create an identity as the 'injured'. This creates what Brown (1995) describes as an attachment to the 'wound', to the point in which the 'wound' comes to stand for identity itself. This does not suggest that individuals are responsible for the injuries inflicted upon them, nor does it ignore the structural issues many communities are facing. Rather, it is a particular observation of the identity formation and markers that occur due to the attachment to these injuries, an attachment which forms particular types of political and personal responses.

While Brown's arguments are about how social minorities such as women form political identity against others, I argue that the manosphere and men's rights groups have adopted a similar positionality and narrative. These groups have actively identified themselves as social minorities, attaching themselves to the 'wound' as a means to form a collective identity as injured subjects.

Men in these spaces in particular identify with a communal sense of failure, which then finds a means through which to avenge and redistribute the pain (Brown, 1995). This occurs through the identification of 'an agent; still more specifically, a *guilty* agent who is susceptible to suffering – in short, some living thing upon which he can, on some pretext or other, vent his affects, actually or in effigy' (Nietzsche, 1989, p. 127). As I will discuss in the case studies below, men in the manosphere and the far-right describe a range of injuries that have been inflicted upon them – including attacks on essential 'masculinity' creating crisis for men and boys, the subjugation of men in a range of legal systems such as the family law courts, and the 'replacement' of white populations from an 'invading' Muslim other. The culprit of this injury, as described by men in the manosphere and the far-right, is a broad notion of feminism, the left, or 'social justice warriors' (SJWs). Each, according to these men, have inflicted a collective injury against men, primarily through feminising society to the point where masculinity is degraded and oppressed.

The Post-feminist Movement

These criticisms of feminism align with a political current of the late twentieth and early twenty-first centuries called 'post-feminism'. Post-feminism describes an economic and social situation wherein feminism is both 'taken into account' and 'undone' at the same time (McRobbie, 2009). Post-feminist movements operate in a number of ways – including a belief that feminism has succeeded and is no longer necessary alongside more popular feminist approaches that are focused more on consumerism than activism. For the purpose of this chapter I study a specific element of post-feminism, which represents a backlash to what is considered the 'excesses' of feminism (Gill, 2009; Ging, 2009), part of a broader history of 'backlash' to feminism (Faludi, 1991). This is not just a movement of men's rights activists, but also consists of mainstream reaction against the so-called excesses of feminism. The rise of the #MeToo movement for example was met with significant backlash, with individuals across the political spectrum arguing that women had taken the movement too far and that it was now targeting 'innocent' men and 'innocent' behaviour (Bates, 2020).

Post-feminism therefore does not necessarily argue against female equality, in fact it recognises many of the victories of feminism (although this is not always entirely true, particularly in the movements/organisations I will discuss below). It says instead that we have moved past a point where feminism is needed and argues that we are living in a post-feminist world in which equality has been achieved (Tasker and Negra, 2007; Ging, 2009). Any attempts therefore to continue to push feminist ideas or ideology represent a push to take things to the extreme, and in turn to inflict unfair injuries against those who are the targets of feminism. Elements of feminism are incorporated into social and political life, but in doing so it is deemed that feminism is no longer necessary, as women have achieved all the rights they require. As McRobbie (2009, p. 12) argues, post-feminism 'positively draws on and involves feminism as that which can be taken into account, to suggest that equality has been achieved, in order to install a whole repertoire of new meanings which emphasise that it is no longer needed, it is a spent force'. It therefore represents 'a taking for granted of feminist ideas alongside a fierce repudiation of feminism' (Gill, 2009, p. 346).

In the next sections I will examine how modern elements of the manosphere and far-right argue that feminism has gone too far, and the injuries they claim that this inflicts upon men. I argue that the ideology of each of these groups is based in a belief that feminism, the left and the social justice warrior have 'feminised' society, softening masculinity to a point that is detrimental to men and society.

The Red Pill and Post-Feminism

The modern men's rights movement is a spin-off from the men's liberation movement, which, in the 1970s and 1980s primarily worked alongside feminist activists with a belief that gender roles negatively impact men as much as they do women (Coston and Kimmel, 2013). In the 1980s and 1990s, however, men's rights groups began to splinter from these roots, with some groups reacting against the discussion about the substantial responsibility individual men held for violence against women, child sexual abuse and sexual assault. Leaders such as Warren Farrell said that feminism was inappropriately targeting men, arguing in his book *The Myth of Male Power* (Farrell, 1993) that the widespread perception that men held all the power in society was false and that, instead, it was men who were systematically disadvantaged, not women.

While men's rights organisations have been around for decades, in recent years, particularly since the rise of the internet and social media platforms, they have begun slowly to be eclipsed by a new iteration called the 'manosphere' (Ribiero et al., 2021). While based on some similar ideas, in particular a reaction against feminism, the manosphere is distinct from men's rights groups through its online activity and primary focus on individual life circumstances rather than political activism. As Mayer and Goetz (this volume) argue, even though focused on individual lives and life circumstances, this anti-feminism is still political in nature, with men critiquing societal structures and the impacts these have on individual men's lives.

This can be evidenced by the ideology that drives the manosphere - the Red Pill. The Red Pill is a concept taken from the film *The Matrix*, based on a scene in which the main character, Neo, is offered the choice of taking a red pill or a blue pill by the leader of the rebellion, Morpheus. The Red Pill represents learning the truth about the world. Taking it frees Neo from the control of the machine. However, the new world he enters is more uncertain, harsher and more difficult. On the flip side, taking the blue pill means remaining in the dream world, staying in the prison that is the Matrix. It means going back to an ignorant but somewhat more comfortable life. The version of the Red Pill spoken about by the manosphere argues that by taking the Red Pill manosphere men learn the truth about women, feminism and society. These truths are uncomfortable and can make life more difficult for the men involved, yet at the same time they allow men to escape and push back against the prison that is the feminist and feminine society.

r/TheRedPill is a subreddit dedicated to Red Pill ideas on the popular news and social sharing site, Reddit. The subreddit has over 300,000 subscribers, with a specific focus on educating men about Red Pill ideas and encouraging them to take up these ideals. r/TheRedPill is based entirely on a belief that things have gone wrong in society, particularly for men. An introductory post to the subreddit starts with the question, 'Why have we grown so quickly', with the author then replying to themselves:

> Because there's truth in the red pill. Because men are realizing that the sexual marketplace has shifted away from what we've been taught. Men who grew up over thirty years ago are discovering the world has changed. Men who are still growing up – from the 80s, 90s, and even the last decade, they're starting to realize that what their parents taught them, what television and chick flicks taught them, what church and sunday school taught them . . . it's all wrong.

Here we can see that it is not just that things have changed (which they have, see de Boise, 2015), but that men have not been brought along for the ride. Similar to Nietzsche's reading of *ressentiment* the complaint is based on a sense of failure – that men had been promised one thing and then delivered another. Everything they had been taught by parents, television, chick flicks, church and Sunday school – it is all wrong!

This feminisation of society, these r/TheRedPill users argue, has two distinct impacts. Individuals open with the argument that feminism has fundamentally changed men by punishing their masculinity – something intrinsic, valuable and idealised to them. While these users do have debates about masculinity, there is an overarching belief that it is something to be valorised, and that it has been unfairly attacked. They argue that masculinity is central to their identity and well-being, and that criticisms of it represent criticisms of men as men.

A user on r/TheRedPill for example makes a post simply titled 'Vagina Envy'. Manosphere men often speak about 'penis envy' – the idea that women are trying to act like men (through focusing on their career, going to the gym, etc.) and that this is disconnecting women from their true feminine essence. Penis envy, apparently, hurts women and fundamentally changes the nature of society. In this post the user flips the script, arguing that men are doing the same via 'vagina envy'. As he argues:

> Vagina envy.
>
> Men are cutting off their own balls, their own masculinity, and acting like they wish they had a vagina.
>
> **The Modern Man:** *I can't wait to find a chick to settle down with. I will sit around doing nothing meaningful with myself, praying for Mrs.

Right to save me from my boring life. I want to cuddle on the couch with her and whisper sweet nothings. My greatest ambition in life is to find the Right One.*

Barf.

This post provides an essentialist understanding of femininity and masculinity with the feminine coded as soft, caring and emotional, while masculinity is rejecting these ideologies. The post is written in a semi-ironic style, which is central to the culture of Reddit (Massanari, 2015), and the manosphere and far-right more generally (Chang, 2019), a style that adds to the attraction of these groups. Femininity is seen as contaminating masculinity, primarily through the rise of feminist ideals. The post, therefore, represents a reaction against what some theorists have described as a 'softening' of masculinity (Forrest, 2010; McCormack, 2012; McCormack and Anderson, 2010; Roberts, 2013), or the rise of the 'new' (Morgan, 1992), or 'metrosexual' (Simpson, 1994) man. These concepts are based on the idea that men are getting 'more in touch' with their emotions (Beynon, 2002; Edwards, 2006; Gill, 2003; de Boise, 2015), and in turn are adopting more 'feminine' traits as a response to changing economic circumstances and the rise of feminism in the late twentieth and early twenty-first centuries (Illouz, 2007; de Boise, 2015). Changing economic circumstances for example have resulted in a decline in manual labour and 'breadwinner' jobs (McDowell, 2000), which have historically been key indicators of many men's masculine identity (de Boise, 2015).

Theorists routinely challenged this notion of the 'new man' and of 'softening masculinity'. As de Boise (2015) points out, for example, there is little evidence of actual changes in male behaviour in, for example, conducting domestic duties. More importantly, research has challenged the notion that men have not previously been 'emotional' or 'sensitive', with strong evidence to suggest that, despite stereotypes, men have always engaged in these behaviours (Dixon, 2005; de Boise and Hearn, 2017; Wester et al., 2002; MacArthur and Shields, 2015).

Despite this, however, these concepts have become common in the popular press and academia alike (de Boise, 2015), and, in turn, have become a point of contention for manosphere men. The concept of a 'softening of masculinity' has become a key claim in the argument of masculinity being in crisis, with men reacting both against economic and social changes, and the impact these have on their perceptions of self (de Boise, 2015; Kimmel, 2018). Central to this has been how the notion of the 'new man' has reinscribed gendered norms, creating an essentialist notion of 'emotions' and 'sensitivity' as being 'feminine' traits, which men are now participating in. Manosphere men react directly against this, arguing that the 'softening' of masculinity turns men into women, denying them their natural manhood. This is emphasised by the very notion of 'vagina envy' in the post above, which creates a direct link between supposedly 'feminine' traits such as 'cuddling on the couch whispering sweet nothings', with an essentialised notion of the 'woman'. These essentialised concepts are symbolised by the vagina, in the case of women, and penis, in the case of men.

The Red Pill therefore valorises an essentialised understanding of masculinity, reinforcing a social structure which Nicholas and Agius (2017) describe as 'global masculinism'. They use the definition from Brittan (1989, p. 4), who argues that:

> masculinism takes it for granted that [1] there is a fundamental difference between men and women, [2] it assumes heterosexuality is normal, [3] it accepts without question the sexual division of labour, and [4] it sanctions the political and dominant role of men in the public and private spheres.

Members of r/TheRedPill claim that feminism has undermined this structure, taking away what it means for men to be men.

This has not just impacted men as individuals. As Mayer and Goetz argue in the introduction, anti-feminists construct gender as a natural given, which in turn stabilises social relations in an 'attempt to restore security that has become precarious' (Hark and Villa, 2015, p. 10). This is not just about individuals, but also national security, with masculinity being spoken about as central to the strength of the West. This aligns with a notion of modern statehood, with masculinity aligned with the strength of the Western nation (Nagel, 1998).

Feminism, r/TheRedPill users argue, has undermined this, weakening both men and the state at the same time. This is evidenced in a post by a user, titled: 'Do your civic duty: LIFT, RUN, and PLAY'. In it, the use states:

> Arguably the best TEDx Talk I've ever seen. Lieutenant General Mark Phillip Hertling on Obesity in America. It's 100% worth a watch. It puts National Health into perspective and highlights why TRP [The Red Pill] is so focused on physical fitness. He touches on a few other topics as well. We often say "Lift" to get your SMV[1] higher but that's only a side-effect. Seeing this was an even bigger kick in the pants for myself to stay fit so I posted it here for others needing the motivation to get fit.
>
> We are literally becoming too fat to defend ourselves and the things we value.

This post is then followed by a range of activities the man encourages others to participate in, including lifting more frequently, running and eating healthier. He concludes the post by saying 'Summary: Your fatass is a threat to National Security.' The feminisation of society, therefore, is not just impacting individual men and their masculinity but is also acting as a threat to national security. r/TheRedPill users frequently, for example, post images and memes about jobs that are commonly undertaken primarily by men – firefighting, construction, police work etc. – arguing that this is evidence that it is men who have built the modern world. I have observed men in the subreddit then joking about women's attempted entry into these professions, suggesting that it simply isn't possible. They at the same time they warn that women attempting to take these roles will result in societal collapse, as women simply cannot do what men can. The feminisation of society therefore presents a threat in particular to the notion of the 'strong nation', and by extension an assumed version of a 'strong West', with a belief that Western nations require masculinity to build and defend itself. It is this latter trend in particular that is prominent in far-right anti-feminist arguments, to which I will now turn my attention.

In these next sections, I am going to examine the similarities between these arguments and those found in the far-right. While anti-feminist ideals are a central part of all elements of the far-right, feminism is often not a direct or main target in the same way that it is for men's rights organisations. In this section, however, through examining the manifesto of the Christchurch shooter, and the website for the Australian far-right organisation the Lads Society, I argue that the idea of the 'feminisation of society' is central to extremist, far-right ideas. This concept is used as an explanation for the 'invasion' of immigrants and the 'replacement' of white populations, which, the far-right argues weaken individual men and society.

Men Have Been Weakened – The Christchurch Shooter

In March 2019 a man[2] opened fire in two mosques in the New Zealand city of Christchurch, murdering fifty-one people and injuring forty others in cold blood. The man livestreamed the massacre on Facebook and posted a manifesto explaining his actions on the image-board 8chan, which hosts several far-right user-created message boards.

The manifesto of the Christchurch shooter mixes anti-Muslim and anti-immigrant rhetoric with internet memes and in-jokes. He claims that Muslims are replacing white communities and culture in the Western world, undermining Western society and values. In response to this, the manifesto primarily acts as a call to action – with the shooter at multiple times decrying the failures of the far-right to properly take up the fight. While the shooter argues that he represents millions of people, at the same time he expresses frustration at the lack of a proper fascist[3] movement. One part of his manifesto is structured in a question-and-answer format, and at one point he asks 'Won't your attack do more harm than good?' to which he responds 'No, there isn't a successful, influential grand movement established just yet, and no leading organizations, so there is no great structure created that could be brought to harm.' At another point he describes his frustration at a lack of action writing in all caps three times on the same page 'WHY WON'T SOMEBODY DO SOMETHING?', to which he then replies, 'WHY DON'T I DO SOMETHING?'

This lack of action, the shooter surmises, comes from a weakness in modern society, one that has particularly infiltrated men. As noted in my introduction, at one point the shooter asks, 'Who is to blame?', to which he replies:

> The people who are to blame most are ourselves, european men. Strong men do not get ethnically replaced, strong men do not allow their culture to degrade, strong men do not allow their people to die. Weak men have created this situation and strong men are needed to fix it.

In another section of the manifesto, he argues that the left and progressives, which themselves are often seen as 'feminine' (Green, 2019), have marched through mainstream institutions in the West, weakening them as they go. He argues that men have been left behind in this process and that men need to do the same as women – take back control. 'BLITZ TO DOMINANT POSITIONS' he says, attempting to rally men to the cause.

Here we can see a direct link to the idea of the feminisation of society, in which the shooter argues that it is a growing weakness in Western men that has allowed others (Muslims, immigrants, etc.) to 'replace them'. The manifesto therefore acts, as Mayer and Goetz describe (this volume) via intersectional means, with racist, sexist and nationalist ideas combining to form a coherent ideology. Part of this is based on a cultural assumption that openness and care are feminine traits (Hanlon, 2012), which in turn aligns immigration with these ideals. The true masculine ideal therefore is strong and bold, it protects its own against the threat of the 'other'. Like anti-abortion movements (Mayer and Goetz, introduction, this volume) the shooter frames himself in a positive light – the hate he feels for Muslims is only because of the love he feels for his community – in particular the white women and children he is seeking to protect. To truly love one's own community, the shooter argues, men must protect it. He claims that 'diversity is not a strength. Unity, purpose, trust, traditions, nationalism and racial nationalism is what provides strength. Everything else is just a catchphrase.'

It is important here to note a significant difference between the mano-sphere and this manifesto. While women are hyper-visible in the mano-sphere, in this manifesto they are virtually invisible. Despite this, however, anti-feminist ideas run throughout the document, with feminism being an invisible bogeyman that is the cause of all the problems the shooter identi-fies. Again, for example, while not specifically talking about feminism, men appear as a central reference point for the shooter throughout the manifesto. The second page of the manifesto for example features a six-verse poem by Dylan Thomas (1914–53) titled 'Do Not Go Gentle Into That Good Night', a famous poem that evokes 'wise men', 'good men' and 'wild men' fighting to the death. At another point, once again posing a self-referential question, 'What do you encourage us to do?', the shooter refers back to men, stating:

> Make your plans, get training, form alliances, get equipped and then act. The time for meekness has long since passed, the time for a political solution has long since passed. Men of the West must be men once more.

Despite his complaints about the lack of a fascist movement, the shooter then argues that recent societal changes will inevitably result in a radicali-sation of white, ethno-European, Western men, stating:

> The radicalisation of young Western men is not just unavoidable, but inevi-table. It should come as no shock that European men, in every nation, and on every continent are turning to radical notions and methods to com-bat the social and moral decay of their nations and the continued ethnic replacement of their people.
>
> Radical, explosive action is the only desired, and required, response to an attempted genocide . . .

It is the failure of men and Western society in general to live up to mas-culine ideals that the Christchurch shooter argues are behind the 'replace-ment' of white people with Muslims in particular. Notably, here he argues that there is a growing difference between Western and Muslim men, with Muslim men maintaining the strength that he desires to see in the West. It is this difference between the two that is facilitating this takeover of the West. At one point for example he mocks the idea of assimilation:

> Expecting immigrants to assimilate to a dying, decadent culture is laugh-able. Who would willing (sic) leave their own strong, dominant and rising

culture to join an elderly, decaying, degenerate culture? What culture would entice a man, one of traditions, beauty, architecture, art and prosperity, to a culture of decay, self-hatred, childlessness, disorder and nihilism?

Muslims are taking advantage of the weakness of the West, according to the Christchurch shooter, driven primarily by the feminisation of men and society. This is similar to the arguments made by other shooters, such as the 2019 Halle Mosque shooting and the El Paso massacre. While he doesn't use the term explicitly, the 'feminisation of society' is a central plank of the belief system of the Christchurch shooter. The shooter argues that Western society and Western men have been weakened, blaming this on the left, mainstream institutions and, by implication, feminism. The shooter therefore valorises a traditional notion of masculinity, one in which men are seen as strong, rational, and protectors of the family and the state. It is this dying masculinity that is the cause of the great replacement, a white nationalist conspiracy myth which states that, with the complicity of 'replacist' elites, white populations are being demographically replaced with non-European peoples. The great replacement requires a radicalisation and backlash from men.

Attacks on the 'Natural Order' – The Lads Society

The Lads Society was a far-right group of men based primarily in Melbourne Australia. Modelled on the US-based group the 'Proud Boys', the Lads Society was founded in 2017, evolving from the now disbanded white nationalist organisation the United Patriots Front. The group was founded by known white supremacists Blair Cottrell, Neil Erikson, Christopher Shortis and Thomas Sewell. Sewell was reported in May 2019 to have corresponded with the Christchurch terrorist about the possibility of joining the Lads Society (Begley, 2019). The Lads Society has since been disbanded, with members moving to form the National Socialist Network. The organisation however is still useful to study as an example of a reaction against the feminisation of society within the far-right in Australia.

The Lads Society acted as a version of a support group, while at the same time calling itself a 'movement'. The organisation had two club houses, one in Melbourne and one in Sydney, which included gyms, informal get-togethers, job networking, skills education seminars, mentoring and community assistance. Key leaders, however, have also been involved in far-right protests, including protesting the construction of a new mosque in the rural town of Bendigo in 2015 (Morris, 2015), and an anti-immigration rally in the Melbourne coastal suburb of St Kilda in 2019 (Martin,

2019). In a highly publicised moment, founder Blair Cottrell and other members publicly harassed a street performer in Melbourne's Federation Square, accusing him of indecently exposing himself in front of kids due to his costume (Butler, 2018).

Similar to the rhetoric of the Christchurch shooter, the ideology of this organisation was underpinned by a fundamental belief that Western society has been weakened and that men are required to respond. This ideology was prominent throughout the society's website, which has not been taken down despite the group's disbandment. However, I have still managed to analyse key texts from it, including landing pages and a series of blog posts written by members. In the 'Who Are You?' section of the Lads Society website, the group started by decrying changes in cultural and social norms.

> We are a group of like-minded people who have grown increasingly concerned over the state of affairs within our nation.
>
> The values of community, personal responsibility and commitment are rapidly being washed away amid a flood of dramatic changes to our home, allowed by our apathy. We are experiencing a greater need to bond together as a cohesive collective for the benefit of the individuals within, and society as a whole.

Here we can see strong similarities between the organisation and the Christchurch shooter, alongside r/TheRedPill, both in terms of a belief that something is changing, as well as an articulation of the failure of men in general to respond to these changes.

This is directly articulated through a number of blog posts featured on the site. In a blog post titled 'Mind, Body and Spirit', they articulate a belief in a fundamental logic that is the foundation of all higher civilisation. As documented by Zuckerberg (2018), many men's rights and far-right organisations use ancient Greek and Roman philosophy and theology as a basis for their own ideology, using this material to justify an argument that there are inherent differences between men and women, and that the success of society is based on masculine ideals. In this post the Lads Society claims that society is based on three fundamental truths, or a 'natural order':

> He was the bearer of a spear, this was not a right but a duty, and it was his duty to protect his tribe and to hunt and fight for his tribe's survival. (Body)

> A man who holds a spear, and only a man who holds a spear has the "right" to debate or dictate the path of the tribe. (Mind)

A man who holds the spear and holds the right to speak must develop his higher purpose and his metaphysical reincarnation through rebirth. (Spirit)

These fundamental truths are based on a hierarchical masculine notion of the world, in which men – the bearers of the spear – have a duty to protect the tribe. Through this protection men then have the right to lead – to debate or dictate the path of the tribe. Men also have a responsibility to develop their own higher purpose, to be strong, rational beings. The post then continues to say, 'the sole purpose of the relationship between Mind, Body and Spirit is self-preservation, just as the purpose of life is the balance between the self-preservation of the micro (one's self) and the macro (one's people)'. Men are there to protect and it is through this protection that society survives.

Like r/TheRedPill and the Christchurch shooter, the Lads Society argues that something has fundamentally changed to challenge this order. In a series of blog posts, they describe the encroachment of 'chaos' into Western society. The notion of chaos being associated with the 'feminine' is common in these spaces. This is often based in religious texts, which link femininity to creation, and, in turn, nature – all of which are seen as elements of chaos. Masculinity, on the other hand, is located within the rational and public spheres, which are ideologies and spaces of order. Chaos is not inherently bad but instead is seen as a notion that is not suitable for the management or protection of society. Intellectual dark web thinker Jordan Peterson, for example, has prominently argued that we now have an overdose of femininity and chaos in our society, stating that 'we have to rediscover the eternal values and then live them out' as an antidote to feminisation, and the chaos it supposedly brings (Peterson cited in Bowles, 2018).

The Lads Society echoes this, arguing that Western society has become dominated by a chaotic energy, one which has undermined the natural order. In a post which exemplifies this, they talk about the idea of democracy, stating that it is 'a word that has been so twisted that it almost means nothing today – was built on the notion that only those Men who had fought or were capable of fighting had a voice. How different our world would be today if this were still the case.' They therefore suggest that some of the most fundamental components of modern liberal society – the right for all to vote – represents such an overdose of chaos. The feminisation of society is not just about softening men, it is the imposition of a range of social programmes that undermine the inherent order of things.

In response to this the Lads Society focuses on creating 'strong, honourable and healthy men', arguing that 'strong Men create strong Families, strong Families create strong Communities and strong Communities make strong Nations'. The focus is on developing individuals, but in doing so they believe that this will redevelop the strength of the Western nation. The goal here is less to be involved in direct political action, and instead to 'create [the] strongest possible organisation resembling Natural Order that we can achieve'. This organisation argues that with the imposition of chaos, Western society has the potential of collapse and that therefore their duty is to develop 'a self-reliant parallel society so that we succeed in our mission whether or not the collapse comes in our life time'.

Men in the group do this by focusing on their own masculinity and personal development, which is very similar to the activities of r/TheRed-Pill. A big focus for example is weightlifting, something men can do to develop and maintain their masculinity. Weightlifting and gyms for example are often a feature of masculine identity, with men seeing 'getting big/thick' as a core way to express their masculine body and ideals (Underwood, 2018). Lads Society men get together and lift weights, and the web page features discussion of different ways to do the activity. The first blog post on the website for example is titled 'Deadlifting 101', in which founder Tom Sewell goes through the technique for one of the formative exercises in weightlifting. The blog features an image of Sewell instructing other members in one of the Lads Society's gyms, with a caption 'Pictured above, Tom Sewell educating young lads on how to become thick, via the correct and safe performance of a crucial weight-lifting movement known as the "deadlift".' Another post features a 'LadSoc fitness standard', a list of exercises men should be doing to achieve the right standard. The exercises include pull-ups, hangs, bench presses, push-ups, deadlifts, the beep test, a run of 2.4 km and a 'pack march'. The post says that the 'purpose of fitness testing is to ensure personal discipline, health and strength is achieved throughout the group. A combination of Strength and Fitness exercises ensures a balance amongst members whilst performing more practical activities as well as members focusing on their weaknesses.'

Fitness is seen as essential both to the individual development of men, but also to the success of the movement. The Lads Society sees strength as core to masculinity and in turn the individual, collective and nation. They state:

> Our movement will not succeed until every man in our cadre is an Übermensch, we will not succeed until all have understood the worldview – Natural Order. Our movement will not succeed until every man is strong and fit and healthy, until he is Aesthetic in both his physicality and his soul.

Notably, they articulate a belief that doing so is an act of love, not hate. As Ahmed (2004) notes, hate is often reframed as a means through which individuals connect with the self, and specifically an identified 'in-group', resulting in a situation in which 'hate is renamed as love' (Ahmed, 2004, p. 123). As Ahmed argues (ibid.), 'The conversion of hate into love allows the groups to associate themselves with "good feeling" and "positive value". Indeed, such groups become the ones concerned with the well-being of others; their project becomes redemptive, or about saving loved others.' The Lads Society exemplifies this relationship between love and hate, stating that their movement is not about hating others, but about loving themselves, their community and traditional Western values. As they say in a blog post:

> Our movement is one of love; we love our culture, our history, its beauty, strength and honour. To love something you must hate that which threatens it, we must be absolutely intolerant and despise anything that threatens the memory of our ancestors, what they built and our future.

Implicit here is a belief that those who are willing to change society – to feminise it and undermine the 'natural order of things' – are the true haters. It is them who want to destroy, while it is these men who want to restore, care for and nurture. This justifies the sense of hatred of those who want to change things so dramatically – why would you not react against those who want to destroy what you love so much.

Conclusion

In the introduction to this volume, Mayer and Goetz argue that three interconnected features render anti-feminist and anti-gender discourses attractive to right-wing politics. As they claim, anti-feminism is 'intersectional', making it easy to link it to racist and national politics. Second, anti-feminism aligns strongly with the populist strategies of right-wing politics, which have been able to frame feminist ideas as the interests of a cultural and social elite that uses them to attack and injure the everyday person. Feminism and so-called 'gender ideology' attack the everyday naturalness of masculinity and femininity, hurting women and men as individuals and collectives. Finally, they argue that anti-feminist discourses offer right-wing actors the opportunity to position themselves as the defender of 'ordinary people', particularly those who maintain the dominant 'natural' order of society.

Through my analysis of r/TheRedPill, the manifesto of the Christchurch shooter, and the website of the Lads Society, we can see this strategy play out. In this context the manosphere functions as a space which men around the world who see their masculinity as threatened can use to exchange and network. Although men often access these spaces for 'local' reasons, it is evident that similar discourses (such as threatened masculinity) are taken up by corresponding groups worldwide, and that they have a great potential for fanaticisation. These groups/individuals are all based in a reaction to the 'feminisation' of society. Manosphere groups argue that this feminisation has weakened men, resulting in their systemic discrimination at the hands of feminism and left-wing institutions. Far-right individuals and organisations such as the Christchurch shooter and the Lads Society say this weakening of society has allowed for the deterioration of traditional Western values. The Christchurch shooter argues that this is the genesis of the 'invasion' of immigrants, primarily from Muslim societies, while the Lads Society reacts against a weakening of society through attempts to build a movement of 'strong' men. Through this work I build on analyses of representations of masculinity within the manosphere and far-right communities to identify a trend of men positioning themselves as 'injured' within the post-feminist society. In this chapter, however, the question remains open as to whether and how these ideas of threatened masculinity are articulated outside the West. In this anthology, for example, Naaz provides insights into constructions of masculinity in India, as does Beeson with regard to South Africa.

It would be easy, at this stage, therefore to claim that men's rights groups provide a potential 'gateway' drug to more extreme elements of the far-right. It is true that some high-profile members of the far-right cut their teeth in the men's rights movement. A number of prominent far- and alt-right figures, particularly in the United States all had their start in men's rights movements. David Futrelle (2017) argues that, for some, men's rights activism is a gateway drug for the alt-right. Reliant upon notions of a white, male, masculine identity, manosphere ideas tap into many of the gendered and racial assumptions behind alt-right ideology. Furtelle claims that both movements appeal to men with fantasies of violent and sometimes apocalyptic redemption. Both also appeal to men who feel socially isolated and alienated, men who see themselves as outside of and oppressed by recent social changes.

However, the suggestion of a 'gateway drug' is difficult to sustain for multiple reasons. First, it suggests a linear pathway from one group to another, which is rarely the trajectory of individuals in the movement. Men's rights and manosphere groups are deeply embedded in racist and far-right ideologies, while far-right and racist organisations are strongly misogynistic. While groups may emphasise one ideology or hatred above another, they are intrinsically linked, and must be examined as such. Similarly, the idea of a 'gateway drug' suggests that misogynistic movements are somewhat less radical, extreme or violent than their racist, or alt-right counterparts. As the number of attacks from self-proclaimed incels (i.e. the Isla Vista shooting in 2014 and the Toronto van attack in 2018) testify to, this is not always the case. While there are variations across individual groups and movements (i.e. r/TheRedPill does not suggest any level of violence compared to the Christchurch shooter), it is important to see these groups along a similar scale.

The examples provided in this chapter exemplify this analysis, and highlight the co-constitution of male and white supremacist ideas in these groups and ideologies. I argue that a full analysis of anti-feminism is central to understanding the ideology and ongoing threats of these groups – from the manosphere to the far-right. Anti-feminism is central to the ideologies of these groups and individuals, even when the term itself and discussion of women more broadly are invisible in materials (as is the case in the manifesto of the Christchurch shooter). Ignoring this, particularly in studies of the far-right (where anti-feminism is often not spoken about at all), therefore misses an essential element of analysis, and in turn a central point in which intervention is required.

Notes

1. Sexual market value.
2. Following the shooting there have been calls from victims not to name the perpetrator as this provides him with undue publicity. I am therefore following these guidelines and will simply refer to him as the Christchurch shooter.
3. The shooter self-identifies as a fascist in his manifesto. At one point in his Q and A section he asks 'Were/are you a fascist?' to which he responds: 'Yes. For once, the person that will be called a fascist, is an actual fascist. I am sure the journalists will love that.'

References

Ahmed, S. (2004). *The Cultural Politics of Emotion*. Routledge.

Bates, L. (2020). *Men Who Hate Women*. Simon and Schuster.

Begley, P. (2019, 2 May). Threats from white extremist group that tried to recruit Tarrant. *The Sydney Morning Herald*. https://www.smh.com.au/national/threats-from-white-extremist-group-that-tried-to-recruit-tarrant-20190501-p51j5w.html

Beynon, J. (2002). *Masculinities and Culture*. Open University Press.

Bowles, N. (2018, 18 May). Jordan Peterson, custodian of the patriarchy. *The New York Times*. https://www.nytimes.com/2018/05/18/style/jordan-peterson-12-rules-for-life.html

Brittan, A. (1989). *Masculinity and Power*. Basil Blackwell.

Brown, W. (1995). *State of Injury: Power and Freedom in Late Modernity*. Princeton University Press.

Butler, G. (2018, 28 June). 'You can't wear that in front of kids, mate': confronting moment leader of far-right group attacks a street performer for wearing a pink mankini in Melbourne. *The Daily Mail.* https://www.dailymail.co.uk/news/article-5881167/Leader-far-right-group-confronts-Melbourne-street-performer-wearing-pink-mankini.html

Chang, W. (2019) The Monstrous-Feminine in the Incel Imagination: Investigating the Representation of Women as 'Femoids' on /r/Braincels. *Feminist Media Studies, 1–17.*

Coston, B. and Kimmel, M. (2013). White Men as the New Victims: Reverse Discrimination Cases and the Men's Rights Movement. *Nevada Law Journal, 13,* 368–85.

de Boise, S. (2015). *Men, Masculinity, Music and Emotions.* Palgrave Macmillan.

de Boise, S. and Hearn, J. (2017). Are Men Getting More Emotional? Critical Sociological Perspectives on Men, Masculinities and Emotions. *The Sociological Review, 65*(4), 779–96.

Dixon, T. (2005). *From Passions to Emotions: The Creation of a Secular Psychological Category.* Cambridge University Press.

Edwards, T. (2006). *Cultures of Masculinity.* Routledge.

Faludi, S. (1991). *Backlash: The Undeclared War Against Women.* Chatto & Windus Ltd.

Farrell, W. (1993). *The Myth of Male Power.* Simon & Schuster.

Forrest, S. (2010). Young Men in Love: The (Re)making of Heterosexual Masculinities Through 'Serious' Relationships. *Sexual and Relationship Therapy, 25*(2), 206–18.

Futrelle, D. (2017, 17 August). Men's-rights activism is the gateway drug for the alt-right. *The Cut.* https://www.thecut.com/2017/08/mens-rights-activism-is-the-gateway-drug-for-the-alt-right.html

Gill, R. (2003). Power and the Production of Subject: A Genealogy of the New Man and the New Lad. *The Sociological Review, 51*(1), 34–56.

Gill, R. (2009). Mediated Intimacy and Postfeminism: A Discourse Analytic Examination of Sex And Relationships Advice in a Women's Magazine. *Discourse & Communication, 3*(4), 345–69.

Ging, D. (2009). All-consuming Images: New Gender Formations in Post-Celtic-Tiger Ireland. In D. Ging, M. Cronin and P. Kirby (eds), *Transforming Ireland: Challenges, Critiques, Resources.* Manchester University Press.

Green, A. (2019). Cucks, Fags and Useful Idiots: The Othering of Dissenting White Masculinities Online. In E. Harmer and K. Lumsden (eds), *Online Othering: Exploring Violence and Discrimination on the Web.* Palgrave Macmillan.

Hanlon, N. (2012). *Masculinities, Care, Equality.* Palgrave Macmillan.

Hark, S. and Villa, P.-I. (Hrsg.). (2015). *Anti-Genderismus: Sexualität und Geschlecht als Schauplätze aktueller politischer Auseinandersetzungen.* Transcript.

Illouz, E. (2007). *Cold Intimacies: The Making of Emotional Capitalism.* Polity Press.

Kimmel, M. (2017). *Angry White Men: American Masculinity at the End of an Era.* Nation Books.

Kimmel, M. (2018). *Healing from Hate: How Young Men Get Into and Out Of Violent Extremism.* University of California Press.

MacArthur, J. and Shields, S. (2015). There's No Crying in Baseball, Or Is There? Male Athletes, Tears, and Masculinity in North America. *Emotional Review, 7*(1), 39–46.

McCormack, M. (2012). *The Declining Significance of Homophobia: How Teenage Boys are Redefining Masculinity and Heterosexuality*. Oxford University Press.

McCormack, M. and Anderson, E. (2010). 'It's just not acceptable any more': The Erosion of Homophobia and the Softening of Masculinity at an English Sixth Form. *Sociology, 44*(5), 843–59.

McDowell, L. (2000). The Trouble with Men? Young People, Gender Transformations and the Crisis of Masculinity. *International Journal of Urban and Regional Research, 24*(1), 201–9.

McRobbie, A. (2009). *The Aftermath of Feminism: Gender, Culture and Social Change*. Sage.

Martin, L. (2019, 5 January). St Kilda beach rally: far-right and anti-racism groups face off in Melbourne. *The Guardian Australia*. https://www.theguardian.com/australia-news/2019/jan/05/far-right-and-anti-racism-groups-face-off-in-melbourne-flashpoint

Massanari, A. (2015). *Participatory Culture, Community, and Play: Learning From Reddit*. Peter Lang.

Morgan, D. (1992). *Discovering Men*. Routledge.

Morris, M. (2015, 12 October). Bendigo's anti-mosque protest: United Patriots Front nationalist group behind demonstration. *ABC News Online*. https://www.abc.net.au/news/2015-10-12/who-was-behind-bendigos-anti-mosque-protests/6848468

Nagel, J. (1998). Masculinity and Nationalism: Gender and Sexuality in the Making of Nations. *Ethnic and Racial Studies, 21*(2), 242–69.

Nicholas, L. and Agius, C. (2017). *The Persistence of Global Masculinism: Discourse, Gender and Neo-Colonial Re-Articulations of Violence*. Palgrave Macmillan.

Nietzsche, N. (1989). *On the Geneaology of Morals and Ecce Homo*. Translated and edited by W. Kaufmann. Vintage Books.

Ribiero, M., Blackburn, J., Bradlyn, B., Cristofaro, E., Stringhini, G., Long, S., Greenberg, S. and Zannettou, S. (2021). The Evolution of the Manosphere Across the Web. 15th International Conference on Web and Social Media (ICWSM). https://arxiv.org/pdf/2001.07600.pdf

Roberts, S. (2013). Boys Will Be Boys . . . Won't They? Change and Continuities in Contemporary Young Working-class Masculinities. *Sociology, 47*(4), 671–86.

Simpson, M. (1994). *Male Impersonators: Men Performing Masculinity*. Routledge.

Tasker, Y. and Negra, D. (2007). *Interrogating Postfeminism: Gender and the Politics of Popular Culture*. Duke University Press.

Underwood, M. (2018). 'We're all gonna make it brah': Homosocial Relations, Vulnerability and Intimacy in an Online Bodybuilding Community. In A. Dobson, B. Robards and N. Carah (eds), *Digital Intimate Publics and Social Media*. Palgrave Macmillan.

Wester, S. R., Vogel, D. L., Pressly, P. K. and Heesacker, M. (2002). Sex Differences in Emotion: A Critical Review of the Literature and Implications for Counseling Psychology. *The Counseling Psychologist, 30*(4), 630–52.

Zuckerberg, D. (2018). *Not All Dead White Men: Classics and Misogyny in the Digital Age*. Harvard University Press.

Part Two

Local Articulations of Global Anti-Feminism

While the first part of our book shed light on broad, transnational trends in contemporary anti-feminism and looked at the possible consequences of these discourses and mobilisations by means of situated analyses, the second part provides a somewhat different perspective. The following chapters focus on specific (mostly national) cases and analyse how anti-feminism is articulated in these contexts. Questions that are dealt with by several authors include the specific political and religious alliances anti-feminism fosters in different situations and the ways in which the intersectionality of anti-feminism as an ideology play out. The latter becoming visible, e.g. in the roles anti-feminism plays for different nationalist movements as well as for conspiracy narratives and so-called gender-critical feminism, i.e. essentialist feminism that opposes the queer-feminist deconstruction of gender and violently excludes trans people.

The section starts with Cristina Vega's analysis of anti-feminist campaigns in Ecuador, which shows the role concrete experiences of faith play for Catholic as well as evangelical groups. Vega goes beyond an analysis of religious doctrine or discourse and looks at everyday practices of believers. Her perspective therefore provides an important complement to the ongoing debate on the role of religion in contemporary anti-feminism and authoritarianism.

The two chapters that follow venture beyond Christian contexts, with Hira Naaz analysing feminist struggles and violent answers of the Hindu Right in India and Kazuyoshi Kawasaka looking at changing strategies of anti-gender movements in Japan since the beginning of the 2000s. Naaz shows how Hindu nationalism builds on anti-feminism's intersectionality, tying the fight against (Hindu) women's emancipation to anti-Muslim agitation and nativism. For European readers, parallels to strategies used by right-wing actors in Europe are striking; but so are differences that clearly show that situated research is a necessity – possibly even more so for post-colonial contexts where (right-wing) nationalist movements show specific dynamics.

The question of global similarities in spite of different local and regional histories is also taken up by Kazuyoshi Kawasaka in his analysis of anti-feminism in Japan. Looking at a twenty-year period, this article provides an in-depth look at the changing salience of questions of gender and sexuality in Japanese politics and on the shifting strategies of feminist and anti-feminist actors. His analysis of how so-called gender-critical feminists today foster the anti-feminist agenda also holds important lessons for feminist movements internationally.

Mareike Fenja Bauer focuses more tightly on a recent phenomenon and analyses the role of anti-feminism in corona conspiracy narratives in Germany. The author shows that staples of anti-feminist argumentation serve several bridging functions within these movements, e.g. linking fearmongering about the dangers of vaccination to anti-abortion and pro-nativist standpoints and using traditional gender identities as a means for mobilisation. Bauer's analysis provides a clear picture of how anti-feminist discourse and corona conspiracy myths are both strengthened by this intermingling of ideologies.

The final chapter in this section is Amber Beeson's intersectional analysis of anti-feminism and its relation to questions of race in the postcolonial context of South Africa. Beeson draws together different strands of analysis, looks at the salience of different issues over time and provides an in-depth account of the most important anti-feminist actors. She thereby shows a comprehensive picture of the challenges South African feminists currently face, but also of the strength of intersectional, Black and anti-racist feminism in the country, which can provide inspiration to feminist activists globally.

This concern with feminist activism and with the exploration of possible pathways to a more equal society, which would provide recognition to everyone, regardless of sex, gender or sexuality, unites most of the chapters in this second part of the book. Understanding how and why anti-feminism seems to be on the rise globally is a first step in this endeavour. Therefore the editors close this volume with some tentative conclusions drawn from this wealth of analyses in an effort to identify some of the main lines of enquiry that these global perspectives open for research on anti-feminism as a global challenge to human emancipation.

SIX

'Original Design' and the Renewal of Patriarchy: Discipleship and Religious Politicisation in an Evangelical Church in Quito (Ecuador)

Cristina Vega

In June 2019, Ecuador's Constitutional Court approved equal marriage, reopening a heated debate that had intensified since 2017 with the Con-MisHijosNoTeMetas (Don't mess with my children) campaign. Under dispute was the 'gender focus' in education, which was integrated into the legislation on violence, and sexual autonomy within health reform, both feminist-backed proposals. This time the evangelical churches actively joined in as a civil force armed with various arguments: from constitutional, pseudo-scientific, nationalist, to biblical authority and civil morality. One of the central religious actors was the Iglesia Evangélica de Iñaquito (IEVI), a place of worship with a long history in Ecuador.

The mobilisation of the IEVI was strengthened by family discipleship and its emphasis on the importance of the traditional family in public and spiritual life. It argues that the normative, heterosexual couple, with identities and attributes based on a binary and essentialised conceptualisation of sexual difference, is endangered by laws that undermine it by recognising gender diversity, different unions and gender changes. The legitimacy of the so-called 'original design' (meaning a couple formed by a man and a woman with traditional attributions) is grounded in biblical literalism.

According to Pérez Guadalupe (2018), the political and social participation of churches overlaps with theological frameworks of meaning through which the faithful operate in the world. These are woven into everyday evangelism, in which pastors offer parishioners guidance on their problems and, more recently, a path to public participation through 'anti-gender' mobilisation. The connection between dogma and practices in the congregation as well as church organisation and politicisation underpins what Vaggione (2017) calls 'religious citizenships'.

This text takes the IEVI in Quito as a case study and examines how these conservative, normative, sometimes radically authoritarian views are actualised in church life, prompting a move into the political arena. It is part of a broader investigation into the anti-gender political agency and subjectivation of evangelical churches and the faithful in Ecuador between 2017 and 2020.[1] In-depth interviews with eleven IEVI pastors and ten members of other churches and actors in the Vida y Familia (Life and Family) movement, as well as observations of services of worship, ministries and other activities, were conducted between 2019 and 2020. The enquiry here focuses on how the beliefs disseminated by IEVI leaders within family discipleship encourage political responses. Rather than delving into the embeddedness of these discourses among parishioners, I am interested in how men and women pastors shape the link between doctrine, discipleship and politicisation.

The contemporary recourse to 'gender' in 'anti-gender' movements, and the consequent invention of 'genderism', has been analysed as a populist-conservative strategy that fashions a penetrating and corrosive enemy, associating it with the socio-economic crisis (Graff and Korolckzuk, 2021). This very act hides or blurs how this concept (gender) accounts for power relations and inequality (Vega, 2017). While 'anti-genderism' is a veiled way of attacking feminism in its struggle for rights, it sometimes openly dialogues with it, to misappropriate it in a distorted way ('anti-gender feminism', 'good and bad feminism', 'pro-life feminism') or to demonise it ('ex-feminist', 'feminine, not feminists'); often both. The presence and legitimacy of feminism in Latin America has contributed to the fact that not all those who call for mobilisation 'against gender' openly identify themselves as anti-feminist, thus acknowledging its protagonism in the struggle for justice.

The first part of this text addresses how the literature has been discussing views and actions on gender and sexuality in the evangelical field. It elaborates how 'anti-gender' and 'anti-feminist' activism contests sexual democracy and any updating of religious citizenship. It then introduces the context of Protestantism in Ecuador and the prominence of the Evangelical Church of Iñaquito. The second part analyses the leaders' views, focusing on women's and men's ministries and family discipling, then addresses public anti-gender activism and offers some conclusions.

Sex-Gender-Desire Order Versus Social Disorder

The expansion of evangelical churches in Latin America has aroused the interest of social scientists in recent decades. They have endeavoured to understand how the subjectification of believers develops in specific historical, social and political contexts, with gender being a central aspect.

Nicolás Panotto (2015) argues that theological discourses constitute frameworks of meaning from which believers make sense of the world and conduct their daily lives. Joaquín Algranti (2008a), an Argentinian scholar, points out that 'The church, with its action networks, its collective representations, its symbols and practises, acts as a formative force of subjectivity, obliged to constantly negotiate with the selective and partial appropriations that subjects make in their religious searches' (p. 197). Churches are a reference point for daily life, establishing a moral standard for the cultivation of faith, a guide for believers, whose 'conduct in itself must also be a testimony to society' (Garma Navarro, 2004). The 'good Christian' conforms his or her behaviour to the doctrine, becoming what Saba Mahmood (2019) refers to as a 'docile subject'. Leaders guide these actions, which bear witness to God's work in their parishioners before the eyes of the community.

The regulation of gender and sexuality is a central aspect here (Algranti, 2008a, 2008b; Cabezas, 2015; Carbonelli, 2009; Ceballos, 2008; Panotto, 2015; Pérez Guadalupe, 2018; Schäfer, 1992). As Sandoval points out, 'at the discursive level, a differentiated relationship of women and men with God is established, which has a practical impact on the church's organisation; daily tasks, as well as on the participation in and experience of religious rituals' (2005, p. 101). For Algranti (2007), Pentecostalism advocates equivalence, 'mirror and reflection' between men and God (Holy Spirit, Prophets, Patriarchs and Apostles). Men interpret the world and intervene in public affairs, while women exalt spiritual sensitivity and care. They take care of the family and the community and are a key part of the congregation. Men are, as is often repeated, the 'head'. Women may be seen as weak and manipulable, prone to sin and to drift away from spiritual life (Sandoval, 2005), but they also embody industriousness, thrift, efficiency, self-control and austerity. Women restrain and lead men to faith through a mixture of humility and subordination. They gain autonomy by going out and participating in the church community, always within the confines of an institution that reinforces their difference and guards their sexuality (Algranti, 2007; Brusco, 1995; Lindhardt, 2009). Violence, in many cases, is hidden behind the paragon of the Christian home, embodied by pastor couples.

The feminine ability to handle crises enables them to endure addictions, infidelity, violence, economic difficulties and other adversities. Hierarchical complementarity, based on determinism and foundationalism,[2] is expressed in all aspects of life, from clothing to economics.

The promotion of this division, which orders and stabilises the family, is the foundation on which 'anti-gender' religious politicisation is promoted today. It is around the preaching, witnessing, engagement, training and daily cultivation of a clear and (self-)regulated binary family regime – the so-called 'family perspective' – that leaders organise and mobilise the community against what they see as threats to sexual integrity, heterosexuality and family cohesion. The deconstructive power of feminism, LGBTI and *queer* movements (Mayer and Goetz, this volume) unifies these fears. 'Gender Ideology' (GI) operates as a *symbolic glue* (Grzebalska et al., 2017) that binds sectors of the alternative right, anti-neoliberals, anti-communists and anti-migrant activism together with religious homophobes and anti-abortionists. In the middle of all this are believers who, without necessarily being fundamentalists, recognise themselves in the patriarchal discourse in defence of the family.

In the church, the interplay between doctrine and groups based on gender and age has proved productive in leading and politicising the faithful. Although families in Ecuador and Latin America, especially in the popular sectors (impoverished, racialised urban groups, usually of migrant origin), are marked by diversity and adversity, appeals to the 'original design' of the whitewashed upper- and middle-class family are attractive as models for the design and patterns of a good life (Vega, 2020). The emphasis on patriarchal[3] order and the naturalisation of sex-gender, associated with national, even anti-colonialist, traditions, is set against market deregulation, loss of sovereignty to the IMF and other international bodies, and the precariousness of life. The ghosts of moral confusion and corruption rise out of everyday uncertainties that emerge from the crisis (Brown, 2018; Fassin, 2009; Vega, 2019).

The deliberate association of 'gender' with neoliberalism, a significant feature of the current conservative offensive (Graff and Korolckzuk, 2021), allows 'ordinary people' to speak. While in the public sphere the dyad feminism/LGBTI and neoliberalism is associated with the diabolical (Vega, 2021) and has an important political impact (Corrêa, 2019; Salazar, 2019; Torres, 2020; Mayer and Goetz, introduction, this volume), within the church and households the battle is waged against internal enemies (alcohol, drugs, infidelity, pregnancy, promiscuity, violence, etc.) derived from modernity, and barely associated with inequalities. The restoration of the safety provided by the (patriarchal) 'original design' in the face of (progressive) state meddling is thus proposed.

Fundamentalist Religious Citizenship and Sexual Democracy

The Latin American feminist and anti-colonial critique of citizenship has revealed the abstraction of who is the bearer of human rights, in reality,

a whitewashed, heteronormative individual, formally bound to and recognised by the state as owner, parent, wage-earner, literate and digitally
connected (Molyneux, 2006; Wade, Urrea and Viveros, 2008).

For Vaggione (2017), in Latin America the practice of citizenship is
based on a *sexual morality* that links the legitimate subject of the nation
to Catholicism. The 'sexualisation of the citizenry' challenged the univer-
salisation of this link and the asymmetries it created. The struggle to separate the two figures – citizen and believer – produced a reaction in the
Church. As the official endeavour of the Catholic nation was interrupted,
the defence of the citizenry's sexual morality was anchored to new mechanisms: the *culture of death* and *gender ideology*, to bring about a refocus on
natural law in legislation.

While religious discourses are being displaced by secularisation in
American republics, they reappear as a means of purifying the public by
appealing to (certain) virtues of private morality (Panotto citing Sennett,
2015). Evangelical fundamentalism has joined the Catholic Church in
promoting the 'sanctity of the private' in the body, sexuality and the family as a strategy of recovery of public life. Faith continues to denominate
'good citizens' (Nyhagen, 2015).

For Eric Fassin (2005), the reaction to *sexual democracy* – sex-gender as
a terrain of diversities, deliberations and social self-determination like any
other, and not of essential and fixed truths – reveals not only the limits of
secularism, but 'the last refuge of an immutable representation of things'.
'The politicisation of sexual norms, based on the naturalistic illusion', Fassin argues, 'is the last frontier of democratic combat' (p. 6).

While the Catholic religion has historically had the privilege of defining citizenship in Latin America, since the mid-2010s we have witnessed a
transnational religious re-politicisation for the 'defence of human nature',
meaning a hierarchical binary complementarity within the heterosexual
family (Bracke and Patternote, 2018; Careaga-Pérez, 2016; Corrêa, 2019;
Pecheny et al., 2016; Vega, 2017; Viveros, 2017). Recent 'anti-gender'
mobilisations in Latin America and Ecuador, led by the nascent Catholic-
Evangelical alliance have had an eminently religious hue.

The fact that this offensive has overlapped with and/or responds to an
intense cycle of feminist street protests in Latin America since 2015 (Gago,
2019) has radicalised the confrontation, which is taking place in an 'anti-
progressive' climate following the decline of progressive governments
(Torres, 2019). Indeed, although these governments have not been consistently favourable towards feminism, anti-gender movements/campaigns
and the allied right have portrayed feminism and LGBTI as examples of
'excesses' of progressivism and 'cultural Marxism' (an alt-right idea that

believes feminism and its 'cultural' critique as an avant-garde substitute for communism). Given the legitimacy and increasing appeal of feminisms, particularly in the struggle against violence, but also in the rejection of dispossession, Latin American and transatlantic authoritarian right-wing efforts through 'anti-gender' campaigns have failed to provoke a complete opposition to feminism.

Evangelical Expansion in Latin America and Ecuador: The Church of Iñaquito

In recent decades, evangelical churches have experienced significant growth in Latin America. Although Catholicism remains the majority religion, the Latinobarómetro (2018) reveals that its base has decreased while evangelical churches have increased. Since the 1970s, growth has accelerated due to these churches' internal structure and organisation, which is less vertical, centralised and monolithic (Guamán, 2011; Pérez Guadalupe, 2018; Schäfer, 1992; Semán, 2019). 'Christian denominations' are a group of national or foreign churches with common organisational, doctrinal and liturgical systems but limited representation in terms of being one body (Semán, 2019). Many churches do not belong to any denomination.

Evangelicalism, on its arrival in Latin America and Ecuador in the mid-nineteenth century, participated in the liberal movements calling for the separation of Church and state and religious freedom (Bastián, 2006; Guamán, 2011). Until the mid-twentieth century, they did not exceed 1 per cent of the population (Pérez Guadalupe, 2018). In this period, characterised by coups d'état and dictatorships, a new conservative, anti-communist and anti-ecumenical Protestantism spread, driven by US missionaries (Pérez Guadalupe, 2018). With the US 'Moral Majority' (1980), they entered the public discourse with sexual conservatism, extending it to Latin America and later associating it with Trump's candidacy and government (Machado et al., 2021).

Between 1910 and 2014, Catholic numbers decreased from 94 per cent to 69 per cent, while Evangelicals grew from 1 per cent to 19 per cent (Semán, 2019, p. 35). Their growth, first in popular sectors and rural areas and then in middle- and upper-class urban environments, is a result of Pentecostal churches and their capacity to adapt to the territory. What makes them unique is their networking, promoting support and salvation for those in difficulty (Semán, 2019).

Pentecostal churches have driven religious politicisation (Pérez Guadalupe, 2018; Schäfer, 1992; Wynarczyk, 2018), most recently in anti-gender mobilisations. In Ecuador, activation has fallen to the so-called independent churches in middle and upper sectors linked to groups with economic and political power, penetrating downwards through them (Pérez Guadalupe, 2018).

The Iglesia Evangélica de Iñaquito (IEVI) is an independent evangelical[4] church located in the north of Quito. It was founded in the 1950s with the Protestant radio station HCJB, La Voz de los Andes. Spiritual support for patients and their families in a medical clinic and shelter developed into prayer and worship groups, and later to a church. During the 1990s, the country experienced a severe economic and social crisis that led to the impoverishment of the population. Many people turned to faith for emotional support (Algranti, 2008a); participation in IEVI rocketed and diversified.

Pastor Carlos Caisapanta estimates current attendance to be some 6,000 people. In addition, 'daughter churches' have been created in popular neighbourhoods linked to IEVI's Pastoral Council, led by Fernando Lay, its senior pastor.

In 2017, Lay made fervent calls for participation in the ConMisHijos-NoTeMetas campaign with the slogan 'defend life and the family'. In the same year, at the Ecuadorian Episcopal Conference, evangelical leaders, with Lay at the forefront, signed a letter calling on the state to end 'Gender Ideology'. In 2019, when equal marriage was passed, they once again called on their followers to act.

Proselytising, social ties and the practice of self-perfection are central to the IEVI. Ministries have been created for specific groups of gender, age and marital status. The organisational structure includes cells and church branches that develop training events, vigils, counselling, etc. Female and male pastors, in couples or independently, are at the head of a church that is funded through tithing and is part of a wider network of resources.

Doctrine, Discipleship and Anti-gender Politicisation

Drawing on in-depth interviews with IEVI pastors and leaders, I will analyse how the deterministic doctrine is modulated as spiritual guidance in the 'family approach (a common expression that refers to chastity, biological reproduction within marriage and traditional gender roles)'. I then address how this is deployed through discipleship. Thirdly, I explore how doctrine and discipleship intersect with reactive politicisation by the leaders in shaping religious citizenship.

'Women of influence' and 'the perfect male'

In Iñaquito, the naturalistic illusion of sex-gender-sexuality comes from biblical literalism. Women and men are conceived as perfectly distinct and therefore complementary beings in the heterosexual couple. Male and female pastors refer to women as sensitive, humble, willing, courageous in their sacrifices, etc., while men are (or should be) eminently protective, 'heads', 'priests of the home', responsible for bringing the word of God to their families. Distinct social places in the church and the home are derived from these qualities and attributes. Natural differences associate some with childcare and housekeeping and others with provision and governance. There is no consideration of the relationship between these roles and inequality. It is within these conventional identities that women become citizens. The asymmetries are further diluted by the recognition of women's importance and of the difficulties they encounter in the face of machismo.

'Women of Influence' is the name of the women's ministry. In 2001, Pastor Teresa de Lay formed a Bible reading space with twelve women. Before she married the pastor, she was aware of her difficulties ('if I hadn't had the Lord Jesus Christ in my life, I would have been in some feminist movement, haha').

> God allowed me to go on a commission of pastors, but I was not part of that commission, we were on our way to the USA with Fernando. And in every church we visited, they identified me as the wife of the head pastor and asked me 'and you sister, do you work with the women?' And I answered 'no'. 'But the work should be done, because it is vital, even for the well-being of the pastor, that the wife is always working with the women, that she is working alongside her husband like that.' (Teresita Lay, interview, 11 June 2019)

The group became a ministry, producing several cells. Women, she argues, 'are just that, women of influence. And if our influence is negative, we can be very destructive because we could lead a family into chaos'. The ministry seeks to:

> Support women not only to grow, of course, in the basic knowledge of the word of God, but also in their issues as women as well as in their roles as a wife, as a mother, as a woman in society, as a citizen, because that is what we are. We are not only wives or mothers, we are also citizens and what is more, citizens of the Kingdom. (Teresa de Lay, 11 June 2019)

Sensitivity in the face of machismo and the promotion of equality before the law do not stand in contradiction to the differences envisaged in the creator's design. The pastor states:

> (...) it was the Lord who moved us to work for women. Looking at the hard, difficult situations they are going through: violence, machismo, injustice, mistreatment. So, practically speaking, we have been working from the

very identity of women. Obviously, all underpinned by biblical principles (. . .) empowering them to exercise the qualities, the talents that God has already placed in them and to exercise them for the benediction of themselves, their homes and the church (. . .) men and women can exercise the same roles. Within the home, obviously not; women exercise their roles and so do men. But within the church we can all do the same. Here in the church, women are involved in everything.

Ministry leaders agree with Pastor Lay: 'equal opportunities' should not be confused with 'wanting to be equal to men, as is proposed by "gender ideology"'.[5]

The ministry offers support through counselling that provides free psychological advice, as well as training on parenting, money management, love, sex and dating, nutrition, entrepreneurship, and also domestic violence. Women not only learn how to run their households, but also to create bonds of affection that strengthen their role through 'friendship' cells in their homes.

Proper parenting and the education of children, derived from traditional values, have grown in emphasis with the 'family approach'. Pastor Lay insists that the task is to 'awaken God-given qualities' and understand where and how to serve. Pastor Flor del Pilar Gómez describes her work in terms of 'care', especially for women and the disadvantaged. The ability to work in a network comes, in her case, from her experience in a multinational company focused on 'self-effort and self-sufficiency', which she applied to 'the word of God'. Becoming a preacher was not, she says, an easy path, being a woman and a single parent (on the margins of 'the family'). From what these leaders say, the struggle to value family diversity is not contradicted by a foundationalist understanding of sexual difference either.

In the pastors' view, it is in men that the greatest challenge is posed. The 'perfect man', far from being a given, as one might expect from the essentialist view, is achieved after an arduous process. If in women the work of self (which is done by the Lord) consists of 'awakening' their gifts, men must be 'restored' and 'perfected' in the Way of Jesus. Women, as the literature points out, bring men closer to the church so that they may assume their responsibilities.

These elements and outlines of 'Faith and Family' have to do with raising the family and, in truth, our priority is marriage and within marriage it is the man, because we have seen that if the man changes, the family changes and if the patriarch of an extended family changes, everyone changes. (Maria del Pilar, interview 16 July 2019)

That has been the cry of many women, to say 'Please! We need you to work with our husbands, our partners', because we are aware that if the image of God is restored in that man, he will assume his role, he will assume his responsibility and the situation will change, the relationship with the wife will change, and obviously the relationship with the children and the situation of the family on all fronts. Economically, emotionally, physically, in all aspects of family life. (Carlos Caisapanta, interview 1 July 2019)

The group Hombres Fieles (Faithful Men) aims to strengthen them as 'heads', re-establishing their authority with love and respect; as Tonny Tamayo, liturgy and communication coordinator, explains, if everyone in the family assumed their role, the Church would have nothing to do.[6]

For Pastor Lay, machismo and violence 'are sins'; authority based on abuse of power and uncontrolled emotions must be rebuilt on other foundations. By involving them in the home as leaders, the church imposes 'moral restrictions on gender abuses such as domestic violence, alcoholism or infidelity' (Algranti, 2008b).

Carlos Caisapanta (interview 1 July 2019) describes the work done in the counselling centres so that single men take on the role of 'intermediaries' between God and their future family. The important thing is to instil a type of manliness which is committed to the running of the household, exemplified by the pastoral couple.

The laws, in line with Christian values, but above all the Church, have the task of preventing, restoring, training and mediating for men. For Pastor Wilson Salguero, they 'are the providers of the family, the priests of the home, those who bring the principles of the Word of God to the family' (interview July 2019). Pastor Joselito Orellana, at the Perfect Man Congress, uses biblical quotations:

> Paul says that the man is the head of the woman, just as Christ is the head of the man and not only that, but the Father is the head of Christ. Submission has only one purpose in the family, the key word being protection. The wife is to submit to the man's authority just as the man submits to Christ. (Joselito Orellana, lecture, June 2019)

Patriarchal subordination is portrayed as a chain of hierarchy that eliminates asymmetries through the love and trust of women (and their sons and daughters) towards their husbands, whose moral and spiritual obligation is to look after them. Despite their gifts, women are thus perceived as physically and intellectually vulnerable.

> Submission is cyclical, it is never unidirectional, which is why Paul in Ephesians 5 says that submission must be mutual. The direct implication in

Colossians is to be like the Lord. I must submit to Christ and in that model, in that paragon, in that example, in that mould, the wife has to submit to me and I have to exercise authority over her, over my children, but with that attitude of tenderness, of protection, understanding that submission, the exercise of authority, is to protect. (Joselito Orellana, conference, June 2019)

It is clear that, more than being 'cyclical' or 'mutual', subjugation is presented as a ladder, with the top rung, the divine, accessible only to men. As Mary Daily once argued, 'if god is man, then man is god' (1973, quoted by Russell 1997). Theological authority, legitimate knowledge and power, whether granted or earned, results in an entrenchment of the patriarchal order that normalises the power structure that runs through society. Male dominance, as feminist theology warns, is sacralised, whilst the connection between difference and inequality is diluted in the Church's project to instil this structure as the way to face life's difficulties.

'Raising the family': the organisational gamble

Naturalised sexual difference, gender traditionalisation and a sex-gender order make sense under the so-called 'family approach',[7] which for the IEVI represents a shift towards education and childhood. The pastors maintain that the modern world is in chaos and that the way to rein that in is to re-establish order in the family and to ensure the transmission of faith from generation to generation. The power for social change shifts from individuals to families.

Our primary task is to restore families and relationships. To restore the image and likeness that God placed in every human being, understanding that the family is the nucleus of society. If we restore, through the Word of God, the image and likeness of God and the relationships in the family, automatically society, the country and its institutions will change. The family is fundamental. (Wilson Salguero, interview 10 July 2019)

Restoration is related to two discourses: theological, which expresses the relationship between the Christian family and God's plan, and social, which seeks to 'heal' society through faith. The men and women pastors view the family, God's primary creation, as immutable and ahistorical. The biblical foundation of what is 'right', 'normal', 'natural' is shaped as a narrative field for interpreting experiences and generates social and political meanings.

It is from this standpoint that, since 2010, IEVI has been reaching out to other churches and pastors through materials based on the principles of 'Faith and Family':[8]

For about three years now, God has been speaking to us in a concrete way . . ., because 99.9% of the counselling was on family issues, family conflicts, difficult situations. God has been directing us in that sense, to be more intentional, to work and disciple families, because a healthy family and a healthy church also contribute to a healthy society. God has been directing us to heal families (. . .) Throughout biblical history, from genesis to apocalypse, God manifests himself through and for families. (Teresita Lay, interview 11 June 2019)

Two arguments are to be found here: first, despite attacks, the traditional family has proved resilient, and, second, it is the best relational structure for achieving 'inner healing', which is crucial in the evangelical world-view (Algranti, 2008b). The discipleship plan, pathway and materials – disseminated on the web as 'Fe y Familia. Hogares Fuertes' (Faith and Family. Strong Homes) – is led by Pastor Ana María Ampuero.[9] For Patricia García, a social outreach worker at IEVI, they involve 'having the guidance and direction of God in the family'.[10]

The approach is underpinned by a 'cellular' structure, imported from Costa Rica (see Arguedas-Ramírez in this volume), which aims to move the church into neighbourhoods and homes in order to form networks under its supervision. As Algranti (2008a) notes, this vision actualises affection and leadership; it expresses 'the capacity to influence daily life, habits, routines and customs that shape the fabric of experience, allowing religions to transcend the model of the *ideal community* to become *real communities*' (p. 184). To this end, different strategies are proposed: counselling, where 'first aid' is practised (the 'Faith and Family Kiosk'), the creation of a 'family altar' in each home, and the formation of local 'cells' from which sister churches are born. For Pastor Carlos Caisapanta, this vision is complex, with misgivings over commitment, training and sharing 'among' families. Furthermore, Iñaquito receives people from all over the city, and has not managed to implement decentralisation. For this reason, the figure of the pastors remains key; in the words of several leaders during the interviews, rather than being 'Christocentric', the organisation remains 'pastor-centric'.

Religious citizenship: 'healing and liberating our society'

The 'degeneration of the family', in domestic violence, infidelity, abandonment or male irresponsibility, is understood to be directly connected to the loss of clear gender identities and roles and homosexual deviance. The activism of ConMisHijosNoTeMetas mobilises ministries and followers against the 'attack on the family and children' in 'gender' legislation (sexual and reproductive rights, sex education, equal marriage). For leaders, all of these go against Natural Law, God's plan and 'original design'.

Contacts with Peruvian fundamentalist evangelicals played their part, as did visits by other political operators from the international far-right, whose speeches shifted from victimhood on behalf of the nation's minors and offended parents, to direct attacks on feminism.[11]

For Pastor Salguero, awareness needs raising about a problem that affects 'the whole of society': 'the dictatorship of gender'. In a fiery sermon, prior to the first mobilisations in 2017, during the constitution of the 'Movimiento Vida y Familia' (Life and Family Movement – MVyF), Fernando Lay warned:

> Brothers, this is hellish and diabolical. What do they tell teenagers? . . . They give 'so-called' sex education, but they are promoting promiscuity, the beginning of very early sexual relations, and teenage pregnancies and venereal diseases are multiplying. And above all this is happening behind parents' backs (. . .) What shall we do for the honour of the Lord and the benediction of our children and future generations? God chose parents, family and adult society to guide and protect children and young people, to bring them to the knowledge of God, to forge their values and character and an eternal purpose in life. And God will call us to account on this . . . In practical terms, we have to protect our rights against this encroachment of the state and the diabolical gender ideology. (17 September 2017)

Religious freedom, the traditional banner of the Protestant camp against Catholic primacy in the state, is pitted against 'the dictatorship'. At the heart of the struggle is the moral regeneration of the citizenry, counterposed, through multiple and extreme examples (marriage with animals, adult males who claim to be girls and are adopted by lesbians, training in the use of condoms in schools or the defence of paedophilia as a 'sexual orientation'), with anti-discrimination legislation or sex education for the prevention of violence or pregnancy. This mission is divided into two ultimately intertwining threads – citizenship and religion.

'Strategic secularism' allows for challenges of public policies and legislative changes (Vaggione, 2005) in the name of children's civil defence and parental rights. It stands against 'ideological colonisation', another transnational appeal particularly effective in Latin America. Pastor and MVyF leader Cesar Parra comments:

> The MVyF is inspired by Christianity, but it is made up of Ecuadorian citizens, in terms of the exercise of freedom of citizenship. Although it comes from the evangelical sector, it is not owned by the evangelical church, it is

owned by the citizens. I, although I am a pastor, I am religious, I am exercising my rights as an Ecuadorian citizen here (. . .) I insist that this is a civil organisation and that it is shaping up to be so. Of Christian inspiration, undeniably. (Interview, 23 April 2019)

In the case of the Constitutional Court's approval of equal marriage, the legal defence invoked the constitution and the rule of law in requesting the proceedings be dismissed and a judge recused. The legal commission presented an appeal for clarification and extension of the sentences before the Constitutional Court, a complaint to the Council for Citizen Participation and Social Control, and an appeal for the president to override it. It invoked 'freedom', 'national sovereignty' and even the 'popular uprising', a term which holds significance for indigenous and popular movements in the country's (post)colonial history. Words like 'rebellion', 'resistance' and 'non-compliance' entered the populist lexicon of protest. The rights of parents over their children (against the state) were placed above the right to identity, equality and non-discrimination, to self-determined (not forced) sexuality and motherhood, and to protection from violence.

Verdi Sulca (2019), a pastor and anti-fundamentalist researcher, explains the composition of the evangelical camp. The initial prominence of coordinated, prominent pastors with media reach, such as Fredy Guerrero, Jaime Cornejo, Fernando Lay and Estuardo López, saw an addition of groups, collectives or foundations 'in favour of citizens' rights', blurring their religious character and political affiliation. The insistence on 'defending rights' and 'not being against anyone' gave them a pluralist, democratic appearance, far removed from fundamentalism and discrimination (Vega, 2017). Other evangelicals, with political and economic power, involved themselves as professionals and businessmen associated with parties with links to the legislature. At the base of this chain were local pastors, less clear-cut, more radicalised and antagonistic in their message, with substantial rallying power. IEVI belongs to the first group but presents itself to be a church which is active on all fronts.

To deal with the merging of the religious with the political, recourse was made to biblical authority, religious cleansing as a brake on the degradation and moral corruption of politics (less so the market) and the healing of public life (Semán, 2019). Christian politicisation was presented as a mission, an exercise in purification; the previous detachment from matters of the world gave way to a lively political interest in the name of the majorities. After the approval of equal marriage, the Sangolquí Declaration, the culmination of a summit that brought together some seventy pastors and national-level leaders of denominations, leaders of la Confraternidad

Evangélica Ecuatoriana (Ecuadorian Evangelical Fellowship) and el Cuerpo de Pastores de Quito (the Quito Pastors' Corps), affirmed:

> That Ecuadorian society is suffering from a moral and legal decadence that threatens the Constitution and the rule of law and makes the approval of equal marriage by the Constitutional Court viable. This calls the Christian church and religious organisations once more to defend the principles and values of our beloved country. (Sangolquí Declaration, 2019, recital 4)

In this way, evangelicals were identified, not as just another voice, but as the one that embodied the moral and civil integrity of the country at a time when the country was in the throes of emergency. The defence of 'the family' reappeared as the foundation of society.

> The Churches, as an institution in concept and structure, actively provide support in the form of people and resources to carry out a grand civil mobilisation to heal and liberate our society, from its fundamental nucleus, which is the family. (Sangolquí Declaration, 2019, recital 5)

Religion, whether Evangelical or Catholic, provides the necessary values against the general political and institutional crisis (Morán Faúndes and Peñas Defago, 2020). This implies ignoring or hiding any kind of internal discussion within the religion, as well as rekindling the struggle against/ for the state through an escalation that ascends from pastoral and ministerial coordination to civil (legal, social, educational, communicational) action and finally to the selection and training of candidates with a political vocation (Vega et al., 2020).

Though in Ecuador the anti-gender movement has not contributed to the formation of an evangelical party, it has relaunched the 'politics of moralisation', which brings believers closer to the 'doings of the world' (Panotto, 2015). This has re-established links between religious operators and political and institutional positions.

The links between state and religious citizenship (of the Kingdom) are at some points laid out.

> It is true that the Church as an institution does not get involved in governing, but Christians as citizens, as children of God, the Lord himself sends us to be the light of the world. The light guides, we are salt of the earth. Salt preserves against corruption. And we do that because we have civil rights and freedom to express our faith. In other words, we have two obligations, not one. Render unto Caesar the things that are Caesar's; and unto God the things that are God's. (Fernando Lay, Sunday service, June 2019)

Religious citizenship, the very advent of the Kingdom of God, inspired by the Old Testament, reworks sovereignty along the lines of the connecting threads between church, state and civil society, establishing a mandate for the believer. The IEVI, in addition to giving spiritual and practical guidance, becomes a civil actor that affirms faith to be the unquestionable foundation for all, independent of beliefs or their consequences.

In sermons and at marches, where self-victimising and/or anti-feminist discourses are more apparent, the climate of polarisation combines pathologisation and deformation of the enemy, exaltation of the supposed national, and/or anti-colonial spirit and Spiritual Warmongering.

> There is a many thousand-year-old war between light and darkness, between God and Satan, and we are there to decide which side we are on. When there is a war and a nation is in danger, let's say Ecuador is being threatened by an attack . . . an Ecuadorian who does not stand up to defend his country is a traitor, a national traitor. And as well as being Ecuadorian citizens, we are citizens of the Kingdom and whoever does not defend the honour of God and the values of the Kingdom of God, is also a traitor. (Fernando Lay, Sunday service, June 2019)

Despite the political stakes and as mobilisations abated, some IEVI leaders rethought the relationship between the church, the word and politics. One woman pastor, whose name is not disclosed by express agreement, for example, acknowledged the pressure exercised over the church services (interview, July 2019). For her, the mission is to 'build bridges', and she acknowledges that 'unprepared' 'anti-gender' positioning closes them off.

Conclusion

The IEVI is a key actor in understanding the current neoconservative take on gender and its eminently religious delineation in Ecuador. Its vision of gender identities, sexuality and the family is not only a particular set of beliefs used to explain and guide believers in their problems, but is also a lever to influence policies and public life. While Catholic fundamentalism has maintained a permanent anti-feminist offensive, which increased in the 1990s, evangelicalism has now joined the fight against 'gender' in the name of defending the family.

In the IEVI, the internal work in ministries and family discipleship lays the doctrinal and social foundations that regulate the 'healing' of the community, which can be extrapolated to the broader society. The problems and difficulties brought about by modernity are seen as the effects of diffuse forces of evil. In the face of these, a model of order is reclaimed, a seemingly benign and tolerant patriarchal scheme, which incorporates a depoliticised version of machismo, which reinstates the asymmetry between women and men and the traditionalisation of gender attributes, disconnecting them from any interplay between power and inequality. It also restores the exclusion and rejection of homosexuality, lesbianism and trans identities, on the assumption that these destroy the self, particularly childhood and youth (which is naturally heterosexual and binary). The subordination of minors is achieved by appealing to paternal responsibility, by promoting sexuality as dangerous, and by denying education as a path to autonomy and self-determination. In this way, the churches ignore the causes and processes that generate inequalities, discrimination and violence, which, in fact, they contribute to deepening.

To face 'evil', their proposition is to strengthen the family according to the 'image and likeness' that God has created. As many pastors repeat, when the perspective of the 'image of God has been lost', when the subjects lack foundation and do not know their origin or purpose, when they 'lose the fear and knowledge of God', they are vulnerable to any ideology, because, as one pastor reminds us, 'the enemy of our God never stops working and those of us who know the truth have let him advance' (interview with Wilson Salguero, 10 July 2019). The 'family approach' is an internal response that provides affection and guidance while weaving connections, always within the margins of what is right. Such an approach, moderate in appearance within the IEVI, has become a pillar of resistance leaning towards the authoritarian.

The doctrine involves rights, laws and programmes that confront 'sexual democracy'. Advocating an anti-state discourse ('less state and more family') while intervening in the social state, speaking secular and pluralist language while propagating reactionary religiosity or moralising politics, by appealing to the righteousness and purification of sex while strengthening vertical and absolutist convictions, are all ways in which the new transnational wave against 'Gender Ideology' contributes to de-democratisation and authoritarian advance, almost always in coalition with extreme right-wing forces. Evangelical fundamentalism thus seeks to interweave itself in the Catholic project of shaping the citizenry.

In many cases, 'anti-gender' campaigns and movements express themselves as an open and conscious offensive against feminism and political actors of sex-gender diversity, whose deformation has been a constant, while on other occasions it does so in a veiled or oblique way through positive reasoning and arguments framed to be in defence of the family, childhood, the nation or morality. Feminist power in the region has made it difficult to popularise the 'anti-feminism' commonly found in other contexts, although this would merit further research.

Notes

1. Lorena Castellanos, Sofía Yépez and Joseph Salazar conducted interviews and contributed to the analysis in the project 'Fundamentalismo religioso y disputas en torno al género y la sexualidad. La avanzada evangélica en el panorama sociopolítico ecuatoriano', Flacso Ecuador.

2. For 'biological determinism', human sexuation, of enormous diversity and physiological complexity, predicts and explains attributes, personality and behaviour which, against all evidence, are presented as immutable. In religious terms, Natural Law establishes both sexual binarism and (compulsory) heterosexuality. 'Foundationalism', while conceding that sexual identity is constructed, assumes that it is constantly constructed across cultures (Nicholson, 2003). Both determinism and foundationalism contribute to 'naturalising' inequalities.

3. Despite criticisms of the universalism of the concept of 'patriarchy' and the 'sex-gender system', I retrieve it here to account for its historical and intersectional character in the current offensive, which appeals to the supremacy and control of the authoritative 'fathers' of the nation.

4. I adopt Shäfer's (1992) typology here, which distinguishes historic Protestantism, Evangelicalism and (neo-)Pentecostalism.

5. Discussion: 'Universal Women's Rights', https://www.facebook.com/watch/?v=403919654403213. Audiovisual programme 'Entre Nos . . .', featuring pastors and IEVI experts.

6. Entre Nos (2021): 'Padre, sublime responsabilidad'. https://www.facebook.com/iglesiaievi/videos/500351964537127

7. This has already appeared in public policy under Rafael Correa, when the sexual and reproductive rights policy, in force since 2012, was repealed and replaced with the Plan Familia (2015), under the influence of Opus Dei.

8. They mention contacts with pastors such as J. Otis Ledbetter in the United States, the exchange of materials, collected on the church's website, and the contribution of the Centro Cristiano de Cuenca and the Cornejo pastors, leaders in 'anti-gender' politicisation.

9. https://www.iglesiaievi.org/sitio/fe-familia/

10. Entre Nos (2021): Derecho Universales Mujer. https://www.facebook.com/watch?ref=search&v=1443782495988685&external_log_id=1f81eb0f-6c19-44e9-8440-a44b3a462de6&q=ievi%20patricia%20garcia%20mujeres%20de%20influencia

11. Among them are the Peruvian pastor Christian Rosas, supposedly an international gender expert, Amparo Medina, an Ecuadorian Catholic self-proclaimed 'pro-life feminist', and the Argentinean reactionary liberal Agustín Laje. All of them are outspoken critics of feminism, radical compared to some IEVI members, as revealed in the debate with the former in 2017 (see www.facebook.com/iglesiaievi/videos/730375010489676). Over time, the anti-feminism of the campaigns becomes more radical, as shown by the exchanges with members of the Spanish

VOX party. See, for example, the forum 'Femenina sí, feminista no', 8 March 2020, https://www.facebook.com/FamiliaEcuador2020/posts/2851073225165169

References

Algranti, J. (2007). Tres posiciones de la mujer cristiana. Estudio sobre las relaciones de género en la narrativa maestra del pentecostalismo. *Ciencias Sociales y Religión, 9*(9), 165–93.

Algranti, J. (2008a). Cuando lo invisible gobierna lo visible: etnografía de los cultos de prosperidad en la iglesia evangélica pentecostal Rey de Reyes. *Perspectivas Latinoamericanas, 5*(12), 37–67.

Algranti, J. (2008b). De la sanidad del cuerpo a la sanidad del alma: estudio sobre la lógica de construcción de las identidades colectivas en el neo-pentecostalismo argentino. *Religião & Sociedade, 28*(2), 179–209.

Bastián, J. P. (2006). De los protestantismos históricos a los pentecostalismos latinoamericanos: Análisis de una mutación religiosa. *Revista de Ciencias Sociales,* (16), 38–54.

Bracke, S. and Paternotte, D. (2018). Desentrañando el pecado del género. In S. Bracke and D. Paternotte (eds), *¡Habemus género! La iglesia católica e ideología de género* (pp. 8–25). Género y política en América Latina.

Brown, W. (2018). Neoliberalism's Frankenstein: Authoritarian Freedom in Twenty-First Century Democracies. *Critical Times, 1*(1), 60–79.

Brusco, E. (1995). *The Reformation of Machismo: Evangelical Conversion and Gender in Colombia.* University of Texas.

Cabezas, M. G. (2015). *Conversiones religiosas en la clase media quiteña: el renacer de una nueva identidad social espiritual cristiana evangélica.* Tesis de Maestría en Ciencias Sociales con mención en Sociología, FLACSO Ecuador.

Carbonelli, M. A. (2009). Desde el barrio: perspectivas acerca de la actividad política de pastores evangélicos en el cono urbano bonaerense. *Ciencias Sociales y Religión/Ciências Sociais e Religião, 11*(1), 107–29.

Carreaga-Pérez, G. (2016). Moral Panic and Gender Ideology in Latin America. *Religion and Gender, 6*(2), 251–5.

Ceballos, R. (2008). Pobreza, desarrollo y espiritualidad en experiencias religiosas pentecostales. In G. Zalpa and H. Egil Offerdal (eds), *¿El reino de Dios es de este mundo?: el papel ambiguo de las religiones en la lucha contra la pobreza.* Siglo del Hombre Editores/Clacso.

Corrêa, S. (ed.). (2019). *Políticas Antigénero en América Latina: Estudios de Caso.* https://sxpolitics.org/GPAL/#

Fassin, E. (2005). *Democracia Sexual, 1–8.* https://es.slideshare.net/estebangalvan/democracia-sexual-por-eric-fassin

Fassin, E. (2009). La democracia sexual y el conflicto de las civilizaciones. *Género, sexualidades y política democrática.* México: UNAM y Pueg/Colmex (Cuadernos Simone de Beauvoir).

Gago, V. (2019). *La potencia feminista. O el deseo de cambiarlo todo.* Tinta Limón.

Garma Navarro, C. (2004). *Buscando el espíritu. Pentecostalismo en Iztapalapa y la Ciudad de México*. Universidad Autónoma Metropolitana.

Graff, A. and Korolczuk, E. (2021). *Anti-Gender Politics in the Populist Moment*. Routledge.

Grzebalska, W., Kováts, E. and Petö, A. (2017). *Gender as Symbolic Glue: How 'Gender' Became an Umbrella Term for the Rejection of the (Neo)Liberal Order*. https:// hal.archives-ouvertes.fr/hal-03232926/document

Guamán, J. (2011). *Evangélicos en el Ecuador. Tipologías y formas institucionales del protestantismo*. Abya – Yala/Universidad Politécnica Salesiana.

Latinobarómetro. (2018). *Las religiones en tiempos del Papa Francisco*. Corporación Latinobarómetro.

Lindhardt, M. (2009). Poder, Género y Cambio Cultural en el Pentecostalismo Chileno. *Revista Cultura y Religión*, 718(4727), 94–112.

Machado, M. das D. C., Mariz, C. L. and Carranza, B. (2021). Articulaciones político-religiosas entre Brasil-USA: derecha y sionismo cristianos. *Ciencias Sociales Y Religión/Ciências Sociais E Religião*, 23(00).

Mahmood, S. (2019). Teoría feminista y el agente social dócil: algunas reflexiones sobre el renacimiento islámico en Egipto. *Papeles del CEIC*, 1(202), 1–31.

Molyneux, M. (2006). Justicia de género, ciudadanía y diferencia en América Latina. Studia historica. *Historia contemporánea*, (28), 181–211.

Morán Faúndes, J. M. and Peñas Defago, M. A. (2020) Una mirada regional de las articulaciones neoconservadoras. In A. Torres (ed.), *Derechos en riesgo en América Latina. 11 estudios sobre grupos neoconservadores*. Fundación Rosa Luxemburgo y Ediciones Desde Abajo.

Nicholson, L. (2003). La interpretación del concepto de género. In S. Tubert (ed.), *Del sexo al género. Los equívocos de un concepto*. Cátedra.

Nyhagen, L. (2015). Conceptualizing Lived Religious Citizenship: A Case-Study of Christian and Muslim Women in Norway and the United Kingdom. *Citizenship Studies*, 19(6–7), 768–84.

Panotto, N. (2015). Religión. Ciudadanía y espacio público: un acercamiento socio-antropológico y teológico. *Perspectivas Internacionales*, 11(1), 64–87.

Pecheny, M., Jones, D. and Ariza, L. (2016). Sexual Politics and Religious Actors in Argentina. *Religion and Gender*, 6(2), 205–25.

Pérez Guadalupe, J. L. (2018). ¿Políticos Evangélicos o Evangélicos Políticos? Los Nuevos Modelos de Conquista Política de los Evangélicos. In J. L. Pérez Guadalupe and S. Grundberger (eds), *Evangélicos y poder en América Latina*, (11–106). Instituto de Estudios Social Cristianos.

Russell, L. M. (1997). *Bajo un techo libertad: la autoridad en la teología*. DEI.

Salazar, J. (2019). *'Ideología de género' y nuevos activismos conservadores en Ecuador. Entre el discurso y la politización de los actores religiosos*. Tesis Maestría en Ciencias Sociales con mención en Género y Desarrollo. FLACSO Ecuador.

Sandoval, M. (2005). *Protestantismo, género y nuevas identidades: sentidos y prácticas en un centro cristiano benéfico en Quito*. Tesis Maestría en Ciencias Sociales con mención en Antropología: FLACSO Ecuador.

Schäfer, H. (1992). *Protestantismo y crisis social en América Central*. Editorial Departamento Ecuménico de Investigaciones.

Semán, P. (2019). ¿Quiénes son? ¿Por qué crecen? ¿En qué creen? Pentecostalismo y política en América Latina. *Nueva sociedad*, 280, 26–46.

Torres, A. (2019). *De la marea rosa a la marea conservadora y autoritaria en América Latina: desafíos feministas*. FES-ILDIS. http://library.fes.de/pdf-files/bueros/quito/15682.pdf

Torres, A. (ed.). (2020). *Derechos en riesgo en América Latina. 11 estudios sobre grupos neoconservadores*. Fundación Rosa Luxemburgo y Ediciones Desde Abajo.

Vaggione, J. M. (2005). Reactive Politicization and Religious Dissidence: The Political Mutations of the Religious. *Social Theory and Practice*, 31(2), 233–55.

Vaggione, J. M. (2017). La Iglesia Católica frente a la política sexual: la configuración de una ciudadanía religiosa. *Cadernos Pagu*, 50. http://www.scielo.br/scielo. php?script=sci_arttext&pid=S0104-83332017000200303&lng=en&nrm=iso>

Vega, C. (2017). ¿Quién teme al feminismo? A propósito de la 'ideología de género' y otras monstruosidades sexuales en Ecuador y América Latina. *Sin Permiso*. www.sinpermiso.info/textos/quien-teme-alfeminismo-a-proposito-de-la-ideologia-de-genero-yotras-monstruosidades-sexuales-en

Vega, C. (2019). La 'ideología de género' y la renaturalización privatizadora de lo social. In M. Maher (ed.), *Fundamentalismos religiosos, derechos y democracia*. FLACSO Ecuador.

Vega, C. (2020). Sexo, vida y familia. La corriente conservadora/fundamentalista en Ecuador. In Grupo Permanente de Trabajo Alternativas al Desarrollo (eds), *Nuevas derechas autoritarias. Conversaciones sobre el ciclo político actual en América Latina*. Fundación Rosa Luxemburgo/Abya Yala.

Vega, C. (2021). El género diabólico. Evangélicos, naturaleza femenina y diseño original. In E. Vázquez, L. Coba and I. Yánez (eds), *Brujas, salvajes y rebeldes. Mujeres perseguidas en entornos de moralización y criminalización en Ecuador*. Instituto de Estudios Ecologistas del Tercer Mundo.

Vega, C., Castellanos, L. and Salazar, J. (2020). Poner orden en la familia y en el país: La politización reactiva y la consolidación de la articulación evangélica en Ecuador. In H. Salazar and D. Castro (eds), *América Latina en tiempos revueltos. Claves y luchas renovadas frente al giro conservador*. Libertad Bajo Palabra y Bajo Tierra.

Verdi Sulca, J. L. (2019). *El sistema discursivo del fundamentalismo evangélico ecuatoriano y su influencia política en contra de la llamada ideología de género*, tesis Maestría en Estudios de la Cultura Mención en Género y Cultura. Universidad Andina Simón Bolívar Ecuador.

Viveros, M. (2017). Deshacer y hacer la Ideología de género. *Sexualidad, Salud y Sociedad. Revista Latinoamericana*. 1984–6487, n. 27–dic., 118–27.

Wade, P., Urrea, F. and Viveros, M. (eds). (2008). *Raza, etnicidad y sexualidades. Ciudadanía y multiculturalismo en América Latina*. Universidad Nacional de Colombia-Centro de Estudios Sociales (CES).

Wynarczyk, H. (2018). Argentina: ¿Vino Nuevo en Odres Viejos? Evangélicos y Política. In J. L. Pérez Guadalupe and S. Grundberger (eds), *Evangélicos y poder en América Latina* (pp. 107–40). Instituto de Estudios Social Cristianos.

SEVEN

The Anti-Feminist Narrative of the Hindu Right in India

Hira Naaz

This chapter focuses on the linkages between anti-feminism and Hindu religious fundamentalism in contemporary India by drawing attention to the activism of 'Pinjra Tod' (Break the Cage), a feminist movement which originated in Delhi in 2015, a year after the right-wing government of Bharatiya Janata Party (BJP, Indian People's Party) ascended to political power in India. The research for this chapter was conducted by consulting texts written by Hindutva ideologues and activists, historical accounts, journalistic pieces, news, survey reports, academic research articles and internet sources. The chapter argues that the Hindu Right, in its bid to construct India as a Hindu nation, weaves a grand anti-feminist narrative that makes the oppression and subjection of women central to its ideology.

Indian Women in Public Spaces

On 16 December 2012, a twenty-two-year-old woman named Jyoti Singh was brutally gang raped in a private bus in Delhi, the capital of India. The horrific incident followed by the victim's death provoked national outrage, sparking countrywide protests with public anger directed at state and central governments on account of their inability to ensure women's safety in Indian cities where rape cases were perennially on the rise (BBC News, 2012). An educated, middle-class, caste Hindu woman, Jyoti was represented by different groups and the Indian media as 'everywoman' whose tragedy became a matter of national shame (Shandilya, 2015). In an ideal scenario, such mobilisations ought to have contributed to creating safer public spaces for women. However, they instead resulted in a heightened and fully legitimised control of women's lives by the institutions of family, school, university and the state. It was women's presence in public spaces and not their ability to access the same without peril and fear that became a matter of public and state concern (Phadke et al., 2013). The onus of their safety was once again put on women themselves, as they were expected to promptly act on security measures such as calling emergency helpline numbers or pressing the panic buttons[1] given on public vehicles if they sensed a potential threat (Soni, 2016).

The growing anxieties about women's safety in city spaces have led to an exponential rise in the installation of smart surveillance solutions such as AI-enabled CCTV cameras in streets, on public transport and in buildings across all major cities of India, even though crime rates refuse to decline (Pankaj, 2022). These mechanisms add to the layers of policing and monitoring that women in India experience in their everyday lives, and become part of the constant patriarchal gaze they are subjected to (Krishnan, 2015). The notion of state responsibility to 'protect' women is intimately linked to the ideologies of paternalistic protectionism at the cost of individual freedom and agency. Instead of analysing the specific structures and ideologies that reproduce violent masculinities and perpetrate the cycle of gendered crimes, the mainstream discourses around women's safety in public spaces have discouraged women's unconditional use of the same (Soni, 2016; Viswanath and Mehrotra, 2007). In this manner, they complement the anti-feminist discourses circulated by political actors who present feminism as a Western concept not applicable to Indian society (Ambekar, 2019) and the rise in sexual crimes against women as by-products of a derivative Western modernity or a failure to emulate Indian values. For instance, a number of Indian politicians have frequently uttered callous remarks on rape by invoking the familiar tradition-versus-modernity trope. A BJP leader named Kailash Vijayvargiya justified rape of modern urban women by citing the example of Sita's abduction[2] in the ancient Sanskrit epic of *Ramayana* to argue that women who cross their boundaries (by travelling alone, going out after dark, etc.) pay the price, that is, get raped (*India Today*, 2013). Another BJP politician, Manohar Lal Khattar, commented: 'If they (women) want freedom, why don't they just roam around naked? Freedom has to be limited. These short clothes are western influences. Our country's tradition asks girls to dress decently' (*The Citizen*, 2014).

Amidst the amplified calls for protection of women by the state, and the rationalisation of sexist restrictions on women's freedom, the movement 'Pinjra Tod' arrived on the scene with a feminist approach to the questions of urban mobility and women's right to the city.

Breaking the Cage: Methods and Challenges

Pinjra Tod, translated as 'Break the Cage', was founded as a collective primarily composed of women students and alumni of colleges across the national capital region of Delhi. It was formed to take collective action against gendered restrictions on women's urban mobility imposed by hostels and paying guest accommodations (Borpujari, 2016). The movement was born in August 2015 when the University of Jamia Millia Islamia in Delhi issued a notice barring the female residents of its hostels from staying out after 8 pm (Kausar, 2015). The incident exposed other similar institutions where women's hostels had stricter rules than men's hostels (Azad, 2015). Authorities at these institutions routinely interfered in the lives of female students, asking them personal questions about their whereabouts and commenting on their dress and lifestyle choices in the guise of concern for their security. This has contributed to a deeply embedded culture of moral policing, victim-blaming and infantilisation of adult females in Indian societies. Since 2016, Pinjra Tod has inspired and supported women from universities and colleges in many other cities to take forward the fight against curfews on women, sexual harassment, sexist dress codes, higher prices for women's hostels, and all other kinds of gender-based discrimination at campuses.

Pinjra Tod's assertion of women's right to freely and safely access public spaces at all times has led to evening rallies, night vigils, protests and public gatherings by the collective's members during curfew hours imposed on women (usually after 7.30 pm). The women marchers carry placards, shout feminist slogans, play drums, sing songs of *azaadi* (freedom) and perform impromptu dances as acts of feminist resistance (BBC News, 2015). In the book *Why Loiter?* (2011), the authors discuss the stakes involved in women's visibility in public spaces in the Indian context.

> 'Respectable' women could be potentially defiled in a public space while 'non-respectable' women are themselves a potential source of contamination to the 'purity' of public spaces and, therefore, the city. For the so-called 'respectable' woman this classification is always fraught with some amount of tension, for should she transgress the carefully policed 'inside-outside' boundaries permitted to her, she could so easily slip into becoming the 'public' woman – the threat to the sacrality of public space. (Phadke et al., 2011, p. 27)

On the night of 23 September 2016, during a night march and vigil by Pinjra Tod in North Delhi, the women participants were interrupted by some male members of the Akhil Bharatiya Vidyarthi Parishad (ABVP, All Indian Student Council). ABVP is a right-wing student organisation that competes in student-body elections in higher education institutions across India, and it is described as the student wing of the Rashtriya Swayamsevak Sangh (RSS, National Self-help Organisation), a Hindu nationalist organisation (Ramachandran, 2017). The women who were present at the Pinjra Tod march reported that some ABVP members arrived at the scene and started harassing them using obscene gestures and words. They made personal attacks on their moral character, and flashed a currency note in front of them to suggest that no 'respectable' woman would be out on streets at that hour (*The Times of India*, 2016). Members of the Pinjra Tod collective have faced such attacks on a regular basis from ABVP. They form part of the larger right-wing attempts to suppress secular, feminist and democratic voices in the university space (Mody, 2016). ABVP has repeatedly adopted violence to silence criticism and wield authority at university campuses. Investigative journalism and the Delhi police both confirmed its involvement in the violent assault on left-wing students that occurred on 5 January 2020 at Jawaharlal Nehru University (Khan and Jain, 2020; *The Wire*, 2020).

ABVP attempts to present itself as a progressive organisation in favour of gender equality. Yet it has inflicted physical violence on students for celebrating the anniversary of gender equality protests and for requests to stop shaming sexual harassment survivors (Malu, 2018). In its 2018 manifesto for the Delhi University Students' Union (DUSU) elections, ABVP stressed the need for women's safety and gender sensitisation by proposing to offer self-defence training courses for women at the campus (*The Pioneer*, 2018). The manifesto treats women's safety as their own responsibility as discussed in the beginning of this chapter, and there is no mention of the challenges faced by members of the LGBTQI communities. It also states ABVP's objective to start lectures on nationalism at the campus for university students (*Hindustan Times*, 2018). In practice, the ABVP works in accordance with the Hindu fundamentalist ideology of its parent organisation, the RSS (discussed later) which is notorious for its ultra-conservative and anti-feminist stance.

In reaction to Pinjra Tod's protests against the ABVP turning the university into a hostile masculine space, the Hindu student organisation has often shouted 'Bharat Maata Ki Jai!' (Victory for Mother India). Such a patriotic slogan would appear to be a fairly misplaced or irrelevant reaction to a feminist protest if one lacks an understanding of the intricate bond between the forces of anti-feminism and Hindu nationalism in India. To delineate the relationship between the two ideologies, the following sections will shed light on the right-wing-led Hindu Nationalism or Hindutva in India.

Hindu Nationalism or Hindutva

Hindutva is a fundamentalist politico-ideological movement of Hinduism that embodies the foundational principles, aims and struggles of the Hindu far-right in India (Chakrabarty and Jha, 2020). It is the predominant form of Hindu nationalism that relies on Hindu majoritarianism and myths of Hindu supremacy. Hindutva joins the ilk of many right-wing populist movements around the world that thrive on the rhetoric of racial/ethnic purity, nativist claims, corrupt foreign influences, and a masculinist protection of territorial, religious and cultural boundaries. The movement has gained traction in contemporary India since the formation of the Bharatiya Janata Party (BJP) as the nation's central ruling government, after its sweeping win in the 2014 general elections and continuation through the next term from 2019 to the present day. Gita Sahgal (2020) has noted that, historically, Hindutva had to wait and struggle for a long time to gain mass appeal, unlike its European contemporaries in Italy, Spain and Germany that rapidly acquired popular support and power in the post-First World War period. It continues to meet with significant resistance from secular and feminist groups like Pinjra Tod, on which I shall elaborate later in this chapter.

Origins and concept

The formation of the All-India Muslim League in 1906 and the colonial Indian government's creation of a separate electorate for Muslims under the Morley-Minto reforms of 1909 served as catalysts for Hindu leaders to generate a force of action against the apparent consolidation of Muslims as a political collectivity in India (Chakrabarty and Jha, 2020). Consequently, the Hindu Mahasabha (All-India Hindu Grand Assembly) was created in 1915, following the formation of several Hindu assemblies at state levels. The Hindu Mahasabha came under the leadership of Vinayak Damodar Savarkar (1883–1966) during the 1930s and the 1940s. While the origins of Hindutva have been traced back to the nineteenth-century religious revivalist movements in India such as the Arya Samaj (discussed later), its ideological moorings lie in the writings of twentieth-century Hindu nationalists like Savarkar that drew heavily on the glorious Hindu past to advocate the establishment of a powerful Hindu state.

Savarkar is generally credited for inventing the fundamentalist political ideology of Hindu nationalism termed as Hindutva. He listed a common nation (Rashtra), a common *jati* (race) and a common civilisation (Sanskriti) as the essentials of Hindutva (Savarkar, 1923). Savarkar conceptualised India as a compact of Hindus which would be established on the basis of 'Hinduness', or the quality of being Hindu. Hindus would be united by the bonds of love to a common fatherland and a common holy land. Muslims and Christians could not belong to this compact of a nation because their holy lands, unlike those of Hindus, were geographically located outside the Indian subcontinent, and hence they were practically aliens or 'others' to the nation. The only way for them to acquire the right to belong to the Hindu *rashtra* (nation) is through the route of reversion. One may re-enter the Hindu fold by going through *shuddhi* or purification rites, an idea first introduced by the Arya Samaj in the nineteenth century (Sahgal, 2020). Envisioned as a reform movement for social reconstruction and national progress, the Arya Samaj was influential in eradicating social evils such as child marriage and illiteracy, but the movement's progressive teachings were driven by deeply patriarchal notions. The campaigns in favour of practices such as remarriage of Hindu widows (particularly of young and virgin widows) and *niyoga*[3] were motivated by a desire to enable all Hindu women to produce male progeny for the nation. Similarly, education for women was promoted to model them into more efficient and enlightened home-makers and mothers. The home was still fashioned as the proper place of a Hindu woman and her domesticity was an object of Hindu reform (Bala, 2014).

Organisations, aims, strategies

The Hindu Right in India has developed a 'vast ecosystem of local, national and international organisations, registered charities, activist groups, think tanks, and a political party' that have worked, in their separate ways as well as in unison, to achieve Hindutva's core goals (Sahgal, 2020, p. 26). Together, they are often grouped under the Hindi term *Sangh Parivar* (Family of Organisations), sharing a common ideology. The charities and funds raised by them locally and internationally are used to train activists and buy resources (including training equipment, weapons, digital media, print media, etc.) for religious campaigns, political activities and electoral success.

Founded in 1925, Rashtriya Swayamsevak Sangh (RSS) is a male paramilitary organisation, and the progenitor and leader of a large number of Hindu right-wing organisations that make up the Sangh Parivar. Like a true patriarch, the RSS not only looks after the functioning and growth of its related organisations, but also acts as 'the operational, strategic and intellectual heart of the Hindutva movement' (Sahgal, 2020, p. 26). One of the largest voluntary movements in the world, it appoints and trains full-time workers, focusing on their physical strength and teaching them martial skills as well as lessons in discipline, religion, patriarchal family values, anti-Muslim hatred and India's overly glorified pre-Islamic heritage.

The RSS admits only men for training and volunteer purposes; however, it does have a women's wing called the Rashtriya Sevika Samiti (National Women Volunteers Committee) where *sevika* refers to a female servant.

Founded in 1936 by a Hindu nationalist woman named Laxmibai Kelkar, the Rashtriya Sevika Samiti is India's largest women-only nationalist group and operated with 2,784 active branches or *shakhas* across India in 2016 (Jha, 2016). The organisation works on three principles: *Matrutva* (Universal Motherhood), *Kartrutva* (Efficiency and Social Activism) and *Netrutva* (Leadership). It trains Hindu girls in yoga and self-defence, in addition to imparting lessons on becoming a good wife and mother, keeping the family together and preserving Indian culture.

The Vishva Hindu Parishad (VHP, World Hindu Assembly) was founded by RSS leaders in 1964 with the objective of protecting the rights of Hindus worldwide (Katju, 2013). It was identified as a militant religious organisation in the *The World Factbook* by the CIA in 2018 (Dua, 2018). VHP has a youth wing called Bajrang Dal which is notorious for its violence in the northern and central parts of India. The VHP also has women's branches such as Durga Vahini where the training of girls is markedly more militaristic, teaching them how to use guns, especially against Muslim men (Sarkar, 2018).

The BJP, the current ruling party of India, is a right-wing political party which was founded in 1980 as the electoral wing of the Sangh. Over the decades, it has maintained close ideological and organisational ties to the RSS. A multitude of ministers, leaders and representatives of the BJP, including the present Prime Minister of India, have previously served as *pracharaks* (preachers) and *sevaks* (servants) for the RSS (Jaffrelot, 2021). The BJP has supported Hindutva and Hindu nationalist activities from the beginning, as reflected in many of its government policies and campaigns. These include the abrogation of the special status of Jammu and Kashmir, backing the Ramjanambhoomi movement to build a Ram temple at the disputed site of Ayodhya, supporting cow slaughter bans, altering Indian history and educational curriculums to further Hindutva myths and narratives, and introducing the Citizenship Amendment Act 2019.

In contemporary India, Hindutva has become a strong mobilising device for electoral victory, Hindu patriarchal hegemony and anti-Muslim sentiment. It has a range of agendas on its elaborate list, aiming at substantial modifications to the social, cultural, political, economic and legal systems of the country. An important goal is to end Christian and Islamic proselytisation, and the demographic growth of non-Hindu populations across India, especially Muslims who make up the largest religious minority community in the country (Jaffrelot, 2009). *'Ghar wapsi'* (return home) is an ongoing programme of Hindutva that invites Indian Muslims and Christians to give up their 'foreign' faiths and return to Hinduism. The movement targets any group, person or idea that potentially threatens the dream of a Hindu nation. Equating Indian culture/identity with Hindu culture/identity, the supporters of Hindutva demand institutional protection of native or holy symbols of Hinduism, such as the cow. The violent anti-cow slaughter campaigns have gained momentum in the country since the rise of the BJP to power (*Telegraph India*, 2018).

Militarised masculinities and sexual violence

Hindutva organisations, particularly the RSS, have made physical and military training of the Hindu youth an integral component of their project's design. M. S. Golwalkar, second RSS leader, regarded the organisation as an important instrument to create virile and masculine Hindu men freed from the emasculation caused by colonialism, Westernisation and secularism (Golwalkar, 1965). Moreover, he was of the view that the Indian constitution should be based on the laws pronounced by *Manusmriti* or *Manava Dharmashastra*, an ancient Hindu legal text that describes a woman as a weak creature who needs to be protected by her father in her childhood, by her husband in her youth, and by her son in her old age; women do not deserve to be independent and their social space is limited.[4]

Chakrabarty and Jha (2020) have detailed how the calls for Hindu militarisation grew quite vociferous in the early twentieth century to counter the supposed militant mindset, aggression and unity of Muslims in British India. The consolidation of the Muslim community as an organised political force that participated in debates about nation building prompted the right-wing Hindu leaders to start preparing for physical clashes and confrontations with Muslims in the future. These leaders pointed out that the Gandhian methods of non-violence and peaceful religiosity had emasculated Hindu men. Thus, non-violence was rejected in favour of a militarist approach built on the ideas of 'manliness', physical fervour and use of violence where required. It was determined that intensive training in wrestling, boxing, rifle shooting, and wielding swords and *lathis* (sticks) to fight the enemy would foster confidence and fearlessness among the Hindu youth. The initiatives for Hindu militarisation – by establishing *akharas*, gymnasiums and military schools – were preceded by calls for a physical regeneration of Hindu youth through proper diet, exercise and discipline. These measures not only played a vital role in the formation of the Hindu *sangathan* (organisation), but also predetermined the collective, practical role of generations of Hindu men as fighters and protectors of the emerging Hindu nation. 'The Hindutva body that is to be re-masculinised is both individual and collective. Individual Hindus, through exercise and service, are to become strong, while the collective

Hindu nation is to react like a viraat purush (one corporate masculine body)' (Anand, 2007, p. 261).

The drive for Hindu men's re-masculinisation and militarisation signify two things that are relevant to our discussion: that violence is indispensable to the Hindutva project; and that an ideal Hindu masculinity can only be cultivated by glorifying physical prowess, dominance and violence in Hindu men, and by discarding the 'soft' traits of compassion, feebleness, passivity, coexistence and dialogue associated with femininity and domesticity. The Hindu male defines his masculinity vis-à-vis his 'others' which chiefly include women and Muslims. This means that an 'anxious Hindu masculinity' (Anand, 2007) must constantly self-validate and reassert itself by attacking all that represents or embodies femininity, including women and members of the LGBTQI community. It is no surprise then that Hindutva leaders have unabashedly made misogynistic and transphobic remarks on multiple occasions. For example, Muslim men have been compared to *hijras* (transgender people) to mock their masculinity (Narasingha Ji, 2005).

Rashmi Varma (2017) has analysed how sexual violence is a fundamental constitutive element of the political project of Hindutva and has come to occupy both the public and private domains of life in unprecedented ways under the right-wing rule of the BJP. It has been noted that fundamentalist movements survive on militarised masculinities for authoritarian power which, in turn, normalises violence, especially violence against women (Yuval-Davis and Al-Ali, 2017). Such masculinities have a proclivity for sadism, which explains the particular corporeal violence that was unleashed on pregnant Muslim women, foetuses and infants during the state-backed anti-Muslim riots in Gujarat in 2002 (Anand, 2007). The masculinity at work in the Gujarat riots was a particular concoction of Hindu religious fundamentalism, gendered nationalism and state power. Its roots again lie, among other things, in the writings of Hindutva ideologues like Savarkar who legitimised the use of rape as a political weapon (Agarwal, 1995).

> The killing and sexual violence against Muslim women that marked Gujarat 2002 were for public consumption (see IIJ 2003 on the rampant pervasiveness of sexual violence during the riots). The audience was both the 'awakened' Hindu community and the victimised Muslims. There were conscious displays of acts of violence as acts of bravado. (Anand, 2007, p. 264)

Controlling love and marriage

The Hindutva movement endeavours to maintain a strict control over love and marriage in the country to ensure the continuation of Hindu majoritarianism and ethnic purity. This is undertaken by means of clan-based regulations, vigilante harassment, policing of relations with low castes and religious minorities, conspiracy theories, spying, kidnapping, police interference, detention, threats, social ostracism, beating and murder.

Khap Panchayats have gained significant traction since the rise of the BJP into power. A *Khap* is a community organisation representing clan-based village associations – particularly among the Jat clans of Haryana and Uttar Pradesh – that considers itself responsible for maintaining gender and caste hierarchies in the name of social propriety among its members (Varma, 2017). Its functions range from settling disputes among clan members to protecting their religion and culture. *Khap* is basically a caste council with its headship either hereditary or given to an elder male member of the clan on an occasion basis (Anand, 2021). *Khap Panchayats* are not affiliated with any democratically elected government body and have no official government authority, yet they exercise significant power and social influence with support from the police and locally elected leaders in rural areas. *Khaps* have carried out all sorts of criminal activities, including ordering the murders of couples who dare flout clan norms by marrying outside their caste or religion, to save the 'honour' of their community, also called honour killing (Mahajan, 2018). The councils are particularly infamous for their regressive statements and the restrictions imposed on women such as strict traditional dress codes, slut-shaming, claiming that consumption of a non-traditional food like *chow mein* causes rapes, and banning the use of mobile phones and mingling with male friends (Dogra, 2013; Saini, 2012).

'Love Jihad' is a contemporary Islamophobic conspiracy theory propagated by Hindu extremist groups and supported by *Khap Panchayats*. It was first advanced in 2009 and was firmly institutionalised in India after the electoral victory of the BJP in 2014 (Farokhi, 2020). The term plays on the Islamic concept of *jihad* (struggle) – commonly interpreted as an Islamic religious war in modern times – to explain the motives of Muslim men behind marrying Hindu women. It purports that those Muslim men systematically target and wed women from Hindu families to bring them into the folds of Islam and increase the demographic strength of Muslims through conversions using either of the various techniques of seduction, deception, blackmail and brainwashing. Hindutva groups have tried to stop, often violently, interfaith marriages between Muslim men and Hindu women by labelling the act as 'Love Jihad' which has caused a number of murders and vigilante assaults on inter-religious couples in the past six to seven years. The theory is essentially patriarchal as it suggests that Hindu women are solely the possessions of the men of their communities and thus objects/territories of conquest for the 'other' Muslim community that aims to steal and defile these women to gain dominance over Hindus. It has been used as a pretext for the state repression of Muslims and to strictly regulate the sexuality of Hindu women. The conspiracy theory was employed as an important promotion tactic in Uttar Pradesh to draw Hindu voters and has contributed to the success of the BJP party in the state (George, 2016).

The phenomenon of curbing the freedom of love and marriage is not just limited to vigilantism but has also entered the domains of administration and law with states like Uttar Pradesh passing ordinances to prohibit interfaith relationships and marriages under the guise of ensuring protection from forced conversions (Sahgal, 2020). There have been many reports of inter-religious couples being harassed by the police in several states under the BJP rule. In many of these cases, the couple was arrested, their parents called, and the adult Hindu woman 'caught' with the Muslim man either sent back to her family, or detained in the so-called women's shelters or correction homes. Sahgal (2020) has noted how even the courts are not a safe space because of the presence of VHP cells and other underground Hindutva networks that regularly check the lists for interfaith court marriages.

Bharat Maata: **Nationalism, Female Sexuality and Hindutva**

The image of *Bharat Maata* (Mother India) as the personification of the Indian subcontinent first appeared in the late nineteenth century, gaining pathos after the Rebellion of 1857 against the British colonisation of India. According to DN Jha (2016), the image was popularised by certain literary texts such as Bankim Chandra Chattopadhyaya's *Anandmath* (1880). In his novel, Bankim Chandra developed a proto-form of Hindu nationalism by portraying the erstwhile Muslim rulers of India as antagonists who gravely disrespected the land and its indigenous people. In the book, India is visually presented as a ten-armed idol placed in a marble temple, resembling a Hindu goddess. It also features the poem *Bande Mataram* – which was later adopted as the national song of India – as a hymn dedicated to the goddess Durga, also addressed as *Maa* (Mother) by Hindu devotees. The novel emphasised the sufferings of the Indian nation-mother-goddess under colonial rule whose children must awaken to her humiliations and come to her rescue. With such anthropomorphism, the Indian nation came to be constructed simultaneously as a mother and as a feminine Hindu deity, captured in the patriotic slogan of 'Bharat Maata Ki Jai'.

In the twentieth century, multiple secular voices in India criticised the conflation of Hindu divinity with the Indian nation that is home to so many different faiths (Jha, 2016). However, the idea was reclaimed and glorified by supporters of Hindutva including Savarkar. Since then, 'Bharat Maata Ki Jai' has become one of the central rallying slogans of the Hindu Right, although not without controversies. In 2016, a BJP legislator pressurised Waris Pathan, a Muslim leader, to chant the slogan at a state-level political assembly (Deshpande, 2016). When Pathan refused to do so on religious grounds, explaining that the monolithic concept of Islam did not allow chanting of slogans associated with the worship of deities, he was suspended from the assembly. The incident demonstrates how the slogan has become predominant in contemporary India as a symbol of Hindu nationalism and powerful evidence of an Indian's patriotism.

The idea of the nation as a mother figure is deeply connected to women's sexuality (Naaz, 2017). The mother's reproductive fertility gets translated to the economic and cultural prosperity of the nation. While as a figurative mother figure, the nation is a nurturing and self-sacrificing entity, it also becomes a site that demands absolute reverence, protection and subservience. It is only the legitimate Hindu sons of the nation who can and must protect their sacred mother from the Muslim and Christian 'others'. In the Hindutva world-view, Mother India can only be served and guarded by protecting the Hindu woman, family and culture, especially against the perceived threats from its Muslim, Christian, feminist and secular foes. BJP rules by the same logic, positioning itself as the ultimate protector of Mother India at the political level. As a result, any discourse, group or individual in present-day India that goes against the party is quickly labelled as 'anti-national'. Voices of dissent are seen as enemies of the nation; they are silenced either by acts of violence, threats of violence, or through arbitrary laws such as the Unlawful Activities (Prevention) Act (UAPA).[5]

The concept of *Bharat Maata* equates the nation with a woman's body and the nation's honour with a woman's honour (Naaz, 2017). However, it is only a particular kind of female body in which this honour can reside – the body of a chaste, upper-caste, middle-/upper-class, able-bodied Hindu woman who has either mothered children already, or will become a mother in future after marrying a Hindu man. This body must be 'pure', which means a body free of all polluting influences such as moral weakness, contact with 'outsiders', sin and desire, especially sexual desire. This body cannot be that of a Dalit woman, a tribal woman, a Muslim woman, or even a lower-class working woman who is seen too often in public spaces and fails to meet the criteria of a 'respectable woman'. As a consequence, while Hindutva strives to protect the body of a Hindu woman by

exercising strict control over her personal freedom and sexuality, it bra-
zenly rationalises and perpetuates violence on the bodies of women that
belong to 'other' communities such as Muslims and Dalits. In this manner, Hindutva upholds and guards 'Brahmanical patriarchy', a term coined
by Indian historian Uma Chakravarti (1993) to explain how the control
over land by high-caste groups in India was executed through a similar
control over women's sexuality. While 'Brahmanical' is a reference to the
uppermost caste of Brahmins in the Hindu social order, the term signifies the confluence of two hegemonic institutions of caste and patriarchy
where each ensures the continuation of the other. The result is silencing,
brutalisation, rape or murder of any female who is the 'other' or a misfit
in the world of Brahmanical patriarchy. The gang rape and killing of a
nineteen-year-old Dalit woman by four upper-caste Hindu men in Hathras district of Uttar Pradesh in 2020 is just one example among many
(*The Indian Express*, 2020). There was no state action taken against the
accused in the first ten days after the crime, and the victim's body was forc-
ibly cremated by the police without proper examination nor the consent
of her family (Rashid, 2020). More recently, in January 2022, more than
100 notable Muslim women were auctioned virtually on 'Bulli Bai', an
online application that displayed the women's morphed images (taken
from social media) and personal information without their knowledge
(Vats, 2022). The Muslim women who were targeted included some who
have consistently criticised Hindutva and the BJP government, such as the
journalist Ismat Ara. The 'Bulli Bai' app had been preceded by an earlier
attempt to belittle and insult Muslim women through a similar version
going by the name of 'Sulli Deals' reported in July 2021. Bulli and Sulli are
both derogatory terms used for Muslim women in India.

Pinjra Tod's struggle against *Bhaarat Maata* is a struggle against Brahmanical patriarchy and Hindutva politics. Owing to the unmistakably
sectarian, patriarchal and casteist logic of the concept of *Bharat Maata*,
the term has been staunchly critiqued and denounced by Pinjra Tod
members and other feminists. Therefore, in response to the chanting of
'Bharat Maata Ki Jai!' by Hindu right-wing groups like ABVP, Pinjra Tod
has loudly proclaimed in its protest events and marches: 'Hum Bharat Ki
Maata Nahi Banenge!' (We Won't Be Mother India). The message is clear:
these women will not allow anyone to turn their bodies into sites where
patriarchal projects of ownership, control and conquest are played out,
masculinities are validated, and sexual violence is justified.

Pinjra Tod strives to struggle against everything that Hindu nationalism
stands for: militarised masculinities; patriarchal control of women's bodies, spaces and relationships; state repression of political dissent; abuse

and assault of women hated or discarded by Hindutva; discrimination and violence against religious minorities, Dalits, tribal people and LGBTQI communities; and violations of constitutional rights. As a movement resisting the right-wing attacks on equality, diversity and democracy in India, Pinjra Tod has been actively involved in the countrywide anti-CAA (Citizenship Amendment Act) protests to save the Indian constitutional values of equality and non-discrimination. The CAA 2019 makes religion a basis for Indian citizenship, and discriminates against Muslim immigrants in bestowing the citizenship status. The non-violent sit-in protests against the CAA have been violently disrupted by the police and some Hindu right-wing groups using physical force on the peaceful protestors (Lokaneeta, 2020). In May 2020, two Pinjra Tod activists, Natasha Narwal and Devangana Kalita, were detained under the UAPA for allegedly being part of a premeditated conspiracy to spark up communal riots amidst the anti-CAA protests in northeast Delhi. After months of imprisonment and lack of evidence, they were granted bail by the Delhi High Court but their arrest has been seen as an act of systematic silencing of feminist voices by the Indian state led by the Hindu Right government of the BJP (Banerjee, 2020).

Conclusion: Weaving a Grand Narrative of Anti-feminism

The RSS: Roadmaps for the 21st Century (2019), written by Sunil Ambekar, the national organising secretary of the ABVP, provides insights into the ongoing programmes, present agendas and long-term goals of the RSS. It also discusses much of the Hindutva ideology and world-view, although in a soft manner. Ambekar writes as a spokesperson for the RSS, stating that the organisation perceives Hindutva as the natural destination of the world. The book suggests a common solution to the multiple problems of sexual harassment, rape, divorce, dysfunctional marriages and juvenile crimes in contemporary India: a move away from Westernisation towards traditional Indian family values. The RSS *pracharak* (preacher) claims: 'Only a close-knit family can discipline the hormonal surges and the vagaries of the minds of young people and give them a certain direction' (Ambekar, 2019, p. 185). He further states: 'The family is our future and we are obligated to preserve and protect it. The example of the superficiality of the West is before us, with tremendous shallowness beneath its external glitter' (p. 193). The superiority of the Indian/Hindu family value system is corroborated by citing statistical examples of an increasing number of divorces, broken families, alienated adults and abandoned children born outside of marriage in the West. A gradually rising similar trend is also noticed in India, with children suffering from the mistakes of their Westernised parents, Ambekar notes. This is a usual trope found in anti-feminist discourses that cover their anxiety to maintain male privileges and a patriarchal gender order under the cloak of saving children and families (Mayer and Goetz, 2019). These concerns emanate from women's increased independence and access to the public sphere and reduced dependence on men. Ambekar also tells the reader that the RSS does not approve of live-in relationships because they have no place in a country like India with a fully functional family system.

The Sangh subscribes to the ideology of familialism and gives unimpeachable sanctity to the institution of marriage, which explains its strong objection to the criminalisation of marital rape in India. Exception 2 of Section 375 of the Indian Penal Code (IPC) decriminalises marital rape by stating that sexual intercourse by a man with his own wife who is above fifteen years of age is not rape. The idea of marital rape poses a considerable threat to the Hindu concept of family by challenging the notion of absolute and implied consent in marriage. 'Rape' within conjugal relationships would suggest that marriage is not a sacred contract where a man's sexual demands are always to be obeyed by his wife for procreation and familial bliss. Therefore, the women's wing of the RSS unequivocally denies the existence of marital rape (Bhardwaj, 2016). The BJP government has consistently sent out pleas to courts against declaring legal punishment for marital rape in India (*Hindustan Times*, 2022). On 29 August 2017, the government submitted an affidavit to the Delhi High Court arguing that India cannot blindly follow the West; marital rape cannot be made a criminal offence as it would destabilise the institution of marriage and become a convenient tool for harassing husbands (*The New Indian Express*, 2017). This is a strategic cover-up to deprive married women of their fundamental human rights to consent, dignity and self-expression. The Hindu Right protects the Hindu family at the cost of a woman's right to have agency and walk away from an abusive marriage. Tanika Sarkar's work on the Rashtriya Sevika Samiti, the women's wing of the RSS, reveals:

> At home, they practise a conservative domesticity which is hostile to divorce, and to love that is not sanctioned by parents. They advise women that domestic peace is their responsibility and they avoid counselling or legal help for battered women on that ground. (Sarkar, 2018, p. 228)

In the world of Hindutva, a woman cannot escape domesticity, nor imagine it as a subject of individual/personal choice. She is 'allowed' to have a career and take on leadership roles, but not without fulfilling her domestic obligations towards the family. In its 2012 national-level campaign against female foeticide in India, ABVP used the slogan 'Ma ke pet mein hi ma ki hatya' (a mother's murder in a mother's womb). Religious fundamentalist movements cannot imagine a woman without her womb; motherhood is incumbent on her identity, which explains their general distaste for abortion rights and reproductive freedom for women. The RSS first and foremost deems itself to be an extended, joint (Hindu) family or sangha where members have different roles and duties to perform. As a conventional figure who nurtures and ties the family together, the mother is crucial to the conceptualisation of the Sangha. The Rashtriya Sevika Samiti was needed eleven years after the formation of the RSS because there cannot truly be a family without women, especially mothers (Sarkar, 1995). But the place of these women within the RSS family is predetermined without undermining their larger significance to the overall vision of the organisation. 'The limits of equality should be noted. The RSS continues to plan and lead every step of the movement and the RSS remains an all-male body. This means that women are necessarily excluded from the highest decision-making bodies' (Sarkar, 1995, p. 211).

The Rashtriya Sevika Samiti used to be politically active, with visible participation in the Ramjanmabhoomi movement. However, since the 1990s the committee has 'reduced to a small, bounded, non-expansive affair like the good, modest, non-competitive Hindu woman' because their primary job is to be the custodians of the essential values of the RSS, which the latter has to often dilute and recast for electoral success in the political arena (Sarkar, 1999, p. 2). 'Like women of the Ku Klux Klan in post-bellum US, they run whisper campaigns in homes, alerting women to the dangerous enemy and preparing them to assist their men in reprisals' (Sarkar, 2018, p. 228). Thus, even the two wings of the RSS have fixed gender roles to perform with a discernible distinction of the public and the private. The RSS expands its political power and influence (in the public domain) by ensuring the BJP's electoral success, while its women's wing is supposed to defend the Indian tradition (in the private domain) against Western culture through proper domestic training of Hindu women who would enjoy the fruits of their labour alongside their men when the dream of Akhand Bharat is achieved. However, there is a snag which constantly obstructs their path to the realisation of this dream: feminism. Ambekar describes feminism as an imported diagnostic tool and a pretentious academic discipline from the West that 'soon degenerated into a fad and reckless lifestyle choices' (p. 208). He writes: 'Feminism is the language of male oppression and class struggle and it shows no flexibility to account for diverse experiences' (p. 207). A religious fundamentalist organisation – which constructs cis-gender, heterosexual, traditional womanhood and gender roles as normative absolutes – accusing feminists for failing to account for the diverse experiences of people is ironical but not a novel phenomenon. This is a common strategy adopted by anti-feminist actors for gaining moral legitimacy and mass appeal (see the introduction). In the same section, Ambekar also blames feminist movements (like Pinjra Tod) for altering the idea of Indian womanhood and focusing unnecessarily on the woman's body and sexual politics. 'For them, the nature-defined role of women as mothers and carers was a model of femininity based on a patriarchal past, like cages associated with a gendered identity' (p. 207). Before attacking feminism in the book, Ambekar devotes a great deal of time and space to elaborate on the organisation's engagement with women for their intended empowerment and well-being. He mentions in extensive detail the profiles and achievements of several Hindu women associated with the RSS and the increasing participation of women volunteers in its activities. One of the overarching arguments in the book is that Hindutva sees men and women equally, and the Hindu *sanskriti* (culture) is enough to protect women's interests; feminism is a futile Western concept, or rather a conspiracy, that must be discarded for good. However, the seemingly pro-women stance of the RSS clearly straitjackets a woman in the traditional gender roles of homemaker and mother which are presented as her most desirable and ultimate destiny while her unpaid domestic labour is glorified.

> The word 'multitasker' is genuinely feminine. The working woman strikes a fine balance between emotion, aspiration and familial duties. She is to be celebrated and supported. If families and society fail to understand this and support her, there is a real possibility of a negative m-curve, which is faced by many developed countries where educated career-oriented women are postponing their decision to become mothers or are averse to it. (Ambekar, 2019, p. 210)

Three components are essential to fulfilling the dream of a Hindu nation: (1) a controlled heterosexual, cis-gender sexuality dedicated to reproducing Hindu posterity, (2) a domesticated Hindu woman committed to her family and the cause of perpetuating Hindutva values, and (3) a militarised Hindu masculinity to protect the Hindu nation against non-Hindus and other foes through violence. In gaining control over these three, the Hindu Right continually weaves a grand anti-feminist narrative by introducing concepts like Bharat Maata and Love Jihad, incorporating plot lines that present feminism as an enemy of familial bliss and security, and silencing feminists through harassment, intimidation and police detention.

Notes

1. See Watson-Lynn (2016) for Modi's 'panic button' policy and why it was criticised by feminists.
2. The ancient Sanskrit epic of *Ramayana* written by Valmiki tells the story of a prince, Rama, and his wife, Sita, both of whom are worshipped as deities in Hinduism. Sita was kidnapped by Ravana, the demon-king of Lanka and suffered a woeful fate because she crossed the *Lakshman Rekha*, a line drawn in front of her house by her husband's brother, Lakshman, for her protection in the men's absence.
3. An ancient Hindu practice to carry on the lineage. In *niyoga* (trans. without union), a childless Hindu woman whose husband is either dead or incapable of begetting a child is allowed to have sexual intercourse with a revered man to get pregnant. However, the woman must do it solely for the sake of birthing an heir and not for sexual pleasure; only then will the act be seen as a duty of *Dharma* (religion).
4. The text makes a number of misogynistic claims. For more, see chapter IX of Manusmriti: *The Laws of Manu* (c. 1500 BC – or later), translated by G. Buhler. http://eweb.furman.edu/~ateipen/ReligionA45/protected/manusmriti.htm
5. UAPA is an Indian law aimed at prevention of unlawful activities directed against the integrity and sovereignty of the Indian state. It presumes guilt and gives the state the power to incarcerate people even before the trial commences. Between 2016 and 2018, many notable human rights activists with secular, feminist and leftist inclinations and from minority, Dalit and tribal communities have been arrested under UAPA. The law is increasingly being misused to silence dissent against the BJP government in India.

References

Agarwal, P. (1995). Surat, Savarkar and Draupadi: Legitimising Rape as a Political Weapon. In T. Sarkar and U. Butalia (eds), *Women and the Hindu Right* (pp. 29–57). Kali for Women.

Ambekar, S. (2019). *The RSS: Roadmaps for the 21st Century*. Rupa Publications India.

Anand, D. (2007). Anxious Sexualities: Masculinity, Nationalism and Violence. *The British Journal of Politics and International Relations, 9*, 257–69.

Anand, A. (2021, 3 March). Khap Panchayats – the role & history of complex social institution in Haryana & western UP. *The Print*. https://theprint.in/india/khap-panchayats-the-role-history-of-complex-social-institution-in-haryana-western-up/613988/

Azad, N. (2015, 30 September). Pinjra Tod: stop caging women behind college hostel bars. *Feminism in India*. http://feminisminindia.com/2015/09/30/pinjra-tod-stop-caging-women-behind-college-hostel-bars/

Bala, I. (2014). Women Issues and Arya Samaj. *International Journal of Science and Research*, 3(7), 549–52.

Banerjee, S. (2020, 3 July). The caging of women's dissent by patriarchal policing in a hyper-masculine regime. *Feminism in India*. https://feminis-minindia.com/2020/07/03/pinjra-tod-uapa-police-arrest-safoora-zargar-natasha-narwal/

BBC News. (2012, 29 December). Protests in India after Delhi gang-rape victim dies. https://www.bbc.com/news/world-asia-india-20863707

BBC News. (2015, 14 October). Claiming Delhi's streets to 'break the cage' for women. https://www.bbc.com/news/world-asia-india-34486891

Bhardwaj, A. (2016, 11 November). Nothing called marital rape, marriage is sacred, says Seetha Annadanam of RSS women's wing. *The Indian Express*. https://tinyurl.com/2p8wavdn

Borpujari, D. (2016, 30 December). How 'Pinjra Tod' spread its wings. *Mint*. https://www.livemint.com/Leisure/z6E69WRoNJAyUuGU5yYwXO/How-Pinjra-Tod-spread-its-wings.html

Chakrabarty, B. and Jha, B. (2020). *Hindu Nationalism in India: Ideology and Politics*. Routledge.

Chakravarti, U. (1993). Conceptualising Brahmanical Patriarchy in Early India: Gender, Caste, Class and State. *Economic and Political Weekly*, 28(14), 579–85.

Deshpande, A. (2016, 16 March). MLA won't chant 'Bharat Mata Ki Jai', suspended. *The Hindu*. https://www.thehindu.com/news/national/MIM-MLA-suspended-from-Maharashtra-Assembly/article60514388.ece

Dogra, C. (2013, 19 October). Jeans, mobiles and khap panchayats. *The Hindu*. https://www.thehindu.com/news/national//article60060450.ece

Dua, R. (2018, 15 June). VHP a militant religious outfit, RSS nationalist: CIA factbook. *The Times of India*. https://timesofindia.indiatimes.com/india/vhp-a-militant-religious-outfit-rss-nationalist-cia-factbook/articleshow/64594295.cms

Farokhi, Z. (2020). Hindu Nationalism, News Channels, and 'Post-truth' Twitter: A Case Study of 'Love Jihad'. In Me. Boler and E. Davis (eds), *Affective Politics of Digital Media: Propaganda by Other Means* (pp. 226–39). Routledge.

George, C. (2016). *Hate Spin: The Manufacture of Religious Offense and its Threat to Democracy*. The MIT Press.

Golwalkar, M. (1965). *Bunch of Thoughts*. Bharat Publications.

Hindustan Times. (2018, 7 September). ABVP's DU student union poll manifesto includes lectures to promote nationalism. https://www.hindustantimes.com/delhi-news/abvp-s-du-student-union-poll-manifesto-includes-lectures-to-promote-nationalism/story-EFn0OcAjyMogCJXJcmL0AM.html

Hindustan Times. (2022, 4 February). Centre urges Delhi high court to halt hearings on marital rape. https://www.hindustantimes.com/india-news/centre-urges-delhi-high-court-to-halt-hearings-on-marital-rape-101643933682592.html

India Today. (2013, 4 January). MP BJP leader says women who cross Laxman-Rekha will be punished. https://www.indiatoday.in/india/north/story/delhi-gangrape-kailash-vijayvargiya-madhya-pradesh-bjp-ramayana-sita-cross-limits-150751-2013-01-04

Jaffrelot, C. (2009). *Conversion and the Arithmetic of Religious Communities. Hindu Nationalism* (pp. 233–54). Princeton University Press.

Jaffrelot, C. (2021, 24 August). How Narendra Modi transformed from an RSS pra-charak to a full-fledged politician and Hindu Hridaysamrat. *The Wire.* https://thewire.in/politics/narendra-modi-rss-pracharak-politician

Jha, D. (2016, 5 April). Far from being eternal, Bharat Mata is only a little more than 100 years old. *Scroll.in.* http://scroll.in/article/805990/far-from-being-eternal-bharat-mata-is-only-a-little-more-than-100-years-old

Katju, M. (2013). *Vishva Hindu Parishad and Indian Politics.* Orient Blackswan.

Kausar, Heena. (2015, 15 August). Jamia sets girls' curfew at 8pm, no such restrictions for boys. *Hindustan Times.* https://www.hindustantimes.com/education/jamia-sets-girls-curfew-at-8pm-no-such-restrictions-for-boys/story-Id8aANuXrBEM2H-HFCbxcYL.html

Khan, J. and Jain, N. (2020, 10 January). JNU tapes: India Today unmasks ABVP attackers in a big sting, Left role also exposed. *India Today.* https://www.india-today.in/india/story/india-today-sting-operation-jawaharlal-nehru-university-violence-jnu-attackers-abvp-delhi-police-aishe-ghosh-1635757-2020-01-10

Krishnan, K. (2015, 28 February). Don't need Big Brother watching us: who says CCTVs will make women safer? *Youth Ki Awaaz.* http://www.youthkiawaaz.com/2015/02/cctv-for-safety-of-women/

Lokaneeta, J. (2020, 29 January). Anti-CAA protests reveal torture remains at the heart of Indian policing. *The Wire.* https://thewire.in/rights/anti-caa-protests-reveal-torture-remains-at-the-heart-of-indian-policing

Mahajan, N. (2018, 27 August). Honour killing continues unabated in Haryana. *The Pioneer.* https://www.dailypioneer.com/2018/state-editions/honour-killing-continues-unabated-in-haryana.html

Malu, P. (2018, 24 September). ABVP members allegedly attack BHU students celebrating gender equality. *CJP – Citizens for Justice and Peace.* https://cjp.org.in/abvp-members-attack-bhu-students-celebrating-gender-equality/

Mayer, S. and Goetz, J. (2019). Mit Gott und Natur gegen geschlechterpolitischen Wandel. Ideologie und Rhetoriken des rechten Antifeminismus. In *Rechtsextrem-ismus Band 3: Geschlechterreflektierte Perspektiven* (pp. 205–47). Mandelbaum.

Mody, A. (2016, 14 February). Why the centre and the ABVP must take classes on citizenship and democracy. *Scroll.in.* http://scroll.in/article/803544/why-the-centre-and-the-abvp-must-take-classes-on-citizenship-and-democracy

Naaz, H. (2017, 14 August). Women's sexuality in the Indian nationalist discourse. *Feminism in India.* https://feminisminindia.com/2017/08/14/womens-sexuality-indian-nationalist-discourse/

Narasingha Ji. (2005, 6 December). Public speech on 'Shaurya Diwas' [Valour Day], Ayodhya, India.

Pankaj, J. (2022, 5 January). CCTV surveillance is rising in India, world, but crime rates remain unaffected. *The Wire*. https://thewire.in/rights/cctv-surveillance-is-rising-in-india-world-but-crime-rates-remain-unaffected

Phadke, S., Khan, S. and Ranade, S. (2011). *Why Loiter? Women and Risk on Mumbai Streets*. Penguin Books.

Phadke, S., Ranade, S. and Khan, S (2013). Invisible Women. *Index on Censorship*, 42(3), 41–5.

Ramachandran, S. (2017, 9 March). The rise of ABVP and why it attracts the youth. *Hindustan Times*. https://www.hindustantimes.com/india-news/the-rise-of-abvp-and-why-it-attracts-the-youth/story-EINVYG4o21aDovqD3f6IcK.html

Rashid, O. (2020, 1 October). Hathras gang rape. Cremation of victim shocked our conscience, says Allahabad High Court. *The Hindu*. https://www.thehindu.com/news/national/other-states/cremation-of-hathras-rape-victim-shocked-our-conscience-says-allahabad-high-court/article32747271.ece

Sahgal, G. (2020). Hindutva Past and Present: From Secular Democracy to Hindu Rashtra. *Feminist Dissent*, (5), 19–49.

Saini, M. (2012, 16 October 16). Haryana khap blames consumption of chowmein for rapes. *The Times of India*. https://timesofindia.indiatimes.com/india/haryana-khap-blames-consumption-of-chowmein-for-rapes/articleshow/16829882.cms

Sarkar, T. (1995). Heroic Women, Mother Goddesses: Family and Organisation in Hindutva Politics. In T. Sarkar and U. Butalia (eds), *Women and the Hindu Right* (pp. 181–215). Kali for Women.

Sarkar, T. (1999). Pragmatics of the Hindu Right: Politics of Women's Organisations. *Economic and Political Weekly*, 34(31), 2159–67.

Sarkar, T. (2018). Who Rules India? A Few Notes on the Hindu Right. *Revista Canaria De Estudios Ingleses*, (76), 223–39.

Savarkar, V. (1923). *Hindutva. Bharati Sahitya Sadan*. 1989 (reprint).

Shandilya, K. (2015). Nirbhaya's Body: The Politics of Protest in the Aftermath of the 2012 Delhi Gang Rape. *Gender & History*, 27(2), 465–86.

Soni, M. (2016). Rethinking the Challenge of Women's Safety in India's Cities. *ORF Issue Brief*, (159), 1–8. https://www.orfonline.org/research/womens-safety-in-indias-cities/#_ednref20

Telegraph India. (2018, 13 December). Law exam question on cow slaughter reflects the BJP's culture of insult and murder. https://www.telegraphindia.com/opinion/law-exam-question-on-cow-slaughter-reflects-the-bjp-s-culture-of-insult-and-murder/cid/1678569

The Citizen. (2014, 22 October). And now Haryana's CM Khattar wants girls to dress 'decently'. https://www.thecitizen.in/index.php/en/newsdetail/index/7/1027/and-now-haryanas-new-cm-khattar-wants-girls-to-dress-decently

The Indian Express. (2020, 1 October). Impunity in Hathras. https://indianexpress.com/article/opinion/editorials/hathras-dalit-woman-gangrape-6654041/

The New Indian Express. (2017, 29 August). Criminalising marital rape will destabilise marriage, government tells HC in affidavit. https://www.newindianexpress.com/nation/2017/aug/29/criminalising-marital-rape-will-destabilise-marriage-government-tells-hc-in-affidavit-1649747.html

The Pioneer. (2018, 7 September). ABVP manifesto stresses on women safety, gender sensitisation, Bharat first. https://www.dailypioneer.com/2018/state-editions/abvp-manifesto-stresses-on-women-safety--gender-sensitisation--bharat-first.html

The Times of India. (2016, 21 October). Pinjra Tod rails against harassment by ABVP. https://timesofindia.indiatimes.com/city/delhi/pinjra-tod-rails-against-harassment-by-abvp/articleshow/54966249.cms

The Wire. (2020, 15 January). JNU attack: Delhi police confirm masked woman is ABVP member Komal Sharma. https://thewire.in/government/jnu-masked-woman-komal-sharma-abvp-delhi-police-confirm

Varma, R. (2017). (Un)Modifying India: Nationalism, Sexual Violence and the Politics of Hindutva. *Feminist Dissent*, (2), 57–83.

Vats, G. (2022, 5 January). Bulli Bai: how yet another sickening virtual auction targetted muslim women. *Feminism in India*. https://feminisminindia.com/2022/01/05/bulli-bai-muslim-women-auction-sulli-deals-updates/

Viswanath, K. and Mehrotra, S. (2007). Shall We Go out? Women's Safety in Public Spaces in Delhi. *Economic and Political Weekly*, 42(17), 1542–8.

Watson-Lynn, E. (2016, 2 May). *Modi's Panic Button for Women's Safety: Pros and Cons*. https://www.lowyinstitute.org/the-interpreter/modi-s-panic-button-women-s-safety-pros-cons

Yuval-Davis, N. and Al-Ali, N. (2017). Introduction to Special Issue on Gender and Fundamentalisms. *Feminist Dissent*, (2), 1–6.

EIGHT

Queers and National Anxiety: Discourses on Gender and Sexuality from Anti-Gender Backlash Movements in Japan since the 2000s[1]

Kazuyoshi Kawasaka

The rise of anti-gender movements in Japan in the early 2000s was interpreted by many feminists as a *bakkurashu* (backlash) against feminist political achievements in the post-war period. English-language scholarship so far has tended to focus on the grass-roots style of these movements and their political campaigns against feminism and sex education (Fujimura-Fanselow and Wakakuwa, 2011; Kano, 2011; Yamaguchi, 2014, 2017). Despite their important contributions, these studies have failed to analyse the hate campaigns against sexual minorities, within the backlash movements, and their significant political impacts. This chapter explores how sexual anxiety, especially homo-/bi-/transphobia, has played a significant role in Japanese ultra-conservative movements, provoking suspicion and mistrust towards feminists, as well as hindering feminist efforts to organise efficient counter-movements. It analyses Japanese anti-gender discourses in the 2000s, focusing on those of two influential ultra-conservative ideologues – Yagi Shūji,[2] a constitutional law scholar, and Nishio Kanji, a specialist in the philosophy of Friedrich Nietzsche. They have been prominent opinion leaders in the ultra-conservative national newspaper *Sankei Shimbun* and other media, and they have organised and led historical revisionist, anti-gender and constitutional reform movements for Japan's remilitarisation.[3]

This chapter will identify and discuss three discursive characteristics of ultra-conservative anti-feminist movements in Japan. First, it analyses how the concept of 'gender' was represented as posing a threat to the foundations of Japanese national identity, that is, the so-called traditional family. Second, it will point out that a sense of national threat and anxiety was embodied by figures of monstrous minorities such as queer people and sexual minorities, sometimes portrayed as snails or other dehumanised creatures. Third, it explores the movements' frequent focus on children who are represented as the fragile future of the nation, which is in danger of being harmed by feminists and LGBTIQ (Lesbian, Gay, Bi, Transgender/-sexual, Intersex, Queer) people.[4] Similar characteristics can be found in European anti-feminist/anti-LGBTIQ rights movements, notably during the heated national arguments over the legislation of same-sex marriage in France. Although these movements developed separately and did not share the same core interest groups or religious beliefs, their similarities shed light on their political development and the role of emotions and homo-/bi-/transphobia. Finally, the chapter will discuss how ultra-conservatives and some 'feminists' are now repeating the transphobic discourses from the backlash movements in the 2000s to attack transgender rights and inclusive LGBTIQ social reforms in contemporary Japan.

The Emergence of Anti-gender Movements in Japan in the Early 2000s

In the 1990s, feminist activism led to the successful implementation of legislation for gender equality and women's rights in Japan. In describing the progress of women's rights, Kano Ayako (2011) notes that 'the 1990s were considered a "lost decade" for the Japanese economy, but for women it could be said to have been a booming decade' (p. 43). The Japanese government adopted international initiatives for women's rights and equality, including the Beijing Declaration and Platform for Action by the Fourth World Conference on Women in 1995. The Cabinet Office's (2001) White Paper on gender equality states that women's equality is 'the essential factor for building a rich and dynamic society and the key to defining our society in the twenty-first century' (p. ii).[5] The Japanese Diet passed numerous important bills for improving gender equality and women's protection, including the Child Care and Family Care Leave Law (1992), Law for Punishing Acts Related to Child Prostitution and Child Pornography and for Protecting Children (1999), Anti-Stalking Law (2000) and Law for the Prevention of Spousal Violence and the Protection of Victims (2001). In particular, the Basic Law for a Gender Equal Society (1999; hereafter 'the Basic Law') was considered one of the most important feminist achievements because it was specifically intended to improve gender equality, and it required all municipal governments to make their own ordinances and plans to promote gender equality.

However, anti-gender (backlash) movements rapidly grew and campaigned to overturn the social impact of the Basic Law. They targeted the concept of gender, especially the term 'gender-free' (*jendā-furī*), which had often been utilised in gender-sensitive education in the 1990s to refer to liberation from compulsory gender roles (Yamaguchi, 2014, p. 542). The term was quickly adapted and spread by feminist scholars and activists, as well as by the government's gender equality projects. Anti-gender campaigners in the 2000s interpreted 'gender-free' as a notion that completely denied all gender divisions and gender roles, including biological sex, traditional ceremonies, the family system, and gender separation in physical education, toilets, shower rooms and public baths (Nishio and Yagi, 2005). Their anti-gender-free campaigns succeeded in attracting general attention, including that of conservative politicians, and they galvanised grass-roots activism to challenge local policies on gender equality and education: both national and local governments eliminated the term 'gender-free' from their projects and some local governments removed books containing the term from their libraries (Ueno, 2006b). As a result, the drafting of each local municipal ordinance bill became a field of struggle between feminist and anti-gender activists: while feminists were institutionalising gender equality in the ordinances, anti-gender activists tried to write them without the term 'gender' and included phrases asserting differences between the biological sexes and emphasising respect for tradition (Ogiue, 2006; Seok, 2016; Yamaguchi, 2014, 2017; Yamaguchi et al., 2012).

The frequent use of 'gender-free' in school education, especially sex education, also became a target of anti-gender movements. In May 2002, Yamatani Eriko, an ultra-conservative politician, raised a question in the Diet about a pamphlet for sex education, *Shishunki no tame no rabu ando bodī BOOK* (Book about love and bodies for adolescents), for junior high school students (12–15 years old). She accused the pamphlet of being 'too extreme', saying it was intended to encourage sexual conduct among minors. Subsequently, campaigns against sex education came from a national political level, from both the ruling and the opposition parties. The government adopted her criticisms, and Yamatani and seventy-eight lawmakers formed a 'study group for healthy education' to 'protect children from extreme gender-free and sex education' (Seok, 2016, p. 85). Local activists pressured regional education committees not to use the pamphlet and the Tokyo Metropolitan Government announced in December 2002 that the pamphlet's publisher, the Tokyo Women's Foundation, would be dissolved. Similar campaigns against sex education followed. For instance, in 2003, a conservative assembly member in

Tokyo accused a special education school for children with disabilities of providing extreme sex education, and the educators were subjected to disciplinary action. Anti-sex education campaigns have become a means for conservative politicians to attract public attention and forge a connection with local grass-roots conservative movements, even though some of these political interventions violated the Japanese Fundamental Law of Education (1947).[6]

The ultra-conservative anti-gender movements focused on another important field: historical revisionism. Since the 1970s, feminist scholars and activists in Japan and other Asian countries have pressured the Japanese government to take responsibility for war crimes of sexual violence against women during the Second World War. They challenged post-war historical views that have long ignored the systemic sexual violation and exploitation of women during the war, the so-called 'wartime comfort women' (*jūgun ianfu*). Following multiple testimonies from victims and former Japanese soldiers, as well as research conducted by Japanese officials, the government issued the so-called Kono Statement in 1993, which confirmed that the Imperial Japanese Army had, directly or indirectly, forced women to work in military-run brothels during the war, and it expressed remorse to all victims. In 2000, the Violence Against Women in War Research Action Center in Tokyo organised the Women's International War Crimes Tribunal on Japan's Military Sexual Slavery, a quasi-international court based on international laws, to verify cases of sexual violations and slavery by the Japanese military. The tribunal convicted Japanese wartime leaders, including Emperor Hirohito, who had escaped prosecution in the International Military Tribunal for the Far East (Lévy, 2014). It issued a statement after four days of deliberations that Hirohito was guilty as the leader of Japan for the wartime sexual slavery policy.

Japanese nationalists regarded feminist activism to expose Japanese war crimes as a threat to national identity and pride. Revising interpretations of Japanese wartime history became part of the ultra-conservative agenda in the following decades, resulting in the so-called 'history wars' (*rekishi-sen*) (Yamaguchi, 2020). For instance, conservative intellectuals formed the Japanese Society for History Textbook Reform (Atarashī Rekishi Kyōkasho o Tsukuru Kai) to promote a nationalistic education that differs from what they criticised as a 'masochistic view of history' in post-war Japanese education (Yagi, 2005, pp. 86–96). Their new narrative rewrote Japan's role in the Second World War, denying Japan's aggression in the war, the Nanjing massacre and sexual slavery. Japanese historical revisionists labelled victims and witnesses, especially former 'comfort women' from Korea, as liars, claiming the women had merely been sex workers who received large salaries from military-run brothels.[7] Nationalist politicians such as Abe Shinzō, who became Japan's longest-serving prime minister (2006–7, 2012–20), have enthusiastically supported these historical revisionist movements and tried to promote such views internationally (Norimatsu, 2020; Yamaguchi, 2020).

New media such as political manga and the internet offered platforms to disseminate revisionist historical views and anti-gender messages to a wider audience (Morris-Suzuki and Rimmer, 2002; Yamaguchi et al., 2012). In the 1990s, Kobayashi Yoshinori, a manga artist and a founding member of the Japanese Society for History Textbook Reform, successfully attracted the younger generation's interest in history and political debates. He viewed the Pacific War as a 'race war' between whites and Asians, led by Japan, to liberate Asia from Western colonisation. Moreover, he attacked and discredited former comfort women's testimonies, depicting them as an attempt to degrade the memories of fallen soldiers, and instead emphasised the soldiers' heroic self-sacrifice to protect the nation and their families. Kobayashi became one of the most influential media figures on this topic, although many Japanese historians repeatedly pointed out 'the numerous mistakes, omissions and distortions of historical facts' in his bestsellers (Morris-Suzuki, 2005, p. 189). As evident in Kobayashi's works, an attempt to restore the soldiers' masculinity is one of the essential factors in Japanese historical revisionist movements (Sakamoto, 2008). This is why the movements attracted a wider audience through popular culture and were closely linked to anti-gender movements. The internet also offered a platform for anti-feminist sentiments in the 2000s. The 2channel, an anonymous text-board (*keijiban*) and a precursor of the US image-board 4chan, became a popular platform for anti-gender messages that labelled feminists as 'feminazis', implying that feminists were oppressors with political power (Kaizuma, 2005; Yamaguchi, 2014, p. 557).

The anti-gender rhetoric grew in national and local politics, education, history debates (historical revisionism) and popular cultures. It attracted interest across generations through different topics, for example, popular culture for the youth, education issues for middle-aged parents, and historical revisionism for the older generation. As the anti-gender rhetoric was sensationalised by various interest groups and individuals, many conservative-leaning politicians and political parties have tried to exploit it. The Japanese anti-gender movements, however, suddenly declined after Prime Minister Abe Shinzō, one of the leading political figures who supported them, lost popularity and resigned in 2007.

The Emotional Politics of Japanese and European Anti-gender Discourses

There are strong similarities between Japanese and European anti-gender discourses, although the anti-gender movements did not collaborate closely or share religious or political organisations such as Catholic and evangelical churches. In particular, Japanese anti-gender discourses have common characteristics with French reactionary discourses against same-sex marriage in the early 2010s, both of which considered that a 'traditional' family model was the centre of national identity. Bruno Perreau (2016) noted that the French protests against reforming same-sex marriage and adoption laws were unprecedented in scope and mobilised people by emphasising the dangers of the abstract notion of gender theory. In the Japanese case, the abstract term 'gender-free' was what triggered wider reactionary movements against gender equality policies and sex education. Perreau (2016) observed that a grey area existed where abstract theories and notion were easily able to expand their polemics into other political disputes (Perreau, 2016, pp. 19–20).

First, a sense of threat to national identity played a significant role in anti-gender discourses. In these discourses, abstract arguments about 'gender' are presented as a problem for national identity, while disseminating the image of the traditional family as the foundation of national identity and integrity. Thus, anti-gender discourses labelled the idea of gender itself as an attack against the nation, both in Japan and in certain European countries. Perreau (2016) pointed out that French anti-gender discourses exploited anti-Americanism (pp. 57–9). Similarly, Japanese anti-gender discourses also targeted the foreignness of gender theory, which was endangering the national identity and its traditional family. Even though Japanese feminist ideas and movements can be traced back to the early years of Japan's modernisation in the late nineteenth century, feminism has often been labelled a 'foreign' concept and movement imported from the West, which would not fit the Japanese social context (Ueno, 1994). Japanese anti-gender discourses also utilised anti-communist sentiments against gender theory. Nishio Kanji and Yagi Shūji, nationalists and leading anti-gender intellectuals, remarked that 'gender-free' was a Marxist project of the Revolutionary Left and thus gender-sensitive education was similar to teaching children radical communist ideas (Nishio and Yagi, 2005, pp. 195–9; Yagi, 2005, p. 102). In another context, they called the pundits who tried to introduce a unisex public toilet for transgender people 'Gestapos' who were imposing the 'soft fascism of sexual perverts' (Nishio and Yagi, 2005, p. 262). With such rhetoric, anti-gender campaigners presented themselves as patriots while portraying feminists as enemies of the nation.

Second, this sense of national threat and anxiety was embodied by figures of monstrous minorities like sexual deviants. Both Japanese and European anti-gender discourses campaigned that gender theory aimed to deny the two biological sexes, suggesting that it degenerated humans into primitive animals such as snails (Perreau, 2016, pp. 62–5; Yamaguchi, 2014, p. 559). This seems more extreme than the 'gender theories' they believe themselves to be criticising, since they are denying differences between species and the theory of evolution, confusing mammals with pulmonata. At the same time, however, anti-gender discourses exploit anxiety over gender and sexual deviance to justify their extremism: they represented homosexuality and bisexuality as symbols of immorality caused by 'gender-free' feminism, which destroys the traditional family. Nishio and Yagi (2005) insisted that respect for the human rights of bisexuals meant that they were able to have an affair with a same-sex person outside of their heterosexual marriage (pp. 299–300). They also claimed that the denial of biological sexes and celebration of genderless people were intended to encourage homosexuality, accusing 'gender-free' feminists of 'envying snails – hermaphroditic animals that they celebrate as ideal gender-free symbols' (p. 284). Though lacking evidence, their assertions appeal not only to the sense of morality about marriage but also the phobia against LGBTIQ people, dehumanising them as genderless creatures by associating them with snails (Kazama, 2008; Maree, 2008). Yamaguchi Tomomi (2017) observed that the religious right, including the Jinja Honchō (Association of Shinto Shrines), Shinsei Bukkyō (literally, 'New-born' Buddhism) and the Unification Church (or 'the Moonies'), were involved in anti-gender movements, and some of them clearly targeted LGBTIQ people rather than the idea of gender itself (pp. 75–7).

Third, both European and Japanese anti-gender movements made school education central to the public debate. Perreau (2016) pointed out two functions of these campaigns: they place the debate on irrational foundations by insinuating that sex and sexuality can be learned, and they seek to mobilise support by spurring fears of the commodification of children (p. 70). The strategy of anti-gender discourses was a political example of Lee Edelman's (2004) 'reproductive futurism', which represents children as the national future but innocent and frail, in need of protection against the queer. Japanese anti-gender movements also effectively utilised school education to inflame fears over children's safety by their irrational discourses, and represented themselves as protecting children from teachers and feminists intervening in school education (Murase, 2006; Seok, 2016; Yamaguchi, 2014).

Japanese and European anti-gender movements strategically utilised similar rhetoric and appealed to political emotions such as nationalism, anxiety and fear. These similarities suggest that it can be fruitful to pay attention to transnational political dynamism and the movements' discursive strategies.

The Failure of Counter-movements against the Backlash in the 2000s

Japanese feminists failed to strategically build a counter-movement against the backlash movements in the 2000s. Mainstream feminists incorrectly assumed that anti-gender movements had misunderstood the concept of gender, rather than intentionally manipulating the wrong interpretation for political means (Inoue, 2008; Wakakuwa et al., 2006). In response, feminist scholars focused on clarifying the concept of gender, dwelling on abstract arguments that enabled extreme discourses by anti-gender intellectuals as discussed above. The failure of feminist counter-movements resulted in setbacks to gender equality policies and human rights such as the gender equality ordinance in Miyakonojō City – the first law including the term 'sexual orientation' in Japan – which was revoked following a municipal consolidation in 2006.

Using their interviews with anti-gender activists and feminist activists, Yamaguchi et al. (2012) criticised the mainstream feminist response against the backlash movements. Kano (2011) summarises institutional progress for women in post-war Japan as 'state policy feminism' and 'bureaucratic feminism' (pp. 42–3); thus, Japanese mainstream feminism relied on its relationship with the government and policymakers. Gender equality policies were introduced from the top down, as was the aforementioned Basic Law. Yamaguchi et al. (2012) believe that the failure of Japanese mainstream feminism was caused by such structural problems and point out three factors why the counter-movement has been insufficient.

First, Japanese feminists presupposed the public's ignorance about gender issues and did not try to understand the backlash movements and their strategy. Yamaguchi (2017) notes that feminists grossly underestimated the role of religious movements, which reached out to rural, working-class people who felt alienated by the top-down gender equality agenda of state feminism (pp. 77–8). As a result, academic feminists misunderstood the backlash movements as an attack against the concept of gender, failing to recognise the importance of the role of sexuality, especially issues of sexual orientation and sex education.

Second, mainstream feminists failed to organise counter-movements at the grass-roots level, and their strong connection with bureaucrats suddenly became ineffectual when ultra-conservative politicians such as Abe Shinzō became influential in the ruling Liberal Democratic Party and government. Conversely, Yamaguchi et al. (2012) emphasised in their ethnographic research how the backlash movements built influence in local politics, reaching out to people at the grass-roots level, especially when gender equality ordinance bills were being written in municipalities (pp. 49–146).

Third, Japanese feminists failed to cope with new media such as the internet and popular culture, which the backlash movements used effectively to spread their messages. Since the 1990s, mainstream feminist movements have relied heavily on government publicity for promoting the idea of gender. Yamaguchi et al. (2012) claim that this close cooperation meant that feminist scholars and activists had to pay very little, if anything, to promote their messages, as their own publicity and community were displaced with state publication. As a result, feminist discourses also became politically moderate and coincided with the government's official views. Yamaguchi et al. (2012) point out that mainstream feminist scholars and organisations opposed using the internet in the late 1990s as they regarded it as a place for pornography and misogynist message boards – such hesitation still prevails (pp. 299–300). Consequently, they were slow to turn to the internet to correct misinformation and spread their own views while the backlash movements dominated the internet media space with their ideas. For these reasons, Yamaguchi et al. (2012) believe that mainstream feminism not only failed to understand why the backlash movements reached out to the wider population in Japan but also missed an opportunity to introduce concrete measures and tackle urgent social problems such as gender-based discrimination and the low-wage temporary work contracts from which many women suffered. They call the 2000s 'a lost decade for feminism' (Yamaguchi et al., 2012, p. v).

Furthermore, there was a notable lack of cooperation and solidarity between mainstream feminism and the LGBTIQ community when the backlash movements tactically confused gender studies with queer subjects and representations, fanning hate and fear against LGBTIQ people to undermine gender-sensitive and sex education in school. Mainstream feminists ignored this exploitation of the phobia against LGBTIQ people and merely denied accusations, such as the idea that they were promoting 'androgynous people' (Iino, 2020). As a result, they indirectly accepted – or at least failed to criticise – the backlash views that LGBTIQ people were damaging society and that teaching LGBTIQ issues to children could be harmful.

For example, Ueno Chizuko (2006a), arguably the most prominent Japanese feminist, interpreted sexuality issues in anti-gender discourses such as the confusion between 'gender-free' and 'free sex' as men's 'dirty jokes' (p. 384), not the strategic usage of moral panic against feminism. Ueno regarded these 'dirty jokes' as aiming to build homosocial solidarity among male activists in the backlash movements through the othering of women. In her understanding, this strategy was intended to form an imaginary community of Japanese men – beyond the class differences that were widening in Japan – in the 2000s due to neoliberal economic reforms (Ueno, 2006a, pp. 383–8). She interpreted the anti-gender movements as struggles between conservative men who were trying to uphold the old society and values and progressive women who wanted to create a new society, thus presenting a historical view underpinned by sexual dualism. Notably, she regarded gay men and transgender people as being on the side of conservative men. In an interview, she made it clear that she preferred the term 'equality between men and women' to 'gender-free' and criticised sex education and the raising of 'gender-free' awareness in school, which includes sexual minorities:

> I don't think at all that sexual minorities presented by 'gender-free' education are people who are liberated from the gender order – that is gender dualism. Heterosexism, homosexuality and transgender – all are merely results of various effects of gender dualism . . . The essence of gender dualism is an identification as a sexual subject by men differentiated from women. I wonder if there is misogyny in gay men and transgender people through the process of their sexual subjectification. Therefore, if someone asks me if feminism can forge a coalition with gay men, I would answer 'yes, if they are not misogynistic'. Gay activists would harshly criticise me if I talk like this, but I cannot imagine gay men who are not misogynistic. The gay men who are not misogynistic would be those who do not romanticise masculinity; if they exist, I want to meet them. (Ueno, 2006a, p. 398)

In this statement, Ueno foreclosed the possibilities of a coalition with queer people who were being targeted and tactically utilised against feminism by the backlash movements. Instead, she constructed a double bind for gay and transgender people. First, while she presented her simplified social and historical view based on the gender dualism between men and women, she declared only those gay and transgender people who were liberated from such gender dualism to be fit to be part of a cooperation with feminist movements – which she clearly considered impossible. In doing so, she erased queer subjects from the history of feminist movements, especially lesbians and transgender people. Second, while the backlash movements targeted LGBTIQ people as threatening the gender dualism, even dehumanising them by comparing them to snails, for example, Ueno excluded gay and transgender people from feminist movements by representing them as being bonded to the old gender order, although her own feminist goal – equality between men and women – was based precisely on this dualism. Thus, even with her radical postmodern rhetoric, Ueno was hand in hand with the discursive strategy of the backlash movements: to keep arguments on gender abstract, to target and exclude social minorities, and to minimise gender equality within traditional family values through the exclusion of sexuality and transgender issues.

Mainstream gay movements were also not interested in working with feminist movements against the backlash. Ironically, with a similar reason to that of Ueno, Fushimi Noriaki, a ground-breaking openly gay writer, agreed with backlash discourses in his book *Yokubō mondai* (The Problems of Desire, 2007), rather than seeking solidarity with feminist movements against homophobic campaigns. In the book, he proposed a new political strategy for gay men to focus on desires and pleasures rather than discrimination and inequality because humans, he said, do not live only for social justice. From the viewpoint of expanding opportunities to fulfil desires and pleasures, he insisted that sexual pleasure stems from sexual differences and therefore the idea and purpose of 'gender-free' movements were wrong. According to the backlash discourses, 'gender-free' feminists were creating a dystopian society by promoting the acceptance of same-sex couples. Fushimi (2007), however, ignored this anti-gay rhetoric and prioritised the distancing of gay politics from 'gender-free' movements, accepting the caricature of the latter as denying the biological sexes altogether (p. 246).

In the 1990s, Japanese feminist and LGBTIQ movements grew by engaging with new ideas, including those of postcolonialism and queer theory, facing differences among women through Japan's colonial past, wartime sexual slavery, challenges to heteronormativity and gender dualism, and sexual rights for LGBTIQ people. As a result, in the early 2000s when Japanese society did not yet embrace the idea of LGBTIQ rights, nationalist backlash ideologues tactically exploited racism, fearmongering about communism and hatred of LGBTIQ people against feminism. In response, however, both Japanese mainstream feminists and gay activists failed to embrace intersectionality and to push back against the backlash movements. Instead, they tried to protect themselves by distancing themselves from each other. Consequently, intersectional issues including class, xenophobia, racism, sexism and homo-/bi-/transphobia were marginalised, such as sexism against Korean residents in Japan, LGBTIQ poverty and xenophobic attitudes towards non-Japanese LGBTIQ people or refugees.

The New Backlash Movements in the Late 2010s

Japanese anti-gender backlash movements suddenly disappeared after the first Abe administration. However, the backlash movements have forced mainstream feminist activists to reconsider their political and media strategy. Ueno Chizuko took the initiative to establish the Women's Action Network (WAN) in 2009 and launched a feminist information site under the same name to increase the feminist presence on the internet. Ueno stated in her opening lecture for the WAN that the organisation intended to implement an aggressive strategy against the backlash movement rather than a passive defence (Yamaguchi et al., 2012, pp. 313–18). Japanese attitudes towards LGBTIQ people also changed after the backlash movements. In the 2010s, LGBTIQ issues became transnationally important political issues and the Obama administration internationally supported LGBTIQ rights in order to demonstrate its progressive values, utilising LGBTIQ rights as a form of soft power. In the Japanese context, the US embassy strategically promoted LGBTIQ rights in Japan (Kawasaka, 2013). Caroline Kennedy, the daughter of John F. Kennedy, became the first US Ambassador to participate in the Tokyo pride parade. Japanese LGBTIQ activism has become mainstream compared to the 2000s and LGBTIQ issues have received positive support in wider society. For example, public support for same-sex marriage has dramatically grown in the 2010s and more than 80 per cent of responders in the twenties and thirtiess age groups expressed support for legalising same-sex marriage in 2019 (Kamano et al., 2020).

Japanese conservative political strategies also changed alongside the new political and social environment. In 2012, Abe Shinzo led the LDP again and won the general election. The second Abe administration kept close relations with the religious right and nationalist groups such as the Nippon Kaigi (Japan Conference) but adjusted their public messages in line with Japan's liberal-leaning allies, especially the Obama administration. Instead of attacking 'gender', the Abe administration adopted 'Womenomics' as their economic growth strategy proposed by Kathy Matsui, a Goldman Sachs economist, which aimed to create economic growth through empowering women while carefully avoiding the term 'gender-free'. On LGBTIQ issues, the Abe administration prioritised maintaining traditional family values by blocking reforms of the Japanese family system, such as allowing married couples to have separate surnames, or legalising same-sex partnerships/marriage. In 2014, however, Abe Akie was the first Japanese first lady to participate in the Tokyo pride parade. During the second Abe administration, gaffes on LGBTIQ issues occasionally came from LDP members; a notorious case was that of Sugita Mio, a lawmaker in the LDP, who opined in the monthly conservative magazine *Shinchō 45* that 'LGBT people are unproductive because they don't make children, therefore the state should not use taxpayers' money for them' (Sugita, 2018, pp. 58–9). However, those gaffes were strongly criticised by the public and did not attract the kind of wider support that the backlash movements did in the early 2000s.

The media environment also changed between the 2000s and 2010s. Owing to the characteristics of the Japanese language, which can express more information with fewer characters than languages using alphabets, Twitter has become one of the most popular media forms in Japan. Especially after the Great East Japan Earthquake in 2011, Twitter has been regarded as an effective media infrastructure to access live and local information during a natural disaster (Doan et al., 2012). The popularity of Twitter has also created a new space for feminist movements. Thanks to social media, many women can speak out about their discontent over sexism and experiences of sexual harassment and violations in an anonymous and safe way such as in the #MeToo and #KuToo movements.[8] The emergence of feminist social media activism as well as feminist popular cultures are now regarded as 'the fourth wave of feminism' in Japan (Kitamura, 2020) and these have started to change the discursive dynamics in society.

In the late 2010s, however, anti-LGBTIQ discourses along with anti-gender criticism have surfaced among feminist social media activities. In 2018 Ochanomizu University, a women's university and one of Japan's top national universities, announced that it would admit transgender students from 2020 onwards. The decision was based on the long-running discussions of LGBTIQ rights in Japan, especially with regard to the rights of education for LGBTIQ children and students. The Science Council of Japan released an advisory report on LGBTIQ rights in 2017, which included the admission of transgender women to women's universities as part of a necessary reform to secure the right to education for transgender people (Takahashi, 2019, p. 35). Just after Ochanomizu University's announcement, however, many 'feminist' Twitter accounts started to express concerns about its trans-inclusion, especially in relation to sexual violence and safety issues in toilets, insisting that the university's definition of 'transgender' was so obscure that it would even include a 'transvestite man' who has a penis (Hori, 2019, p. 8). These discourses employed typical transphobia – being a transgender person was tied to being a deceiver, criminal or sexual predator – to encourage oppostition to the university's decision. To counter these discourses, transgender and trans-inclusive feminist accounts pointed out the transphobia in these tweets and corrected misinformation about trans rights and trans-women's situations in Japan. Some of these responses labelled transphobic feminists as TERFs (trans-exclusionary radical feminists), such as is found in English online arguments. Trans-inclusive issues have become tense arguments on Japanese Twitter.

In this context, Japanese mainstream feminists again failed to show a consensus against the problematic transphobia expressed by some 'feminist' accounts. Senda Yuki, a feminist scholar and a WAN board member, described the 'TERF war' on Japanese Twitter as a bitter squabble (Senda, 2020, pp. 246–7). She was more concerned about the derogatory term TERF being used against feminists than about transphobic views and exclusion from 'feminist' discourses. Furthermore, WAN published an essay titled, 'It's Not That We Are Excluding Transgender People', by an author calling herself Ishigami Uno (2020), a manga character, for anonymity. The essay reveals three stances on trans-inclusive issues. First, the author calls herself gender-critical, claiming that 'sex is real' and biological sexes exist (Ishigami, 2020) – thus, biological sex is taken to be an essential factor to decide one's attribution, either man or woman.[9] Second, trans-women are deemed to invade women-only spaces and threaten cis-women's safety. The author repeatedly insists that she wants to ensure safety in women-only spaces such as toilets, public baths, dressing rooms and rape crisis centres, and does not intend to exclude transgender women from women-only spaces if they have changed their legal sex or actually live in society as a woman. She cannot endure the idea that 'a man with a penis would enter a women's spa space' (Ishigami, 2020). As Japanese law requires a transgender person to have sex reassignment surgery to change their legal sex, this misgendering rhetoric functions to repeat the message that trans-women without sex reassignment surgery – especially transgender minors who legally cannot receive surgery – are not women and should not be allowed to access women-only spaces. Third, while repeatedly misgendering trans-women as men and using extreme examples of situations such as sharing a public bath house, the author denounces the derogatory term 'TERF' for attracting online abuse and threats against people such as J. K. Rowling.

The Feminism and Transgender Rights Study Group, which was organised by feminists opposing discrimination against transgender people, denounced this anonymous essay as fuelling discrimination and misbehaviour – such as misgendering – and publicly criticised the WAN's editorial decision to post it ('Kōkai shitsumonjō', 2020). WAN dismissed the criticism, claiming that editorial control was given to volunteers for editorial works and that they had released the text to 'open up free discussions' ('Kōkai shitsumon jō e no kaitō', 2020).

WAN's decision to publish the essay exposed Japanese mainstream feminism's ambiguous attitude towards LGBTIQ rights and domestic political position in Japan. In the context of transnational discursive flows, the essay reflects the emergence of gender-critical feminism, especially in the UK. As the author calls herself a gender-critical feminist and mentions J. K. Rowling's polemic over transgender rights, she clearly tries to introduce gender-critical feminist discourses to Japan, where the institutionalisation of LGBTIQ rights and activism is far behind the UK's. Due to the lack of an equality act that bans discrimination based on sexual orientation and gender identity in Japan, gender-critical feminist discourses can directly threaten the dignity and social lives of transgender people as seen in the rise of anti-transgender discourses against the trans-inclusive policies of a women's university. Furthermore, these discourses are similar to those of the backlash movements in the early 2000s. When these backlash movements campaigned against the concept of gender in feminism, they spread discourses that 'gender-free' denied biological sexes, encouraged homosexuality and transgenderism, and abolished safe spaces including toilets, for example saying that 'they tried to reform toilets to make them gender-free' (Nishio and Yagi, 2005, p. 261). WAN, which was purportedly established to counter anti-gender movements in the future, ironically now encourages similar discourses on its site in the name of opening up 'free discussions'.

Unsurprisingly, ultra-conservative actors now exploit anti-transgender discourses for their agenda against LGBTIQ rights. The Japanese government was under international and domestic pressure to pass an equality act, including a ban on discrimination based on sexual orientation and gender identity, before the 2020 Tokyo Olympics and Paralympics (postponed to 2021). Although opposition parties agreed to pass the bill, the ruling Liberal Democratic Party failed to forge a consensus within its own party because of opposition from ultra-conservatives about the language of the bill, which stated that 'discrimination based on sexual orientation and gender identity shall not be tolerated'. Yamatani Eriko, a leading politician in the backlash movements in the 2000s, commented: 'It is ridiculous that there are those that have a male body, but say they are women and therefore should be allowed to use the women's restroom, or like in the US, participate in women's sports and win tons of medals' (Bell, 2021). Because of this opposition, the bill was not read in the Diet for voting, and thus was repealed.

The ultra-conservative anti-LGBTIQ movements are again part of their anti-gender equality politics too. Just before abandoning the LGBT Equality Act, the same social conservative group in the LDP opposed and politically 'postponed' a marriage reform, which allowed a couple to choose different family names. Thus, the ultra-conservatives are tactically opposing socially liberal policies in general while inflaming anxiety and fear over social changes including the marriage system and LGBTIQ rights. Japanese social progressive reforms are now again under attack by recycled discursive campaigns of the same political groups as in the early 2000s. However, what is new in the contemporary Japanese situation is that anti-gender conservatives and mainstream feminists sometimes share similar anti-transgender discourses. Consequently, mainstream feminists who failed to recognise the significance of homo-/bi-/transphobia in the backlash discourses in the 2000s have re-energised ultra-conservative political forces against gender and sexual progressive politics in contemporary Japan.

Conclusion

Anxiety over gender and sexuality, especially surrounding LGBTIQ issues, was a significant factor in Japanese anti-gender backlash movements in the 2000s. These movements tactically exploited the phobia towards LGBTIQ people, who were often depicted as dehumanised creatures and tied to moral decay, a national crisis and the end of the traditional family. Such discourses often had illogical, extremist features like '"gender-free" feminists celebrating snails as their ideal creature' (Nishio and Yagi, 2005, p. 284). But manufactured emotions such as anger, anxiety and disgust over feminists and LGBTIQ people distracted the public from the absurdity of these discourses. As a result, these movements had significant political impacts on gender equality policies in Japan. Today, this anxiety over gender and sexuality is again being fuelled by anti-gender discourses, some of which are also being driven by gender-critical feminists. Although their political goals differ, the discourses and rhetoric of such feminists strikingly resemble those of the ultra-conservative movements in the 2000s. Thus, the manufactured anxiety over gender and sexuality remains a clear and coherent feature of anti-gender discourses from the 2000s to the 2020s.

Sexual anxiety also exposes similarities in the discursive characteristics of transnational anti-gender movements. This chapter examined such similarities between Japanese anti-gender and anti-LGBTIQ movements in the 2000s and French movements in the 2010s, which do not share a similar culture, history, religion or political interest groups. The uncanny similarity offers the potential for transnational comparative studies of anti-gender movements beyond cultural, regional and social differences, although this suggestion should not minimise the importance of local contexts. Owing to the development of online social networks, extreme discourses can transgress cultural and linguistic barriers more easily, thereby translating into other social contexts. Thus we are witnessing a rapid transnational spread of gender-critical and other social conservative discourses. Emotions, which are transnationally shared by online communications, can also be a factor in the transnational dynamics of anti-gender movements.

Notes

1. This chapter is based on research funded by the Deutsche Forschungsgemein-schaft in the framework of 'Sexual Diversity and Human Rights in 21st Century Japan: LGBTIQ Activisms and Resistance from a Transnational Perspective' (KA 5082/2-1).
2. All Japanese names in this chapter are presented in Japanese order: family name first, followed by the given name.
3. Yagi, in particular, is influential among conservative groups in the Liberal Democratic Party (LDP) and was appointed government advisor on educational reform (2013–21) by the second Abe administration.
4. In Japan, activists argued over whether intersex or disorders/differences of sex development (DSD) should be included in LGBTQ movements in the early 2000s, and intersex activists in particular have challenged the idea of including intersex. This is why the term 'LGBTIQ' has rarely been used in Japan since the late 2000s and why 'LGBT' is much more popular. In this chapter, however, I use the term 'LGBTIQ' in line with international human rights discourses and also because the Japanese anti-gender backlash has clearly expressed a fear towards the ambiguity of biological sexes.
5. All translations in this chapter are mine, unless otherwise indicated.
6. In 2008, the District Court of Tokyo ruled that the politicians' intervention and the Tokyo Board of Education's decision of disciplinary action against educators in a special education school in 2003 was an abuse of their discretion and violated the autonomy of education. For details, see Yamaguchi (2014, pp. 559–64).
7. Similar historical revisionist views have been disseminated by Japanologists such as John Mark Ramseyer (2021). For historians' criticisms of Ramseyer's lack of evidence, see Gordon (2021) and Lee et al. (2021).
8. #KuToo is an online movement against the high-heel policy in workplaces in Japan.
9. For an analysis of discourses of gender-critical feminism in the UK, see Zanghellini (2020).

References

Bell, B. C. (2021, 21 July). Summer Olympics put fight for Japanese LGBTQ legal protections under the microscope. *Outsports*. https://www.outsports.com/olympics/2021/7/21/22585942/2020-summer-olympics-tokyo-lgbtq-rights

Cabinet Office. (2001). *Danjo kyōdō sankaku hakusho*. [White Paper on gender equality]. https://www.gender.go.jp/about_danjo/whitepaper/h13/zentai/2001-index.html

Doan, S., Vo, B.-K. H. and Collier, N. (2012). An Analysis of Twitter Messages in the 2011 Tohoku Earthquake. In P. Kostkova, M. Szomszor and D. Fowler (eds), *Electronic Healthcare, 91*. Springer Berlin Heidelberg.

Edelman, L. (2004). *No Future: Queer Theory and the Death Drive*. Duke University Press.

Fujimura-Fanselow, K. and Wakakuwa, M. (2011). Backlash against Gender Equality after 2000. In K. Fujimura-Fanselow (ed.), *Transforming Japan: How Feminism and Diversity are Making a Difference* (pp. 337–59). The Feminist Press at the City University of New York.

Fushimi, N. (2007). *Yokubō mondai* [The Problems of Desire]. Potto shuppan.

Gordon, A. (2021). *Statement by Andrew Gordon and Carter Eckert*. [Data set]. Harvard Dataverse.

Hori, A. (2019). Bundan sareta seisabetsu [Divided Sexism]. *Onnatachi no nijūisseiki, 98*, 6–10.

Iino, Y. (2020). Feminizumu wa bakkurasshu to no tatakai no naka de saiyō shita mizukara no 'senryaku' o minaosu jiki ni kiteiru [It's Time for Feminism to Re-examine its Strategy in Fighting the Backlash]. *Etosetora, 4*, 85–93.

Inoue, T. (2008). Bakkurasshu ni yoru seibetsu nigensei ideorogī no saikōchiku [Reconstructing the Ideology of Sexual Dualism in the Backlash]. *Joseigaku, 15*, 14–22.

Ishigami, U. (2020, 12 August). Toransujendā o haijo shiteiru wakedewanai [It's not that we are excluding transgender people]. *WAN*. https://wan.or.jp/article/show/9075

Kaizuma, K. (2005). Taikō bunka to shite no 'han "femi-nazi"' ['Anti-"femi nazi"' as a Counterculture]. In R. Kimura (ed.), *Jendā furī toraburu* [Gender-free Trouble] (pp. 35–54). Hakutakusha.

Kamano, S., Ishida, H., Hiramori, D. and Kawaguchi, K. (2020). *Seiteki mainoritī nitsuite no ishiki: 2019 zenkoku chōsa hōkokukai haifu shiryō* [Attitudes Towards Sexual Minorities in Japan: The 2019 National Survey Report].

Kano, A. (2011). Backlash, Fight Back, and Backpedaling: Responses to State Feminism in Contemporary Japan. *International Journal of Asian Studies, 8*(1), 41–62.

Kawasaka, K. (2013). Amerika-ka sareru LGBT no kenri: 'Gei no kenri wa jinken dearu' enzetsu to shimpo no naratibu [Americanized LGBT Human Rights: The Narrative of Progress and the Speech 'Gay rights are human rights']. *Gender and Sexuality, 8*, 5–28.

Kazama, T. (2008). 'Chūsei ningen' to wa dareka? [Who are Androgynous People?]. *Joseigaku, 15*, 23–33.

Kitamura, S. (2020, 17 August). Nami o yomu [Reading Waves]. *Gendai shisō, 48*, 48–56.

'Kōkai shitsumonjō' [An Open Letter]. (2020). Feminism-Trans-rights Study Group. https://femizemitrans.blogspot.com/2020/08/blog-post.html

'Kōkai shitsumon jō e no kaitō' [A Response to the Open Letter]. (2020, 31 August). *WAN*. https://wan.or.jp/article/show/9108

Lee, Y.-S., Saito, N. T. and Todres, J. (2021). The Fallacy of Contract in Sexual Slavery: A Response to Ramseyer's 'Contracting for Sex in the Pacific War'. *Michigan Journal of International Law*, 42(2), 291–319.

Lévy, C. (2014). The Women's International War Crimes Tribunal, Tokyo 2000: A Feminist Response to Revisionism? *Clio*, 39.

Maree, C. (2008). Bakkurasshu ni okeru samazama na fobia no kaidoku [Reading Phobias in the Backlash]. *Joseigaku*, 15, 34–9.

Morris-Suzuki, T. (2005). *The Past Within Us: Media, Memory, History.* Verso.

Morris-Suzuki, T. and Rimmer, P. (2002). Virtual Memories: Japanese History Debates in *Manga* and Cyberspace. *Asian Studies Review*, 26(2), 147–64.

Murase, Y. (2006, 2 November). Sex Education Bashing in Japan. *CGS Online.* http://web.icu.ac.jp/cgs_e/2006/11/sex-education-bashing-in-japan.html

Nishio, K. and Yagi, S. (2005). *Shin-kokumin no yudan: 'jendā furī' 'kageki na seikyōiku' ga nihon wo horobosu* [New Alert to Citizens: 'Gender Free' and 'Radical Sex Education' Will Ruin Japan]. PHP.

Norimatsu, S. O. (2020). Canada's 'History Wars': The 'Comfort Women' and the Nanjing Massacre. *The Asia-Pacific Journal Japan Focus*, 18(6:4). https://apjjf.org/2020/6/Norimatsu.html

Ogiue, C. (2006). Seiken yotō no bakkurashu [The Backlash from a Ruling Party]. In Sōfūsha Editorial Committee (ed.), *Bakkurashu!* (pp. 357–70). Sōfūsha.

Perreau, B. (2016). *Queer Theory: The French Response.* Stanford University Press.

Ramseyer, J. M. (2021). Contracting for Sex in the Pacific War. *International Review of Law and Economics*, 65, 105971.

Sakamoto, R. (2008). 'Will you go to war? Or will you stop being Japanese?' Nationalism and History in Kobayashi Yoshinori's *Sensoron. The Asia-Pacific Journal Japan Focus*, 6(1). https://apjjf.org/-Rumi-SAKAMOTO/2632/article.html

Senda, Y. (2020). 'Onna' no kyōkai o hikinaosu [Redefining the Boundaries of 'Women']. *Gendai shisō*, 4, 246–56. Seidosha.

Seok, H. (2016). *Jendā bakkurasshu to wa nani datta no ka* [What Was the Gender Backlash?]. Inpakuto shuppan.

Sugita, M. (2018). 'LGBT' shien no do ga sugiru [Support for 'LGBT' People is Too Excessive]. *Shinchō 45*, 8, 57–60.

Takahashi, Y. (2019). Toransujendā gakusei no ukeire to joshi daigaku no mission [Acceptance of Transgender Women and Missions of Women's Universities]. *Onnatachi no nijūisseiki*, 98, 31–6.

Ueno, C. (1994). Chakuchi suru shisō [Landing Thoughts]. In C. Ueno and Y. Nakamura (eds), *Ningen wo koete* [Beyond Humans] (pp. 185–201). Kawade-bunko.

Ueno, C. (2006a). Fuanna otoko tachi no kimyōna rentai [A Strange Solidarity among Anxious Men]. In *Bakkurasshu!* [Backlash!] (pp. 378–439). Sōfūsha.

Ueno, C. (2006b). 'Kachū no hito' kara [From 'Personal Experience']. In M. Wakakuwa, S. Katō, M. Minakawa and C. Akaishi (eds), *Jendā no kiki o koeru!* [Overcoming the Threat to Gender!] (pp. 20–34). Sekikyūsha.

Wakakuwa, M., Katō, S., Minakawa, M. and Akaichi, C. (eds). (2006). *'Jendā' no kiki o koeru!* [Overcoming the Threat to Gender!]. Sekikyūsha.

Yagi, S. (2005). *Kokumin no shisō* [Citizens' Thoughts]. Sankei Shinbunsha.

Yamaguchi, T. (2014). 'Gender Free' Feminism in Japan: A Story of Mainstreaming and Backlash. *Feminist Studies, 40*(3), 541–72.

Yamaguchi, T. (2017). The Mainstreaming of Feminism and the Politics of Backlash in Twenty-first-Century Japan. In J. C. Bullock, A. Kano and J. Welker (eds), *Rethinking Japanese Feminisms* (pp. 68–86). University of Hawai'i Press.

Yamaguchi, T. (2020). The 'History Wars' and the 'Comfort Woman' Issue: Revisionism and the Right Wing in Contemporary Japan and the US. *The Asia-Pacific Journal Japan Focus, 18*(6:3). https://apjjf.org/2020/6/Yamaguchi.html

Yamaguchi, T., Satō, M. and Ogiue, C. (2012). *Shakai undō no tomadoi: Feminizumu no ushinawareta jidai to kusanone undō* [Confusion in Social Movements: The Lost Decade of Feminism and Grassroots Conservative Movements]. Keisōsha.

Zanghellini, A. (2020). Philosophical Problems with the Gender-Critical Feminist Argument against Trans Inclusion. *SAGE Open* (May).

NINE

Anti-Feminism in the Context of Corona Conspiracy Theories in Germany

Mareike Fenja Bauer

Anti-feminist narratives and conspiracy theories are closely intertwined. Not only can these narratives take the form of conspiracy theories themselves, they are also instrumental for conspiracy theories in relation to different topics (Astapova et al., 2020; Höcker et al., 2020). Since the beginning of the COVID-19 pandemic in spring 2020, corona conspiracy theories, questioning the existence, the origin of and the risks resulting from the coronavirus spread in Germany as well as internationally (Stein et al., 2021). Therefore, this chapter asks in what way anti-feminist narratives emerge in the context of corona conspiracy theories in Germany and examines the functions and dynamics associated with these narratives.

First studies indicate that the so-called Anti-Corona-Protests – protests that mobilised against the measures to contain the pandemic – were instrumental in spreading corona conspiracy theories in Germany (Nachtwey et al., 2020). The so-called *Corona Rebellen* played a crucial role in organising the Anti-Corona-Protests (Salheiser and Richter, 2020). Therefore, as a case-study, this research deals with a Telegram chat of the so-called *Corona Rebellen* to analyse anti-feminist narratives in the context of corona conspiracy theories in Germany. To do so, a qualitative content analysis (Kuckartz, 2018) combined with dialogical narrative analysis (Riessmann, 2008) is applied.

First, an overview of the complex relationship between anti-feminism and conspiracy theories, in general, is given before widespread anti-feminist narratives in Germany are described, as these narratives act as an analytical lens for the following analysis. In addition, the spread of corona conspiracy theories in Germany is described briefly. Further, the Telegram chat and the applied methods are presented. The analysis of the Telegram chat reveals that various anti-feminist narratives fulfil different functions within the contexts of the chat and the corona conspiracy theories. Anti-feminist narratives play a major role in identity and othering mechanisms are closely linked to calls for action and fulfil bridging functions inter alia for the incorporation of corona conspiracy theories in far-right ideologies. This study also shows that there is a growing risk of radicalisation of discourse and homogenisation towards anti-feminist ideas that could perpetuate beyond the COVID-19 pandemic.

Anti-feminism and Conspiracy Theories

What defines a conspiracy theory and whether to call it a conspiracy theory, conspiracy myth or conspiracy narrative is open to ongoing public and academic debate (Byford, 2011; McKenzie-McHarg, 2020). For this study, the term conspiracy theory is used as it has a long history in academic discourse, and while it is true that conspiracy theories have nothing to do with science, they can still be falsified and proven wrong – even if people who believe in conspiracy theories tend to not accept the falsification (McKenzie-McHarg, 2020). Further, for this study conspiracy theories are defined as normative narratives that explain phenomena or events by pointing to (alleged) plots of (supposedly) powerful persons or groups (Sunstein and Vermeule, 2009). Conspiracy theories not only create a malevolent 'other' but, for conspiracy theorists – individuals who consume, discuss and diffuse such narratives – conspiracy theories do play a crucial role in identity mechanisms (Leone et al., 2020).

In recent years anti-feminist positions have often been expressed through conspiracy theories about a powerful 'gender lobby' operating in secret to take over the world (Astapova et al., 2020). Marchlewska et al. (2019) propose the term 'gender conspiracy beliefs' to categorise conspiracy theories claiming that gender-equality activists and gender studies are part of a secret plot to promote a so-called 'gender ideology'. Conspiracy theories containing anti-feminist narratives are also closely interlinked with sexism, misogyny and LGBTIQ+ hostility. Anti-feminist ideas of 'deviant' sexualities and/or genders are prominent in many conspiracy theories and play a major role in 'othering' mechanisms (Thiem, 2020). The relationship between anti-feminist ideas and conspiracy narratives is illustrated by the following example from this study:

> You don't really know who is a friend or an enemy [. . .] You can grow from the rising resistance. So be like a warrior, man. Get back to life and aim for your goals. [. . .] Embrace your soul and the tears of truth begin to flow, you see the meaning . . . . (Chat member S.3, 17 June 2020, 8.39 pm)

Phrases such as 'You don't really know who is a friend or an enemy' and 'the tears of truth begin to flow' emphasise the idea of a secret plan behind the COVID-19 pandemic and the urge to find the 'truth' as this is a fundamental feature of conspiracy theories. This search for the 'truth' is directly connected to the identity of men as 'warriors', which is a common anti-feminist conception of masculinity.

Further, anti-feminism and the belief in conspiracy theories share some relevant characteristics as they both relate to everyday experiences and both act as coping strategies for feelings of uncertainty. Therefore, they both increase in times of crisis (Byford, 2011; Graff and Korolczuk, 2021; Klein and Nera, 2020; Siapera, 2019).

As shown, anti-feminism expresses itself through conspiracy narratives and anti-feminist ideas play a significant role in othering processes within different conspiracy theories. In addition, anti-feminism and the belief in conspiracy theories share some significant features. Taking this reciprocal relationship of anti-feminism and conspiracy theories (Graff and Korolczuk, 2021; Höcker et al., 2020) as its starting point this study is going to examine anti-feminist narratives in the context of corona conspiracy theories in Germany.

Anti-feminist narratives in Germany

This study uses widespread anti-feminist narratives as an analytical lens, namely: narratives of anti-political-correctness, anti-genderism, masculinism, family-centred anti-feminism, Christian fundamentalist anti-feminism, and far-right anti-feminist narratives.

Narratives of anti-political-correctness claim that the public space is a space in which it is no longer possible to speak the 'truth' due to 'political correctness', which is equated with 'feminism' or an alleged 'gender ideology' (Blum, 2019; Siri, 2015). In line with this narrative, an overreaching and powerful feminist elite is imagined that wants to influence social life by, for example, demanding discrimination-free speech (Culina, 2018). The narrative of a restriction on the freedom of speech and expression is accompanied by a self-identification as taboo breakers (Gesterkamp, 2010).

In recent years the spread of so-called anti-genderism has increased (Hark and Villa, 2015). Within anti-gender narratives the term 'gender' is used with a pejorative intention and as a proxy for several feminist positions and various types of gender equality policies (Näser-Lather et al., 2019). According to these narratives, policies of gender equality are part of a secret feminist conspiracy of a so-called 'gender lobby' that aims to promote homosexuality, fight Christian values and abolish the sexes (Näser-Lather, 2019; Astapova et al., 2020). Among other things, gender studies are discredited as 'pseudo-science', 'pseudo-religious dogmatism', an ideology, and are denied any scientificity as well as portrayed as irrelevant (Hark and Villa, 2015). This discourse is connected to populist logic and anti-etatist positions as gender studies are portrayed as part of an indoctrination from 'above' (ibid.).

The narrative of an overreaching and powerful feminism is also part of masculinist narratives, in which men are pictured as superior based on an assumed masculine biological strength (Gesterkamp, 2010; Claus, 2014). Masculinist narratives are closely linked with homophobia, misogyny and sexism (ibid.). An imagined powerful and omnipresent feminism is portrayed as a threat to the alleged 'natural' gender roles and especially to men and masculinity (Gesterkamp, 2012).

Family-centred anti-feminist narratives focus on the married and cis-heteronormative family, which is framed as 'natural' and acts as a symbol for heterosexuality and the gender binary (Blum, 2019; Näser-Lather et al., 2019). At the same time, this idea of family is pictured as threatened by feminism or the so-called 'gender-ideology' (Blum, 2019). Family-centred anti-feminist narratives primarily use the emotionally and morally loaded image of children to mobilise for their causes (Näser-Lather et al., 2019). Family-centred anti-feminist narratives appear primarily in attacks on inclusive and gender-reflective pedagogical approaches, which are seen as a threat to 'the family' as they deconstruct hetero- and cis-normativity (Laumann and Debus, 2018).

Within Christian fundamental anti-feminist narratives, the fight against reproductive rights and the regulation of (female) sexuality is central. A sexual morality is propagated that is solely oriented towards procreation and sexuality is only accepted within the 'sacred institution' of heterosexual marriage (Sanders et al., 2014). Feminism is perceived as responsible for increased divorce rates, a loss of sexual morality and abortions (ibid.). In line with narratives of a 'gender lobby' a so-called 'homo lobby' is imagined, which allegedly are both part of the so-called 'abortion industry' (Sanders et al., 2014).

Reproductive rights and an alleged demographic change are also part of narratives of far-right anti-feminism. Within far-right ideologies, family is described as cis-gendered, heteronormative and white, as well as an entity to preserve a 'racially pure people' (Blum, 2019; Näser-Lather et al., 2019). However, it is perceived as threatened from 'inside', by feminism and reproductive rights, but is also threatened from 'outside' by migration (Höcker et al., 2020). The latter is often linked with pseudo-feminist arguments that can be described as femonationalism (Farris, 2011), e.g. constructing white German women as threatened by Muslim men. This threat scenario serves as a call to action for 'manly' white men to protect 'their women', thereby strengthening traditional gender stereotypes of men as strong and women as weak (Mayer, 2021). Further, a dichotomy of 'our Western' culture as modern, equal and emancipated in distinction to Islam portrayed as homophobic, pre-modern, non-enlightened, sexist and patriarchal is constructed (ibid.). The self-perception as an equal and emancipated society also serves to delegitimise feminist demands. These are dismissed as exaggerated since equality has already been achieved (Schutzbach, 2016).

Although these anti-feminist narratives stem from different ideological perspectives they can be interlinked and interwoven with each other. Within this study, these narratives are brought to the analysis of corona conspiracy theories.

Corona conspiracy theories in Germany

Since the beginning of the global COVID-19 pandemic in spring 2020, not just the coronavirus but also corona conspiracy theories have spread on a national and international level. The pandemic itself and the measures against it became the subject of conspiracy theories (Stein et al., 2021; Rubin and Wilson, 2021).

All over the world measures to contain the pandemic were taken, such as obligations to wear a mask in public or new home office regulations. In Germany, these kinds of government measures and regulations were accompanied by nationwide protests, the so-called Anti-Corona-Protests (Grande et al., 2021), which started in March 2020 (Hövermann, 2020) and spread all over Germany. The protests reached their peak at mass demonstrations in Berlin on 1 August and 29 August, in which around 38,000 people took part (Oswald, 2020). Initial studies show that the participants of these protests are not a homogenous political group. Even the self-appointed *Corona Rebellen* are not organised political groups but rather loosely connected individuals (Nachtwey et al., 2020). Telegram groups of the so-called *Corona Rebellen* received a lot of media attention because they are not only considered central places for mobilising protest participants but also because content glorifying violence was repeatedly found in them (Potter, 2020). Well-known German national anti-feminists such as the journalist Birgit Kelle, who draws especially on Christian fundamentalist narratives, and right-wing anti-feminist politicians like Beatrix von Storch participated in the protests (Blum and Rahner, 2020). Additionally, Eva Herman, a well-known anti-feminist of the far-right expressed sympathy for the protests and spread corona conspiracy theories through her social media channels (ibid.). Concerning corona conspiracy theories in Germany, the messenger service Telegram has emerged as a place of exchange, networking and organisation for conspiracy believers (Salheiser and Richter, 2020). Telegram chats and channels generate mono-thematic networks of like-minded people that exchange ideas and create identities (Prucha, 2016). The effect of echo chambers is therefore likely to be particularly high in this digital space (Solopova et al., 2021).

Case Study: Telegram Chat of the *Corona Rebellen*

This study analyses anti-feminist narratives in the context of corona conspiracy theories by looking at the biggest nationwide public chat of the *Corona Rebellen* as of January 2021 (time of data collection). At that time, 4,888 Telegram users were part of the chat, which was formed in April 2020. According to the chat self-description, it was initiated to connect protest participants who identifed themselves as part of the *Corona Rebellen* across Germany and act as a place for exchange. Even though the chat deals with different issues a clear majority of the postings includes positive references to conspiracy theories. Especially the most active chat members (members with ten or more messages) spread conspiracy theories and are also characterised by discriminatory, aggressive and anti-feminist as well as antisemitic, racist, homophobic content.

Data collection and data preparation

The data collection was done on 15 January 2021. Covering the time frame from 1 April 2020 to 31 December 2020 a total of 63,998 messages were exported. Messages and Telegram accounts deleted up to this point were no longer shown in the data. To identify anti-feminist narratives within the chat a systematic search for key words, which derived from research literature as well as from the material itself in an iterative process, was performed. In total, seventy-seven key words were part of the search, whereas only the root of words was used. For example, a search with the word 'fem' leads to messages containing words such as 'feminist', 'feminism' or 'female' and so on. Through this systematic search, sixty dialogical sequences and 360 single messages were identified. A dialogical sequence is defined as an exchange between two or more members of the chat. A single message is a message that did contain an anti-feminist key word but was not part of a conversation (that is, the message is not an answer or reaction to previous messages and none of the following messages reacts to it). Obviously, sixty dialogical sequences and 360 single messages are a small number compared to the 63,998 messages in total. This might be a result of the organisational character of the chat and its aim of connecting members of the *Corona Rebellen* all over Germany. Further, messages that did not include any written text, for example, share-pics or voice messages were not considered as part of the analysis. Additionally, as other research on Telegram shows, such as that by Guhl et al. (2020), Telegram's search functions are non-transparent. Therefore, it is not clear how Telegram determines search hits and how comprehensive the displayed results are. This intransparency of the search function cannot be eliminated at this point and represents a general difficulty in investigations of larger platforms (Guhl et al., 2020).

Qualitative content analysis and dialogical narrative analysis

The 360 single messages and sixty dialogical sequences were analysed using a content-structuring qualitative content analysis according to Kuckartz (2018) in combination with a dialogical/performative narrative analysis according to Riessmann (2008).

First, a qualitative content analysis was applied to the complete corpus. The main categories were constructed on the basis of research on anti-feminist narratives in Germany but also derived inductively from the material. In a second coding process sub-categories to the main categories were formed. At this point the messages containing anti-feminist narratives were also analysed for conspiracy theories. A final coding process was applied to adjust the sub- and main categories.

Through dialogical narrative analysis, the dialogic sequences were additionally considered as a unit of analysis each. Their analysis was guided primarily by questions of the narrative context:

What for? (What purpose do the messages serve? Why is the conversation being held? etc.)

Who is talking? (Are they active members of the chat? Have people already attracted attention because of other anti-feminist statements? Can development be observed? etc.)

How are they talking? (How do users talk to each other? What rhetorical strategies are used? What is the conversational tone? etc.)

Results of these analyses are shown in the following.

Dynamics and Functions of Anti-feminist Narratives

Anti-feminist narratives within the context of corona conspiracy theories create certain meanings and explanations for the pandemic and the associated political, social and economic crisis and fulfil several functions.

Identity and othering mechanisms

Within the chat, identity constructions and othering mechanisms based on anti-feminist narratives occur, which do not only appear in relation to corona conspiracy theories but also independently.

On the one hand, family-centred identities, built on the idea of family as a cis-gender, heteronormative entity with many children, are constructed by addressing users as 'concerned parents' or families and women as mothers or potential mothers. Through the idealisation of this concept of family other forms of families are devalued. In addition, men are addressed as fighters and soldiers whereas women are portrayed as potential victims.

On the other hand, an overreaching feminism and political correctness as well as a so-called 'gender madness' are portrayed as threat scenarios and feminists, LGBTIQ+ persons, Jews and Muslims as 'other'.

Families and female fertility are imagined as threatened by reproductive rights and abortions, which are directly linked to the current pandemic. The so-called 'abortion industry' is constructed as part of an alleged corona conspiracy by claiming that aborted foetuses are part of the COVID-19 vaccine production: 'Cell line from aborted foetuses in Corona vaccine [. . .] it consists of fibroblastic cells originally from the lungs of a 14-week-old male foetus . . .' (Chat Member X.3, 17 November 2020, 11.15 am).[1]

Moreover, other messages also claim that vaccines cause female infertility: 'Corona vaccine! Pregnancy is no longer possible! [. . .] Infertility!' (Chat Member T.2, 5 November 2020, 12.49 am). In an alarming tone, the chat member claims that the COVID-19 vaccines lead to female infertility, thereby portraying them as a threat to women (who are addressed as mothers) and families. This narrative appeals primarily to a vaccine-sceptical audience and reinforces the construction of women as mothers. The conspiracy theory of an 'abortion industry' as part of a secret corona conspiracy as well as the conspiracy theory of the vaccines causing female infertility are the most common anti-feminist corona conspiracy theories within the chat.

However, these threat scenarios are also reinforced by portraying pregnant women and families in general as victims of the corona measures. For example, it is claimed that the corona measures are instrumental for the conspiracy to abolish the family:

> Babies are separated from their mothers because of corona. No hugging, no eye contact [. . .] what this means for new-borns: that they are carried into a box completely without warmth and affection [. . .] destruction of the family [. . .] The corona lie is merely an accelerant for these goals. (Chat member X.3, 13 November 2020, 6.43 pm)

Besides the construction of threat scenarios this message also reinforces chat members' identity as concerned parents.

In the chat the narrative of a powerful and omnipresent feminism and terms such as feminism, gender and political correctness are linked to the COVID-19 pandemic. For example, feminism is implied as part of a secret plan behind the COVID-19 pandemic to 'restructure' society:

> . . . Covid 20 and Covid 21 are planned for next year. All of this is just a cheap farce to restructure everything [. . .] Why do you think we are still supposed to work, shop and send our kids to school? So we all stay silent! [. . .] But why are demonstrations of [. . .] feminism and demonstration for abortion still allowed? (Chat member U.6, 13 November 2020, 7.42pm)

This message relies on the corona conspiracy theory of a planned pandemic and suspects a plan to 'restructure everything' without further specifying the actors and the motivations of this alleged secret plan. Rhetorical questions are raised that imply that feminism as well as abortions are playing a part in it because demonstrations for these topics are still allowed regardless of the coronavirus. The use of rhetorical questions is a common method within the chat to spread conspiracy theories.

Anti-feminist narratives are also linked to the conspiracy theory of the so-called 'Great Reset'. The Great Reset is an initiative by the World Economic Forum with the aim to explore how countries might recover from the economic damages followed by the COVID-19 pandemic (Goodmann and Carmichael, 2020). However, current corona conspiracy theories claim that the Great Reset is in fact a plot by a global elite under the cover of COVID-19 to implement a one-world government and destroy capitalism (ibid.).

> Do you actually know what the 'Great Reset' is?

> All government measures, from the gender madness [. . .] and last but not least the corona measures serve the great plan [. . .] They say the world has to start over. A reset is needed. A 'transformation '! (Chat member F.9, 15 November, 2.42 am)

The message claims to explain the 'Great Reset' as the question 'Do you actually know what the "Great Reset" is?' is asked and at the same time answered, thus portraying 'gender madness' and the 'corona measures' as part of a bigger conspiracy.

Gender and political correctness are also perceived as a restriction to the freedom of speech, as the following message shows:

> I know Jews who were called anti-Semites for saying something against the corona measures [. . .] from the crazy gender crap to the fact that you're not allowed to name criminals if they're Jews [. . .] You first have to get away from all this political correctness crap . . . . (Chat member O.4, 23 October 2020, 7.56 pm)

Within this message 'the crazy gender crap' is linked to the claim 'you're not allowed to name criminals if they're Jews' implying that 'gender' is a restriction of the freedom of speech and expression. The message also rejects the accusation of antisemitism – but is at the same time implying that 'Jews' are 'criminals' *who are* somehow related to the COVID-19 pandemic. Throughout the whole chat the connection between antisemitic and anti-feminist claims stays rather vague.

Moreover, throughout the whole chat women are mainly described as weak, whereas in contrast men are referred to as strong. Concepts of masculinity as militant and soldierly are propagated primarily by the most active chat members. However, within the chat anti-feminist narratives are also interwoven with explicitly misogynistic and sexist ideas, for example, the term 'woman' is used as an insult. Personal attacks concentrate on feminist and LGBTIQ+ persons as individuals. Partly, women as a group are also described as playing a part in a supposed secret corona conspiracy, with women being referred to as malevolent in a blanket manner. This portrayal of women seems to contradict the aforementioned construction of women as victims. However, within the chat, this supposed contradiction is not addressed and misogynistic statements remain without rebuttal.

In addition to the anti-feminist idea of an omnipresent feminism, a supposedly powerful homosexual elite is imagined, which is also portrayed as a group of conspirators in the COVID-19 pandemic. This narrative is closely linked to a distrust towards governmental and intergovernmental institutions:

> Lobbying through the bedroom? 'The mid-thirties, same-sex married, childless, extremely ambitious, highly networked' pattern seems to be emerging in the corona pandemic as a punchline for influential people in the health sector [. . .] unfortunately, Streeck's flawless varnishes [. . .] The reason is the connections of his husband [. . .] who is a diplomat in Brussels in charge of

the United Nations Population Fund (UNFPA) [. . .] 'UNFPA supports pro-
grams that help women, men and young people with family planning and
prevent unwanted pregnancies'. With this agenda, the Fund is pursuing virtually the same interests as the world's largest, most financially powerful Bill
and Melinda Gates Foundation, which promotes vaccination, sterilisation
and birth control [. . .] The success dynamic behind this gay power couple
is true teamwork: . . . is Gates the key? (Chat member K.3, 27 September
2020, 3.43 pm)

The message first indicates that homosexual couples do play a crucial role
within the pandemic. Then it uses the UNFPA to personally attack the
virologist Henrik Streeck and his husband by associating the organisation with the widespread corona conspiracy theory that Bill and Melinda
Gates are part of the COVID-19 pandemic in order to control and gradually reduce the population. At the same time, the anti-feminist threat
scenario of abortion and birth control appears. Therefore, anti-feminist
ideas, homophobic statements and corona conspiracy theories are interwoven with each other as well as with distrust towards institutions.

In line with femonationalism, anti-Muslim and anti-migration narratives, which claim to be in defence of women's rights, occur within the
context of corona conspiracy theories.

2,300 years ago, long before Islam, the Arabs discovered that forcing people
to cover their nose and mouth broke their will and individuality and deper-
sonalised them. It made them submissive [. . .] Then Islam transformed
it into a woman's symbol of submission to Allah, the man who owns a
harem [. . .] The mask is the beginning of the erasure of individuality. (Chat
member T.2, 4 November 2020, 1.05 pm)

In this message hygiene masks are equated with the niqab, which on the other
hand is framed as a symbol of the oppression of women. Thus, within this
example, Islam is not just constructed as a threat to women, but is used as a
symbol or short-cut to claim oppression. Further, Muslim men are portrayed
as over-sexualised as they follow a religion whose God is portrayed as a 'man
who owns a harem'. Sexualised violence is also described in the chat as an
external problem that is due to migration. Thus, othering mechanisms are at
play. The image of Muslim or migrant men as a threat to (German) women
indirectly leads to an identity construction as a protector of 'our women'.

Mobilising strategies and calls to action

In the chat, some identity constructions are closely linked to mobilising
strategies and calls to action. For example, within the following message

a call for a demonstration is directly linked to the scenario of threatened children, thereby calling upon family-centred identity constructions as mothers or concerned parents: '. . . they can take away your children [. . .] They will take EVERYTHING away from you, force genetically modified [. . .] RNA vaccines into you [. . .]! YOU HAVE TO COME TO BERLIN ON 18.11!' (Chat member C.10, 10 October 2020, 2.44 pm).

Pointing to the threat scenario of children who are taken away from their families the message addresses 'concerned parents' and calls to mobilise for a demonstration in Berlin. Through phrases like 'They will take EVERYTHING away from you' an unspecified and powerful 'They' is constructed, as is common in conspiracy theories.

Descriptions of women as weak and potential victims, as well as of men as strong and soldierly, are also directly linked to calls to action. Women are portrayed as victims of the corona measures and in contrast men are called upon to fight these measures and the associated conspirators. Thus, these identity constructions are used to mobilise men specifically, as the following shows:

> Let's storm health offices and town halls with angry mobs. Beat up all employees and make it clear to them that they will hang from trees in the future if they continue to do Gates' dirty work [. . .] People prefer to demonstrate in masks and film women being led away. (Chat member O.4, 27 October 2020, 2.55 pm)

This message is a direct call to violence, which is connected to the idea of Gates being the centre of a supposed conspiracy. At the same time the statement that 'women being led away' at demonstrations portrays women as victims. In addition, the message reveals a criticism of the demonstrations, which are perceived as too peaceful. Instead, there is a call for violence to protest against the measures; thus, a call to radicalise the protests. Over the analysed period of time, the calls to action became more and more violent within the chat.

Identity constructions as fighters for the freedom of speech and expression and the mentioned othering mechanisms of feminist, LGBTIQ+ persons, Jews and Muslims also appeared alongside calls to action within the chat, but these calls to action did not show any corona conspiracy theory content.

Delegitimise criticisms

Criticism and counter-arguments in relation to the anti-feminist narratives were also found. However, these discussions could hardly develop before they stopped abruptly. Discussions were ended in three ways: by insulting chat members, by referencing the narrative of the supposed restriction of speech and expression, or by recalling common goals and the supposed current oppression in the wake of the COVID-19 pandemic. Chat members who did express criticism of anti-feminist, homophobic or misogynist statements were personally attacked, as can be seen in the following discussion on reproductive rights that took place on 30 December 2020. The discussion started as one person shared a news article on the legalisation of abortions in Argentina containing pictures of demonstrators celebrating the new law. The reactions to this post were the following:

> Chat member T.5: Well, if women didn't murder unborn life, they would continue to live. No sympathy for women who die during abortions.
>
> Chat member P.8: [. . .] how dare you to judge these women without knowing the reasons why women take this step [. . .] You obviously haven't learned to respect opinions and actions that are legal in other countries for good reason.
>
> Chat member D.12: Are you mental?
>
> Chat member T.5: You can see how perverse and unnatural society has become when the murder of the unborn is seen as social progress. Cunts who advocate such things are welcome to get vaccinated. Better if they become infertile.

Person T.5 reacts to the post and calls abortion murder, for which the death of women seems to be a deserved consequence. Chat member P.8 disagrees, attacks T.5 and refers positively to the legalisation of abortion by stating that it is legal 'for good reason'. Another person joins in and attacks P.8 by asking in a devaluating and rhetorical way 'Are you mental?' Chat member T.5 also insults P.8 personally using a sexist slur, before turning to the alleged consequences for societies. In addition, T.5 refers to the conspiracy theory of infertility as a consequence of vaccination. Chat member P.8 did not react to these insults, instead the discussion ended abruptly at this point.

Criticism – both from outside as well as from other chat members – was also delegitimised through the narrative of the restriction of speech and expression. Moreover, internal debates, discussions and criticism of discriminating behaviour or language use are impeded by referring to the shared goal of fighting for the freedom of speech and expression and the associated identity construction as fighters for democratic values. These identity constructions also legitimise one's actions. Thus, disagreements are quickly resolved or made impossible, as can be seen in the following discussion that took place on 3 November 2020:

Chat member C.7: I am glad that generations of women have fought so that I can live like this today.

Chat member T.5: [. . .] I've also heard from women that feminism doesn't give them any space to be female anymore because that's something bad for feminists.

Chat member C.7: [. . .] Without this movement, I would not have the same opportunities today. That is why I am grateful to all the women for their struggle. But enough about the topic, this is actually about the current oppression and it affects everyone, whether man or woman.

The discussion starts[2] with person C.7 referring to feminism as something positive and showing gratitude to the feminist movement, to which person T.5 reacts by portraying feminism as a threat to women's femininity. Person C.7 then answers and again positively refers to feminism, but also ends the discussion by pointing to the alleged 'current oppression' and its supposed effects on 'everyone, whether man or woman'. This way of covering up disagreements by referring to the supposed current oppression is seen again and again in the chat.

The analysis of the narratives also indicates that disagreement and criticism among the chat members were becoming less and less frequent over time, i.e. the chat is becoming more and more homogeneous. Throughout the chat, especially active chat members dominated discussions and dismissed criticism. Thus, chat members who are particularly active in spreading anti-feminist narratives and conspiracy theories also dominated discussions and dismissed criticism of their statements not only by referring to freedom of speech and expression but also by personally insulting and attacking other chat members.

Bridging functions

Anti-feminist narratives also fulfil bridging functions as they enable right-wing actors to spread their ideas in the Telegram chat as well as to incorporate current corona conspiracy theories into their narratives. Moreover, by telling anti-feminist stories chat members also reference well-known anti-feminist actors, thus, introducing them to the chat. Further, the anti-feminist dismissal of gender studies is closely interwoven with a general rejection of science.

First, as already mentioned anti-feminist narratives are partially interwoven with corona conspiracy theories and criticisms of the corona measures. Thus, anti-feminist narratives provide a link that enables far-right actors to incorporate current corona conspiracy theories into their

ideological narratives. For example, identity constructions such as 'protector of our women', which are widespread within far-right narratives,
come into play when constructions of a threatening Islam are interwoven with the corona conspiracy discourse. Further, anti-feminist narratives fulfil a bridging function by placing well-known anti-feminist
actors as trustworthy sources within the context of conspiracy theories.
How users of the Telegram chat are pointed towards well-known anti-
feminists such as the Canadian author Jordan Peterson can be seen in
the following message:

> . . . There's nothing to be said against emancipation. But the pendulum
> swings too far, as is so often the case, and then it becomes absurd or per-
> verted [. . .] Men are often insecure. What is masculine? What am I still
> allowed to do or say? The man is supposed to show feelings and be strong
> at the same time. Then concepts and terms are created like toxic masculin-
> ity [. . .] I recommend Jordan Peterson on the subject. (Chat member Z.3,
> 3 November 2020, 7.35 pm)

Chat member Z.3 adds to the narrative of an overreaching feminism. The
person portrays men as victims of feminism and especially dismisses concepts that question certain forms of masculinity. The chat member then
refers to Jordan Peterson as a trustworthy source 'on the subject'. Also,
Telegram channels of well-known anti-feminists do get promoted through
forwarded messages, for example from well-known German anti-feminists
such as Eva Herman.

In the context of corona conspiracy theories, anti-feminist narratives are
also concerned with the devaluation of gender studies, which are depicted
as a part of a supposed corona conspiracy. The anti-feminist attacks on gender studies within the chat serve to strengthen a general rejection of science:

> Christian Drosten – in court? [. . .]

> Are scientists, who have repeatedly interfered in politics in recent years,
> liable for the consequences of their interference? This question can be spec-
> ified as mimicry subjects have been installed at universities, such as gender
> studies, which have nothing even remotely to do with science, but whose
> aim is explicitly to bring social change, for example by procuring pseudo-
> scientific legitimacy for political measures such as quotas for women or
> discrimination programs such as the female professor program (which is
> to be sold as scientific justification). One should also think of supposed
> scientists who call for a comprehensive societal restructuring because of the
> allegedly man-made climate change [. . .].' (Chat member K.3, 23 Decem-
> ber 2020, 1.31 pm)

The message's title refers to Christian Drosten, a German virologist who had been all over the media during the COVID-19 pandemic and was part of a scientific council for the German government at the beginning of the pandemic. The message refers to this advisory role by asking the rhetorical question: 'Are scientists, who have repeatedly interfered in politics in recent years, liable for the consequences of their interference?' The message then jumps to gender studies as an alleged example of a 'pseudo-scientific' science, which is supposed to 'bring social change' rather than scientific progress. Climate research is devalued as well, as it also aims for societal changes. Even though the post refrains from an open denial of science it doubts the social and political relevance of scientific – including virologic – knowledge using the anti-feminist devaluation of gender studies as its main argument. Furthermore, distrust of politics is expressed, as it would be steered by the scientists, which in turn would primarily represent ideological interests.

Discussion

As Graff and Korolczuk (2021) and others show, anti-feminism can be expressed through conspiracy theories. This study asked in what way anti-feminist narratives emerge in the context of corona conspiracy theories and examined the functions and dynamics associated with these narratives. By means of qualitative content analysis and narrative analysis, this study showed that several anti-feminist narratives are intertwined with corona conspiracy theories, for example through the story of an alleged 'abortion industry' as part of a corona conspiracy. Further, within the context of corona conspiracy theories, anti-feminist narratives fulfil several functions. Anti-feminist narratives are part of mobilising strategies and calls to action, they lead to identity and othering mechanisms and they are used to delegitimise criticism. Moreover, they serve as bridges between corona conspiracy theories, far-right ideologies and anti-feminist movements.

In the chat, several different anti-feminist narratives interlink. For example, narratives of anti-political correctness refer to alleged restrictions of the freedom of speech and expression due to feminism or political correctness (Blum, 2019), which are further linked to narratives of anti-genderism that resemble narratives that Marchlewska et al. (2019) call gender conspiracy beliefs. Anti-gender narratives are also used to strengthen a general rejection of science by devaluating gender studies. Also, gender studies are portrayed as an indoctrination from 'above' as is common in anti-genderism (Hark and Villa, 2015).

Anti-etatist positions are also expressed through the construction of a so-called 'homo-lobby' that allegedly dominates international institutions and the EU. Heteronormative ideas also form the basis of narratives that resemble masculinism such as concepts of a soldierly masculinity (Gesterkamp, 2012). In line with family-centred anti-feminism, the family – as a patriarchal and heteronormative entity – is portrayed as threatened (Blum 2019; Näser-Lather et al., 2019). These anti-feminist narratives are integrated into corona conspiracy narratives, e.g. the narrative of female infertility through vaccination. Moreover, narratives of an 'abortion industry' as part of an alleged corona conspiracy are similar to Christian fundamentalist anti-feminism (Sanders et al., 2014). However, these anti-feminist narratives also occur in the chat without intertwining with corona conspiracy theories.

As the belief in conspiracy theories plays a crucial role in the construction of identities (Leone et al., 2020) this study shows that anti-feminist narratives also do play a major role. Individual identities are constructed by addressing women as caring mothers and men as warlike and soldierly, therefore promoting anti-feminist concepts of manhood and womanhood. Furthermore, collective identities, such as 'concerned parents' or 'fighters for the freedom of speech and expression and democratic values', are constructed, which emphasises the importance of the digital space for conspiracy theorists to establish new social contacts and communities (Douglas et al., 2019). The latter identity is essential for different narratives, for example for narratives of anti-political-correctness, anti-genderism and far-right anti-feminism (Blum, 2019; Näser-Lather, 2019; Mayer, 2021).

Family-centred identity constructions of mothers and 'concerned parents' are the most common identity construction within the chat. They are also part of calls to action that are interwoven with corona conspiracy theories. These constructions of 'concerned parents' also resemble anti-feminist attacks on sexual education and gender-reflective pedagogical approaches, which are seen as a threat to children and families as well (Laumann and Debus, 2018). The family-centred anti-feminist narratives are also similar to other conspiracy theories such as the QAnon conspiracy theory, which is widespread in the chat and also increasingly argues with an alleged concern for children. Supporters of the QAnon conspiracy theory are known for the slogan 'Save the children' as the conspiracy theory claims that an unspecified powerful elite kidnaps and abuses children (Virchow and Häusler, 2020, p. 25f.). One strategy of spreading the QAnon conspiracy theory is to address chat members in their roles as 'concerned parents' or mothers. Thus, using identity constructions which are also central in anti-feminist narratives.

Corresponding to these identity mechanisms are othering processes. Through narratives of an omnipresent and powerful feminism, a malicious other is constructed, and through the idealisation of the cis-gender, heteronormative family, other concepts of living as well as LGBTIQ+ persons are devalued as they negate the biologistic perception of gender as binary (Thiem, 2020). Additionally, anti-feminist narratives were closely linked to sexism and misogyny (Astapova et al., 2020). Right-wing femonationalism is linked to corona measures and corona conspiracy theories by framing migration and Islam as a threat.

Anti-feminist narratives are also linked to calls to action and calls to violence. For example, family-centred anti-feminists narratives address chat users as 'concerned parents', who have to act on behalf of their children. Calls for violence are especially addressing men as fighters and soldiers to fight the corona measures and the alleged conspirators, which strengthens anti-feminist stereotypes of men as soldierly and strong. Therefore, a close relation of anti-feminist ideas of masculinity and violence becomes apparent, which reveals the potential for a radicalisation of the discourse within corona conspiracy theories, especially as calls for violence appear more frequently over time.

The narrative of restrictions on the freedom of speech and expression is also used to shut down or prevent discussion and criticism of antisemitic, misogynous or racist comments. This reveals a limited understanding of democracy, which excludes political minorities. A safeguarding of one's own privileges is performed as one's own freedom of speech and expression is defended while the freedom of the other is denied. Even though criticism and disagreements show that different opinions are represented in the chat, over the course of time an increasing homogenisation of the chat happens, with less and less criticism and debate. Thus, as with Grande et al. (2021) this study shows a growing risk of radicalisation within the context of corona conspiracy theories. In addition to the risk of homogenisation and radicalisation posed by the technical structure of the platform Telegram and its tendency to construct echo chambers (Solopova et al., 2021), the chat members themselves add to this risk by preventing criticism and discussion.

Furthermore, anti-feminist narratives fulfil a bridging function as they enable far-right ideologies to incorporate current corona conspiracy theories into their narratives. As with Grande et al. (2021), this study therefore shows a potential mobilising effect for far-right movements through corona conspiracy theories. Moreover, anti-feminist narratives introduce well-known anti-feminist actors as trustworthy sources to chat users. Anti-feminist content is thus coupled with corona conspiracy theories in two ways: on the one hand, anti-feminist actors participate in the protests or publicly spread corona conspiracy theories, on the other hand anti-feminist narratives are interwoven with corona conspiracy theories in the Telegram chat. As well-known anti-feminist actors participated in the protests it can be assumed that some of the protesters already had an anti-feminist world-view. However, previous studies indicate a heterogeneous composition of the protest participants (Grande et al., 2021). This study now shows the danger of an increasing homogenisation of participants' views towards anti-feminist ideas. While the corona-centred narratives are likely to lose their mobilising power as the pandemic subsides, anti-feminist narratives show a certain timelessness, since they do not refer to a specific situation but, with topics such as sexuality and gender, touch on essential societal issues (Thiem, 2020). Therefore, there is a growing danger of sustained anti-feminist politicisation reaching beyond the current COVID-19 crisis.

In conclusion, this study showed that anti-feminism and the belief in conspiracy theories co-occur and are closely intertwined with each other as anti-feminist narratives fulfil different functions within the context of corona conspiracy theories. Due to the limitation of the research material and the specific context of the corona conspiracy theories in Germany, further research is necessary to understand the complex relationship between anti-feminism and conspiracy theories.

Notes

1. All of the chat messages shown here have been translated by the author of the study.
2. The message itself is a response to another previous message that has been deleted or is from a deleted account at the time of the data analysis.

References

Astapova, A., Bergmann, E., Dyrendal, A., Rabo, A., Rasmussen, K. G., Thórisdóttir, H. and Önnerfors, A. (2020). *Conspiracy Theories and the Nordic Countries* (1st edition). Routledge.

Blum, R. (2019). *Angst um die Vormachtstellung. Zum Begriff und zur Geschichte des deutschen Antifeminismus.* Marta Press UG.

Blum, R. and Rahner, J. (2020). Triumph of the Women? The Female Face of Right-wing Populism and Extremism Case Study: Anti-feminism in Germany During the Coronavirus Pandemic. *Friedrich-Ebert-Stiftung.* http://library.fes.de/pdf-files/dialog/17098.pdf

Byford, J. (2011). *Conspiracy Theories.* Palgrave Macmillan.

Claus, R. (2014). Maskulismus. Antifeminismus zwischen vermeintlicher Salonfähig-keit und unverhohlenem Frauenhass. *Friedrich-Ebert-Stiftung.* http://library.fes.de/pdf-files/dialog/10861.pdf

Culina, K. (2018). Verschwörungsdenken, Antifeminismus, Antisemitismus. Die Zeitschrift Compact als antifeministisches Diskursorgan. In J. Lang and U. Peters (eds), *Antifeminismus in Bewegung. Aktuelle Debatten um Geschlecht und sexuelle Vielfalt* (pp. 91–116.). Marta Press UG.

Douglas, K. M., Uscinski, J. E., Sutton, R. M., Cichocka, A., Nefes, T., Siang Ang, C. and Deravi, F. (2019). Understanding Conspiracy Theories. *Advances in Political Psychology, 40*(1), 3–35.

Farris, S. (2011). Die politische Ökonomie des Femonationalismus. *Feministische Studien, 29*(2), 321–34.

Gesterkamp, T. (2010). Geschlechterkampf von rechts: wie Männerrechtler und Familienfundamentalisten sich gegen das Feindbild Feminismus radikalisieren. *Friedrich-Ebert-Stiftung.* http://library.fes.de/pdf-files/wiso/07054.pdf

Gesterkamp, T. (2012). 'Die Männerbewegung' zwischen Geschlechterdialog und Antifeminismus. In A. Kemper (ed.), *Die Maskulisten* (pp. 79–100). Unrast Verlag.

Goodman, J. and Carmichael, F. (2020). The Coronavirus Pandemic 'Great Reset' Theory and a False Vaccine Claim Debunked. BBC. https://www.bbc.com/news/55017002

Graff, A. and Korolczuk, E. (2021). *Anti-Gender Politics in the Populist Moment* (1st edition). Routledge.

Grande, E., Hutter, S., Hunger, S. and Kanol, E. (2021). Alles Covidioten? Poli-tische Potenziale des Corona-Protests in Deutschland. WZB Discussion Paper, ZZ 2021-601. http://hdl.handle.net/10419/234470

Guhl, J., Ebner, J. and Rau, J. (2020). The Online Ecosystem of the German Far-Right. *Institute for Strategic Dialogue.* https://www.isdglobal.org/wp-content/uploads/2020/02/ISD-The-Online-Ecosystem-of-the-German-Far-Right-Eng-lish-Draft-11.pdf

Hark, S. and Villa, P. I. (2015). Eine Frage an und für unsere Zeit. Verstörende Gender Studies und symptomatische Missverständnisse. In S. Hark and P. I. Villa (eds), *Anti-Genderismus. Sexualität und Geschlecht als Schauplätze aktueller politischer Auseinandersetzungen* (pp. 15–39). Transcript Verlag.

Höcker, C., Pickel, G. and Decker, O. (2020). Antifeminismus – das Geschlecht im Autoritarismus? Die Messung von Antifeminismus und Sexismus in Deutsch-land auf der Einstellungsebene. In O. Decker and E. Brähler (eds), *Autoritäre Dynamiken. Neue Radikalität – alte Ressentiments. Leipziger Autoritarismus-Studie 2020* (pp. 249–82). Psychosozial-Verlag.

Hövermann, A. (2020). Corona-Zweifel, Unzufriedenheit und Verschwörungsmy-then: Erkenntnisse aus zwei Wellen der HBS-Erwerbspersonenbefragung 2020 zu Einstellungen zur Pandemie und den politischen Schutzmaßnahmen. *Hans-Böckler-Stiftung.* https://www.boeckler.de/fpdf/HBS-007886/p_wsi_pb_48_2020.pdf

Klein, O. and Nera, K. (2020). Social Psychology of Conspiracy Theories. In M. Butter and P. Knight (eds), *Routledge Handbook of Conspiracy Theories* (pp. 121–34). Routledge.

Kuckartz, U. (2018). Qualitative Inhaltsanalyse. Methoden, Praxis, Computerunterstützung. Beltz Juventa.

Laumann, V. and Debus, K. (2018). 'Frühsexualisierung' und 'Umerziehung'? Pädagogisches Handeln in Zeiten antifeministischer Organisierung und Stimmungsmache. In J. Lang and U. Peters (eds), *Antifeminismus in Bewegung, Aktuelle Debatten um Geschlecht und sexuelle Vielfalt* (pp. 275–302). Marta Press UG.

Leone, M., Madisson, M. L. and Ventsel, A. (2020). Semiotic Approaches to Conspiracy Theories. In M. Butter and P. Knight (eds), *Routledge Handbook of Conspiracy Theories* (pp. 43–55). Routledge.

McKenzie-McHarg, A. (2020). Conceptual History and Conspiracy Theory. In M. Butter and P. Knight (eds), *Routledge Handbook of Conspiracy Theories* (pp. 16–27). Routledge.

Marchlewska, M., Cichocka, A., Łozowski, F., Górska, P. and Winiewski, M. (2019). In Search of an Imaginary Enemy: Catholic Collective Narcissism and the Endorsement of Gender Conspiracy Beliefs. *The Journal of Social Psychology*, 159(6), 766–79.

Mayer, S. (2021). Anti-Gender-Diskurse – vom 'gesunden Menschenverstand' zur 'Politik mit der Angst'. In S. A. Strube, R. Perintfalvi, R. Hemet, M. Metze and C. Sahbaz (eds), *Anti-Genderismus in Europa* (pp. 35–50). Transcript Verlag.

Nachtwey, O., Schäfer, R. and Frei, N. (2020). *Politische Soziologie der Corona-Proteste.* (SocArXiv, Dezember 2020).

Näser-Lather, M. (2019). 'Wider den Genderismus!' Kritik und Polemiken gegen die Gender Studies in akademischen Kontexten. In M. Näser-Lather, A. L. Oldemeier and D. Beck (eds), *Backlash?! Antifeminismus in Wissenschaft, Politik und Gesellschaft* (pp. 105–27). Ulrike Helmer Verlag.

Näser-Lather, M., Oldemeier, A. L. and Beck, D. (2019). Die Geschichte des Janus. Antifeminismus zwischen Backlash und Moderne. In M. Näser-Lather, A. L. Oldemeier and D. Beck (eds), *Backlash?! Antifeminismus in Wissenschaft, Politik und Gesellschaft* (pp. 7–38). Ulrike Helmer Verlag.

Oswald, B. (2020). *Querdenker: Wer sie sind – und wie sich die Bewegung entwickelt.* https://www.br.de/nachrichten/deutschland-welt/die-querdenker-eine-heterogene-protestbewegung,SO9TvdX

Potter, Nicholas (2020, 13 August). Telegram-Leaks. Hinter der Maske der besorgten 'Corona-Rebellen' lauern Gewaltfantasien. *Belltower – Netz für digitale Zivilgesellschaft.* https://www.belltower.news/telegram-leaks-hinter-der-maske-der-besorgten-corona-rebellen-lauern-gewaltfantasien-102519/

Prucha, N. (2016). IS and the Jihadist Information Highway – Projecting Influence and Religious Identity via Telegram. *Perspectives on Terrorism, 10*(6), 48–58.

Riessmann, C. K. (2008). *Narrative Methods for the Human Sciences.* SAGE Publications.

Rubin, D. I. and Wilson, F. A. (2021). *A Time of Covidiocy: Media, Politics, and Social Upheaval.* Brill.

Salheiser, A. and Richter, C. (2020). Die Profiteure der Angst? Rechtspopulismus und die COVID-19-Krise in Europa. Deutschland. *Friedrich-Ebert-Stiftung.* http://library.fes.de/pdf-files/bueros/paris/16937.pdf

Sanders, E., Jentsch, U. and Hansen, F. (2014). 'Deutschland treibt sich ab'. Organisierter 'Lebensschutz'. Christlicher Fundamentalismus. Antifeminismus. Unrast Verlag.

Schutzbach, F. (2016). Der Heidi-Komplex: Gender, Feminismus und der Ekel vor der Gleichmacherei. *PROKLA. Zeitschrift für Kritische Sozialwissenschaft, 46*(185), 583–97.

Siapera, E. (2019). Online Misogyny as Witch Hunt: Primitive Accumulation in the Age of Techno-capitalism. In D. Ging and E. Siapera (eds), *Gender Hate Online.* Palgrave Macmillan.

Siri, J. (2015). Paradoxien konservativen Protests Das Beispiel der Bewegungen gegen Gleichstellung in der BRD. Paradoxien konservativen Protests. Das Beispiel der Bewegungen gegen Gleichstellung in der BRD. In S. Hark and P. I. Villa (eds), *Anti-Genderismus. Sexualität und Geschlecht als Schauplätze aktueller politischer Auseinandersetzungen* (pp. 239–55). Transcript Verlag.

Solopova, V., Scheffler, T. and Popa-Wyatt, M. (2021). A Telegram Corpus for Hate Speech, Offensive Language, and Online Harm. *Journal of Open Humanities Data, 7*(8), 1–15.

Stein, R. A., Ometa, O., Pachtman Shetty, S., Katz, A., Popitiu, M. I. and Brotherton, R. (2021). Conspiracy Theories in the Era of COVID-19: A Tale of Two Pandemics. *International Journal of Clinical Practice, 75*(e13778).

Sunstein, C. R. and Vermeule, A. (2009). Conspiracy Theories: Causes and Cures. *Journal of Political Philosophy, 17*(2), 202–27.

Thiem, A. (2020). Conspiracy Theories and Gender and Sexuality. In M. Butter and P. Knight (eds), *Routledge Handbook of Conspiracy Theories* (pp. 292–303). Routledge.

Virchow, F. and Häusler, A. (2020). Pandemie-Leugnung und extreme Rechte in Nordrhein-Westfalen. *Netzwerk für Extremismusforschung in Nordrhein-Westfalen.* https://www.bicc.de/uploads/tx_bicctools/CoRE_Kurzgutachten3_2020.pdf

South African Anti-Feminism: Race, Gender and Sexuality in the Opposition to Feminist Activism

Amber Beeson

On Thursday, 5 September 2018, thousands of South African men and women gathered in Cape Town to protest the widespread violence faced by women and members of the LGBTIQ+ community. The hashtags #NotIn-MyName, #AmINext and #SAShutDown were deployed by countless Twitter users who utilised the social media platform to speak out against the domestic violence, rape and femicide endemic in the country. These social media campaigns and organised protests have become common-place in South Africa as feminist activists push for real change and urge the South African government and police force to take gender inequality and violence against women seriously. Though South Africa has a long and vibrant history of women's rights activism, there continues to be a flood of issues facing women in the country today, including employment discrimination, harassment and overwhelmingly commonplace instances of rape and violence. How do we account for the vast discrepancy between women's rights and protections on paper and the actual lived experiences of South African women? It is obvious that progressive legislation does not automatically translate into a more progressive culture. This chapter attempts to answer that question by analysing the impacts of various anti-feminist actors in the state, both secular and religious, who have played a significant role in the perpetuation of gender inequality and violence against women that continue to plague the country despite the long list of legal protections that have been passed in recent decades.

History of Feminism and Women's Rights Activism in South Africa

In order to more comprehensively understand the ways that feminist activism is being combatted in South Africa, it is important to briefly examine the history of feminism in the country. Feminism in the South African context is an inherently contentious topic, which has in turn resulted in less feminist analysis in scholarship on South Africa compared to scholarship on feminisms in Europe and the United States. Scholarship on gender and feminism has proliferated since about the mid-1990s, however – an upward trajectory which scholars Robert Morrell and Lindsay Clowes from the University of Cape Town argue is 'likely explained by the growth of academic interest in gender in the North and its spread to the South, new publishing opportunities, and the increase of interest in gender by students and researchers in South Africa' (Morrell and Clowes, 2016, p. 2). As scholarship on African feminisms grows, so too do the definitions of what exactly 'African feminism' is. As feminist scholar Desiree Lewis (2001, p. 4) asserts, 'essentialist evocations of geographical, national or racial criteria as decisive grounds for defining African feminism are especially untenable in our current context of intensified globalisation'. One of the predominant voices on African feminisms in the late 190s was Gwendolyn Mikell, who in 1997 argued that 'the slowly emerging African feminism is distinctly heterosexual, with many "bread, butter, culture, and power" issues' (Mikell, 1997, p. 4). Mikell's definition of African feminism has been criticised by some scholars in the years since its publication, with scholars such as Josephine Ahikire arguing that 'in the current period, such a perspective on feminism in Africa is not only conservative, but does a disservice to the women's movements, and to the generations that have been dedicated to pursuing more audacious and radical agendas, especially in the fraught arenas of sexuality, culture, and religion' (Ahikire, 2014, p. 9). Over the past couple of decades, prominent scholars of feminism in South Africa such as Desiree Lewis (2001, 2007), Shireen Hassim (2006) and Gabeba Baderoon (2021) have begun to work to deepen understandings of South African feminisms and the various nuances that exist within South Africa's rich history of feminist activism.

Women's experiences in South Africa are in many ways determined by their race, class, gender identity and sexual orientation – intricacies which complicate scholarly examinations of feminism in the country. As prominent South African feminist Desiree Lewis (2007, p. 20) has argued: 'It is no longer possible to get away with exploring gender relations without simultaneously examining the numerous other identities to which they are linked as well as the associated complexities around how to perform them.' Many Black and Coloured women in South Africa have traditionally been sceptical of the feminist label, believing it to essentially be a White woman's luxury.[1] While there was certainly an overarching, 'hegemonic feminism' practised by middle- and upper-class White women in South

Africa during apartheid, there are multitudinous examples of intersectional cooperation, and it would be a major scholarly oversight to limit the scope of South African feminisms to one specific group of women or type of activism. During the apartheid era, shared interests in women's rights bridged the gaps between women of different races, ethnicities and classes, and despite rigid legislation regulating multiracial interactions throughout South African society during apartheid, a number of prominent organisations boasted multiracial membership, including the African National Congress Women's League (ANCWL), the Federation of South African Women (FSAW) and the Black Sash. Also, despite the scepticism of some women of colour in South Africa regarding 'feminism', there were other women of colour who embraced the label and started their own organisations such as Women Against Repression (WAR) which was founded in 1987 by Coloured woman Rozena Maart. Although women's rights activism during the twentieth century has long been eclipsed in scholarship by the broader anti-apartheid movement, women across the socio-demographic spectrum were in fact working in tandem throughout the twentieth century and into the post-apartheid era to secure gender specific rights and protections, including legal protections against sexual and domestic violence and the right to obtain safe and legal abortions.

The large-scale gender-based violence (GBV) protests in 2018 come over sixty years after the first significant women's march in South Africa, the 1956 Women's March in Pretoria, in which nearly 20,000 women from all socio-demographic backgrounds gathered to protest restrictive legislative changes to the Group Areas Act and the imposition of pass laws onto South African women of colour.[2] The 1956 Women's March is considered to have been a 'spectacular success', as it paved the way for the wide-scale feminist activism that would follow it and served as a catalyst for interracial organising among South African women (South African History Online, 2016). Women's rights activism had many victories in subsequent decades, and women were afforded significant freedoms and protections in the country's progressive 1996 constitution, which was lauded internationally for being one of the most progressive constitutions in the world at the time. Crucial legislation was passed between 1996 and 1998 which intended to promote gender equality and women's safety, including the Domestic Violence Act 116, Choice on Termination of Pregnancy Act, and the Employee Equity Act 55. The 1990s were a beacon of hope for South African women's rights activists, and it seemed as if everything were changing for the better.

Though feminist activism achieved significant success at the end of the apartheid era, much women's rights legislation has proved to be largely symbolic in the years that have followed, as many South African women remain underpaid, underemployed, undereducated, and at serious risk of domestic and sexual violence. South Africa has been found at the top of the list of rape statistics in numerous studies in recent years. Failures of the police and the criminal justice system to take violence against women seriously has led many South African women – especially women of colour – to not report violent crimes, and a 2018 study regarding violence against women found that people of colour were four times less likely to trust police in cases of domestic and sexual violence (Maluleke, 2018). Only about half of abortions procured in South Africa are safe and legal, and are disproportionately accessible to middle- and upper-class White women.

Furthermore, studies conducted by the World Bank over the past decade have named South Africa 'The World's Most Unequal Country' due to its immense wealth disparity which has led to inaccessibility to proper health care, education and employment for poor women, and has contributed to the high levels of violence that continue to be a threat (Beaubien, 2018). Additionally, anti-feminism – or, the opposition to feminism and female advancement – is rife in the South African context.

Theoretical Framework and Methodology

Statistics show that women in South Africa continue to face inequality, discrimination and violence, despite the extensive rights and protections guaranteed to them in South Africa's constitution. In order to understand this phenomenon, scholars need to re-conceptualise power in the South African context. In order to do so, this project uses French philosopher Michel Foucault's theory of power as a starting point to examine disparities between the legal rights and lived experiences of South African women. Placing too much emphasis on the influence of the top-down power structure, with the government at the apex, is limiting and does not adequately elucidate the issues facing South Africa today. Whereas power has classically been understood as stemming from government or law, Foucault argued that power relations in human societies are far more complex and multidimensional. In *The History of Sexuality*, Foucault (1978) contests the 'juridico-discursive' conception of power as it portrays power as being largely negative, oppressive and restrictive. It is more useful to understand power relations as a complex web, wherein a multitude of societal actors are at play, rather than to conceptualise power as being a top-down, vertically linear phenomenon, which is largely reductive. Power is not only a product of legislation and government, but is also deployed within the home, romantic relationships, educational and religious institutions, workplaces, friendships, and beyond. In regards to anti-feminism in the South African context, certain actors in positions of power in political, educational and religious organisations wield their influence to spread anti-feminist rhetoric. Furthermore, Foucault conceptualises power as having the ability to be both a repressive and a productive force, which can be seen in the way that many people in South Africa have gravitated towards powerful and influential groups with explicitly anti-feminist ideologies in search of community and solidarity.

South Africa is one of the most racially and ethnically diverse nations in the world. In order to more comprehensively understand the impacts of anti-feminism in the South African context, this chapter uses Kimberlé Crenshaw's (1991) theory of intersectionality to examine the ways in which multiple layers of identity affect the lived experiences of South Africans. To look at anti-feminism in the South African context without considering the significance of factors of identity such as race, gender and sexuality would be limiting and would produce an incomplete analysis.

This chapter examines current anti-feminisms in South Africa by looking at newspaper articles, online blogs, interviews, sociological studies and government documents in order to understand the nuances within anti-feminist activism and discourse in the country today. By utilising these sources and engaging with Foucauldian theories of power and Kimberlé Crenshaw's theory of intersectionality, this chapter will build upon earlier studies of feminism and masculinism to argue that despite the many legislative successes of women's rights activism, various anti-feminist actors have played integral roles in the perpetuation of gender-based violence and inequality that remain endemic to the country today. First, the chapter will look at the right-wing religious organisations the Mighty Men Conference and the Worthy Woman's Conference to demonstrate the way that their widespread discourse has worked to combat feminist progress in the country. Then, the chapter will look at the ways that anti-feminism is deployed at the state level by politicians who have spoken out against gender equality and have spread misinformation about sexual and domestic violence. This will be followed by a discussion of anti-choice activism that is trying to dismantle abortion laws in the country. Finally, the chapter will examine the experiences of South Africa's LGBTIQ+ community with anti-feminism.

'Muscular Christianity' and 'Formenism'

Two major right-wing anti-feminist ideologies in South Africa are masculinism and formenism. Masculinist groups have been hugely influential in the dissemination of anti-feminist rhetoric around the globe, and

South Africa is no exception. Scholars Melissa Blais and Francis Dupuis-Déri define masculinism as an ideology that 'focuses primarily on masculinity and the place of white heterosexual men in North America and European societies [that is] concerned with the supposed ramifications of feminism and the alleged domination of women in both the public and private spheres' (Blais and Dupuis-Déri, 2012, p. 25). Masculinism is still a burgeoning field of study, and the majority of scholars that look at masculinist ideologies focus on the United States and Europe. However, there is a growing literature on masculinities in the global South, and studies of masculinities in South Africa are proliferating, led by scholars such as Kopano Ratele (2008, 2015) and Malose Langa (2020). Following the fall of apartheid and the increased rights afforded to women in the 1996 constitution, masculinism in South Africa has been on the rise and has manifested itself in various ways, including in 'muscular Christianity' groups such as the Mighty Men Conference (MMC) which has risen to great prominence since its inception in 2004 and, despite its predominately White membership, has attracted members of all racial and ethnic backgrounds along the way.

Masculinist rhetoric is generally characterised by a fear of feminism and female power, and masculinist groups typically call for a return to 'traditional' family values and for women to return to their secondary place in society and within the household. Some of the most prominent examples of masculinist anti-feminism in the country are 'Muscular Christianity' groups, which frequently deploy such rhetoric in the face of increased women's rights and feminist activism. One of the primary masculinist groups in South Africa is the Mighty Men Conference, which was started in 2004 by South African farmer and evangelist preacher Angus Buchan. Buchan's preachings have repeatedly come under fire for their controversiality, as he calls for women's submissiveness in society and the home, condemns homosexuality, and has said that only Jews and Afrikaners will ever see the Kingdom of Heaven (Mahlangu, 2019).[3] Buchan relentlessly preaches the need for South African men to re-establish their masculinity and reclaim their rightful place as 'prophets, priests, and kings' (Buchan, 2019) within the home and for South African women to willingly submit to the men in their lives. Discourse circulated by influential figures such as Buchan validates the toxic patriarchal structure of South African society that has perpetuated since the nation's inception and continues to complicate the progress of feminist activism towards gender equality and an end to discrimination and gender-based violence.

By looking at South African masculinism through a Foucauldian lens, it becomes obvious that discourse created and employed by anti-feminist evangelical ministers like Buchan puts them in a unique position of power and allows them to attract mass following. As prominent South African masculinities scholar Kopano Ratele (2008, p. 5) asserts, 'two important coordinates show themselves to be vital to bear in mind when trying to understand masculinity: power and meaning'. South Africa's long-standing patriarchal tradition at times validates the placement of men like Buchan in positions of influence and power; in turn, these men use their platforms to assign meaning to their ideologies of male superiority and other anti-feminisms. The Mighty Men Conference is a prominent node of power in South African society, with extensive reach. Estimates for the attendance at the 2010 Mighty Men Conference range between 140,000 to 350,000 (Staff Reporter, 2010; Nadar and Potgieter, 2010, p. 142). Buchan also preaches internationally, and has several other popular programmes within South Africa. Buchan told BizNews in a 2012 interview, 'I'm on TV every single day of the week. I do 10 programmes a week, that's 40 programmes a month. I'm preaching full-out. I'm doing columns for *Farmer's Weekly, Landbouweekblad, Vision* . . . I'm still writing books. I've written over 35 books' (Davis, 2017). Foucault (1978) asserts that it is within discourse that 'power and knowledge are joined together', and that discourse 'transmits and produces power' (p. 101). The case of Angus Buchan's preachings shows that within the right hands, anti-feminist discourse can be circulated far and wide, even from the grass-roots level.

Prior to 1996, women of colour were not considered equal citizens under the law; rather, customary law relegated them to the position of perpetual legal minors, under the authority of their fathers or husbands. While married, White women were also limited when it came to their legal freedoms, and had little to no economic autonomy or guardianship rights. On paper, rights for women of all racial and ethnic groups improved dramatically with the adoption of the new Bill of Rights in South Africa in 1996. The Mighty Men Conference's massive following can largely be attributed to men's increasing anxieties about the role of women in post-apartheid South African society as women have secured more rights and are entering higher education and the work force in higher numbers than ever before. Buchan plays heavily on these anxieties in order to increase the organisation's membership. In his book *Faith Like Potatoes,* Buchan laments, 'it is very hard for a husband to love his wife when she insists on wearing the trousers and refusing to submit. The children become traumatised when the wife belittles the so-called head of the house, or he beats up his wife so that she will submit. The result is rebellious children' (Buchan, 2006, p. 170). The hypocrisy in this sentiment is staggering in the way that it places blame on outspoken women for their children's trauma, rather than blaming the violence they see inflicted upon their mothers. While the vast majority of

Buchan's followers are White, nearly 20 per cent are men of colour, despite Buchan being open about his views on White supremacy and his controversial statements about Afrikaners and Jews being the only groups of people who will be allowed into heaven. This irony can be explained by Foucault's conceptualisation of power as being productive; large numbers of men across the racial spectrum in South Africa gravitate towards the Mighty Men Conference and the teachings of men like Buchan in search of solidarity, understanding and community. In some cases, the ideas that men of colour have about gender in South Africa align with those held by people like Buchan, and they search for brotherhood within his organisation even though he has deployed racist rhetoric openly in the past.

The idea that women should be subservient to men is not only prevalent among religious men in South Africa, but is also commonplace in some women's religious groups as well. The Mighty Men Conference's female counterpart, the Worthy Woman's Conference (WWC), also focuses on biblical notions of male authority and women's 'rightful place' within the home and outside of it. Scholars Sarojini Nadar and Cheryl Potgieter define the WWC as being 'formenist', an ideology that is feminism's antithesis. Nadar and Potgieter conceptualise formenism as an ideology that 'subscribes to a belief in the inherent superiority of men over women (in other words, only men can be leaders), but unlike masculinism, it is not an ideology developed and sustained by men, but one constructed, endorsed, and sustained by *women*' (Nadar and Potgieter, 2010, p. 141). The Worthy Woman's Conference was founded by White Afrikaner motivational speaker Gretha Wiid, and the vast majority of the WWC's membership are White women. Wiid has come under fire in South African media for her sexist, homophobic and Islamophobic rhetoric in her videos and publications. In discussing male authority and Christianity during the 2009 Worthy Woman's Conference, Wiid proclaimed, 'Jesus' authority has harmed nobody. If you have a husband like that, who doesn't want to be submissive? This is the function of the role that God has given to the wife: to be submissive' (Pretorius, 2018). Prominent figures like Wiid work to sustain hetero-patriarchal cultural behaviours and practices, especially in White, Afrikaner culture, that protect and, in many ways, justify gender inequality and violence against women. These attitudes contribute to the perpetuation of toxic patriarchy in South Africa, especially when they find their way onto far-reaching platforms such as the Mighty Men Conference and the Worthy Women Conference.

The objective of this project is not to condemn religion or place blame on religion for the gender-based atrocities that continue to occur in contemporary South Africa. Religion and patriarchy are not synonymous in this context. Many religious institutions in South Africa, including the influential Anglican Church, have been beacons of hope even in the darkest parts of the country's recent history, and have worked alongside different feminist activists and women's groups to help procure women's rights. However, other religious sects take a more traditional and patriarchal approach to their teachings, delivering a sort of 'palatable patriarchy' that uses religion to justify anti-feminist rhetoric and actions (Nadar, 2009). Over 85 percent of South Africans consider themselves to be religious, yet one in four men admit to having committed a rape, a statistic that illuminates the sometimes complicated relationship between patriarchy, religion and violence in the country (Nadar and Potgieter, 2010). Scholars like Sarojini Nadar argue that South Africa's deeply traditional religious beliefs help facilitate the nation's endemic violence against women, as gendered expectations of male authority and female submission remain deeply pervasive. Alongside social and cultural forces, traditional Christian beliefs have played a role in the creation and perpetuation of deep-seated patriarchy in South Africa. This 'profoundly macho culture' has fuelled the activism of a number of anti-feminist organisations and actors, both male and female, that work to keep women relegated to the position of second-class citizens (Smith, 2013).

State Anti-feminism

On paper, women in South Africa have extensive rights and protections in education, employment, health care and within personal relationships and in the home. As discussed throughout this chapter, however, these legal rights and protections have yet to be fully realised in contemporary South Africa. While within the government there are not currently any tangible, organised threats to dismantle existing women's rights legislation, there is an element of state anti-feminism present in South African governmental institutions. Francis Dupuis-Déri defines state anti-feminism as an ideology that 'signifies the actions of agents or agencies of the state that slow, stop, or push back the mobilisations of the feminist movement' (Dupuis-Déri, 2016, p. 23). Criticism of feminist activism and sexist comments have been deployed in recent years by notable political figures in South Africa, such as former president Jacob Zuma and former amaXhosa king Mpendulo Zwelonke Sigcawu.

Jacob Zuma has garnered international attention and media scrutiny for an abundance of transgressions in recent years, several of which are directly detrimental to the women in South Africa and combative towards feminist progress in the country. In 2005, two years before his ascension to the presidency, Zuma was accused of rape by Fezekile Ntsukela Kuzwayo, the daughter of an ANC member who had been imprisoned on Robben Island with Zuma for ten years. Zuma was found not guilty following his rape trial, while Kuzwayo was deemed a 'bitch' by the African National Congress Women's League, bombarded with death threats, and had her home burned down (Thamm, 2016). Kuzwayo was also HIV-positive, a fact that Zuma apathetically brushed off in his statements. Zuma asserted that it was not easy for men to contract the disease, and that he showered after the act in order to lower his risk of infection. His casual dismissal of the risks of HIV is particularly harmful in a nation with one of the largest HIV epidemics in the entire world.

Zuma's vocal misconceptions surrounding HIV/AIDS, and the relative silence of the South African government following the statements adds to the vast misinformation on HIV/AIDS in South Africa, leading AIDS denialists to cite Zuma's comments and behaviours in defence of their positions on the disease, in turn 'increasing public confusion about the issue' (Sidley, 2006). During his presidency, Zuma also criticised women for being overly sensitive to comments from men, complaining that 'When men compliment you innocently, you say it's harassment. You will miss out on good men and marriage' (Claymore, 2016), a sentiment that is blatantly ignorant to the lived realities of South African women who exist under constant threat of harassment and assault. Zuma's rhetoric downplays the seriousness of sexual harassment and frames men who do sexually harass women as being 'good men' while also reinforcing the long-standing patriarchal notion that marriage should be women's primary goal in life. This sort of dialogue coming from a character as influential and controversial as Jacob Zuma has a long reach in South Africa as it validates the patriarchal structure of South African society and the various threats that women face as a result of such pervasive patriarchy.

Women in government also continue to deal with sexism, even as female representation within government institutions improves. Although South Africa has some of the highest rates in the world of women holding government positions – in 2021, for instance, 51.2 per cent of the country's parliamentary members were women (Parliamentary Monitoring Group, 2021) – masculinist discourse surrounding women in politics is commonplace in South Africa. Lindiwe Mazibuko, a Black woman who became the parliamentary leader of the country's Democratic Alliance Party, said in an interview in 2014 that she had 'experienced sexism of every different kind' (Smith, 2014) as her age, appearance and gender were criticised by various political actors. While Mazibuko viewed the fervent criticism she and other female politicians faced as a 'signal' that women in politics were 'a threat' and 'a force to be reckoned with', she also lamented that it is 'depressing to be in a parliament that has so many female members willing to condone their male counterparts resorting to sexism and ageism and all kinds of other divisive tactics simply to score political points' (Smith, 2013). In 2017, the amaXhosa king at the time, Mpendulo Zwelonke Sigcawu, publicly stated that 'The country's problems have overwhelmed leaders who are men, how much more for a woman?' (Margolis, 2017). The same year, it was reported that male members of parliament would yell derogatory terms at female MPs as they took the stage, and that some male members of parliament made cat noises at female MPs while they spoke, an apparent 'tradition' in the South African parliament according to some news sources (Margolis, 2017). While women in South Africa are afforded significant representation in government, there are still issues within the government that perpetuate sexist attitudes and behaviours and keep women from achieving true equality.

Abortion Rights and Anti-choice Activism

On 7 May 2018, dozens of anti-choice activists formed a 'pro-life chain' blocking traffic in one of South Africa's capital cities, Pretoria. Participants held signs that read 'Abortion: God calls it murder' and 'One dead, one wounded' (Matshili, 2018). Those involved in the demonstration were not only adults, as children also were a part of the chain and passed out pamphlets to drivers and passers-by (Matshili, 2018). This example is one of many anti-choice demonstrations that have taken place in South Africa in the post-apartheid era, as those who oppose abortion strive to dismantle abortion laws and combat the feminist activism that helped legalise abortion in the first place. South Africa is home to dozens of anti-choice organisations such as Pro Life South Africa and Christians for Truth that have worked to make abortions harder to secure. Furthermore, in the country there are over fifty affiliates of Heartbeat International, an American right-wing Christian organisation that operates around the world to combat pro-choice activism (Cullinan et al., 2020).

Abortion activists have been met with anti-choice pushback for decades, and anti-choice organising has proliferated following the Termination of Pregnancy Act of 1996. The progressive legislation was shocking in the country, as many South Africans held very conservative views on the subject. Some South Africans were outraged by the legislation, especially among medical workers and religious groups. Soon after the passing of the act, a doctor in northern KwaZulu Natal began keeping two foetuses in bottles on his desk to 'act as a deterrent' (Russell, 1997). Twenty-five years after the legalisation of abortion, only 7 per cent of clinics in the country offer abortion services, which disproportionately affects poor, rural women and women of colour. The clinics that do provide abortion services are sometimes swarmed by anti-choice activists who harass patients, and at times even threaten violence. Misinformation is also spread by these activists and organisations. The University of Cape Town's Students for Life organisation states on the 'Introducing the South African Pro-Life Struggle' section on their website that 'Nine out of ten South Africans believe abortion is wrong, which makes us one of the most strongly pro-life countries in the world', a number that differs significantly from the statistics collected by the 2013 Social Attitudes Survey which found that only about 55 per cent of South Africans thought abortion to be 'always wrong' even in cases of familial poverty and foetal abnormality (Mosley et al., 2017). Abortion stigma is a significant factor in the inaccessibility of safe and legal abortions in South Africa today.

In addition to anti-choice organisations around the country, prominent politicians and religious leaders also contribute to the discourse surrounding abortion rights in South Africa. Evangelist Angus Buchan is vocally anti-abortion, which is obvious in his sermons and blog posts. At his notable 2016 appearance in Kilkenny, Buchan preached, 'I love families and I hate divorce. I think abortion is legalised murder. Why? Because the Bible tells me that' (Boland, 2016). In his video series 'The A–Z's of Christian Living', Buchan laments, 'I know of young people who have been very poor, have not been able to go to a proper doctor as it were, and they have died in the process of having an abortion. But the worst part is, you are going against the word of God' (Buchan, 2021). To his followers, Buchan stresses that the real tragedy of women dying as result of illicit abortions is not their actual death, but their defiance of Christian teachings. Pieter Groenewald, a parliament member and leader of South Africa's white, Afrikaner, far-right political party Freedom Front Plus, is also a notable figure who condemns abortion in South Africa. Groenewald has attended anti-abortion demonstrations in South Africa, including a 2019 march in Cape Town wherein participants held 'a funeral-like proceeding involving prayers for the souls of the unborn babies that have been aborted over the years since the legalisation of abortion in South Africa' (Yuku, 2019). Activists lamented that they had been pushing for their government to address the issue of abortion for years, but now 'carry on with faith that one day, members of parliament will hear their cry and realise the aftermath that comes with abortion' (Yuku, 2019). While it is unlikely that abortion rights in South Africa will be altered legally any time soon, a parliamentary member such as Groenewald's attendance at and support of events such as this help fuel the anti-feminist activism that continues to make safe and legal abortions in South Africa more difficult to procure.

The weight of anti-choice activism falls most heavily on the country's most marginalised populations, who typically have the highest need to procure safe and legal abortions due to poverty, pregnancy as a result of rape, and high rates of HIV transmission among poor people of colour. This phenomenon can be understood by utilising Crenshaw's theory of intersectionality, as those who find themselves at the nexus of several oppressed identities – i.e. race, class and gender – are the most heavily affected by abortion stigma and have the least accessibility to legal and safe abortions. The rate of teenage pregnancies in the country is extremely high, with at least four out of ten girls becoming pregnant at least once in their teenage years (Majavu, 2009). Adolescent girls in South Africa often-times have little negotiating power in sexual experiences, and little to no sexual and reproductive health education, both factors that have led to the country's high rates of adolescent pregnancies (Mchunu et al., 2012). Get-ting pregnant while still in school can be a huge roadblock for South Afri-can adolescents, and especially working-class girls of colour, who often do not have the resources or support systems necessary to go back to school after giving birth. Former South African president Jacob Zuma asserted in 2009 that teenage mothers should be sent away from their children after giving birth to finish their schooling, unable to return until they had com-pleted a degree (Maclean, 2015). Young women in South Africa continue to be blamed for getting pregnant, and face stigma in every direction, be it for becoming pregnant in the first place, for not finishing school, or for obtaining an abortion. The increased difficulties that young women of colour face in procuring safe abortions in the first place contribute heavily to their experiences as young mothers and the lack of opportunities that they have access to both in their adolescent years and beyond (Feltham-King and Macleod, 2021).

Scholars examined the 2013 Social Attitudes Survey in order to determine the impacts of socio-demographic differences on attitudes towards abor-tion, finding that non-Xhosa Africans and Coloured participants expressed anti-abortion attitudes at much higher rates than Xhosas and whites, and that participants with lower education levels tended to be far more opposed to abortion than their educated counterparts (Mosley et al., 2017).[4] They engage heavily with Crenshaw's work on intersectionality and Earnshaw and Kalichman's (2013) theory of intersectional stigma when analysing the attitudes of low-income women regarding abortion in South Africa. Poor Black women in particular often find themselves at the intersection of both economic and abortion stigma, which leads them to experience increased discrimination. The Social Attitudes Survey also shows that the lack of access to 'normative forms of status-building, identity-development, and meaning-making' leads to increased emphasis on the importance of motherhood in marginalised communities, which heightens the abortion stigma felt within such communities (Mosley et al., 2017). The intersections of race, class and religion play heavily on the consequences of anti-choice activism on South African women.

Anti-feminism and South Africa's LGBTIQ+ Community

Women who belong to the LGBTIQ+ community in South Africa are faced with a unique set of anti-feminisms. As in many other cases of gendered oppression in the country, White South Africans in the LGBTIQ+ community face the least stigma and discrimination within their families, communities and South African society more broadly, while people of colour face the brunt of homophobic and transphobic rhetoric and actions. Right-wing anti-feminism affects lesbians, bisexuals and transgendered people of colour significantly more so than it does cis-gendered White women. One of the most prevalent hate crimes against the queer community in South Africa is corrective rape, wherein men rape lesbians and bisexual women in an attempt to 'cure' them of their homosexuality. In 2011, it was estimated that an average of ten lesbian women are sexually assaulted a week in cases of corrective rape in Cape Town alone (Fihlani, 2011). Many perpetrators of corrective rape operate on the misconception that lesbian women have never been sexually satisfied by a man. Corrective rape is also sometimes used as a punishment by conservative South African men who believe homosexuality to be a sin, or a specifically un-African transgression. The notion that homosexuality is un-African has proliferated as gay right's movements have become more commonplace in Africa. Although rights and protections for South Africa's LGBTIQ+ community have been included in the country's constitution since its drafting in the mid-1990s, homophobia continues to '[operate] in violation of the law' with leaders like Jacob Zuma condemning homosexuality as a 'disgrace to the nation and to God' (Msibi, 2011). A 2012 report by In On Africa stated that 'When a lesbian presents her preferred orientation to community leaders, she may be correctively raped by members of the same tribe or township. Instead of being punished for the act, the rapist is exalted and venerated. Lesbians victimised by rape endure social persecution and report feelings of self-hate following the incident' (IOA, 2012). Violence, including rape, is a frequent threat to transwomen in South Africa as well. In a 2010 interview, trans-woman Vanya recounted multiple experiences of rape and sexual assault since coming out as transgender, which led her to develop a smoking habit, miss a semester of school, and seek counselling because of the extreme resulting depression (Morgan et al., 2009). Queer women who are victims of sexual violence are also at extremely high risk of HIV transmission, as it is estimated that nearly one-fifth of male rapists in South Africa are HIV-positive (IOA, 2012).

Progress

While much still needs to be done to combat gender-based violence in South Africa, many groups and individuals have been working tirelessly to realise the full potential of women's rights activism in the country. South Africa has a strong history of LGBTIQ+ rights activism that has been working to secure and protect rights for this community since the late 1980s, and has been a beacon of hope for other gay rights movements around the continent. The National Girl Child Movement of South Africa has educated over 1,000 South African boys and girls in 'anti-racism, anti-bullying and anti-sexism', and has taught girls empowerment through gardening and by emphasising their own unique abilities. The Girl Child Movement teaches girls that 'if she wants to become a pilot instead of a mother, she can do that' (Majavu, 2009). The non-profit organisation Sonke Gender Justice's 'One Man Can' campaign hosts workshops, commissions murals, holds door-to-door campaigns and hosts large public events in order to work towards educating communities about the harms of sexism and gender-based violence in the country, working to help men 'change their belief on gender norms, [take] an active stand against domestic and sexual violence, and [sustain] these changes in their personal lives' (van den Berg et al., 2013). Gender-based violence marches take place frequently, with both men and women involved. Male students at universities such as the University of KwaZulu-Natal have organised meetings regarding gender-based violence, which have had influential keynote speakers such as Rozena Maart, the woman who founded the country's first Black feminist group, WAR, and who is currently the Director for the Centre for Critical Research on Race and Identity. Large-scale organising that can be seen in protests and marches in recent years, such as the 2018 march against gender-based violence, demonstrates that great strides are being made to ensure the safety of women in South Africa. While there is still a long way to go, and a number of anti-feminist actors pushing back against women's rights, dedicated activists and organisations continue to push for gender equality and an end to gender-based violence in South Africa today.

There is still much work to be done. Hopefully this research helps to spark more in-depth examinations of the impacts of anti-feminist actors on contemporary South African society, especially in townships and rural areas that continue to be plagued by violence against women and disproportionately low access to economic and educational opportunities. In a 2020 interview, prominent feminist scholar Susan Faludi urges all people to 'dissect and try to understand how anti-feminist and other reactionary backlashes operate'. Faludi passionately urges academics in fields such as history, sociology and political science to address anti-feminism as 'true public intellectuals' who 'write and speak with clarity and in an accessible style to reach a large audience' (Faludi et al., 2020). This project attempts to answer that call.

Conclusions

This chapter has examined various nodes of anti-feminist influence in South Africa today to attempt to answer the question 'How do we account for the vast discrepancy between women's rights and protections on paper and the actual lived experiences of South African women?' Although South Africa has a long and vibrant history of women's rights and queer activism which has culminated in extensive protections and rights being incorporated into the country's progressive constitution, these groups continue to face inequality, discrimination and violence at alarming rates. Analysing the anti-feminist activism and discourse of right-wing grass-roots religious organisations, politicians and anti-choice groups brings clarity to the disparity between constitutional rights and the lived experiences of women and LGBTIQ+ persons.

To understand the disconnect between law and lived experiences, it is important to look not only at the power and influence of South African law and government, but to look also at the influence wielded by both secular and religious anti-feminist groups in the country. This chapter utilises Michel Foucault's theories of power as a starting point to re-conceptualise power in the South African context as a complex web of relations rather than a top-down structure in order to show how realities of gender-based discrimination and violence in South Africa are not products of the law; rather, they work in violation of the law. Furthermore, this chapter uses Kimberlé Crenshaw's theory of intersectionality to evaluate the ways that different layers of identity affect both those who wield anti-feminist power and those who fall victim to anti-feminist activism. In a country as diverse as South Africa, it is imperative to look at the ways in which identity factors such as race, ethnicity, gender, sexuality, class and religion intersect when examining issues in the country today, including the discrimination, violence and inequality that continue to plague women and members of the LGBTIQ+ community.

South African feminist activists continue to be met with pushback from a variety of anti-feminist actors, both religious and secular. Right-wing grass-roots Christian organisations such as the Mighty Men Conference and the Worthy Woman's Conference call for a return to 'traditional' gender relations, push for female submission, downplay the severity of relationship violence, and condemn abortion and homosexuality. Women in government continue to face sexism from some of their male counterparts. Anti-choice organisations like Pro Life South Africa and Christians for Truth campaign and protest against South Africa's progressive abortion legislation in an effort to dismantle the current abortion laws. Anti-feminist discourse emanates from each of these nodes of power, all of which wield considerable influence over public opinion in the country. The anti-feminist activism and discourse of these groups and individuals affects poor women of colour the most direly, as the accessibility of resources and support decreases with each added layer of oppression.

Anti-feminism in South Africa aids in the perpetuation of heteropatriarchal power structures in the country that allow for persistent gender discrimination and inequality. In turn, women and LGBTIQ+ persons continue to face consequent issues, including violence, harassment and inaccessibility to resources and support. If the underlying causes of sexual harassment and assault, relationship violence, the corrective rape of lesbians and inaccessible abortions are not addressed, such problems will persist, and South Africa will remain one of the most dangerous countries in the world for such vulnerable groups. In order to protect the rights of women and LGBTIQ+ persons in South Africa today, and to work towards true equality, we must address the anti-feminism deployed by politicians and right-wing groups both religious and secular that are actively working to combat feminist and queer progress in the country.

Notes

1. Throughout this chapter, in relation to race I use several different terms to describe different groups. Under apartheid, South Africans were categorised into four different racial classifications: White, Black, Coloured, and Indian. Whites were of European descent, Africans were of African descent, Indians of Indian descent, and Coloured acted as a sort of ambiguous blanket term that covered persons of mixed descent and also groups indigenous to South Africa such as the Khoi and the San. Both in apartheid legislation

and in historiography, 'Black' can sometimes refer to any non-white person, including people belonging to the coloured and Indian communities. When referring specifically to people who racially identify as 'coloured', I will refer to them as 'coloured'. Though I acknowledge that this classification is loaded with apartheid-era implications, it is still the most widely-accepted term for this purpose. When speaking about people who are not white, I will refer to them as people 'of colour' rather than non-white people.

2. The Group Areas Act No. 41 was enacted in 1950 by the apartheid government to separate different racial groups into specific zones where they could live and work. The result was ultimately that whites had prime real estate within cities while people of colour were relegated to the outskirts in neighbourhoods that were often overcrowded and had disproportionately low access to resources.

3. Afrikaners are descendants of early Dutch settlers in South Africa who speak Afrikaans.

4. Xhosa is one of the nine primary ethnic groups that make up South Africa's Black population.

References

Ahikire, J. (2014). African Feminism in Context: Reflections on the Legitimation Battles, Victories and Reversals. *Feminist Africa*, 19, 7–23.

Baderoon, G. and Lewis, D. (2021). *Surfacing: On Being Black and Feminist in South Africa*. Wits University Press.

Beaubien, J. (2018, 2 April). 'The country with the world's worst inequality is . . .' . *NPR*. https://www.npr.org/sections/goatsandsoda/2018/04/02/598864666/the-country-with-the-worlds-worst-inequality-is

Blais, M. and Dupuis-Déri, F. (2012). Masculinism and the Anti-feminist Counter-movement. *Social Movement Studies*, 11(1), 21–39.

Boland, R. (2016, 25 August). Kilkenny protest over claim to cure homosexuality via prayer. *The Irish Times*. https://www.irishtimes.com/news/social-affairs/kilkenny-protest-over-claim-to-cure-homosexuality-via-prayer-1.2767468.

Buchan, A. (2006). *Faith Like Potatoes*. Monarch Books.

Buchan, A. (2019, 14 August). The Intimacy of God. Angus' Desk. https://www.angusbuchan.co.za/angus-desk/2019/8/14/the-intimacy-of-god

Buchan, A. (2021, 1 April). What Does the Bible Say About Abortion? Angus' Desk. https://www.angusbuchan.co.za/a-to-z-of-christian-living/abortion

Claymore, E. (2016, 3 June). Women are too sensitive, mistake compliments for harassment. Zuma. *The South African*. https://www.thesouthafrican.com/news/women-are-too-sensitive-mistake-complimentsfor-harassment-zuma/

Crenshaw, K. (1991). Mapping the Margins: Intersectionality, Identity Politics, and Violence against Women of Color. *Stanford Law Review*, 43(6), 1241–99.

Cullinan, K., Modjadji, M. and Nortier, C. (2020, 11 February). Revealed: US-linked Anti-abortion Centres 'Violating the Law' in South Africa. *Open Democracy*.

https://www.opendemocracy.net/en/5050/revealed-us-linked-anti-abortion-centres-violating-the-law-in-south-africa/

Davis, R. (2017, 24 April). Analysis: The Gospel According to Angus Buchan. *Daily Maverick*. https://www.dailymaverick.co.za/article/2017-04-24-analysis-the-gospel-according-to-angus-buchan/

Dupuis-Déri, F. (2016). State Antifeminism. *International Journal for Crime, Justice and Social Democracy, 5*(2), 21–35.

Earnshaw, V. and Kalichman, S. (2013). Stigma Experienced by People Living with HIV/AIDS. In P. Liamputtong (ed.), *Stigma, Discrimination, and Living with HIV/AIDS: A Cross-Cultural Perspective*. Springer.

Faludi, S. et al. (2020). A Conversation with Susan Faludi on Backlash, Trumpism, and #MeToo. *Journal of Women in Culture and Society, 45*(2), 336–45.

Feltham-King, T. and Macleod, C. (2021, 11 October). South Africa's Stance on Teenage Pregnancy Needs a Radical Review: What it Would Look Like. *The Conversation*. https://theconversation.com/south-africas-stance-on-teenage-pregnancy-needs-a-radical -review-what-it-would-look-like-169032

Fihlani, P. (2011, 30 June). South Africa's Lesbians Fear 'Corrective Rape'. BBC News. https://www.bbc.com/news/world-africa-13908662

Foucault, M. (1978). *The History of Sexuality*. Pantheon.

Hassim, S. (2006). *Women's Organizations and Democracy in South Africa: Contesting Authority*. University of Wisconsin Press.

In On Africa (IOA). (2012, 20 September). *The 'L' Word: An Evaluation of Corrective Rape in South Africa*. Polity.

Langa, M. (2020). *Becoming Men: Black Masculinities in a South African Township*. Wits University Press.

Lewis, D. (2001). Introduction: African Feminisms. *Agenda: Empowering Women for Gender Equity, 50*, 4–10. http://www.jstor.org/stable/4066

Lewis, D. (2007). Feminism and the Radical Imagination. *Agenda (Durban), 21*(72), 18–31.

Maclean, R. (2015, 12 March). Zuma calls for teenage mothers to be sent to Robben Island. *The Times*. https://www.thetimes.co.uk/article/zuma-calls-for-teenage-mothers-to-be-sent-to-robben-island-qcmhzp0c7bw

Mahlangu, S. (2019, 10 November). God Loves Black People, Even If Angus Buchan Doesn't Agree. *Independent Online*. https://www.iol.co.za/news/opinion/god-loves-black-people-even-if-angus-buchan-doesnt-agree-36970123

Majavu, M. (2009, 10 July). South Africa: Fighting Sexism to Curb Out of Wedlock Births. *Global Information Network*.

Maluleke, R. (2018, June). Crime Against Women in South Africa: An In-depth Analysis of the Victims of Crime Survey Data 2018. *Statistics South Africa*. https://www.justice.gov.za

Margolis, H. (2017, 13 March). 17 times politicians have resorted to wildly sexist speech over the last year. *The New York Times*. https://www.hrw.org/news/2017/03/13/17-times-politicians-have-resorted-wildly-sexist-s peech-over-last-year

Matshili, R. (2018, 7 May). Pro-life Chain Formed in Anti-abortion Protest in City. *IOL.* https://www.iol.co.za/pretoria-news/pro-life-chain-formed-in-anti-abortion-protest-in-city-14817750

Mchunu, G., Peltzer, K., Tutshana, B. and Seutlwadi, L. (2012). Adolescent Pregnancy and Associated Factors in South African Youth. *African Health Sciences,* *12*(4), 426–34.

Mikell, G. (1997). *African Feminism: The Politics of Survival in Sub-Saharan Africa.* University of Pennsylvania Press.

Morgan, R., Marais, C. and Wellbeloved, J. R. (eds). (2009). *Trans: Transgender Life Stories from South Africa.* Jacana Media.

Morrell, R. and Clowes, L. (2016). The Emergence of Gender Scholarship in South Africa – Reflections on Southern Theory. University of Cape Town, Faculty of Humanities, Aids and Society Research Unit. http://hdl.handle.net/11427/21594

Mosley, E. A., King, E. J., Schulz, A. J., Harris, L. H., De Wet, N. and Anderson, B. A. (2017). Abortion Attitudes Among South Africans: Findings From the 2013 Social Attitudes Survey. *Culture, Health & Sexuality, 19*(8), 918–33.

Msibi, T. (2011). The Lies we Have Been Told: On (Homo) Sexuality in Africa. *Africa Today, 58*(1), 54–77.

Nadar, S. (2009). Palatable Patriarchy and Violence Against Wo/Men in South Africa: Angus Buchan's Mighty Men Conference as a Case Study of Masculinism. *Scriptura, 102*, 51–61.

Nadar, S. and Potgieter, C. (2010). Liberated through Submission?: The Worthy Woman's Conference as a Case Study of Formenism. *Journal of Feminist Studies in Religion, 26*(2), 141–51.

Parliamentary Monitoring Group. (2021, 16 August). Representation and Participation of Women in Parliament. Parliamentary Monitoring Group. https://pmg.org.za/blog/Representation%20and%20Participation%20of%20Women%20in%20Parliament

Pretorius, E. (2018). Mans se rol in die stryd om gendergeregtigheid: 'n Historiese oorsig van antifeminisme en profeminisme. *Tydskrif Vir Geesteswetenskappe, 58*(4–2), 887–904.

Ratele, K. (2008). Masculinities, Maleness and (Illusive) Pleasure. Africa Regional Sexuality Resource Center.

Ratele, K. (2015). Working Through Resistance in Engaging Boys and Men Toward Gender Equality and Progressive Masculinities. *Culture, Health and Sexuality, 17*(2), 144–58.

Russell, A. (1997, 19 November). Abortion Law, 'a hot potato' in South Africa. *Daily Telegraph.* https://www.proquest.com/docview/252499657?pq-origsite=primo

Sidley, P. (2006). Zuma's Trial Leaves Confused Messages on AIDS. *BMJ: British Medical Journal, 332*(7550), 1112.

Smith, A. (2013, 17 February). South Africa's macho society, where attacks on women are the norm. *The Observer.* https://www.theguardian.com/world/2013/feb/17/south-africa-macho-society-oscar-pistorious

Smith, D. (2014, 8 February). Lindiwe Mazibuko: The insults are a signal that we're having a huge impact. *The Observer*. https://www.theguardian.com/politics/2014/feb/09/lindiwe-mazibuko-south-africa-democ ratic-alliance

South African History Online. (2016). The 1956 Women's March, Pretoria, 9 August. South African History Online. sahistory.org.za/article/1956-womens-march-pretoria-9-august

Staff Reporter. (2010, 1 April). The wrong kind of power. *Mail and Guardian*. https://mg.co.za/article/2010-04-01-the-wrong-kind-of-power/

Thamm, M. (2016, 10 October). 'Khwezi', the woman who accused Jacob Zuma of rape, dies. *The Guardian*. https://www.theguardian.com/world/2016/oct/10/khwezi-woman-accused-jacob-zuma-south-african-president-aids-activist-fezekile-ntsukela-kuzwayo

van den Berg, W., Hendricks, L. Hatcher, A., Peacock, D. Godana, P. and Dworkin, S. (2013). 'One man can': Shifts in Fatherhood Beliefs and Parenting Practices Following a Gender-transformative Programme in Eastern Cape, South Africa. *Gender and Development*, 21(1), 111–25.

Yuku, N. (2019, 7 February). Anti-abortion Bible-thumpers March to Parly. *News24*. https://www.news24.com/news24/SouthAfrica/Local/City-Vision/anti-abortion-bible-thumpers-march-to-parly-20190206

Global Articulations of Anti-Feminism

Judith Goetz and Stefanie Mayer

The starting point of this anthology was the realisation that a global perspective on anti-feminism is mostly missing. Unlike previous anthologies, which mostly referred to case studies from Europe, Russia and the US (see inter alia Graff and Korolczuk, 2021; Kováts et al., 2015; Kuhar and Paternotte, 2017), this publication has two central objectives: on the one hand, it wants to broaden the perspective and to include analyses of topics, countries or groups which are not European based. On the other hand, it aims to identify the transnational ideological similarities between anti-feminist actors and movements, with regard to their shared strategies and discourses as well as their underlying ideology and to analyse how these are articulated in different local contexts. Thus, both approaches contribute to closing relevant research gaps. Also, we wanted to include the significant contributions by scholars from e.g. Ecuador, Costa Rica, India and Ghana, thus raising awareness of the fact that anti-feminism is being researched globally. Therefore, we have compiled ten contributions from and about five continents, which provide in-depth insights into the global dimension of anti-feminist policies and their different national forms of expression; they show that the phenomenon of organised anti-feminism is not limited to Europe, Russia or the US, and that similar developments with comparable strategies and discursive elements can be observed all over the world.

The chapters were chosen to present different approaches to the analysis of a broad range of anti-feminist actors, topics and policies. Thus, the individual texts cover varying topics ranging from national politics to online exchanges and show the diversity of contemporary anti-feminism, and although they come from different perspectives applying different approaches regarding methodology and theoretical background, they can be put together as pieces of one large jigsaw puzzle.

As the table of contents already reveals, we tried to order the different chapters not for their geographical but their topical closeness. Accordingly, the anthology starts with a first part, which examines anti-feminist discourses, common discursive elements and transnational aspects ('gender ideology', Comprehensive Sexuality Education, masculinist discourse) and their spaces of political resonance (e.g. backlash against feminist body positive activism) as well as distinct ideologies (political Christianity). In the second part, country-specific case studies address relevant topics such as the link between nationalism and anti-feminism, the role of religion, heteronormativity and anti-trans discourses as more recent elements of anti-feminism, the importance of conspiracy myths, and the role and function of state policies. These topics are analysed against the background of specific geographical, national and political contexts (religiously motivated anti-feminist campaigns in Ecuador, the role of Hindu nationalism in spreading anti-feminism in India, changing strategies of anti-gender movements in Japan since the turn of the century, anti-feminism in COVID-19-related conspiracy narratives in Germany, and counter-movements against feminism in South Africa).

Based on our understanding of anti-feminism as an intersectional ideology between continuity and change, we would like to use these concluding remarks for discussing the chapters in their relationship with each other, noting relevant similarities and differences and giving impulses for further discussion and research. In this context, the insight that many foundations of anti-feminist ideology have originated from countries that see themselves as part of the so-called 'West' seems particularly relevant. As the contributions to this anthology show, many of the argumentative models and (rhetorical) strategies were 'invented' by right-wing, conservative and, most of all, Christian actors in the so-called West; after that, they were not only taken over by non-religious groups but also transmitted globally, where they have become powerful in e.g. postcolonial and non-Christian contexts as well. Surprisingly, as several chapters demonstrate, anti-feminist actors in different regions have embedded this discourse in an anti-Western rhetoric.

Anti-feminism Between Continuity and Change

In our introduction, we tried to develop a shared analytical understanding of anti-feminism as an ideology and a political movement against the emancipation of women and LGTBIQ+ persons on an individual as well as collective level; this understanding is also the common basis of this anthology's individual chapters. Importantly, we wanted to describe anti-feminism as an intersectional ideology with a long history which, in its current form, has been directed mainly against queer-feminism (Kawasaka, amongst others), deconstructivist gender theories and gender research.

However, anti-feminism is not a new phenomenon, despite its changed facade since its appearance as an organised political force around the turn of the nineteenth century. Anti-feminism is rooted in a long and versatile history and has been an integral part of conservative and right-wing thought throughout the twentieth century – often interwoven with other ideologies like antisemitism or racism as well as nationalism and classism. Aside from long-standing discursive patterns which have determined anti-feminist ideology for a long time, we found it important to take a look at innovations, such as the rejection of gender theories and, in close connection, the invention of the so-called 'gender ideology' (Arguedas-Ramírez). Precisely because deconstructivist feminisms attack the alleged naturalness and implicitness of gender dualism and heteronormativity, more recent anti-feminist attempts often oppose gender diversity (Fuller) as well as legal reform in favour of LGBTIQ+ persons (Kawasaka). In our assessment, these phenomena are highly relevant for an understanding of anti-feminism in its current forms of appearance and for detecting changes; at the same time, we thought it important not to limit our perspective by focusing solely on anti-gender policies. Particularly, the texts on India (Naaz) and also on Russia, Kyrgyzstan and Kazakhstan (Wiedlack and Zabolotny) demonstrate that the presence of women or female bodies in the public sphere has remained a key bone of contention for 'traditional' anti-feminist mobilisations that aim at limiting the autonomy and participation of women and at forcing them into traditional women's roles. In South Africa as well, women's rights activism still faces protests by anti-feminists against the involvement of women in public affairs. In these case studies, an anti-gender rhetoric plays a secondary role at best for attacks on feminist groups while anti-feminist actors rather rely on traditional anti-feminist ideas in order to delegitimise feminist efforts.

A Western Export and its Global Articulations

One of the key questions when defining anti-feminism is how to differentiate it from more general and widespread phenomena like sexism, misogyny, heteronormativity or LGBTIQ+ hostility. This question becomes especially pertinent when doing research with a global perspective as the assumption might arise that anti-feminism is more widespread, more dangerous and more deadly the more traditional a society's gender order is. But as various chapters in this anthology show, such a view that equates the everyday articulations of sexism with organised anti-feminism would be far too simplistic.

First, several chapters demonstrate the consistent danger posed by organised and ideologically grounded anti-feminism in all parts of the world, not least the so-called West. They show that women who do not conform to the roles assigned to them or (try to) break free from them, who fight gender- and sexuality-related discrimination or people who do not position themselves within the binary heteronormative system, face massive verbal, sometimes legal and also physical threats by anti-feminists globally. In addition, a number of deadly right-wing terrorist attacks in the so-called West have been fuelled by anti-feminism as well as other hateful ideologies, including e.g. attacks in Christchurch (see chapter by Copland), El Paso (US), Utøya (Norway), Hanau or Halle (Germany). Creating a hierarchy of threats and setting them up against one another therefore not only alludes to unwarranted feelings of Western superiority, but also serves to downplay the threat anti-feminism poses in the so-called West. In contrast, this anthology's texts demonstrate that anti-feminism is a global phenomenon, which is based on traditional and conservative concepts of gender orders and society in general, but which is not necessarily more virulent in more traditional societies.

Second, the analyses confirm the decisive role of so-called Western societies in the development and dissemination of current anti-feminist concepts and discourses. Thus, it is mostly Christian actors in Europe and the US (see Arguedas-Ramírez and Vega) and their networks like Agenda Europa (Mayer and Goetz) or also the manosphere (Copland) that flesh out these reactionary ideologies and provide the argumentative blueprints which are then distributed transnationally and re-articulated in different contexts. In this sense, Arguedas-Ramírez for example shows in her chapter that 'the US neoconservative project' in Latin America has fallen on 'a fertile ground'. According to her this might be due to the fact that it is a region which 'historically [has been] dominated by the conservative idea that the state has a moral purpose and that this purpose must be guided by religious institutions'. Vega also points out that the 'coups d'état and dictatorships' of the twentieth century in Latin America had led to the dissemination of a 'new conservative, anti-communist and anti-ecumenical Protestantism [. . .] driven by US missionaries'. In the same vein, the contributions by Naaz or Beeson not only illustrate the brutality of anti-feminist actors, but also show that those actors reference many of the argumentative patterns originating from the so-called West.

Despite their similarities with regard to anti-feminist strategies and arguments, a look at postcolonial contexts, in particular, demonstrates that even though the respective discourses are taken from the West, they are clad in an anti-colonial rhetoric. Anti-feminist actors criticise feminism, gender theories and LGBTIQ+ rights as 'Western imports' which were forced on societies against the population's will and in opposition to their traditional, moral and national values. In other words, anti-feminist discourses originating from the West are articulated in an anti-Western and anti-colonial frame. Naaz, for example, shows in her text not only the 'glorification of an "authentic" Indian culture over Western culture' but also demonstrates that all over the country, political actors disseminate anti-feminist discourses which 'present feminism as a Western concept not applicable to Indian society and the rise in sexual crimes against women as by-products of a derivative Western modernity and a failure to emulate Indian values'. In this context, Naaz refers inter alia to the national organising secretary of the ABVP, Sunil Ambekar, and his text *The RSS: Roadmaps for the 21st Century* (2019) in which he describes feminism as 'an imported tool and a pretentious academic discipline from the West' that 'degenerated into a fad and reckless lifestyle choices'. Thus, anti-feminist actors often see 'a move away from Westernisation towards traditional Indian family values' as a 'common solution to the multiple problems of sexual harassment, rape, divorce, and dysfunctional marriages in contemporary India', ironically mirroring a strategy of Western anti-feminists, who often clad their ideology in an alleged protective stance for ('real') women.

Similarly, Vega characterises the anti-feminist resistance against 'ideological colonisation' as 'another transnational appeal particularly effective in Latin America' where 'the emphasis on patriarchal order and the naturalisation of sex-gender, [is] associated with national, even anti-colonialist, traditions'. The example of Japan is especially telling as the country is economically closely linked to the West, but remains culturally distinct. Still, anti-feminist arguments are charged with an anti-Western rhetoric in order to construct feminism as 'foreign', 'threatening' and incompatible with supposedly traditional, moral and national values, ironically thereby devaluating the long and distinct tradition of Japanese feminism. In this sense, Kawasaka points out that in Japan, feminism 'often [has] been labelled as "foreign" thought and movement which was imported to Japan from the West, and therefore it would not fit the Japanese social context although Japanese feminist thought and movements can be traced back to the beginning of Japanese modernisation in the late 19th century'. Wiedlack and Zabolotny in their analysis of different post-Soviet contexts also find it no accident that 'part of the discourses that position morality and so-called "traditional values" positively against gender equality, abortion, reproductive rights, sex education and the acceptance of homosexuality and trans*gender identification, among other things, is a decidedly anti-Western stance', particularly as 'the analytical concept of "gender" is understood as Western ideology and opposed to "traditional values"'.

Even though feminism is painted as a (highly successful) Western export in postcolonial as well as other non-Western contexts, anti-feminists in the West find it dangerous for broadly similar reasons as their counterparts. The construction of feminism as a threat to Western societies themselves can be seen clearly in the chapter by Copland; he shows with regard to the manosphere that the weakening of a (valiant) masculinity is also imagined as presenting a danger for national security and the West's strength: 'This aligns with a notion of modern statehood, with the masculinity aligned with strength of the Western nation.' When it comes to Agenda Europe and the paper *Restoring the Natural Order* (RTNO) (Mayer and Goetz), these ultra-conservative Christian actors also refer to the decline of the West, especially in their doomsday narrative of societies allegedly transformed (or rather 'deformed') by a sexual and cultural revolution during the past decades.

Concluding, a pattern becomes obvious: although anti-feminist actors globally take their discursive strategies and arguments largely from concepts which have been 'imported' from Europe and/or the US, those very same persons delegitimise feminism as a tool of Western imperialism. This way, a hostile stance against 'the West' and allegedly 'Western imports' like (queer) feminism becomes a key driving force for anti-feminist policies and narratives, which are used by religious and political actors in order to gain and/or maintain political power. While in the Anglo-American world and Western Europe, anti-feminists see feminism, political and sexual correctness, gender and queer theories as well as LGBTIQ+ rights as a (leftist and/or liberal) threat from inside (Mayer and Goetz, Copland) or as a deplorable 'US import', comparable groups in Eastern Europe employ the notion of a 'dictate from Brussels' (Korolczuk and Graff, 2018), whereas these same phenomena are seen as an expression of the 'decadent West' in Russia (Wiedlack and Zabolotny; Moss, 2017) and as a 'colonial impertinence' in the global South (Vega, Naaz). These different framings notwithstanding, anti-feminist rhetoric shares the idea of an (international) elite, whose members are said to be state or lobby group actors, setting the agenda 'from above', 'forcing' their (queer) feminist and LGBTIQ+ friendly views on 'us' and on ordinary people. These common features highlight the anti-modern thrust of the anti-feminist ideology, even if it is articulated differently according to political and historical contexts. This common baseline already hints at some of the reasons why anti-feminism is so attractive for right-wing political projects as it allows them to highlight alleged differences ('our way of life') while still providing a shared goal on an international level.

'Gender Ideology' as a Global Enemy

An illustrative example of anti-feminism's transnational travel success is the figure of 'gender ideology' – a bogeyman and conspiracy myth invented by the Vatican and by Catholic intellectuals in the 1990s. Various anti-feminist actors all over the world, from religiously motivated activists and churches to supporters of conspiracy myths, right-wing extremist and right-wing conservative parties and masculinists, use this rhetorical strategy. They discredit 'gender' as an ideology, which threatens heteronormativity and the resulting dichotomous conception of complementary genders, therefore threatening traditional concepts of family. In short, an ideology, which either endangers the divine order or the 'natural' order of society. In the chapter by Arguedas-Ramírez, the examples of Mexico, Brazil and Columbia show how the narrative of 'gender ideology' was promoted by Christian actors and travelled from the Vatican to Latin America, and how it has been used by political and religious (ultra-)conservative movements as a rhetorical strategy in a fight for hegemony. In her chapter, Vega also points out the impact of the spectre of 'gender ideology' in Ecuador. At the same time, the author stresses its function as a 'symbolic glue' (Kováts et al., 2015), which unites a very diverse set of actors as it appeals inter alia to a vague anti-neoliberal sentiment. Similarly, Bauer and Copland demonstrate in their respective chapters how anti-feminism is woven into (non-religious) political ideologies by way of the narrative of 'gender ideology', taking right-wing extremism and conspiracy myths as their examples. Thus, the various chapters show how this narrative is an extremely versatile discursive strategy, shared from Europe to Latin America, and from Christian groups to the manosphere.

Interestingly, it is also possible to detect similarities independently of direct networks between anti-feminist actors from different regions. The contribution by Kawasaka shows that anti-feminists in Japan use similar patterns of discourse as their European counterparts, even though there is no evidence of direct contacts. In the words of Kawasaka:

There are strong similarities between Japanese and European anti-gender discourses, although the anti-gender movements did not collaborate closely or share religious or political organisations such as Catholic and evangelical churches. In particular, Japanese anti-gender discourses have common characteristics with French reactionary discourses against same-sex marriage in the early 2010s, both of which considered that a 'traditional' family model was the centre of national identity.

Yet the contributions also point out the importance of local and national contexts, which shape the ways anti-feminist sentiments are articulated. Wiedlack and Zabolotny in their chapter on post-Soviet contexts show that 'although anti-feminism is the transnationally and discursively shared sentiment and discourse, the specific local conditions that allowed for the erupting of anti-feminism, its rhetorical foci and goals are rooted in local contexts and are not imported from elsewhere' – this includes Russia and the Russian Orthodox Church, which have often been regarded as central producers of anti-feminist ideologies. Therefore, the authors stress that their

> discourse analysis does not support widespread theories of a direct and state-ordered Russian influence in the post-Soviet regions of Kazakhstan and Kyrgyzstan. Rather the violent incidences analysed should be understood as regionally enacted measures in support of patriarchal authoritarian social structures that are globally connected through anti-feminism.

Another striking aspect connecting several chapters is the analyses of globally repeated hate figures including – in addition to 'gender ideology' – (individual) women, feminists, researchers in the field of gender, LGBTQI+ persons (trans persons in particular) and the 'homosexual lobby' as well as weak men, feminity, 'genderism' and sex education. The patterns of anti-feminist discourses and the rhetorical strategies employed also share many parallels, as several chapters of this anthology describe. One example is discursive strategies of depreciation, ranging from discrediting women (Wiedlack and Zabolotny, Beeson, Naaz), LGBTQI+ persons (Kawasaka, Vega, Beeson), feminism (Copland) or gender-policy measures (Mayer and Goetz, Fuller) to the rejection of feminity (Copland, Wiedlack and Zabolotny). Although the composition of actors varies by country, anti-feminist actors globally use campaign work, shared scenarios of societal decline and shared constructions of enemies as well as similar discursive strategies in order to build alliances between different political and religious spectra.

All these similarities notwithstanding, the analyses in this anthology also show the flexibility of anti-feminist discourses and their usability for different short- or long-term political goals. As Beeson points out in her chapter, anti-feminism in South Africa can be understood largely as a reaction to the political engagement and the successes of women's movements. Also, Wiedlack and Zabolotny demonstrate in their study how specific instances of feminist activism are followed by anti-feminist reactions, even though the authors point out the difference between trigger events and underlying root causes. Mayer and Goetz highlight how conservative Christian actors understand themselves to be resisting not only feminism but also broader societal process of democratisation and pluralisation. This shows that while anti-feminism defines itself as a reactive ideology in pursuit of the re-creation of an imagined traditional order, it is at the same time a central tool in establishing a new right-wing and/or religious hegemony that aims to profoundly change society in an authoritarian direction.

The Role of Religion and Strategic Secularisation

Almost all analyses in this anthology show the importance of religious actors for current anti-feminism. Although the individual chapters cover quite specific aspects such as e.g. attacks on sex education (Fuller), abortion (Beeson) or LGBTQI+ rights (Vega), religion seems to be a motivating factor in many contexts, thereby meriting closer attention. While Arguedas-Ramírez follows the spreading of the 'gender ideology' discourse in Latin America, the chapter by Mayer and Goetz deals with the ultra-conservative Christian network 'Agenda Europe' and its strategy of seemingly secularising its religiously grounded anti-feminist discourse. Taking interviews with pastors of an independent church in the north of Quito as her starting point, Vega writes about the relationship between Evangelical teachings on gender, family and sexuality, their everyday dissemination within the church and the participation in Ecuadorian anti-gender campaigns. Beeson stresses that 'Christian beliefs have played a role in the creation and perpetuation of deep-seated patriarchy in South Africa'. Among other factors, she describes the growing trend of masculinism, for example in the form of 'Muscular Christianity' groups, as a key element of current anti-feminist attacks. Fuller also shows the influence of Christian and, to a lesser degree, Islamic leaders on the pushback of Comprehensive Sexuality Education in Ghana, thereby providing a first insight that the link between anti-feminism and religion reaches beyond Christianity. For Japan, Kawasaka underlines that 'the religious right including the Association of Shinto Church (Jinja honcho), "New-born" Buddhism (Shinsei bukkyō) and the Unification Church (Tōitsu kyōkai or "the Moonies") were involved in anti-gender movements'. Naaz, in turn, focuses on the Hindu nationalist right in India as an especially striking example of the intersecting of religious zeal and nationalism.

Interestingly, the significance of religion becomes obvious even in contributions where it is not in the foreground. This holds true for opponents of COVID-19 measures in Germany who, as Bauer points out in her analysis, not only disseminate antisemitic and anti-Muslim racism in the analysed Telegram groups, but also stress that they wouldn't be prepared to accept any other religion but Christianity. Not only have leading fundamentalist Christian actors participated in the protests, but the disseminated conspiracy myths contain elements of Christian anti-feminism. One example is the narrative of an 'abortion industry' – a term frequently used by Christian actors such as e.g. Agenda Europe – being part of an alleged corona conspiracy. Copland mentions in his chapter that actors involved in the manosphere, such as the Lads Society, as well as the subreddit r/TheRedPill and the Christchurch shooter, assume the supposedly natural order of society being increasingly turned upside down, resulting in 'chaos' making its way into Western societies. According to Copland, the related association of chaos with the 'female principle' is based on 'religious texts, which link femininity to creation, and in turn, nature, which are seen as elements of chaos'. Only Wiedlack and Zabolotny found that the Russian Orthodox Church, 'which is often seen as strong proponent within anti-feminist agitation', had no leading role in the examples described in their chapter. Analyses of the influence of religion are further complicated by strategies developed by religious actors in order to gain respectability and influence in secularised debates. As Mayer and Goetz claim with regard to the programme of Agenda Europe:

> Although our analysis showed that the secularisation of Christian discourse within the paper (*Restoring the natural Order*; RTNO) remains superficial and does not pertain to the argumentative logic, these superficial changes might have consequences both with regards to conservative Christian's ability to form alliances with secular right-wing extremist forces and with regards to their influence on broader public and political discourse especially in the domain of human rights.

With regard to Latin America, Vega also sees a 'strategic secularism' being used within the framework of 'challenges of public policies and legislative changes'. Her description of strategies echoes those employed in the RTNO paper:

> The doctrine and its development, as well as beliefs, involves rights, laws, programmes that confront sexual democracy. Advocating an anti-state discourse (less state and more family) while intervening in the social state, speaking secular and pluralist language while propagating reactionary religiosity, or moralising politics by appealing to the righteousness and purification of sex while strengthening vertical and absolutist convictions, are all ways in which the new transnational wave against gender ideology contributes to de-democratisation and authoritarian advance, almost always in coalition with extreme right-wing forces.

Accordingly, non-religious anti-feminist actors increasingly use arguments shaped by Christian discourse, as for example Copland shows in the case of right-wing groups in the manosphere. This makes obvious that even secular right-wing extremist actors have adopted elements of religious discourse, integrating them into their own nativist (völkisch) racist ideology in order to establish a common frame of reference with debates in society at large.

Anti-feminism and the Struggle for Hegemony

Corresponding to the strategic secularisation of religious discourses on gender and sexuality and their use in right-wing politics, it should not be surprising that anti-feminist discourses link the rejection of feminism, equal rights and gender as well as sexual diversity with questions of national as well as religious identity. As Fuller points out: 'Religious leaders in Ghana used the sex education debates to affirm Ghana as a Christian, heterosexual nation and to promote anti-homosexual politics.' The widespread topoi of societal decline and devastation attached to the 'gender ideology' discourse have been powerful tools for political mobilisation. Additionally, the importance of anti-feminism's bridging function becomes obvious, as anti-feminist discourses unite various political actors and provide common enemies as well as a common goal. As Fullers mentions, e.g. Christian and Muslim leaders in Ghana cooperate when it comes to rejecting sex education just as Catholic and Evangelical groups work together in Latin America. Turning to a very different political spectrum, also the very heterogeneous group of opponents of anti-COVID-19 measures in Germany is united by shared images of the enemy, including feminism and 'gender ideology'. Using the example of COVID-19 conspiracy myths Bauer shows that anti-feminist narratives work as 'mobilising strategies and calls to action' as well as 'bridges between corona conspiracy theories, far-right ideologies and anti-feminist movements', motivating various actors to take to the streets together. Copland, in turn, shows how the idea of a 'feminisation' of society serves as an ideological link between online manosphere and the extreme right.

The present anthology illustrates the decisive role played by the Vatican as a transnational actor that uses its global reach in order to spread the specific modernised form of 'anti-gender' anti-feminism that we find dominant today. Even though an in-depth examination of Muslim as well as Jewish religious groups is not covered by this anthology, through its global outlook the book also shows that Christianity is not the only religion that matters in this respect. Not only do all world religions contain anti-feminist ideas, but they are also actively engaged in anti-feminist discourses and political mobilisations.

Of course, this close relationship between religion and anti-feminism is no coincidence. The texts by Mayer and Goetz as well as Arguedas-Ramírez demonstrate the anti-Enlightenment orientation of (conservative) Christianity, which is fundamentally opposed to the emancipation of women and LGBTIQ+ persons (which in turn is based on the concept of equality and individual human rights). In part, their growing political influence can be attributed to a weak and incomplete secularisation as Arguedas-Ramírez argues in relation to a number of Latin American countries. Understanding current anti-feminism as a symptom of the ongoing struggle of the (Catholic) church against processes of social and institutional secularisation appears to be a fruitful line of thought in order to grasp the importance of the current boom of anti-feminism, which can be complemented by an analysis of anti-feminism's relevance for secular political actors. The chapters by Kawasaka and Arguedas-Ramírez show that religious anti-Enlightenment stances contain anti-democratic principles which foster the cooperation of religious and right-wing political actors partly rendering them indistinguishable as political aims and strategies coalesce. Anti-feminism and 'politicised homophobia' (Fuller) serve as strategies in this multifaceted struggle for political hegemony, in which religious and secular political actors might target gender equality and sexual liberation for different reasons (e.g. as sinful in one case and as detrimental to the biological reproduction of the ethnic nation in the other) but find common ground as they construct similar enemies and both strive for rigid social and gender order.

The growing importance of religion therefore not only shows that religious actors of various orientations work on increasing their political influence and halting secularisation, but that secular political actors are increasingly willing to openly confront the basic tenets of liberal democracy. Thus, current anti-feminist policies cannot be understood simply as reactions to feminist or LGBTIQ+ successes but need to be regarded in the broader framework of struggles for political hegemony targeting the most basic democratic values, i.e. equality and individual freedom. For a future research agenda that means that analyses of politically active religious groups on one hand and secular reactionary political forces on the other hand, need to be systematically integrated rather than treated as two independent fields of research.

Anti-feminism as an Intersectional Ideology

Several contributions to this anthology also take a look at the great importance of the link between nationalism, right-wing extremism and anti-feminism. As Kawasaka points out, 'anti-gender discourses labelled the idea of gender itself an attack against a nation both in Japan and some European countries'. The chapters by Copland as well as by Wiedlack and Zabolotny show how secular actors integrate anti-feminism in nationalist ideologies, using it for their own ends, while the chapters by Naaz and Fuller make visible the relationship between anti-feminism, nationalism and religion. Wiedlack and Zabolotny come to the conclusion that in all analysed cases 'questions of national representation and national values were brought forward with regards to individual female body representations'. Naaz shows for India how political (nationalist) actors merge religion and nationalism in order to convey anti-feminist ideas, while Fuller deals in her text with religious actors who use nationalism for their own moral agenda. Fuller also demonstrates that the rejection of homosexuality by political leaders is based on the claim that 'Ghana as a conservative religious, heterosexual nation' was incompatible with homosexuality, showing once more how religious sentiments define national identity.

These examples establish that anti-feminism as an intersectional ideology can easily be connected with racism and nationalism, and that anti-feminism itself has been infused with other, often actor-specific ideologies of inequality in an intersectional manner. Moreover, the presentation of feminism, body positive activism or LGBTIQ+ rights as contrary to national (and religious) values contributes to a national construction of normalcy and identity; all those who do not conform to the norm are declared 'deviant' others and excluded from the national collective, thus creating a central basis for discrimination. Constructing a danger for the nation not only kindles fear but also prepares the stage for fighting societal change as well as individual 'culprits' by all means. The violent extremes of this defence of heteronormative and male notions of superiority are also covered by several contributions (Copland, Beeson, Kawasaka, Naaz).

This shows that various anti-feminist actors use a politics of fear (Wodak, 2015), in the form of horror scenarios and doomsday fantasies, in order to delegitimise feminist ideas. In a (conscious) misunderstanding the claim is made that feminism, and first all gender theories, were prone to abolish biological sexes, thereby endangering the very basis of society. Concerns about the concept of gender and gender identities themselves are closely intertwined with normative notions of sexuality and desire, making visible another intersectional component of anti-feminist ideology. This is even more pronounced when an anti-feminist agenda is linked with a nativist (völkisch) and nationalist population policy so that conservative family policies serve a racist agenda. As Copland points out, taking the topos of fear 'feminisation of society' as an example, it is not only masculinity and (heterosexual, patriarchal) gender relations that are presented as being under attack, but also and most of all the family (Mayer and Goetz, Vega, Kawasaka, Bauer). The family in turn provides a discursive link to moral religious discourses as well as to conservative, classist or caste-based visions of a hierarchically ordered society and to ethnicised racist and antisemitic population policies.

The alleged threat to families is easily broadened to a threat to children, a rhetoric figure uniquely suited to emotionalise discourse and to provide another common point of reference for actors with differing political ideologies. The narrative of endangered children can be seen in several chapters of this anthology as the figure of the innocent and immature child is perfectly suited in order to delegitimise sex education (Fuller), liberal LGBTQI+ rights (Kawasaka, Vega) or body positivity activism (Wiedlack and Zabolotny). The fact that in right-wing extremism men are called upon to protect ('our') children and women becomes especially visible in the chapter by Copland on the Christchurch attacker, who included this point into his reasoning for the attack, but examples of such a rhetoric of safeguarding 'our' women and children, while 'others' are attacked or even killed, abound in all contexts.

Restoring the Natural Order

As we have just argued, anti-feminism serves as a means to establish an 'us' vs. 'them' dichotomy, but this is not the only function it fulfils as it also entails a specific vision of what societies should look like with regard to their inner structures and hierarchies. This becomes most obvious in the chapter by Mayer and Goetz, who show how Agenda Europe targets the judicial order as well as the ethics and values of European societies in their attempt to completely redefine the meaning of equality and justice. It is interesting to see that the term 'natural order', which Agenda Europe used in the title of its programmatic paper *Restoring the Natural Order*, is yet another notion that is taken up broadly and by very different actors. The term is e.g. also used by the Lads Society analysed by Copland and referenced by Evangelical pastors interviewed by Vega. Both adhere to the notion 'that the modern world is in chaos'. While the pastors try 'to re-establish order in the family and to ensure the transmission of faith from generation to generation' in order to contain this chaos, the Lads Society wants to 'create [the] strongest possible organisation resembling Natural Order that we can achieve'.

Even though a systematic comparison of the different 'natural orders' envisioned by anti-feminist actors is beyond the scope of this chapter, we can at least discern some common elements. Arguedas-Ramírez shows that the neoconservative alliance in Latin America she is researching has three main political goals, one of them being the promotion of a 'process of de-secularisation of society, at large, that consequently will restore legitimacy to a traditional patriarchal gender hierarchy'. This is seconded by Wiedlack and Zabolotny, who demonstrate how 'anti-feminists call upon the state and its institutions to reinforce the patriarchal social order and punish the [feminist activist] women for taking action'. Naaz explains the significance of gender-specific metaphors and religious references for rationalising the surveillance and control of women and to assign to them their position within a patriarchal framework of roles. So, first of all, anti-feminists, no matter if they employ the new topoi of anti-gender rhetoric or more traditional strategies, aim to (re-)establish patriarchal gender hierarchies.

In Fuller's text we see how the rejection of sex education is linked to the criminalisation of sexualities that do not conform to the heteronormative model. Kawasaka shows an even more specific strategy, which uses so-called 'gender-critical' – i.e. transphobic – feminism for anti-feminist positions. Both can be deciphered as ways to re-naturalise a binary sex-gender system which relies on heteronormativity as the basic ordering principle of society. Heteronormative and patriarchal gender relations, enshrined in (legally secured) family structures, are analysed as the main pillar of anti-feminism's 'natural order' – and as we have shown above, the intersectionality of anti-feminism lets those be quite 'naturally' linked to exclusionary racism, antisemitism and to rigid policing of class or caste borders. The flip side to this is the superiority anti-feminism grants to some (but as the intersectional reasoning shows, by no means all) men. Women on the other hand pay a high price for conforming to this 'natural order' as Naaz shows in her text with regards to the politics of respectability, while those deemed deviant 'others' have to fear discrimination and even legal as well as violent persecution.

Violence is not only inscribed in the hierarchical and exclusionary structures of the alleged 'natural order'. As several contributions highlight, anti-feminist actors do not hesitate to use force in order to push through their political aims. Accordingly, the individual case studies mention anything from harassment, censorship and intimidation, violence and corrective rape, to organised assassinations. Wiedlack and Zabolotny, for example, point out a (male) desire to punish and discipline: 'The bodies were addressed as a battlefield for gendered norms themselves, open for disciplining practices and traditionalist inscriptions, and framing non-normative sexual behaviour as unacceptable.' Beeson also describes alarming developments in South Africa: 'The widespread appeal of masculinist and formenist rhetoric in South Africa reinforces toxic notions of masculine superiority and the expectation for female submission, which has the potential to validate and in turn perpetuate commonplace violence in the country.' Beeson cites 'corrective rape, wherein men rape lesbians and bisexual women in an attempt to "cure" them of their homosexuality' as 'one of the most prevalent hate crimes against the queer community in South Africa'.

However, as we have shown above, the current danger emanating from anti-feminist policies goes beyond their intrinsically violent character and beyond the examples of violence as an anti-feminist strategy, encompassing everything from mockery and shaming, to harassment, (sexual) violence against individuals and terrorist attacks. Precisely because anti-feminism plays an important role within a larger hegemony project of religious (ultra-)conservative and secular right-wing activists, anti-feminism also threatens the project of the unfinished democratisation of societies.

References

Graff, A. and Korolczuk, E. (2021). *Anti-Gender Politics in the Populist Moment.* Routledge.

Korolczuk, E. and Graff, A. (2018). Gender as 'Ebola from Brussels': The Anticolonial Frame and the Rise of Illiberal Populism. *Signs: Journal of Women in Culture and Society*, 43(4), 797–821.

Kováts, E. and Põim, M. (2015). Gender as Symbolic Glue: The Position and Role of Conservative and Far Right Parties in the Anti-gender Mobilization in Europe. *Foundation for European Progressive Studies: Friedrich-Ebert-Stiftung.* http://library. fes.de/pdf-files/bueros/budapest/11382.pdf

Kuhar, R. and Paternotte, D. (eds). (2017). *Anti-gender Campaigns in Europe: Mobilizing against Equality.* Rowman & Littlefield.

Moss, K. (2017). Russia as the Saviour of European Civilization: Gender and the Geopolitics of Traditional Values. In R. Kuhar and D. Paternotte (eds), *Anti-gender Campaigns in Europe: Mobilizing against Equality* (S. 195–214). Rowman & Littlefield International, Ltd.

Wodak, R. (2015). *The Politics of Fear. What Right-Wing Populist Discourses Mean.* Sage.

NOTES ON CONTRIBUTORS

Gabriela Arguedas-Ramírez is Associate Professor of Bioethics at the School of Philosophy of the University of Costa Rica. She is also a researcher at the Women's Studies Research Center, where she coordinates the Reproductive Rights Observatory. She has been working as a consultant for the Inter-American Human Rights Institute for several years, in areas related to human rights, poverty, gender and sexuality. Her latest book is a translation into Spanish of Dr Steven Miles' book, *Doctors who Torture: The Pursue of Justice*. Her translation was published in 2022 by the University of Costa Rica Press, under the title *Médicos que torturan: en búsqueda de la justicia*. Gabriela participates in several academic networks and working groups such as the Independent Research Group on Global Health Justice (IRG-GHJ) and the International Network on Biolaw.

Mareike Fenja Bauer is a PhD candidate at the European New School of Digital Studies/European University Viadrina Frankfurt (Oder). Her dissertation focuses on anti-feminism in visual social media content. Her research interests include social media studies, protests and movements studies, science and technology studies and feminist theory.

Amber Beeson is a PhD candidate at the University of Arkansas in Fayetteville, Arkansas. Her master's thesis focused on intersectionality in women's rights activism and feminism during the apartheid era in South Africa. She is currently researching contemporary South African anti-feminisms and masculinist groups, as well as examining the intersections of race, class, gender and sexuality in countercultural movements in the country. Her dissertation will analyse changes over time in South Africa's punk scene from the late 1970s to the present.

Simon Copland is a PhD candidate in sociology at the Australian National University (ANU), studying online men's rights groups and communities' 'manosphere'. He has research expertise in masculinity, the far-right, online hate and digital media platforms.

Regina Fuller is a doctoral candidate in educational policy studies at the University of Wisconsin-Madison. Her ethnographic dissertation explores debates around gender and sexuality within sex education policy in Ghana from 2018 to 2020. Her work draws on African feminist studies, African studies and anthropology of education. Fuller holds a masters in African Studies and Gender from the University of Ghana-Legon.

Judith Goetz holds degrees in Comparative Literature and Political Science and is currently pursuing a PhD at the Department of Education at the University of Innsbruck. She is also a member of FIPU (research group ideologies and policies of inequality, www.fipu.at) and the German Research Network 'women and right-wing extremism'. Her interests and research focus on right-wing extremism and women*/gender and anti-feminism. Most recently, she co-edited the anthologies (in German) *Right-wing Extremism as a Challenge for Journalism* (2021) and *Continuities of the Stigmatisation of 'Asociality'. Perspectives of Socio-critical Political Education* (2021).

Kazuyoshi Kawasaka is a principal investigator of a DFG-funded project at the Institute for Modern Japanese studies in Heinrich Heine University Düsseldorf, Germany ('Sexual Diversity and Human Rights in 21st Century Japan: LGBTIQ Activisms and Resistance from a Transnational Perspective', 2020–3). His research focuses on the history of LGBTQ activism and ethno-nationalism in Japan. Kawasaka is the author of 'Mishima Yukio and the Homoeroticisation of the Emperor of Japan' in *Feminist Encounters: A Journal of Critical Studies in Culture and Politics*, 2(2) 23, 1–11 and 'Contradictory Discourses on Sexual Normality and National Identity in Japanese Modernity' in *Sexuality & Culture*, 22(2), 593–613. He received his D. Phil from the University of Sussex in 2016.

Stefanie Mayer is a political scientist at the Institut für Konfliktforschung/ Institute of Conflict Research (IKF, Austria). Her main research interests are critical studies of right-wing extremism and populism, racism and anti-feminism as well as research into feminist politics, activism and theory. She published her PhD thesis on feminist activism in Vienna (2018, in German) as well as a number of articles on anti-feminism together with Edma Ajanovic and Birgit Sauer.

Hira Naaz is an independent researcher and a writing/communication professional based out of Delhi (India), working in the development sector and focused on women's rights and well-being in South Asia. After completing her undergraduate studies in English Literature at Delhi University, she pursued a master's degree by research in Gender Studies at Ambedkar University Delhi. She has previously interned at the Department of Women and Child Development, Government of Delhi. She contributes articles for Feminism in India, an award-winning online feminist platform. Her broad research interests have gravitated towards global and transnational feminist theory, South Asian studies, cultural studies and urban theory.

Cristina Vega is a research professor in the Department of Sociology and Gender Studies of FLACSO Ecuador and coordinates the master's degree in Gender Studies (2020–3). Her research focuses on the analysis of work, reproduction and care. She is currently studying the conservative and fundamentalist reaction in terms of gender and sexuality.

Katharina Wiedlack is a post-doctoral researcher at the University of Vienna. Her research interests are queer and feminist theory, popular culture, post-socialist, decolonial, disability studies and transnational American studies. She has published on queer-feminist countercultures, media discourses as well as on feminist and queer activism in the context of the USA and Russia, among other things. Her current arts-based research project 'The Magic Closet and the Dream Machine' (AR 567, 2020–4) investigates issues around post-Soviet queerness, archiving and the art of resistance. It is conducted by Katharina Wiedlack, in collaboration with Masha Godovannaya, Ruthia Jenrbekova and Iain Zabolotny, and is funded by the Austrian Science Fund.

Iain Zabolotny is an activist, translator and researcher. Coming from Novosibirsk, Russia, and currently living in Vienna, Austria, they are active in queer-feminist activism in both countries. They hold a diploma in public relations, a BA in transcultural communications and are currently studying translation and interpreting at the University of Vienna. As part of the arts-based research project 'The Magic Closet and the Dream Machine' in collaboration with Katharina Wiedlack, Masha Godovannaya and Ruthia Jenrbekova, they focus on questions of in/visibility, queer ways of living, community building, and archiving within the post-Soviet space.

INDEX

Abe Shinzô, 186, 190, 193–4
abortion
  abortion rights in South Africa, 226, 227
  Agenda Europe narratives of, 98, 100, 101
  anti-abortion legislation, 38, 42, 95
  anti-choice activism in South Africa,
    234–7, 240
  corona conspiracy theories and, 209,
    214, 217, 218, 254
  opposition to in Brazil, 54–5
  pro-life mobilisations, 8–9, 234, 235
  religious political actors' opposition to,
    41, 54–5, 103
  in *Restoring the Natural Order* (RTNO),
    103, 104, 106, 107
Adolphe, Jane, 33
Africa
  Christian heterosexual nationalism, 51,
    52–3, 56, 58, 62, 65–6
  LGBTIQ+ as culturally un-African, 60–2,
    237
  myth of cultural heterosexuality, 61–2
  politicized homophobia, 52, 55–6, 60
  public religions, 52, 63–4
  sex education debates, 50–1, 55–7, 65–6
  sex education policy and sexual politics,
    56–7
  see also Ghana; South Africa
African feminism, 52, 225
Agenda Europe
  Agenda Europe Insiders, 99
  anti-abortion narratives, 98, 100, 101
  Natural Law concept, 100, 258
  overview, 98–9
  Restoring the Natural Order (RTNO), 96,
    98
  transnational actors (Luminaries), 98–9

  as an ultra-conservative Christian
    network, 96, 110–11
  see also *Restoring the Natural Order*
    (RTNO)
Ahmed, Sara, 131–2
Akhil Bharatiya Vidyarthi Parishad (ABVP,
    All Indian Student Council), 162–3
Ambekar, Sunil, 173–4, 175, 176, 249
anti-feminism
  as anti-genderism, 9, 140, 142
  anti-'Western' discourses of, 17, 248–51
  concept, 72–3
  conspiracy theories and, 202–4, 210–11
  continuities in, 3–4, 6, 7–8, 12
  the culture wars and, 11–12
  as defenders of families, 4, 8–9, 16,
    257–8
  as discourse and ideology, 12–18
  elitist conspiracy agenda, 4–5
  ethnicisation of sexism, 17
  far-right political agendas and, 1, 4, 132
  gender ideology discourses and, 44–5
  as a global phenomenon, 1–2, 245–6,
    247–8
  as an intersectional ideology, 16–18,
    236, 246–7, 256–8
  local contexts, 2, 3, 86–7, 252
  'natural order' discourses, 4, 6, 14–15,
    258–9
  political nature of, 7, 8, 10–11, 232–4
  queer-feminist theory and, 13–15
  as a reactive ideology, 10–11
  scholarship on, 1, 6–12
  at a supra-national European level, 95–6
  term, 15–16
  transnational discourses, 1–3, 25–6,
    86–7, 245–6

EU representative:
Easy Access System Europe
Mustamäe tee 50, 10621 Tallinn, Estonia
Gpsr.requests@easproject.com

www.ingramcontent.com/pod-product-compliance
Lightning Source LLC
Chambersburg PA
CBHW070842300326
41935CB00039B/1377